A SELECTION FROM THE WORKS OF WILLIAM E. CHANNING, D.D.

A

SELECTION

FROM THE WORKS

OF

WILLIAM E CHANNING, D.D.

BOSTON:
AMERICAN UNITARIAN ASSOCIATION,
21 BROMFIELD STREET.
1855.

PREFACE.

THE circulation in this country of more than one hundred and twenty thousand volumes of the works of the late William Ellery Channing, D. D., attests the interest that is felt among us in these writings. Many editions in England, and recent translations in France, Germany, and Italy, give proof that their influence is not confined to this country. In the general unsettling of old opinions, in the growing disposition to look at Christianity from new and higher points of view, we may find reasons to believe that few authors are destined to have a wider influence; while the rational basis on which he rests his faith in Christianity, the profound reverence with which he surveys its claims, and the primitive simplicity to which he restores its substance, point him out as one of the most needed and beneficent teachers of this age.

The American Unitarian Association, in order to place the most characteristic religious publications of this author within the reach of all readers at a greatly reduced cost, have caused the following selection to be made. It contains all the clearest and fullest statements he gave of his views concerning theology and religion. The Discourses which attracted the widest attention and date a new era in the history of religious opinions, and the elaborate Treatises on the Evidences of Christianity, are here presented at a cost a little exceeding that of two pamphlets.

The six volume edition of these works, on good paper and neatly bound, the Association will continue to supply at the low price of two dollars. But some readers may prefer a selection from the productions of this celebrated writer and divine in smaller compass and more compact form. To them the following volume is now offered. There are high motives which may plead for assistance in promoting its circulation. In a style of singular simplicity and beauty, an eloquent voice wins us to feel the paternal character of God, the divinity of the mission of Jesus Christ, the greatness and attractiveness of a holy life. Some of the most original and brilliant thoughts that have been contributed by the literature of the age are scattered through these pages. No better service can be rendered to a young man who may be sceptical as to the truth of Christianity than to place this volume in his hands; and thousands, repelled from all religion by formalism and bigotry, may, by this book, be led to a believing and devout life.

It remains only to be added, that in the arrangement of the contents of this volume reference has been had to three general topics: 1, the basis on which the author rested his belief in Christianity; 2, what he understood the essential and important features of Christianity to be; 3, the high ideal of duty and piety which he believed Christianity presents.

H. A. M.

N. B. This volume is one of a series proposed to be published by the Book Fund of the Association, and is accordingly lettered as the first of the *Theological Library*. The second volume in that library will soon be published, and will be entitled "*Unitarian Principles confirmed by Trinitarian Testimonies*." Other volumes will follow.

CONTENTS.

PAGE

INTRODUCTORY REMARKS. 1

CHRISTIANITY A RATIONAL RELIGION. 27

EVIDENCES OF REVEALED RELIGION. 63

EVIDENCES OF CHRISTIANITY. 95

UNITARIAN CHRISTIANITY. 179

UNITARIAN CHRISTIANITY MOST FAVORABLE TO PIETY. 225

OBJECTIONS TO UNITARIAN CHRISTIANITY CONSIDERED. . 269

MORAL ARGUMENT AGAINST CALVINISM. 287

LETTER ON CATHOLICISM. 313

LETTER ON CREEDS. 341

THE CHURCH. 351

SELF-CULTURE. 399

IMITABLENESS OF CHRIST'S CHARACTER. 465

INTRODUCTORY REMARKS.

THE following tracts, having passed through various editions at home and abroad, are now collected to meet the wishes of those, who may incline to possess them in a durable form. In common with all writings, which have obtained a good degree of notice, they have been criticized freely; but as they have been published not to dictate opinions, but to excite thought and inquiry, they have not failed of their end, even when they have provoked doubt or reply. They have, I think, the merit of being earnest expressions of the writer's mind, and of giving the results of quiet, long-continued thought.

Some topics will be found to recur often, perhaps the reader may think too often; but it is in this way, that a writer manifests his individuality, and he can in no other do justice to his own mind. Men are distinguished from one another, not merely by difference of thoughts, but often more by the different degrees of relief or prominence, which they give to the same thoughts. In nature, what an immense dissimilarity do we observe in organized bodies, which consist of the same parts or elements, but in which these are found in great diversity of proportions! So, to learn what a man is, it is not enough to dissect his mind, and see separately the thoughts and feelings which successively possess him. The question is, what thoughts

A

and feelings predominate, stand out most distinctly, and give a hue and impulse to the common actions of his mind? What are his great ideas? These form the man, and by their truth and dignity he is very much to be judged.

The following writings will be found to be distinguished by nothing more, than by the high estimate which they express of human nature. A respect for the human soul breathes through them. The time may come for unfolding my views more fully on this and many connected topics. As yet, I have given but fragments; and, on this account, I have been sometimes misapprehended. The truth is, that a man, who looks through the present disguises and humbling circumstances of human nature, and speaks with earnestness of what it was made for and what it may become, is commonly set down by men of the world as a romancer, and what is far worse, by the religious, as a minister to human pride, perhaps as exalting man against God. A few remarks on this point seem, therefore, a proper introduction to these volumes.

It is not, however, my purpose in this place to enter far into the consideration of the greatness of human nature, and of its signs and expressions in the inward and outward experience of men. It will be sufficient here to observe, that the greatness of the soul is especially seen in the intellectual energy which discerns absolute, universal truth, in the idea of God, in freedom of will and moral power, in disinterestedness and self-sacrifice, in the boundlessness of love, in aspirations after perfection, in desires and affections, which time and space cannot confine, and the world cannot fill. The soul, viewed in these lights, should fill us with awe. It is an immortal germ, which may be said to contain now within itself what endless ages are to unfold. It is truly an image of the infinity of God, and no words can do justice to its grandeur

There is, however, another and very different aspect of our nature. When we look merely at what it now is, at its present developement, at what falls under present consciousness, we see in it much of weakness and limitation, and still more, we see it narrowed and degraded by error and sin. This is the aspect, under which it appears to most men; and so strong is the common feeling of human infirmity, that a writer, holding higher views, must state them with caution, if he would be listened to without prejudice. My language, I trust, will be sufficiently measured, as my object at present is not to set forth the greatness of human nature, but to remove difficulties in relation to it, in the minds of religious people.

From the direction, which theology has taken, it has been thought, that to ascribe any thing to man, was to detract so much from God. The disposition has been, to establish striking contrasts between man and God, and not to see and rejoice in the likeness between them. It has been thought, that to darken the creation, was the way to bring out more clearly the splendor of the Creator. The human being has been subjected to a stern criticism. It has been forgotten, that he is as yet an infant, new to existence, unconscious of his powers; and he has been expected to see clearly, walk firmly, and act perfectly. Especially in estimating his transgressions, the chief regard has been had, not to his finite nature and present stage of developement, but to the infinity of the being against whom he has sinned ; so that God's greatness, instead of being made a ground of hope, has been used to plunge man into despair.

I have here touched on a great spring of error in religion, and of error among the most devout. I refer to the tendency of fervent minds, to fix their thoughts exclusively or unduly on God's infinity. It is said, in devotional writings, that exalted and absorbing views of

God enter into the very essence of piety; that our grand labor should be, to turn the mind from the creature to the creator; that the creature cannot sink too low in our estimation, or God fill too high a sphere. God, we are told, must not be limited; nor are his rights to be restrained by any rights in his creatures. These are made to minister to their Maker's glory, not to glorify themselves. They wholly depend on him, and have no power which they can call their own. His sovereignty, awful and omnipotent, is not to be kept in check, or turned from its purposes, by any claims of his subjects. Man's place is the dust. The entire prostration of his faculties is the true homage, he is to offer God. He is not to exalt his reason or his sense of right against the decrees of the Almighty. He has but one lesson to learn, that he is nothing, that God is All in All. Such is the common language of theology.

These views are exceedingly natural. That the steady, earnest contemplation of the Infinite One, should so dazzle the mind as to obscure or annihilate all things else, ought not to surprise us. By looking at the sun, we lose the power of seeing other objects. It was, I conceive, one design of God in hiding himself so far from us, in throwing around himself the veil of his works, to prevent this very evil. He intended that our faculties should be left at liberty to act on other things besides himself, that the will should not be crushed by his overpowering greatness, that we should be free agents, that we should recognise rights in ourselves and in others as well as in the Creator, and thus be introduced into a wide and ever enlarging sphere of action and duty. Still the idea of the Infinite is of vast power, and the mind, in surrendering itself to it, is in danger of becoming unjust to itself and other beings, of losing that sentiment of self-respect, which should be inseparable from a moral nature, of degrading the intellect by the forced belief of contradictions which God is supposed to sanction, and of losing that distinct consciousness of moral freedom, of power over itself, without which the interest of life and the sense of duty are gone.

Let it not be imagined from these remarks, that I would turn the mind from God's Infinity. This is the grand truth ; but it must not stand alone in the mind. The finite is something real as well as the infinite. We must reconcile the two in our theology. It is as dangerous to exclude the former as the latter. God surpasses all human thought ; yet human thought, mysterious, unbounded, "wandering through eternity," is not to be contemned. God's sovereignty is limitless ; still man has rights. God's power is irresistible ; still man is free. On God, we entirely depend ; yet we can and do act from ourselves, and determine our own characters. These antagonist ideas, if so they may be called, are equally true, and neither can be spared. It will not do for an impassioned or an abject piety, to wink one class of them out of sight. In a healthy mind they live together ; and the worst error in religion has arisen from throwing a part of them into obscurity.

In most religious systems, the tendency has been to seize exclusively on the idea of the Infinite, and to sacrifice to this the finite, the created, the human. This I have said is very natural. To the eye of sense, man is such a mote in the creation, his imperfections and sins are so prominent in his history, the changes of his life are so sudden, so awful, he vanishes into such darkness, the mystery of the tomb is so fearful, all his outward possessions are so fleeting, the earth which he treads on so insecure, and all surrounding nature subject to such fearful revolutions, that the reflective and sensitive mind is prone to see Nothingness inscribed on the human being and on all things that are made, and to rise to God as the only reality. Another more influential feeling contributes to the same end. The mind of man, in its present infancy and blindness, is apt to grow servile through fear, and seeks to propitiate the Divine Being by flattery and self-depreciation. Thus deep are the springs of religious error. To admit all the elements of truth into our system, at once to adore the infinity of God and to give due importance to our own free moral nature, is no very easy work. But it must be done. Man's free activity is as important to religion as God's infinity. In the kingdom of Heaven, the moral power of the subject is as essential as the omnipotence of the sovereign. The rights of both have the same sacredness. To rob man of his dignity is as truly to subvert religion, as to strip God of his perfection. We must believe in man's agency as truly as in the Divine, in his freedom as truly as in his dependence, in his individual being as truly as in the great doctrine of his living in God. Just as far as the desire of exalting the Divinity obscures these conceptions, our religion is sublimated into mysticism or degraded into servility.

In the Oriental world, the human mind has tended strongly to fix on the idea of the Infinite, the Vast, the Incomprehensible. In its speculations it has started from God. Swallowed up in his greatness, it has annihilated the creature. Perfection has been thought to lie in self-oblivion, in losing one's self in the Divinity, in establishing exclusive communion with God. The mystic worshipper fled from society to wildernesses, where not even nature's beauty might divert the soul from the Unseen. Living on roots, sleeping on the rocky floor of his cave, he hoped to absorb himself in the One and the Infinite. The more the consciousness of the individual was lost, and the more the will and the intellect became passive or yielded to the universal soul, the more perfect seemed the piety.

From such views naturally sprung Pantheism. No being was at last recognised but God. He was pronounced the only reality The universe seemed a succession of shows, shadows, evanescent manifestations of the One, Ineffable Essence. The human spirit was but an emanation, soon to be reabsorbed in its source. God, it was said, bloomed in the flower, breathed in the wind, flowed in the stream, and thought in the human soul. All our powers were but movements of one infinite force. Under the deceptive spectacle of multiplied individuals intent on various ends, there was but one agent. Life, with its endless changes, was but the heaving of one and the same eternal ocean.

This mode of thought naturally gave birth or strength to that submission to despotic power, which has characterized the Eastern world. The sovereign, in whom the whole power of the state was centred, became an emblem of the One, Infinite Power, and was worshipped as its representative. An unresisting quietism naturally grew out of the contemplation of God as the all-absorbing and irresistible energy. Man, a bubble, arising out of the ocean of the universal soul, and fated soon to vanish in it again, had plainly no destiny to accomplish, which could fill him with hope or rouse him to effort. In the East the individual was counted nothing. In Greece and Rome he was counted much, and he did much. In the Greek and the Roman the consciousness of power was indeed too little chastened by religious reverence. Their gods were men. Their philosophy, though in a measure borrowed from or tinctured with the Eastern, still spoke of man as his own master, as having an independent happiness in the energy of his own will. As far as they thus severed themselves from God, they did themselves great harm; but in their recognition, however imperfect, of the grandeur of the soul, lay the secret of their vast influence on human affairs.

In all ages of the church, the tendency of the religious mind to the exclusive thought of God, to the denial or forgetfulness of all other existence and power, has come forth in various forms. The Catholic church, notwithstanding its boasted unity, has teemed with mystics, who have sought to lose themselves in God. It would seem as if the human mind, cut off by this church from free, healthful inquiry, had sought liberty in this vague contemplation of the Infinite. In the class, just referred to, were found many noble spirits, especially Fenelon, whose quietism, with all its amiableness, we must look on as a disease.

In Protestantism, the same tendency to exalt God and annihilate the creature has manifested itself, though in less pronounced forms. We see it in Quakerism, and Calvinism, the former striving to reduce the soul to silence, to suspend its action, that in its stillness God alone may be heard; and the latter, making God the only power in the universe, and annihilating the free will, that one will alone may be done in heaven and on earth.

Calvinism will complain of being spoken of as an approach to Pantheism It will say, that it recognises distinct minds from the Divine. But what avails this, if it robs these minds of self-determining force, of original activity; if it makes them passive recipients of the Universal Force; if it sees in human action only the necessary issues of foreign impulse. The doctrine, that God is the only Substance, which is pantheism, differs little from the doctrine, that God is the only active power of the universe. For what is substance without power? It is a striking fact, that the philosophy, which teaches that matter is an inert substance, and that God is the force which pervades it, has led men to question, whether any such thing as matter exists ; whether the powers of attraction and repulsion, which are regarded as the indwelling Deity, be not its whole essence. Take away force, and substance is a shadow and might as well vanish from the universe. Without a free power in man, he is nothing. The divine agent within him is every thing. Man acts only in show. He is a phenomenal existence, under which the one Infinite power is manifested ; and is this much better than Pantheism ?

One of the greatest of all errors, is the attempt to exalt God, by making him the sole cause, the sole agent in the universe, by denying to the creature freedom of will and moral power, by making man a mere recipient and transmitter of a foreign impulse. This, if followed out consistently, destroys all moral connexion between God and his creatures. In aiming to strengthen the physical, it ruptures the moral bond, which holds them together. To extinguish the free will is to strike the conscience with death, for both have but one and the same life. It destroys responsibility. It puts out the light of the universe ; it makes the universe a machine. It freezes the fountain of our moral feelings, of all generous affection and lofty aspirations. Pantheism, if it leave man a free agent, is a comparatively harmless speculation ; as we see in the case of Milton. The denial of moral freedom, could it really be believed, would prove the most fatal of errors. If Edwards's work on the will could really answer its end, if it could thoroughly persuade men that they were bound by an irresistible necessity, that their actions were fixed links in the chain of destiny, that there was but one agent, God, in the universe ; it would be one of the most pernicious books ever issued from our press. Happily it is a demonstration which no man believes, which the whole consciousness contradicts.

It is a fact worthy of serious thought and full of solemn instruction, that many of the worst errors have grown out of the religious tendencies of the mind. So necessary is it to keep watch over our whole nature, to subject the highest sentiments to the calm, conscientious reason. Men starting from the idea of God, have been so dazzled by it, as to forget or misinterpret the universe. They have come to see in him the only force in creation and in other beings only signs, shadows, echoes of this. Absolute dependence is the only relation to God, which they have left to human beings. Our infinitely nobler relations, those which spring from the power of free obedience to a moral law, their theory dissolves. The moral nature, of which freedom is the foundation and essence, which confers rights and imposes duties, which is the ground of praise and blame, which lies at the foundation of self-respect, of friendship between man and man, of spiritual connexion between man and his maker, which is the spring of holy enthusiasm and heavenly aspiration, which gives to life its interest, to creation its glory, this is annihilated by the mistaken piety, which, to exalt God, to make him All in All, immolates to him the powers of the universe.

This tendency, as we have seen, gave birth in former ages to asceticism, drove some of the noblest men into cloisters or caverns, infected them with the fatal notion, that there was an hostility between their relations to God and their relations to his creatures, and of course persuaded them to make a sacrifice of the latter. To this we owe systems of theology degrading human nature, denying its power and grandeur, breaking it into subjection to the priest through whom alone God is supposed to approach the abject multitude, and placing human virtue in exaggerated humiliations. The idea of God, the grandest of all, and which ought above all to elevate the soul, has too often depressed it and led good minds very far astray, a consideration singularly fitted to teach us tolerant views of error, and to enjoin caution and sobriety in religious speculation.

I hope, that I shall not be thought wanting in a just tolerance, in the strictures now offered on those systems of theology and philosophy, which make God the only power in the universe and rob man of his dignity. Among the authors of these, may be found some of the greatest and best men. To this class belonged Hartley, whose work on Man carries indeed the taint of materialism and necessity, but still deserves to be reckoned among the richest contributions ever made to the science of mind, whilst it breathes the profoundest piety. Our own Edwards was as eminent for religious as for intellectual power. The consistency of great error with great virtue is one of the lessons of universal history. But error is not made harmless by such associations. The false theories of which I have spoken, though not thoroughly believed, have wrought much evil. They have done much, I think, to perpetuate those abject views of human nature, which keep it where it is, which check men's aspirations, and reconcile them to their present poor modes of thought and action as the fixed unalterable laws of their being.

Many religious people fall into the error, which I have wished to expose, through the belief that they thus glorify the creator. "The glory of God," they say, "is our chief end ;" and this is accomplished as they suppose by taking all power from man and transferring all to his Maker. We have here an example of the injury done by imperfect apprehension and a vague, misty use of Scripture language. The "glory of God," is undoubtedly to be our end ; but what does this consist in ? It means the shining forth of his perfection in his creation, especially in his spiritual offspring ; and it is best promoted by awakening in these their highest faculties, by bringing out in ourselves and others the image of God in which all are made. An enlightened, disinterested human being, morally strong, and exerting a wide influence by the power of virtue, is the clearest reflexion of the divine splendor on earth, and we glorify God in proportion as we form ourselves and others after this model. The glory of the Maker lies in his work. We do not honor him by breaking down the human soul, by connecting it with him only by a tie of slavish dependence. By making him the author of a mechanical universe, we ascribe to him a low kind of agency. It is his glory that he creates beings like himself, free beings, not slaves; that he forms them to obedience, not by physical agency, but by moral influences; that he confers on them the reality, not the show of power; and opens to their faith and devout strivings a futurity of progress and glory without end. It is not by darkening and dishonoring the creature, that we honor the creator. Those men glorify God most, who look with keen eye and loving heart on his works, who catch in all some glimpses of beauty and power, who have a spiritual sense for good in its dimmest manifestations, and who can so interpret the world, that it becomes a bright witness to the divinity.

To such remarks as these it is commonly objected, that we thus obscure, if we do not deny, the doctrine of Entire Dependence on God, a doctrine which is believed to be eminently the foundation of religion. But not so. On the contrary, the greater the creature, the more extensive is his dependence; the more he has to give thanks for, the more he owes to the free gift of his Creator. No matter what grandeur or freedom we ascribe to our powers, if we maintain, as we ought, that they are bestowed, inspired, sustained by God; that he is their life; that to him we owe all the occasions and spheres of their action and all the helps and incitements by which they are perfected On account of their grandeur and freedom they are not less his gifts ; and in as far as they are divine, their natural tendency is not towards idolatrous self-reliance, but towards the grateful, joyful recognition of their adorable source. The doctrine of dependence is in no degree impaired by the highest views of the human soul.

Let me farther observe, that the doctrine of entire dependence is not, as is often taught, the fundamental doctrine of religion, so that to secure this, all other ideas must be renounced. And this needs to be taught, because nothing has been more common with theologians than to magnify our dependence, at the expense of every thing elevated in our nature. Man has been stripped of freedom, and spoken of as utterly impotent, lest he should trench on God's sole, supreme power. To eradicate this error, it should be understood, that our dependence is not our chief relation to God, and that it is not the ground of religion, if by religion we understand the sentiment of faith, reverence, and love towards the Divinity. That piety may exist, it is not enough to know that God alone and constantly sustains all beings. This is not a foundation for moral feelings towards him. The great question on which religion rests, is, *What kind* of a universe does he create and sustain ? Were a being of vast power to give birth to a system of unmeasured, unmitigated evil, dependence on him would be any thing but a ground of reverence. We should hate it, and long to flee from it into nonexistence. The great question, I repeat it, is, what is the nature, the end, the purpose of the creation which God upholds. On this and on the relations growing out of this, religion wholly rests. True, we depend on the Creator ; and so does the animal ; so does the clod ; and were this the only relation, we should be no more bound to worship than they. We sustain a grander relation, that of rational, moral, free beings to a Spiritual Father. We are not mere material substances, subjected to an irresistible physical law, or mere animals subjected to resistless instincts; but are souls, on which a moral law is written, in which a divine oracle is heard. Take away the moral relation of the created spirit to the universal spirit, and that of entire dependence would remain as it is now; but no ground, and no capacity of religion would remain; and the splendor of the universe would fade away.

We must start in religion from our own souls. In these is the fountain of all divine truth. An outward revelation is only possible and intelligible, on the ground of conceptions and principles, previously furnished by the soul. Here is our primitive teacher and light. Let us not disparage it. There are, indeed, philosophical schools of the present day, which tell us, that we are to start in all our speculations from the Absolute, the Infinite. But we rise to these conceptions from the contemplation of our own nature; and even if it were not so, of what avail would be the notion of an Absolute, Infinite existence, an Uncaused Unity, if stripped of all those intellectual and moral attributes, which we learn only from our own souls. What but a vague shadow, a sounding name, is the metaphysical Deity, the substance without modes, the being without properties, the naked unity, which performs such a part in some of our philosophical systems. The only God, whom our thoughts can rest on, and our hearts can cling to, and our consciences can recognise, is the God whose image dwells in our own souls. The grand ideas of Power, Reason, Wisdom, Love, Rectitude, Holiness, Blessedness, that is, of all God's attributes, come from within, from the action of our own spiritual nature. Many indeed think that they learn God from marks of design and skill in the outward world; but our ideas of design and skill, of a determining cause, of an end or purpose, are derived from consciousness, from our own souls. Thus the soul is the spring of our knowledge of God.

These remarks might easily be extended, but these will suffice to show, that in insisting on the claims of our nature to reverence, I have not given myself to a subject of barren speculation. It has intimate connexions with religion ; and deep injury to religion has been the consequence of its neglect. I have also felt and continually insisted, that a new reverence for man was essential to the cause of social reform. As long as men regard one another as they now do, that is as little better than the brutes, they will continue to treat one another brutally. Each will strive, by craft or skill, to make others his tools. There can be no spirit of brotherhood, no true peace, any farther than men come to understand their affinity with and relation to God and the infinite purpose for which he gave them life. As yet these ideas are treated as a kind of spiritual romance ; and the teacher, who really expects men to see in themselves and one another the children of God, is smiled at as a visionary. The reception of this plainest truth of Christianity would revolutionize society, and create relations among men not dreamed of at the present day. A union would spring up, compared with which our present friendships would seem estrangements. Men would know the import of the word Brother, as yet nothing but a word to multitudes. None of us can conceive the change of manners, the new courtesy and sweetness, the mutual kindness, deference, and sympathy, the life and energy of efforts for social melioration, which are to spring up, in proportion as man shall penetrate beneath the body to the spirit, and shall learn what the lowest human being is. Then insults, wrongs, and oppressions, now hardly thought of, will give a deeper shock than we receive from crimes, which the laws punish with death. Then man will be sacred in man's sight ; and to injure him will be regarded as open hostility toward God. It has been under a deep feeling of the intimate connexion of better and juster views of human nature with all social and religious progress, that I have insisted on it so much in the following tracts, and I hope that the reader will not think that I have given it disproportioned importance.

I proceed to another sentiment, which is expressed so habitually in these writings, as to constitute one of their characteristics, and which is intimately connected with the preceding topic. It is reverence for Liberty, for human rights ; a sentiment, which has grown with my growth, which is striking deeper root in my age, which seems to me a chief element of true love for mankind, and which alone fits a man for intercourse with his fellow-creatures. I have lost no occasion for expressing my deep attachment to liberty in all its forms, civil, political, religious, to liberty of thought, speech, and the press, and of giving utterance to my abhorrence of all the forms of oppression. This love of freedom I have not borrowed from Greece or Rome. It is not the classical enthusiasm of youth, which, by some singular good fortune, has escaped the blighting influences of intercourse with the world. Greece and Rome are names of little weight to a Christian. They are warnings rather than inspirers and guides. My reverence for human liberty and rights has grown up in a different school, under milder and holier discipline. Christianity has taught me to respect my race, and to reprobate its oppressors. It is because I have learned to regard man under the light of this religion, that I cannot bear to see him treated as a brute, insulted, wronged, enslaved, made to wear a yoke, to tremble before his brother, to serve him as a tool, to hold property and life at his will, to surrender intellect and conscience to the priest, or to seal his lips or belie his thoughts through dread of the civil power. It is because I have learned the essential equality of men before the common Father, that I cannot endure to see one man establishing his arbitrary will over another by fraud, or force, or wealth, or rank, or superstitious claims. It is because the human being has moral powers, because he carries a law in his own breast, and was made to govern himself, that I cannot endure to see him taken out of his own hands and fashioned into a tool by another's avarice or pride. It is because I see in him a great nature, the divine image, and vast capacities, that I demand for him means of self-developement, spheres for free action; that I call society not to fetter, but to aid his growth. Without intending to disparage the outward, temporal advantages of liberty, I have habitually regarded it in a higher light, as the birthright of the soul, as the element, in which men are to put themselves forth, to become conscious of what they are, and to fulfil the end of their being.

Christianity has joined with all history in inspiring me with a peculiar dread and abhorrence of the passion for power, for dominion over men. There is nothing in the view of our divine teacher so hostile to his divine spirit, as the lust of domination. This we are accustomed to regard as eminently the sin of the Archfiend. "By this sin fell the angels." It is the most Satanic of all human passions, and it has inflicted more terrible evils on the human family than all others. It has made the names of king and priest the most appalling in history. There is no crime, which has not been perpetrated for the strange pleasure of treading men under foot, of fastening chains on the body or mind. The strongest ties of nature have been rent asunder, her holiest feelings smothered, parents, children, brothers murdered, to secure dominion over man. The people have now been robbed of the necessaries of life, and now driven to the field of slaugh ter like flocks of sheep, to make one man the master of millions. Through this passion, government, ordained by God, to defend the weak against the strong, to exalt right above might, has up to this time been the great wrong doer. Its crimes throw those of private men into the shade. Its murders reduce to insignificance those of the bandits, pirates, highwaymen, assassins, against whom it undertakes to protect society. How harmless at this moment are all the criminals of Europe, compared with the Russian power in Poland. This passion for power, which in a thousand forms, with a thousand weapons, is warring against human liberty, and which Christianity condemns as its worst foe, I have never ceased to reprobate with whatever strength of utterance God has given me. Power trampling on right, whether in the person of king or priest, or in the shape of democracies, majorities and republican slaveholders, is the saddest sight to him who honors human nature and desires its enlargement and happiness.

So fearful is the principle of which I have spoken, that I have thought it right to recommend restrictions on power, and a simplicity in government, beyond what most approve. Power, I apprehend, should not be suffered to run into great masses. No more of it should be confided to rulers, than is absolutely necessary to repress crime and preserve public order. A purer age may warrant larger trusts ; but the less of government now the better, if society be kept in peace. There should exist, if possible, no office to madden ambition. There should be no public prize tempting enough to convulse a nation. One of the tremendous evils of the world, is the monstrous accumulation of power in a few hands. Half a dozen men may, at this moment, light the fires of war through the world, may convulse all civilized nations, sweep earth and sea with armed hosts, spread desolation through the fields and bankruptcy through cities, and make themselves felt by some form of suffering through every household in Christendom. Has not one politician recently caused a large part of Europe to bristle with bayonets? And ought this tremendous power to be lodged in the hands of any human being? Is any man pure enough to be trusted with it? Ought such a prize as this to be held out to ambition? Can we wonder at the shameless profligacy, intrigue, and the base sacrifices of public interests, by which it is sought, and when gained, held fast. Undoubtedly great social changes are required to heal this evil, to diminish this accumulation of power. National spirit, which is virtual hostility to all countries but our own, must yield to a growing humanity, to a new knowledge of the spirit of Christ. Another important step is, a better comprehension by communities, that government is at best a rude machinery, which can accomplish but very limited good, and which, when strained to accomplish what individuals should do for themselves, is sure to be perverted by selfishness to narrow purposes, or to defeat through ignorance its own ends. Man is too ignorant to govern much, to form vast plans for states and empires. Human policy has almost always been in conflict with the great laws of social well being; and the less we rely on it the better. The less of power, given to man over man, the better. I speak, of course, of physical, political force. There is a power which cannot be accumulated to excess, I mean moral power, that of truth and virtue, the royalty of wisdom and love, of magnanimity and true religion. This is the guardian of all right. It makes those whom it acts on, free. It is mightiest when most gentle. In the progress of society this is more and more to supersede the coarse workings of government. Force is to fall before it.

It must not be inferred from these remarks, that I am an enemy to all restraint. Restraint in some form or other, is an essential law of our nature, a necessary discipline, running through life, and not to be escaped by any art or violence. Where can we go, and not meet it? The powers of nature are, all of them, limits to human power. A never-ceasing force of gravity chains us to the earth. Mountains, rocks, precipices, and seas forbid our advances. If we come to society, restraints multiply on us. Our neighbour's rights limit our own. His property is forbidden ground. Usage restricts our free action, fixes our manners, and the language we must speak, and the modes of pursuing our ends. Business is a restraint, setting us wearisome tasks, and driving us through the same mechanical routine day after day. Duty is a restraint, imposing curbs on passion, enjoining one course and forbidding another, with stern voice, with uncompromising authority. Study is a restraint, compelling us, if we would learn any thing, to concentrate the forces of thought, and to bridle the caprices of fancy. All law, divine or human, is, as the name imports, restraint. No one feels more than I do, the need of this element of human life. He, who would fly from it, must live in perpetual conflict with nature, society, and himself.

But all this does not prove, that liberty, free action, is not an infinite good, and that we should seek and guard it with sleepless jealousy. For if we look at the various restraints of which I have spoken, we shall see that liberty is the end and purpose of all. Nature's powers around us hem us in, only to rouse a free power within us. It acts that we should react. Burdens press on us, that the soul's elastic force should come forth. Bounds are set, that we should clear them. The weight, which gravitation fastens to our limbs, incites us to borrow speed from winds and steam, and we fly where we seemed doomed to creep. The sea, which first stopped us, becomes the path to a new hemisphere. The sharp necessities of life, cold, hunger, pain, which chain man to toil, wake up his faculties, and fit him for wider action. Duty restrains the passions, only that the nobler faculties and affections may have freer play, may ascend to God, and embrace all his works. Parents impose restraint, that the child may learn to go alone, may outgrow authority. Government is ordained, that the rights and freedom of each and all may be inviolate. In study thought is confined, that it may penetrate the depths of truth, may seize on the great laws of nature, and take a bolder range. Thus freedom, ever-expanding action, is the end of all just restraint. Restraint, without this end, is a slavish yoke. How often has it broken the young spirit, tamed the heart and the intellect, and made social life a standing pool. We were made for free action. This alone is life, and enters into all that is good and great. Virtue is free choice of the right; love, the free embrace of the heart; grace, the free motion of the limbs; genius, the free, bold flight of thought; eloquence, its free and fervent utterance. Let me add, that social order is better preserved by liberty, than by restraint. The latter, unless most wisely and justly employed, frets, exasperates, and provokes secret resistance; and still more, it is rendered needful very much by that unhappy constitution of society, which denies to multitudes the opportunities of free activity. A community, which should open a great variety of spheres to its members, so that all might find free scope for their powers, would need little array of force for restraint. Liberty would prove the best peace-officer. The social order of New England, without a soldier and almost without a police, bears loud witness to this truth. These views may suffice to explain the frequent recurrence of this topic in the following tracts.

I will advert to one topic more, and do it briefly, that I may not extend these remarks beyond reasonable bounds. I have written once and again on War, a hackneyed subject, as it is called, yet, one would think, too terrible ever to become a commonplace. Is this insanity never to cease ? At this moment, whilst I write, two of the freest and most enlightened nations, having one origin, bound together above all others by mutual dependence, by the interweaving of interests, are thought by some to be on the brink of war. False notions of national honor, as false and unholy as those of the duellist, do most toward fanning this fire. Great nations, like great boys, place their honor in resisting insult and in fighting well. One would think, the time had gone by, in which nations needed to rush to arms, to prove that they were not cowards. If there is one truth, which history has taught, it is, that communities in all stages of society, from the most barbarous to the most civilized, have sufficient courage. No people can charge upon its conscience, that it has not shed blood enough in proof of its valor. Almost any man, under the usual stimulants of the camp, can stand fire. The poor wretch, enlisted from a dram-shop and turned into the ranks, soon fights like a "hero." Must France, and England, and America, after so many hard-fought fields, go to war to disprove the charge of wanting spirit ? Is it not time, that the point of honor should undergo some change, that some glimpses at least of the true glory of a nation should be caught by rulers and people ? "It is the honor of a man to pass over a transgression," and so it is of states. To be wronged is no disgrace. To bear wrong generously, till every means of conciliation is exhausted ; to recoil with manly dread from the slaughter of our fellow-creatures ; to put confidence in the justice, which other nations will do to our motives ; to have that consciousness of courage, which will make us scorn the reproach of cowardice ; to feel that there is something grander than the virtue of savages ; to desire peace for the world as well as ourselves, and to shrink from kindling a flame, which may involve the world ; these are the principles and feelings, which do honor to a people. Has not the time come, when a nation professing these, may cast itself on the candor of mankind ? Must fresh blood flow for ever, to keep clean the escutcheon of a nation's glory ? For one, I look on war with a horror, which no words can express. I have long wanted patience to read of battles. Were the world of my mind, no man would fight for glory ; for the name of a commander, who has no other claim to respect, seldom passes my lips, and the want of sympathy drives him from my mind. The thought of man, God's immortal child, butchered by his brother ; the thought of sea and land stained with human blood by human hands, of women and children buried under the ruins of besieged cities, of the resources of empires and the mighty powers of nature all turned by man's malignity into engines of torture and destruction ; this thought gives to earth the semblance of hell. I shudder as among demons. I cannot now, as I once did, talk lightly, thoughtlessly of fighting with this or that nation. That nation is no longer an abstraction to me. It is no longer a vague mass. It spreads out before me into individuals, in a thousand interesting forms and relations. It consists of husbands and wives, parents and children, who love one another as I love my own home. It consists of affectionate women and sweet children. It consists of Christians, united with me to the common Saviour, and in whose spirit I reverence the likeness of his divine virtue. It consists of a vast multitude of laborers at the plough and in the workshop, whose toils I sympathize with, whose burden I should rejoice to lighten, and for whose elevation I have pleaded. It consists of men of science, taste, genius, whose writings have beguiled my solitary hours, and given life to my intellect and best affections. Here is the nation which I am called to fight with, into whose families I must send mourning, whose fall or humiliation I must seek through blood. I cannot do it, without a clear commission from God. I love this nation. Its men and women are my brothers and sisters. I could not, without unutterable pain, thrust a sword into their hearts. If, indeed, my country were invaded by hostile armies, threatening without disguise its rights, liberties, and dearest interests, I should strive to repel them, just as I should repel a criminal, who should enter my house to slay what I hold most dear, and what is intrusted to my care. But I cannot confound with such a case the common instances of war. In general, war is the work of ambitious men, whose principles have gained no strength from the experience of public life, whose policy is colored if not swayed by personal views or party interests, who do not seek peace with a single heart, who, to secure doubtful rights, perplex the foreign relations of the state, spread jealousies at home and abroad, enlist popular passions on the side of strife, commit themselves too far for retreat, and are then forced to leave to the arbitration of the sword, what an impartial umpire could easily have arranged. The question of peace and war, is too often settled for a country by men, in whom a Christian, a lover of his race, can put little or no trust; and at the bidding of such men, is he to steep his hands in human blood? But this insanity is passing away. This savageness cannot endure, however hardened to it men are by long use.

The hope of waking up some from their lethargy has induced me to recur to this topic so often in my writings.

I might name other topics, which occupy a large space in the following tracts, but enough has been said here. I will only add, that I submit these volumes to the public with a deep feeling of their imperfections. Indeed, on such subjects as God, and Christ, and Duty, and Immortality, and Perfection, how faint must all human utterance be! In another life, we shall look back on our present words as we do on the lispings of our childhood. Still these lispings conduct the child to higher speech. Still, amidst our weakness, we may learn something, and make progress, and quicken one another by free communication. We indeed know and teach comparatively little; but the known is not the less true or precious, because there is an infinite unknown. Nor ought our ignorance to discourage us, as if we were left to hopeless skepticism. There are great truths, which every honest heart may be assured of. There *is* such a thing, as a serene, immovable conviction. Faith is a deep want of the soul. We have faculties for the spiritual, as truly as for the outward world. God, the foundation of all existence, may become to the mind the most real of all beings. We can and do see in virtue an everlasting beauty. The distinctions of right and wrong, the obligations of goodness and justice, the divinity of conscience, the moral connexion of the present and future life, the greatness of the character of Christ, the ultimate triumphs of truth and love, are to multitudes, not probable deductions, but intuitions accompanied with the consciousness of certainty. They shine with the clear, constant brightness of the lights of heaven. The believer feels himself resting on an everlasting foundation. It is to this power of moral or spiritual perception, that the following writings are chiefly addressed. I have had testimony, that they have not been wholly ineffectual, in leading some minds to a more living and unfaltering persuasion of great moral truths. Without this, I should be little desirous to send them out in this new form. I trust that they will meet some wants. Books which are to pass away, may yet render much service, by their fitness to the intellectual struggles and moral aspirations of the times in which they are written. If in this or in any way I can serve the cause of truth, humanity, and religion, I shall regard my labors, as having earned the best recompence which God bestows on his creatures.

W. E. C.

BOSTON, *April* 18*th*, 1841.

CHRISTIANITY A RATIONAL RELIGION.

ROMANS i. 16: "I am not ashamed of the Gospel of Christ."

SUCH was the language of Paul; and every man will respond to it, who comprehends the character and has felt the influence of Christianity. In a former discourse, I proposed to state to you some reasons for adopting as our own the words of the Apostle, for joining in this open and resolute testimony to the gospel of Christ. I observed, that I was not ashamed of the gospel, first because it is True, and to this topic the discourse was devoted. I wish now to continue the subject, and to state another ground of undisguised and unshaken adherence to Christianity. I say, then, I am not ashamed of the gospel of Christ, because it is a *rational* religion. It agrees with reason; therefore I count it worthy of acceptation, therefore I do not blush to enrol myself among its friends and advocates. The object of the present discourse will be the illustration of this claim of Christianity. I wish to show you the harmony which subsists between the light of God's word, and that primitive light of reason, which he has kindled within us to be our perpetual guide. If, in treating this subject, I shall come into conflict with any class of Christians, I trust I shall not be considered as imputing to them any moral or intellectual defect. I judge men by their motives, dispositions, and lives, and not by their speculations or peculiar opinions ; and I esteem piety and virtue equally venerable, whether found in friend or foe.

Christianity is a Rational religion. Were it not so, I should be ashamed to profess it. I am aware that it is the fashion with some to decry reason, and to set up revelation as an opposite authority. This error though countenanced by good men, and honestly maintained for the defence of the Christian cause, ought to be earnestly withstood ; for it virtually surrenders our religion into the hands of the unbeliever. It saps the foundation to strengthen the building. It places our religion in hostility to human nature, and gives to its adversaries the credit of vindicating the rights and noblest powers of the mind.

We must never forget that our rational nature is the greatest gift of God. For this we owe him our chief gratitude. It is a greater gift than any outward aid or benefaction, and no doctrine which degrades it can come from its Author. The developement of it is the end of our being. Revelation is but a means, and is designed to concur with nature, providence, and God's spirit, in carrying forward reason to its perfection. I glory in Christianity because it enlarges, invigorates, exalts my rational nature. If I could not be a Christian without ceasing to be rational, I should not hesitate as to my choice. I feel myself bound to sacrifice to Christianity property, reputation, life ; but I ought not to sacrifice to any religion, that reason which lifts me above the brute and constitutes me a man. I can conceive no sacrilege greater than to prostrate or renounce the highest faculty which we have derived from God. In so doing we should offer violence to the divinity within us. Christianity wages no war with reason, but is one with it, and is given to be its helper and friend.

I wish, in the present discourse, to illustrate and confirm the views now given. My remarks will be arranged under two heads. I propose, first, to show that Christianity is founded on, and supposes, the authority of reason, and cannot therefore oppose it without subverting itself. My object in this part of the discourse will be to expose the error of those who hope to serve revelation by disparaging reason. I shall then, in the second place, compare Christianity and the light of reason, to show their accordance; and shall prove, by descending to particulars, that Christianity is eminently a rational religion. My aim, under this head, will be to vindicate the Gospel from the reproaches of the unbeliever, and to strengthen the faith and attachment of its friends. — Before I begin, let me observe that this discussion, from the nature of the subject, must assume occasionally an abstract form, and will demand serious attention. I am to speak of Reason, the chief faculty of the mind; and no simplicity of language in treating such a topic can exempt the hearer from the necessity of patient effort of thought.

I am to begin with showing that the Christian revelation is founded on the authority of reason, and consequently cannot oppose it; and here it may be proper to settle the meaning of the word Reason. One of the most important steps towards the truth is to determine the import of terms. Very often fierce controversies have sprung from obscurity of language, and the parties, on explaining themselves, have discovered that they have been spending their strength in a war of words. What, then, is reason?

The term Reason is used with so much latitude, that to fix its precise limits is not an easy task. In this respect it agrees with the other words which express the intellectual faculties. One idea, however, is always attached to it. All men understand by reason the highest faculty or energy of the mind. Without laboring for a philosophical definition that will comprehend all its exercises, I shall satisfy myself with pointing out two of its principal characteristics or functions.

First, it belongs to reason to comprehend Universal truths. This is among its most important offices. There are particular and there are universal truths. The last are the noblest, and the capacity of perceiving them is the distinction of intelligent beings; and these belong to reason. Let me give my meaning by some illustrations. I see a stone falling to the ground. This is a particular truth; but I do not stop here. I believe that not only this particular stone falls towards the earth, but that every particle of matter, in whatever world, tends, or, as is sometimes said, is attracted towards all other matter. Here is a universal truth, a principle extending to the whole material creation, and essential to its existence. This truth belongs to reason. — Again, I see a man producing some effect, a manufacture, a house. Here is a particular truth. But I am not only capable of seeing particular causes and effects; I am sure that every thing which begins to exist, no matter when or where, must have a cause, that no change ever has taken place or ever will take place without a cause. Here is a universal truth, something true here and everywhere, true now and through eternity; and this truth belongs to reason.—Again, I see with my eyes, I traverse with my hands, a limited space; but this is not all. I am sure, that, beyond the limits which my limbs or senses reach, there is an unbounded space; that, go where I will, an infinity will spread around me. Here is another universal truth, and this belongs to reason. The idea of Infinity is indeed one of the noblest conceptions of this faculty.—Again, I see a man conferring a good on another. Here is a particular truth or perception. But my mind is not confined to this. I see and feel that it is right for all intelligent beings, exist when or where they may, to do good, and wrong for them to seek the misery of others. Here is a universal truth, a law extending from God to the lowest human being; and this belongs to reason. I trust I have conveyed to you my views in regard to the first characteristic of this highest power of the soul. Its office is to discern universal truths, great and eternal principles. But it does not stop here. Reason is also exercised in applying these universal truths to particular cases, beings, events. For example, reason teaches me, as we have seen, that all changes without exception require a cause; and in conformity to this principle, it prompts me to seek the particular causes of the endless changes and appearances which fall under my observation. Thus reason is perpetually at work on the ideas furnished us by the senses, by consciousness, by memory, associating them with its own great truths, or investing them with its own universality.

I now proceed to the second function of reason, which is indeed akin to the first. Reason is the power which tends, and is perpetually striving, to reduce our various thoughts to Unity or Consistency. Perhaps the most fundamental conviction of reason is, that all truths agree together; that inconsistency is the mark of error. Its intensest, most earnest effort is to bring concord into the intellect, to reconcile what seem to be clashing views. On the observation of a new fact, reason strives to incorporate it with former knowledge. It can allow nothing to stand separate in the mind. It labors to bring together scattered truths, and to give them the strength and beauty of a vital order. Its end and delight is harmony. It is shocked by an inconsistency in belief, just as a fine ear is wounded by a discord. It carries within itself an instinctive consciousness, that all things which exist are intimately bound together; and it cannot rest until it has connected whatever we witness with the infinite whole. Reason, according to this view, is the most glorious form or exercise of the intellectual nature. It corresponds to the unity of God and the universe, and seeks to make the soul the image and mirror of this sublime unity.

I have thus given my views of reason; but, to prevent all perversion, before I proceed to the main discussion, let me offer a word or two more of explanation. In this discourse, when I speak of the accordance of revelation with reason, I suppose this faculty to be used deliberately, conscientiously, and with the love of truth. Men often baptize with the name of reason their prejudices, unexamined notions, or opinions adopted through interest, pride, or other unworthy biasses. It is not uncommon to hear those who sacrifice the plainest dictates of the rational nature to impulse and passion, setting themselves up as oracles of reason. Now when I say revelation must accord with reason; I do not mean by the term the corrupt and superficial opinions of men who have betrayed and debased their rational powers. I mean reason, calmly, honestly exercised for the acquisition of truth and the invigoration of virtue.

After these explanations, I proceed to the discussion of the two leading principles to which this Discourse is devoted.

First, I am to show that revelation is founded on the authority of reason, and cannot therefore oppose or disparage it without subverting itself. Let me state a few of the considerations which convince me of the truth of this position. The first is, that reason alone makes us capable of receiving a revelation. It must previously exist and operate, or we should be wholly unprepared for the communications of Christ. Revelation, then, is built on reason. You will see the truth of these remarks if you will consider to whom revelation is sent. Why is it given to men rather than to brutes? Why have not God's messengers gone to the fields to proclaim his glad tidings to bird and beast? The answer is obvious. These want reason; and, wanting this, they have no capacity or preparation for revealed truth. And not only would revelation be lost on the brute; let it speak to the child, before his rational faculties have been awakened, and before some ideas of duty and his own nature have been developed, and it might as well speak to a stone. Reason is the preparation and ground of revelation.

This truth will be still more obvious, if we consider, not only to whom, but in what way, the Christian revelation is communicated. How is it conveyed? In words. Did it make these words? No. They were in use ages before its birth. Again I ask, Did it make the ideas or thoughts which these words express ? No. If the hearers of Jesus had not previously attached ideas to the terms which he employed, they could not have received his meaning. He might as well have spoken to them in a foreign tongue. Thus the ideas which enter into Christianity subsisted before. They were ideas of reason ; so that to this faculty revelation owes the materials of which it is composed.

Revelation, we must remember, is not our earliest teacher. Man is not born with the single power of reading God's word, and sent immediately to that guide. His eyes open first on another volume, that of the creation. Long before he can read the Bible, he looks round on the earth and sky. He reads the countenances of his friends, and hears and understands their voices. He looks, too, by degrees within himself, and acquires some ideas of his own soul. Thus his first school is that of nature and reason, and this is necessary to prepare him for a communication from Heaven. Revelation does not find the mind a blank, a void, prepared to receive unresistingly whatever may be offered ; but finds it in possession of various knowledge from nature and experience, and, still more, in possession of great principles, fundamental truths, moral ideas, which are derived from itself, and which are the germs of all its future improvement. This last view is peculiarly important. The mind does not receive every thing from abroad. Its great ideas arise from itself, and by those native lights it reads and comprehends the volumes of nature and revelation. We speak, indeed, of nature and revelation as making known to us an intelligent First Cause ; but the ideas of intelligence and causation we derive originally from our own nature. The elements of the idea of God we gather from ourselves. Power, wisdom, love, virtue, beauty, and happiness, words which contain all that is glorious in the universe and interesting in our existence, express attributes of the mind, and are understood by us only through consciousness. It is true, these ideas or principles of reason are often obscured by thick clouds, and mingled with many and deplorable errors. Still they are never lost. Christianity recognises them, is built on them, and needs them as its interpreters. If an illustration of these views be required, I would point you to what may be called the most fundamental idea of religion. I mean the idea of right, of duty. Do we derive this originally and wholly from sacred books? Has not every human being, whether born within or beyond the bounds of revelation, a sense of the distinction between right and wrong? Is there not an earlier voice than revelation, approving or rebuking men according to their deeds? In barbarous ages is not conscience heard? And does it not grow more articulate with the progress of society? Christianity does not create, but presupposes the idea of duty; and the same may be said of other great convictions. Revelation, then, does not stand alone, nor is it addressed to a blank and passive mind. It was meant to be a joint worker with other teachers, with nature, with Providence, with conscience, with our rational powers; and as these all are given us by God, they cannot differ from each other. God must agree with himself. He has but one voice. It is man who speaks with jarring tongues. Nothing but harmony can come from the Creator; and, accordingly, a religion claiming to be from God, can give no surer proof of falsehood than by contradicting those previous truths which God is teaching by our very nature. We have thus seen that reason prepares us for a divine communication, and that it furnishes the ideas or materials of which revelation consists. This is my first consideration.

I proceed to a second. I affirm, then, that revelation rests on the authority of reason, because to this faculty it submits the evidences of its truth, and nothing but the approving sentence of reason binds us to receive and obey it. This is a very weighty consideration. Christianity, in placing itself before the tribunal of reason and in resting its claims on the sanction of this faculty, is one of the chief witnesses to the authority and dignity of our rational nature. That I have ascribed to this faculty its true and proper office, may be easily made to appear. I take the New Testament in hand, and on what ground do I receive its truths as divine? I see nothing on its pages but the same letters in which other books are written. No miraculous voice from Heaven assures me that it is God's word, nor does any mysterious voice within my soul command me to believe the supernatural works of Christ. How, then, shall I settle the question of the origin of this religion? I must examine it by the same rational faculties by which other subjects are tried. I must ask what are its evidences, and I must lay them before reason, the only power by which evidence can be weighed. I have not a distinct faculty given me for judging a revelation. I have not two understandings, one for inquiring into God's word and another into his works. As with the same bodily eye I now look on the earth, now on the heavens, so with the same power of reason I examine now nature, now revelation. Reason must collect and weigh the various proofs of Christianity. It must especially compare this system with those great moral convictions, which are written by the finger of God on the heart, and which make man a law to himself. A religion subverting these, it must not hesitate to reject, be its evidences what they may. A religion, for example, commanding us to hate and injure society, reason must instantly discard, without even waiting to examine its proofs. From these views we learn, not only that it is the province of reason to judge of the truth of Christianity, but, what is still more important, that the rules or tests by which it judges are of its own dictation. The laws which it applies in this case have their origin in itself. No one will pretend, that revelation can prescribe the principles by which the question of its own truth should be settled ; for, until proved to be true, it has no authority. Reason must prescribe the tests or standards, to which a professed communication from God should be referred ; and among these none are more important than that moral law, which belongs to the very essence, and is the deepest conviction, of the rational nature. Revelation, then, rests on reason, and, in opposing it, would act for its own destruction.

I have given two views. I have shown that revelation draws its ideas or materials from reason, and that it appeals to this power as the judge of its truth. I now assert, thirdly, that it rests on the authority of reason, because it needs and expects this faculty to be its interpreter, and without this aid would be worse than useless. How is the right of interpretation, the real meaning, of Scriptures to be ascertained ? I answer, By reason. I know of no process by which the true sense of the New Testament is to pass from the page into my mind without the use of my rational faculties. It will not be pretended that this book is so exceedingly plain, its words so easy, its sentences so short, its meaning so exposed on the surface, that the whole truth may be received in a moment and without any intellectual effort. There is no such miraculous simplicity in the Scriptures. In truth, no book can be written so simply as to need no exercise of reason. Almost every word has more than one meaning, and judgment is required to select the particular sense intended by the writer. Of all books, perhaps the Scriptures need most the use of reason for their just interpretation ; and this, not from any imperfection, but from the strength, boldness, and figurative character of their style, and from the distance of the time when they were written. I open the New Testament and my eye lights on this passage ; "If thy hand offend thee, cut it off and cast it from thee." Is this language to be interpreted in its plainest and most obvious sense ? Then I must mutilate my body, and become a suicide. I look again, and I find Jesus using these words to the Jews ; "Fill ye up the measure of your iniquities." Am I to interpret this according to the letter, or the first ideas which it suggests ? Then Jesus commanded his hearers to steep themselves in crime, and was himself a minister of sin. It is only by a deliberate use of reason, that we can penetrate beneath the figurative, hyperbolical, and often obscure style of the New Testament, to the real meaning. Let me go to the Bible, dismissing my reason and taking the first impression which the words convey, and there is no absurdity, however gross, into which I shall not fall. I shall ascribe a limited body to God, and unbounded knowledge to man, for I read of God having limbs, and of man knowing all things. Nothing is plainer, than that I must compare passage with passage, and limit one by another, and especially limit all by those plain and universal principles of reason, which are called common sense, or I shall make revelation the patron of every folly and vice. So essential is reason to the interpretation of the Christian records. Revelation rests upon its authority. Can it then oppose it, or teach us to hold it in light esteem?

I have now furnished the proofs of my first position, that revelation is founded on reason; and in discussing this, I have wished not only to support the main doctrine, but to teach you to reverence, more perhaps than you have done, your rational nature. This has been decried by theologians, until men have ceased to feel its sacredness and dignity. It ought to be regarded as God's greatest gift. It is his image within us. To renounce it would be to offer a cruel violence to ourselves, to take our place among the brutes. Better pluck out the eye, better quench the light of the body, than the light within us. We all feel, that the loss of reason, when produced by disease, is the most terrible calamity of life, and we look on a hospital for the insane as the receptacle for the most pitiable of our race. But, in one view, insanity is not so great an evil as the prostration of reason to a religious sect or a religious chief; for the first is a visitation of Providence, the last is a voluntary act, the work of our own hands.

I am aware, that those who have spoken most contemptuously of human reason, have acted from a good motive; their aim has been to exalt revelation. They have thought that by magnifying this as the only means of divine teaching, they were adding to its dignity. But truth gains nothing by exaggeration; and Christianity, as we have seen, is undermined by nothing more effectually, than by the sophistry which would bring discredit on our rational powers. Revelation needs no such support. For myself I do not find, that, to esteem Christianity, I must think it the only source of instruction to which I must repair. I need not make nature dumb, to give power or attraction to the teaching of Christ. The last derives new interest and confirmation from its harmony with the first. Christianity would furnish a weapon against itself, not easily repelled, should it claim the distinction of being the only light vouchsafed by God to men; for, in that case, it would represent a vast majority of the human race as left by their Creator without guidance or hope. I believe, and rejoice to believe, that a ray from Heaven descends on the path of every fellow-creature. The heathen, though in darkness when compared with the Christian, has still his light; and it comes from the same source as our own, just as the same sun dispenses, now the faint dawn, and now the perfect day. Let not nature's teaching be disparaged. It is from God as truly as his word. It is sacred, as truly as revelation. Both are manifestations of one infinite mind, and harmonious manifestations; and without this agreement the claims of Christianity could not be sustained.

In offering these remarks, I have not forgotten that they will expose me to the reproach of ministering to "the pride of reason"; and I may be told, that there is no worse form of pride than this. The charge is so common, as to deserve a moment's attention. It will appear at once to be groundless, if you consider, that pride finds its chief nourishment and delight in the idea of our own superiority. It is built on something pecuiar and distinctive, on something which separates us from others and raises us above them, and not on powers which we share with all around us. Now, in speaking, as I have done, of the worth and dignity of reason, I have constantly regarded and represented this faculty as the common property of all human beings. I have spoken of its most important truths as universal and unconfined, such as no individual can monopolize or make the grounds of personal distinction or elevation. I have given, then, no occasion and furnished no nutriment to pride. I know, indeed, that the pride of reason or of intellect exists ; but how does it chiefly manifest itself? Not in revering that rational nature, which all men have derived from God ; but in exaggerating our particular acquisitions or powers, in magnifying our distinctive views, in looking contemptuously on other minds, in making ourselves standards for our brethren, in refusing new lights, and in attempting to establish dominion over the understandings of those who are placed within our influence. Such is the most common form of the pride of intellect. It is a vice confined to no sect, and perhaps will be found to prevail most where it is most disclaimed.

I doubt not that they who insist so continually on the duty of exalting Scripture above reason, consider themselves as particularly secured against the pride of reason. Yet none, I apprehend, are more open to the charge. Such persons are singularly prone to enforce their own interpretations of Scripture on others, and to see peril and crime in the adoption of different views from their own. Now, let me ask, by what power do these men interpret revelation ? Is it not by their reason ? Have they any faculties but the rational ones, by which to compare Scripture with Scripture, to explain figurative language, to form conclusions as to the will of God? Do they not employ on God's word the same intellect as on his works? And are not their interpretations of both equally results of reason? It follows, that in imposing on others their explications of the Scriptures, they as truly arrogate to themselves a superiority of reason, as if they should require conformity to their explanations of nature. Nature and Scripture agree in this, that they cannot be understood at a glance. Both volumes demand patient investigation, and task all our powers of thought. Accordingly it is well known, that as much intellectual toil has been spent on theological systems as on the natural sciences; and unhappily it is not less known, that as much intellectual pride has been manifested in framing and defending the first as the last. I fear, indeed, that this vice has clung with peculiar obstinacy to the students of revelation. Nowhere, I fear, have men manifested such infatuated trust in their own infallibility, such overweening fondness for their own conclusions, such positiveness, such impatience of contradiction, such arrogance towards the advocates of different opinions, as in the interpretation of the Scriptures; and yet these very men, who so idolize their own intellectual powers, profess to humble reason, and consider a criminal reliance on it as almost exclusively chargeable on others. The true defence against the pride of reason, is, not to speak of it contemptuously, but to reverence it as God's inestimable gift to every human being, and as given to all for never-ceasing improvements of which we see but the dawn in the present acquisitions of the noblest mind.

I have now completed my views of the first principle, which I laid down in this discourse; namely, that the Christian revelation rests on the authority of reason Of course, it cannot oppose reason without undermining and destroying itself. I maintain, however, that it does not oppose, that it perfectly accords with reason. It is a rational religion. This is my second great position, and to this I ask your continued attention. This topic might easily be extended to a great length. I might state, in succession, all the principles of Christianity, and show their accordance with reason. But I believe that more general views will be more useful, and such only can be given within the compass of a discourse.

In the account which I gave you of reason, in the beginning of this discourse, I confined myself to two of its functions, namely, its comprehension of universal truths, and the effort it constantly makes to reduce the thoughts to harmony or consistency. Universality and Consistency are among the chief attributes of reason. Do we find these in Christianity? If so, its claim to the character of a rational religion will be established. These tests I will therefore apply to it, and I will begin with Consistency.

That a religion be rational, nothing more is necessary than that its truths should consist or agree with one another, and with all other truths, whether derived from outward nature or our own souls. Now I affirm, that the Christian doctrines have this agreement; and the more we examine, the more brightly this mark of truth will appear. I go to the Gospel, and I first compare its various parts with one another. Among these I find perfect harmony; and what makes this more remarkable is, that Christianity is not taught systematically, or like a science. Jesus threw out, if I may so speak, his precepts and doctrines incidentally, or as they were required by the occasion, and yet, when they are brought together, they form a harmonious whole. I do not think it necessary to enlarge on this topic, because I believe it is not questioned by infidelity. I will name but one example of this harmony in Christianity. All its doctrines and all its precepts have that species of unity, which is most essential in a religion, that is, they all tend to one object. They all agree in a single aim or purpose, and that is to exalt the human character to a height of virtue never known before. Let the skeptic name, if he can, one Christian principle which has not a bearing on this end. A consistency of this kind is the strongest mark of a rational religion which can be conceived. Let me observe, in passing, that, besides this harmony of the Christian doctrines with one another, there is a striking and beautiful agreement between the teachings of Jesus and his character, which gives confirmation to both. Whatever Jesus taught, you may see embodied in himself. There is perfect unity between the system and its Founder. His life republished what fell from his lips. With his lips he enjoined earnestly, constantly a strong and disinterested philanthropy; and how harmoniously and sublimely did his cross join with his word in enforcing this exalted virtue! With his lips he taught the mercy of God to sinners; and of this attribute he gave a beautiful illustration in his own deep interest in the sinful, in his free intercourse with the most fallen, and in his patient efforts to recover them to virtue and to filial reliance on their Father in Heaven. So, his preaching turned much on the importance of raising the mind above the world; and his own life was a constant renunciation of worldly interests, a cheerful endurance of poverty that he might make many truly rich. So, his discourses continually revealed to man the doctrine of immortality; and in his own person he brought down this truth to men's senses, by rising from the dead and ascending to another state of being.—I have only glanced at the unity which subsists between Jesus and his religion. Christianity, from every point of view, will be found a harmonious system. It breathes throughout one spirit and one purpose. Its doctrines, precepts, and examples have the consistency of reason.

But this is not enough. A rational religion must agree not only with itself, but with all other truths, whether revealed by the outward creation or our own souls. I take, then, Christianity into the creation, I place it by the side of nature. Do they agree? I say, Perfectly. I can discover nothing, in what claims to be God's word, at variance with his works. This is a bright proof of the reasonableness of Christianity. When I consult nature with the lights modern science affords, I see continually multiplying traces of the doctrine of One God. The more I extend my researches into nature, the more I see that it is a whole, the product of one wisdom, power, and goodness. It bears witness to one Author, nor has its testimony been without effect; for although the human mind has often multiplied its objects of worship, still it has always tended towards the doctrine of the divine unity, and has embraced it more and more firmly in the course of human improvement. The Heathen, while he erected many altars, generally believed in one Supreme Divinity, to whom the inferior deities were subjected and from whom they sprung. Need I tell you of the harmony which subsists between nature and revelation in this particular? To Christianity belongs the glory of having proclaimed this primitive truth with new power, and of having spread it over the whole civilized world. — Again. Nature gives intimation of another truth, I mean of the universal, impartial goodness of God. When I look round on the creation, I see nothing to lead me to suspect that its Author confines his love to a few. The sun sends no brighter beam into the palace of the proudest king, than into the hut of the meanest peasant. The clouds select not one man's fields rather than his neighbour's, but shed down their blessings on rich and poor, and, still more, on the just and the unjust. True, there is a variety of conditions among men; but this takes place, not by any interposition of God, but by fixed and general laws of nature. Impartial, universal goodness is the character in which God is revealed by his works, when they are properly understood; and need I tell you how brightly this truth shines in the pages of Christianity, and how this religion has been the great means of establishing it among men? — Again. When I look through nature, nothing strikes me more than the union which subsists among all its works. Nothing stands alone in the creation. The humblest plant has intimate connexions with the air, the clouds, the sun. Harmony is the great law of nature, and how strikingly does Christianity coincide here with God's works; for what is the design of this religion, but to bring the human race, the intelligent creation of God, into a harmony, union, peace, like that which knits together the outward universe? I will give another illustration. It is one of the great laws of nature, that good shall come to us through agents of God's appointment; that beings shall receive life, support, knowledge, and safety through the interposition and labors and sufferings of others. Sometimes whole communities are rescued from oppression and ruin chiefly by the efforts and sacrifices of a wise, disinterested, and resolute individual. How accordant with this ordination of nature is the doctrine of Christianity, that our Heavenly Father, having purposed our recovery from sin and death, has instituted for this end the agency and mediation of his Son; that he has given an illustrious deliverer to the world, through whose toils and sufferings we may rise to purity and immortal life. — I say, then, that revelation is consistent with nature, when nature is truly interpreted by reason. I see it bringing out with noonday brightness the truths which dawn in nature; so that it is reason in its most perfect form.

I have thus carried Christianity abroad into nature. I now carry it within, and compare it with the human soul; and is it consistent with the great truths of reason which I discover there? I affirm, that it is. When I look into the soul, I am at once struck with its immeasurable superiority to the body. I am struck with the contrast between these different elements of my nature, between this active, soaring mind, and these limbs and material organs which tend perpetually to the earth, and are soon to be resolved into dust. How consistent is Christianity with this inward teaching! In Christianity, with what strength, with what bold relief, is the supremacy of the spiritual nature brought out! What contempt does Jesus cast on the body and its interests, when compared with the redemption of the soul! —

Another great truth dawns on me when I look within. I learn more and more, that the great springs of happiness and misery are in the mind, and that the efforts of men to secure peace by other processes than by inward purification, are vain strivings ; and Christianity is not only consistent with, but founded on, this great truth ; teaching us, that the kingdom of heaven is within us, and proposing, as its great end, to rescue the mind from evil, and to endue it with strength and dignity worthy its divine origin. — Again, when I look into the soul I meet intimations of another great truth. I discern in it capacities which are not fully unfolded here. I see desires which find no adequate good on earth. I see a principle of hope always pressing forward into futurity. Here are marks of a nature not made wholly for this world ; and how does Christianity agree with this teaching of our own souls ? Its great doctrine is that of a higher life, where the spiritual germ within us will open for ever, and where the immortal good after which the mind aspires will prove a reality. — Had I time, I might survey distinctly the various principles of the soul, the intellectual, moral, social, and active, and might show you how Christianity accords with them all, enlarging their scope and energy, proposing to them nobler objects, and aiding their developement by the impulse of a boundless hope. But, commending these topics to your private meditation, I will take but one more view of the soul. When I look within, I see stains of sin, and fears and forebodings of guilt ; and how adapted to such a nature is Christianity, a religion which contains blood-sealed promises of forgiveness to the penitent, and which proffers heavenly strength to fortify us in our conflict with moral evil. — I say, then,

Christianity consists with the nature within us, as well as with nature around us. The highest truths in respect to the soul are not only responded to, but are carried out by Christianity, so that it deserves to be called the perfection of reason.

I have now shown, in a variety of particulars, that Christianity has the character of Consistency, and thus satisfies the first demand of reason. It does not divide the mind against itself, does not introduce discord into the intellect, by proposing doctrines which our consciousness and experience repel. But these views do not exhaust the present topic. It is not enough to speak of Christianity as furnishing views which harmonize with one another, and with all known truth. It gives a new and cheering consistency to the views with which we are furnished by the universe. Nature and providence, with all their beauty, regularity, and beneficence, have yet perplexing aspects. Their elements are often seen in conflict with one another. Sunshine and storms, pleasure and pain, success and disaster, abundance and want, health and sickness, life and death, seem to ordinary spectators to be mixed together confusedly and without aim. Reason desires nothing so earnestly, so anxiously, as to solve these discordant appearances, as to discover some great, central, reconciling truth, around which they may be arranged, and from which they may borrow light and harmony. This deep want of the rational nature, Christianity has supplied. It has disclosed a unity of purpose in the seemingly hostile dispensations of providence, and opened to the mind a new world of order, beauty, and benevolent design. Christianity, revealing, as it does, the unbounded mercy of God to his sinful creatures; revealing an endless futurity, in which the inequalities of the present state are to be redressed, and which reduces by its immensity the sorest pains of life to light and momentary evils; revealing a Moral Perfection, which is worth all pain and conflicts, and which is most effectually and gloriously won amidst suffering and temptation; revealing in Jesus Christ the sublimity and rewards of tried and all-enduring virtue; revealing in Him the founder of a new moral kingdom or power, which is destined to subdue the world to God; and proffering the Holy Spirit to all who strive to build up in themselves and others the reign of truth and virtue; Christianity, I say, by these revelations, has poured a flood of light over nature and providence, and harmonized the infinite complexity of the works and ways of God. Thus it meets the first want of the rational nature, the craving for consistency of views. It is reason's most effectual minister and friend. Is it not, then, eminently a Rational Faith?

Having shown that Christianity has the character of consistency, I proceed to the second mark or stamp of reason on a religion, that is, Universality; and this I claim for Christianity. This indeed is one of the most distinguishing features of our religion, and so obvious and striking as to need little illustration. When I examine the doctrines, precepts, and spirit of Christianity, I discover, in them all, this character of Universality. I discover nothing narrow, temporary, local. The Gospel bears the stamp of no particular age or country. It does not concern itself with the perishable interests of communities or individuals; but appeals to the Spiritual, Immortal, Unbounded principle in human nature. Its aim is to direct the mind to the Infinite Being, and to an Infinite good. It is not made up, like other re-igions, of precise forms and details; but it inculcates immutable and all-comprehending principles of duty, leaving every man to apply them for himself to the endless variety of human conditions. It separates from God the partial, limited views of Judaism and heathenism, and holds him forth in the sublime attributes of the Universal Father. In like manner, it inculcates philanthropy without exceptions or bounds; a love to man as man, a love founded on that immortal nature of which all men partake, and which binds us to recognise in each a child of God and a brother. The spirit of bigotry, which confines its charity to a sect, and the spirit of aristocracy, which looks on the multitude as an inferior race, are alike rebuked by Christianity; which, eighteen hundred years ago, in a narrow and superstitious age, taught, what the present age is beginning to understand, that all men are essentially equal, and that all are to be honored, because made for immortality and endued with capacities of ceaseless improvement. The more I examine Christianity, the more I am struck with its universality. I see in it a religion made for all regions and all times, for all classes and all stages of society. It is fitted, not to the Asiatic or the European, but to the essential principles of human nature, to man under the tropical or polar skies, to all descriptions of intellect and condition. It speaks a language which all men need and all can understand; enjoins a virtue, which is man's happiness and glory in every age and clime; and ministers consolations and hopes which answer to man's universal lot, to the sufferings, the fear, and the self-rebuke, which cleave to our nature in every outward change. I see in it the light, not of one nation, but of the world; and a light reaching beyond the world, beyond time, to higher modes of existence and to an interminable futurity. Other religions have been intended to meet the exigencies of particular countries or times, and therefore society in its progress has outgrown them; but Christianity meets more and more the wants of the soul in proportion to the advancement of our race, and thus proves itself to be Eternal Truth. After these remarks, may I not claim for Christianity that character of universality which is the highest distinction of reason? To understand fully the confirmation which these views give to the Gospel, you must compare it with the religions prevalent in the age of Christ, all of which bore the marks of narrow, local, temporary institutions. How striking the contrast! And how singular the fact, that amid this darkness there sprung up a religion so consistent and universal, as to deserve to be called the perfection of reason!

I do and must feel, my friends, that the claim of Christianity to the honor of being a rational religion, is fully established. As such I commend it to you. As such it will more and more approve itself, in proportion as you study and practise it. You will never find cause to complain, that by adopting it you have enslaved or degraded your highest powers. Here, then, I might stop, and might consider my work as done. But I am aware that objections have been made to the rational character of our religion, which may still linger in the minds of some of my hearers. A brief notice of these may aid the purpose, and will form a proper conclusion, of this discourse.

I imagine that were some who are present to speak,

they would tell me, that if Christianity be judged by its fruits, it deserves any character but that of rational. I should be told that no religion has borne a more abundant harvest of extravagance and fanaticism. I should be told that reason is a calm, reflecting, sober principle, and I should be asked whether such is the character of the Christianity which has overspread the world. Perhaps some of you will remind me of the feverish, wild, passionate religion, which is now systematically dispersed through our country, and I shall be asked whether a system under which such delusions prevail can be a rational one.

To these objections I answer, You say much that is true. I grant that reason is a calm and reflecting principle, and I see little calmness or reflection among many who take exclusively the name of Christ. But I say, you have no right to confound Christianity with its professors. This religion, as you know, has come down to us through many ages of darkness, during which it must have been corrupted and obscured. Common candor requires that you should judge of it as it came from its Founder. Go, then, to its original records; place yourselves near Jesus; and tell me if you ever found yourselves in the presence of so calm a teacher. We indeed discern in Jesus great earnestness, but joined with entire self-control. Sensibility breathes through his whole teaching and life, but always tempered with wisdom. Amidst his boldest thoughts and expressions, we discover no marks of ungoverned feeling or a diseased imagination. Take, as an example, his longest discourse, the Sermon on the Mount. How weighty the thoughts! How grave and dignified the style! You recollect, that the multitude were astonished, not at the passionate vehemence, but at the authority, with which he spoke. Read next the last discourse of Jesus to his disciples in St. John's Gospel. What a deep, yet mild and subdued tenderness mingles with conscious greatness in that wonderful address. Take what is called the Lord's Prayer, which Jesus gave as the model of all prayer to God. Does that countenance fanatical fervor, or violent appeals to our Creator? Let me further ask, Does Jesus anywhere place religion in tumultuous, ungoverned emotion? Does he not teach us, that obedience, not feeling, marks and constitutes true piety, and that the most acceptable offering to God is to exercise mercy to our fellow-creatures? When I compare the clamorous preaching and passionate declamation, too common in the Christian world, with the composed dignity, the deliberate wisdom, the freedom from all extravagance, which characterized Jesus, I can imagine no greater contrast; and I am sure that the fiery zealot is no representative of Christianity.

I have done with the first objection; but another class of objections is often urged against the reasonable character of our religion. It has been strenuously maintained, that Christianity contains particular doctrines which are irrational, and which involve the whole religion to which they are essential, in their own condemnation. To this class of objections I have a short reply. I insist that these offensive doctrines do not belong to Christianity, but are human additions, and therefore do not derogate from its reasonableness and truth. What is the doctrine most frequently adduced to fix the charge of irrationality on the Gospel? It is the Trinity. This is pronounced by the unbeliever a gross offence to reason. It teaches that there is one God, and yet that there are three divine persons. According to the doctrine, these three persons perform different offices, and sustain different relations to each other. One is Father, another his Son. One sends, another is sent. They love each other, converse with each other, and make a covenant with each other; and yet, with all these distinctions, they are, according to the doctrine, not different beings, but one being, one and the same God. Is this a rational doctrine? has often been the question of the objector to Christianity. I answer, No. I can as easily believe that the whole human race are one man, as that three infinite persons, performing such different offices, are one God. But I maintain, that, because the Trinity is irrational, it does not follow that the same reproach belongs to Christianity; for this doctrine is no part of the Christian religion. I know, there are passages which are continually quoted in its defence; but allow me to prove doctrines in the same way, that is, by detaching texts from their connexion and interpreting them without reference to the general current of Scripture, and I can prove any thing and every thing from the Bible. I can prove, that God has human passions. I can prove transubstantiation, which is taught much more explicitly than the Trinity. Detached texts prove nothing. Christ is called God; the same title is given to Moses and to rulers. Christ has said, "I and my Father are one;" so he prayed that all his disciples might be one, meaning not one and the same being, but one in affection and purpose. I ask you, before you judge on this point, to read the Scriptures as a whole, and to inquire into their general strain and teaching in regard to Christ. I find him uniformly distinguishing between himself and God, calling himself, not God the Son, but the Son of God, continually speaking of himself as sent by God, continually referring his power and miracles to God. I hear him saying, that of himself he can do nothing, and praying to his Father under the character of the only true God. Such I affirm to be the tenor, the current, the general strain of the New Testament; and the scattered passages, on which a different doctrine is built, should have no weight against this host of witnesses. Do not rest your faith on a few texts. Sometimes these favorite texts are no part of Scripture. For example, the famous passage on which the Trinity mainly rests, "There are three that bear record in Heaven, the Father, the Word, and the Holy Ghost, and these three are one," — this text, I say, though found at present in John's Epistle, and read in our churches, has been pronounced by the ablest critics a forgery; and a vast majority of the educated ministers of this country are satisfied, that it is not a part of Scripture. Suffer no man, then, to select texts for you as decisive of religious controversies. Read the whole record for yourselves, and possess yourselves of its general import. I am very desirous to separate the doctrine in question from Christianity, because it fastens the charge of irrationality on the whole religion. It is one of the great obstacles to the propagation of the Gospel. The Jews will not hear of a Trinity. I have seen in the countenance, and heard in the tones of the voice, the horror with which that people shrink from the doctrine, that God died on the cross. Mahometans, too, when they hear this opinion from Christian missionaries, repeat the first article of their faith, "There is one God;" and look with pity or scorn on the disciples of Jesus, as deserters of the plainest and greatest truth of religion. Even the Indian of our wilderness, who worships the Great Spirit, has charged absurdity on the teacher who has gone to indoctrinate him in a Trinity. How many, too, in Christian countries, have suspected the whole religion for this one error. Believing, then, as I do, that it forms no part of Christianity, my allegiance to Jesus Christ calls me openly to withstand it. In so doing I would wound no man's feelings. I doubt not, that they who adopt this doctrine intend, equally with those who oppose it, to render homage to the truth and service to Christianity. They think that their peculiar faith gives new interest to the character and new authority to the teaching of Jesus. But they grievously err. The views, by which they hope to build up love towards Christ, detract from the perfection of his Father; and I fear, that the kind of piety, which prevails now in the Christian world, bears witness to the sad influence of this obscuration of the true glory of God. We need not desert reason or corrupt Christianity, to insure the purest, deepest love towards the only true God, or towards Jesus Christ, whom he has sent for our redemption.

I have named one doctrine, which is often urged against Christianity as irrational. There is one more on which I would offer a few remarks. Christianity has often been reproached with teaching, that God brings men into life totally depraved, and condemns immense multitudes to everlasting misery for sins to which their nature has irresistibly impelled them. This is said to be irrational, and consequently such must be the religion which teaches it. I certainly shall not attempt to vindicate this theological fiction. A more irrational doctrine could not, I think, be contrived; and it is something worse; it is as immoral in its tendency, as it is unreasonable. It is suited to alienate men from God and from one another. Were it really believed (which it cannot be), men would look up with dread and detestation to the Author of their being, and look round with horror on their fellow-creatures. It would dissolve society. Were men to see in one another wholly corrupt beings, incarnate fiends, without one genuine virtue, society would become as repulsive as a den of lions or a nest of vipers. All confidence, esteem, love, would die; and without these, the interest, charm, and worth of existence would expire. What a pang would shoot through a parent's heart, if he were to see in the smiling infant a moral being continually and wholly propense to sin, in whose mind were thickly sown the seeds of hatred to God and goodness, and who had commenced his existence under the curse of his Creator? What good man could consent to be a parent, if his offspring were to be born to this infinitely wretched inheritance? I say, the doctrine is of immoral tendency; but I do not say that they who profess it are immoral. The truth is, that none do or can hold it in its full and proper import. I have seen its advocates smile as benignantly on the child whom their creed has made a demon, as if it were an angel; and I have seen them mingling with their fellow-creatures as cordially and confidingly as if the doctrine of total depravity had never entered their ears. Perhaps the most mischievous effect of the doctrine is the dishonor which it has thrown on Christianity. This dishonor I would wipe away. Christianity teaches no such doctrine. Where do you find it in the New Testament? Did Jesus teach it, when he took little children in his arms and blessed them, and said "Of such is the kingdom of God"? Did Paul teach it, when he spoke of the Gentiles, who have not the law, or a written revelation, but who do by nature the things contained in the law? Christainity indeed speaks strongly of human guilt, but always treats men as beings who have the power of doing right, and who have come into existence under the smile of their Creator.

I have now completed my vindication of the claim of the Gospel to the character of a rational religion; and my aim has been, not to serve a party, but the cause of our common Christianity. At the present day, one of the most urgent duties of its friends is, to rescue it from the reproach of waging war with reason. The character of our age demands this. There have been times when Christianity, though loaded with unreasonable doctrines, retained its hold on men's faith; for men had not learned to think. They received their religion as children learn the catechism; they substituted the priest for their own understandings, and cared neither what nor why they believed. But that day is gone by, and the spirit of freedom, which has succeeded it, is subjecting Christianity to a scrutiny more and more severe; and if this religion cannot vindicate itself to the reflecting, the calm, the wise, as a reasonable service, it cannot stand. Fanatical sects may, for a time, spread an intolerant excitement through a community, and impose silence on the objections of the skeptical. But fanaticism is the epidemic of a season; it wastes itself by its own violence. Sooner or later the voice of reflection will be heard. Men will ask, What are the claims of Christianity? Does it bear the marks of truth? And if it be found to war with nature and reason, it will be, and it ought to be abandoned. On this ground, I am anxious that Christianity should be cleared from all human additions and corruptions. If indeed irrational doctrines belong to it, then I have no desire to separate them from it. I have no desire, for the sake of upholding the Gospel, to wrap up and conceal, much less to deny, any of its real principles. Did I think that it was burdened with one irrational doctrine, I would say so, and I would leave it, as I found it, with this millstone round its neck. But I know none such. I meet, indeed, some difficulties in the narrative part of the New Testament; and there are arguments in the Epistles, which, however suited to the Jews, to whom they were first addressed, are not apparently adapted to men at large; but I see not a principle of the religion, which my reason, calmly and impartially exercised, pronounces inconsistent with any great truth. I have the strongest conviction, that Christianity is reason in its most perfect form, and therefore I plead for its disengagement from the irrational additions with which it has been clogged for ages.

With these views of Christianity, I do and I must hold it fast. I cannot surrender it to the cavils or scoffs of infidelity. I do not blush to own it, for it is a rational religion. It satisfies the wants of the intellect as well as those of the heart. I know that men of strong minds have opposed it. But, as if Providence intended that their sophistry should carry a refutation on its own front, they have generally fallen into errors so gross and degrading, as to prove them to be any thing rather than the apostles of reason. When I go from the study of Christianity to their writings, I feel as if I were passing from the warm, bright sun into a chilling twilight, which too often deepens into utter darkness. I am not, then, ashamed of the Gospel. I see it glorified by the hostile systems which are reared for its destruction. I follow Jesus, because he is eminently "the Light"; and I doubt not, that, to his true disciples, he will be a guide to that world, where the obscurities of our present state will be dispersed, and where reason as *well* as virtue will be unfolded under the quickening influence and in the more manifest presence of God.

THE

EVIDENCES OF REVEALED RELIGION.

DISCOURSE

BEFORE THE

UNIVERSITY IN CAMBRIDGE, AT THE DUDLEIAN LECTURE,

14th MARCH, 1821.

JOHN iii. 2: "The same came to Jesus by night, and said unto him, Rabbi, we know that thou art a teacher come from God; for no man can do these miracles that thou doest, except God be with him."

THE evidences of revealed religion are the subject of this lecture, a subject of great extent, as well as of vast importance. In discussing it, an immense variety of learning has been employed, and all the powers of the intellect been called forth. History, metaphysics, ancient learning, criticism, ethical science, and the science of human nature, have been summoned to the controversy, and have brought important contributions to the Christian cause. To condense into one discourse what scholars and great men have written on this point, is impossible, even if it were desirable; and I have stated the extent of speculation into which our subject has led, not because I propose to give an abstract of others' labors, but because I wish you to understand, that the topic is one not easily despatched, and because I would invite ycu to follow me in a discussion, which will require concentrated and continued attention. A subject more worthy of attention, than the claims of that religion which was impressed on our childhood, and which is acknowledged to be the only firm foundation of the hope of immortality, cannot be presented; and our minds must want the ordinary seriousness of human nature, if it cannot arrest us.

That Christianity has been opposed, is a fact, implied in the establishment of this lecture. That it has had adversaries of no mean intellect, you know. I propose in this discourse to make some remarks on what seems to me the great objection to Christianity, on the general principle on which its evidences rest, and on some of its particular evidences.

The great objection to Christianity, the only one which has much influence at the present day, meets us at the very threshold. We cannot, if we would, evade t, for it is founded on a primary and essential attribute of this religion. The objection is oftener felt than expressed, and amounts to this, that miracles are incredible, and that the supernatural character of an alleged fact is proof enough of its falsehood. So strong is this propensity to doubt of departures from the order of nature, that there are sincere Christians, who incline to rest their religion wholly on its internal evidence, and to overlook the outward extraordinary interposition of God, by which it was at first established. But the difficulty cannot in this way be evaded; for Christianity is not only confirmed by miracles, but is in itself, in its very essence, a miraculous religion. It is not a system which the human mind might have gathered, in the ordinary exercise of its powers, from the ordinary course of nature. Its doctrines, especially those which relate to its founder, claim for it the distinction of being a supernatural provision for the recovery of the human race. So that the objection which I have stated still presses upon us, and, if it be well grounded, it is fatal to Christianity.

It is proper, then, to begin the discussion with inquiring, whence the disposition to discredit miracles springs, and how far it is rational. A preliminary remark of some importance is, that this disposition is not a necessary part or principle of our mental constitution, like the disposition to trace effects to adequate causes. We are indeed so framed, as to expect a continuance of that order of nature which we have uniformly experienced; but not so framed as to revolt at alleged violations of that order, and to account them impossible or absurd. On the contrary, men at large discover a strong and incurable propensity to believe in miracles. Almost all histories, until within the two last centuries, reported seriously supernatural facts. Skepticism as to miracles is comparatively a new thing, if we except the Epicurean or Atheistical sect among the ancients; and so far from being founded in human nature, it is resisted by an almost infinite preponderance of belief on the other side.

Whence, then, has this skepticism sprung? It may be explained by two principal causes. 1. It is now an acknowledged fact, among enlightened men, that in past times and in our own, a strong disposition has existed and still exists to admit miracles without examination. Human credulity is found to have devoured nothing more eagerly than reports of prodigies. Now it is argued, that we discover here a principle of human nature, namely, the love of the supernatural and marvellous, which accounts sufficiently for the belief of miracles, wherever we find it; and that it is, consequently, unnecessary and unphilosophical to seek for other causes, and especially to admit that most improbable one, the actual existence of miracles. This sweeping conclusion is a specimen of that rash habit of generalizing, which rather distinguishes our times, and shows that philosophical reasoning has made fewer advances than we are apt to boast. It is true, that there is a principle of credulity as to prodigies in a considerable part of society, a disposition to believe without due scrutiny. But this principle, like every other in our nature, has its limits; acts according to fixed laws; is not omnipotent, cannot make the eyes see, and the ears hear, and the understanding credit delusions, under all imaginable circumstances; but requires the concurrence of various circumstances and of other principles of our nature in order to its operation. For example, the belief of spectral appearances has been very common; but under what circumstances and in what state of mind has it occurred? Do men see ghosts in broad day, and amidst cheerful society? Or in solitary places; in grave-yards; in twilights or mists, where outward objects are so undefined, as easily to take a form from imagination; and in other circumstances favorable to terror, and associated with the delusion in question? The principle of credulity is as regular in its operation, as any other principle of the mind; and is so dependent on circumstances and so restrained and checked by other parts of human nature, that sometimes the most obstinate incredulity is found in that very class of people, whose easy belief on other occasions moves our contempt. It is well known, for example, that the efficacy of the vaccine inoculation has been encountered with much more unyielding skepticism among the vulgar, than among the improved; and in general, it may be affirmed, that the credulity of the ignorant operates under the control of their strongest passions and impressions, and that no class of society yield a slower assent to positions, which manifestly subvert their old modes of thinking and most settled prejudices. It is, then, very unphilosophical to assume this principle as an explanation of all miracles whatever. I grant that the fact, that accounts of supernatural agency so generally prove false, is a reason for looking upon them with peculiar distrust. Miracles ought on this account to be sifted more than common facts. But if we find, that a belief in a series of supernatural works, has occurred under circumstances very different from those under which false prodigies have been received, under circumstances most unfavorable to the operation of credulity; then this belief cannot be resolved into the common causes, which have blinded men in regard to supernatural agency. We must look for other causes, and if none can be found but the actual existence of the miracles, then true philosophy binds us to believe them. I close this head with observing, that the propensity of men to believe in what is strange and miraculous, though a presumption against particular miracles, is not a presumption against miracles universally, but rather the reverse; for great principles of human nature have generally a foundation in truth, and one explanation of this propensity so common to mankind is obviously this, that in the earlier ages of the human race, miraculous interpositions, suited to man's infant state, were not uncommon, and, being the most striking facts of human history, they spread through all future times a belief and expectation of miracles.

I proceed now to the second cause of the skepticism in regard to supernatural agency, which has grown up, especially among the more improved, in later times. These later times are distinguished, as you well know, by successful researches into nature ; and the discoveries of science have continually added strength to that great principle, that the phenomena of the universe are regulated by general and permanent laws, or that the Author of the universe exerts his power according to an established order. Nature, the more it is explored, is found to be uniform. We observe an unbroken succession of causes and effects. Many phenomena, once denominated irregular, and ascribed to supernatural agency, are found to be connected with preceding circumstances, as regularly as the most common events. The comet, we learn, observes the same attraction as the sun and planets. When a new phenomenon now occurs, no one thinks it miraculous, but believes, that, when better understood, it may be reduced to laws already known, or is an example of a law not yet investigated.

Now this increasing acquaintance with the uniformity of nature begets a distrust of alleged violations of it, and a rational distrust too ; for, while many causes of mistake in regard to alleged miracles may be assigned, there is but one adequate cause of real miracles, that is, the power of God ; and the regularity of nature forms a strong presumption against the miraculous exertion of this power, except in extraordinary circumstances, and for extraordinary purposes, to which the established laws of the creation are not competent. But the observation of the uniformity of nature produces, in multitudes, not merely this rational distrust of alleged violations of it, but a secret feeling, as if such violations were impossible. That attention to the powers of nature, which is implied in scientific research, tends to weaken the practical conviction of a higher power ; and the laws of the creation, instead of being regarded as the modes of Divine operation, come insensibly to be considered as fetters on his agency, as too sacred to be suspended even by their Author. This secret feeling, essentially atheistical, and at war with all sound philosophy, is the chief foundation of that skepticism, which prevails in regard to miraculous agency, and deserves our particular consideration.

To a man whose belief in God is strong and practical, a miracle will appear as possible as any other effect, as the most common event in life ; and the argument against miracles, drawn from the uniformity of nature, will weigh with him, only as far as this uniformity is a pledge and proof of the Creator's disposition to accomplish his purposes by a fixed order or mode of operation. Now it is freely granted, that the Creator's regard or attachment to such an order may be inferred from the steadiness with which he observes it ; and a strong presumption lies against any violation of it on slight occasions, or for purposes to which the established laws of nature are adequate. But this is the utmost which the order of nature authorizes us to infer respecting its Author. It forms no presumption against miracles universally, in all imaginable cases ; but may even furnish a presumption in their favor.

We are never to forget, that God's adherence to the

order of the universe is not necessary and mechanical, but intelligent and voluntary. He adheres to it, not for its own sake, or because it has a sacredness which compels him to respect it, but because it is most suited to accomplish his purposes. It is a means, and not an end ; and, like all other means, must give way when the end can best be promoted without it. It is the mark of a weak mind, to make an idol of order and method ; to cling to established forms of business, when they clog instead of advancing it. If, then, the great purposes of the universe can best be accomplished by departing from its established laws, these laws will undoubtedly be suspended ; and, though broken in the letter, they will be observed in their spirit, for the ends for which they were first instituted will be advanced by their violation. Now the question arises, For what purposes were nature and its order appointed ? and there is no presumption in saying, that the highest of these is the improvement of intelligent beings. Mind (by which we mean both moral and intellectual powers) is God's first end. The great purpose for which an order of nature is fixed, is plainly the formation of Mind. In a creation without order, where events would follow without any regular succession, it is obvious, that Mind must be kept in perpetual infancy ; for, in such a universe, there could be no reasoning from effects to causes, no induction to establish general truths, no adaptation of means to ends ; that is, no science relating to God, or matter, or mind ; no action ; no virtue. The great purpose of God, then, I repeat it, in establishing the order of nature, is to form and advance the mind ; and if the case should occur, in which the interests of the mind could best be advanced by departing from this order, or by miraculous agency, then the great purpose of the creation, the great end of its laws and regularity, would demand such departure ; and miracles, instead of warring against, would concur with nature.

Now, we Christians maintain, that such a case has existed. We affirm, that, when Jesus Christ came into the world, nature had failed to communicate instructions to men, in which, as intelligent beings, they had the deepest concern, and on which the full developement of their highest faculties essentially depended ; and we affirm, that there was no prospect of relief from nature ; so that an exigence had occurred, in which additional communications, supernatural lights, might rationally be expected from the Father of spirits. Let me state two particulars, out of many, in which men needed intellectual aids not given by nature. I refer to the doctrine of one God and Father, on which all piety rests ; and to the doctrine of Immortality, which is the great spring of virtuous effort. Had I time to enlarge on the history of that period, I might show you under what heaps of rubbish and superstition these doctrines were buried. But I should repeat only what you know familiarly. The works of ancient genius, which form your studies, carry on their front the brand of polytheism, and of debasing error on subjects of the first and deepest concern. It is more important to observe, that the very uniformity of nature had some tendency to obscure the doctrines which I have named, or at least to impair their practical power, so that a departure from this uniformity was needed to fasten them on men's minds.

That a fixed order of nature, though a proof of the One God to reflecting and enlarged understandings, has yet a tendency to hide him from men in general, will appear, if we consider, first, that, as the human mind is constituted, what is regular and of constant occurrence, excites it feebly ; and benefits flowing to it through fixed, unchanging laws, seem to come by a kind of necessity, and are apt to be traced up to natural causes alone. Accordingly, religious convictions and feelings, even in the present advanced condition of society, are excited, not so much by the ordinary course of God's providence, as by sudden, unexpected events, which rouse and startle the mind, and speak of a power higher than nature. — There is another way, in which a fixed order of nature seems unfavorable to just impressions respecting its Author. It discovers to us in the Creator, a regard to general good rather than an affection to individuals. The laws of nature, operating, as they do, with an inflexible steadiness, never varying to meet the cases and wants of individuals, and inflicting much private suffering in their stern administration for the general weal, give the idea of a distant, reserved sovereign, much more than of a tender parent ; and yet this last view of God is the only effectual security from superstition and idolatry. Nature, then, we fear, would not have brought back the world to its Creator. — And as to the doctrine of Immortality, the order of the natural world had little tendency to teach this, at least with clearness and energy. The natural world contains no provisions or arrangements for reviving the dead. The sun and the rain, which cover the tomb with verdure, send no vital influences to the mouldering body. The researches of science detect no secret processes for restoring the lost powers of life. If man is to live again, he is not to live through any known laws of nature, but by a power higher than nature ; and how, then, can we be assured of this truth, but by a manifestation of this power, that is, by miraculous agency, confirming a future life ?

I have labored in these remarks to show, that the uniformity of nature is no presumption against miraculous agency, when employed in confirmation of such a religion as Christianity. Nature, on the contrary, furnishes a presumption in its favor. Nature clearly shows to us a power above itself, so that it proves miracles to be possible. Nature reveals purposes and attributes in its Author, with which Christianity remarkably agrees. Nature too has deficiencies, which show that it was not intended by its Author to be his whole method of instructing mankind ; and in this way it gives great confirmation to Christianity, which meets its wants, supplies its chasms, explains its mysteries, and lightens its heart-oppressing cares and sorrows.

Before quitting the general consideration of miracles, I ought to take some notice of Hume's celebrated argument on this subject ; not that it merits the attention which it has received, but because it is specious, and has derived weight from the name of its author. The argument is briefly this, — "that belief is founded upon and regulated by experience. Now we often experience testimony to be false, but never witness a departure from the order of nature. That men may deceive us when they testify to miracles, is therefore more accordant with experience, than that nature should be irregular ; and hence there is a balance of proof against miracles, a presumption so strong as to outweigh the strongest testimony." The usual replies to this argument I have not time to repeat. Dr. Campbell's work, which is accessible to all, will show you that it rests on an equivocal use of terms, and will furnish you with many fine remarks on testimony and on the conditions or qualities which give it validity. I will only add a few remarks which seem to me worthy of attention.

1. This argument affirms, that the credibility of facts or statements is to be decided by their accordance with the established order of nature, and by this standard only. Now, if nature comprehended all existences and all powers, this position might be admitted. But if there is a Being higher than nature, the origin of all its powers and motions, and whose character falls under our notice and experience as truly as the creation, then there is an additional standard to which facts and statements are to be referred; and works which violate nature's order, will still be credible, if they agree with the known properties and attributes of its author; because for such works we can assign an adequate cause and sufficient reasons, and these are the qualities and conditions on which credibility depends.

2. This argument of Hume proves too much, and therefore proves nothing. It proves too much; for if I am to reject the strongest testimony to miracles, because testimony has often deceived me, whilst nature's order has never been found to fail, then I ought to reject a miracle, even if I should see it with my own eyes, and if all my senses should attest it; for all my senses have sometimes given false reports, whilst nature has never gone astray; and, therefore, be the circumstances ever so decisive or inconsistent with deception, still I must not believe what I see, and hear, and touch, what my senses, exercised according to the most deliberate judgment, declare to be true. All this the argument requires; and it proves too much; for disbelief, in the case supposed, is out of our power, and is instinctively

pronounced absurd ; and what is more, it would subvert that very order of nature on which the argument rests ; for this order of nature is learned only by the exercise of my senses and judgment, and if these fail me, in the most unexceptionable circumstances, then their testimony to nature is of little worth.

Once more ; this argument is built on an ignorance of the nature of testimony. Testimony, we are told, cannot prove a miracle. Now the truth is, that testimony of itself and immediately, proves no facts whatever, not even the most common. Testimony can do nothing more than show us the state of another's mind in regard to a given fact. It can only show us, that the testifier has a belief, a conviction, that a certain phenomenon or event has occurred. Here testimony stops ; and the reality of the event is to be judged altogether from the nature and degree of this conviction, and from the circumstances under which it exists. This conviction is an effect, which must have a cause, and needs to be explained ; and if no cause can be found but the real occurrence of the event, then this occurrence is admitted as true. Such is the extent of testimony. Now a man, who affirms a miraculous phenomenon or event, may give us just as decisive proofs, by his character and conduct, of the strength and depth of his conviction, as if he were affirming a common occurrence. Testimony, then, does just as much in the case of miracles, as of common events ; that is, it discloses to us the conviction of another's mind. Now this conviction in the case of miracles requires a cause, an explanation, as much as in every other ; and if the circumstances be such, that it could not have sprung up and been established but by the reality of the alleged miracle, then that great and fundamental principle of human belief, namely, that every effect must have a cause, compels us to admit the miracle.

It may be observed of Hume and of other philosophical opposers of our religion, that they are much more inclined to argue against miracles in general, than against the particular miracles on which Christianity rests. And the reason is obvious. Miracles, when considered in a general, abstract manner, that is, when divested of all circumstances, and supposed to occur as disconnected facts, to stand alone in history, to have no explanations or reasons in preceding events, and no influence on those which follow, are indeed open to great objection, as wanton and useless violations of nature's order; and it is accordingly against miracles, considered in this naked, general form, that the arguments of infidelity are chiefly urged. But it is great disingenuity to class under this head the miracles of Christianity. They are palpably different. They do not stand alone in history; but are most intimately incorporated with it. They were demanded by the state of the world which preceded them, and they have left deep traces on all subsequent ages. In fact, the history of the whole civilized world, since their alleged occurrence, has been swayed and colored by them, and is wholly inexplicable without them. Now, such miracles are not to be met and disposed of by general reasonings, which apply only to insulated, unimportant, uninfluential prodigies.

I have thus considered the objections to miracles in general; and I would close this head with observing, that these objections will lose their weight, just in proportion as we strengthen our conviction of God's power over nature and of his parental interest in his creatures.

The great repugnance to the belief of miraculous agency is founded in a lurking atheism, which ascribes supremacy to nature, and which, whilst it professes to believe in God, questions his tender concern for the improvement of men. To a man, who cherishes a sense of God, the great difficulty is, not to account for miracles, but to account for their rare occurrence. One of the mysteries of the universe is this, that its Author retires so continually behind the veil of his works, that the great and good Father does not manifest himself more distinctly to his creatures. There is something like coldness and repulsiveness in instructing us only by fixed, inflexible laws of nature. The intercourse of God with Adam and the patriarchs suits our best conceptions of the relation which he bears to the human race, and ought not to surprise us more, than the expression of a human parent's tenderness and concern towards his offspring.

After the remarks now made to remove the objection to revelation in general, I proceed to consider the evidences of the Christian religion in particular; and these are so numerous, that should I attempt to compress them into the short space which now remains, I could give but a syllabus, a dry and uninteresting index. It will be more useful to state to you, with some distinctness, the general principle into which all Christian evidences may be resolved, and on which the whole religion rests, and then to illustrate it in a few striking particulars.

All the evidences of Christianity may be traced to this great principle, — that every effect must have an adequate cause. We claim for our religion a divine

G*

original, because no adequate cause for it can be found in the powers or passions of human nature, or in the circumstances under which it appeared; because it can only be accounted for by the interposition of that Being, to whom its first preachers universally ascribed it, and with whose nature it perfectly agrees.

Christianity, by which we mean not merely the doctrines of the religion, but every thing relating to it, its rise, its progress, the character of its author, the conduct of its propagators, — Christianity, in this broad sense, can only be accounted for in two ways. It either sprung from the principles of human nature, under the excitements, motives, impulses of the age in which it was first preached; or it had its origin in a higher and supernatural agency. To which of these causes the religion should be referred, is not a question beyond our reach; for being partakers of human nature, and knowing more of it than of any other part of creation, we can judge with sufficient accuracy of the operation of its principles, and of the effects to which they are competent. It is indeed true, that human powers are not exactly defined, nor can we state precisely the bounds beyond which they cannot pass; but still, the disproportion between human nature and an effect ascribed to it, may be so vast and palpable, as to satisfy us at once, that the effect is inexplicable by human power. I know not precisely what advances may be made by the intellect of an unassisted savage; but that a savage in the woods could not compose the "Principia" of Newton, is about as plain as that he could not create the world. I know not the point at which bodily strength must stop; but that a man cannot carry Atlas or Andes on his shoulders, is a safe position. The question, therefore, whether the principles of human nature, under the circumstances in which it was placed at Christ's birth, will explain his religion, is one to which we are competent, and is the great question on which the whole controversy turns.

Now we maintain, that a great variety of facts belonging to this religion, — such as the character of its Founder; its peculiar principles; the style and character of its records; its progress; the conduct, circumstances, and sufferings of its first propagators; the reception of it from the first on the ground of miraculous attestations; the prophecies which it fulfilled and which it contains; its influence on society, and other circumstances connected with it; are utterly inexplicable by human powers and principles, but accord with, and are fully explained by, the power and perfections of God.

These various particulars I cannot attempt to unfold. One or two may be illustrated to show you the mode of applying the principles which I have laid down. I will take first the character of Jesus Christ. How is this to be explained by the principles of human nature? — We are immediately struck with this peculiarity in the Author of Christianity, that, whilst all other men are formed in a measure by the spirit of the age, we can discover in Jesus no impression of the period in which he lived. We know with considerable accuracy the state of society, the modes of thinking, the hopes and expectations of the country in which Jesus was born and grew up; and he is as free from them, and as exalted above them, as if he had lived in another world, or with every sense shut on the objects around him. His character has in it nothing local or temporary. It can be explained by nothing around him. His history shows him to us a solitary being, living for purposes which none but himself comprehended, and enjoying not so much as the sympathy of a single mind. His Apostles, his chosen companions, brought to him the spirit of the age; and nothing shows its strength more strikingly, than the slowness with which it yielded in these honest men to the instructions of Jesus.

Jesus came to a nation expecting a Messiah; and he claimed this character. But instead of conforming to the opinions which prevailed in regard to the Messiah, he resisted them wholly and without reserve. To a people anticipating a triumphant leader, under whom vengeance as well as ambition was to be glutted by the prostration of their oppressors, he came as a spiritual leader, teaching humility and peace. This undisguised hostility to the dearest hopes and prejudices of his nation; this disdain of the usual compliances, by which ambition and imposture conciliate adherents; this deliberate exposure of himself to rejection and hatred, cannot easily be explained by the common principles of human nature, and excludes the possibility of selfish aims in the Author of Christianity.

One striking peculiarity in Jesus is the extent, the vastness, of his views. Whilst all around him looked for a Messiah to liberate God's ancient people, whilst to every other Jew, Judea was the exclusive object of pride and hope, Jesus came, declaring himself to be the deliverer and light of the world, and in his whole teaching and life, you see a consciousness, which never forsakes him, of a relation to the whole human race. This idea of blessing mankind, of spreading a universal religion, was the most magnificent which had ever entered man's mind. All previous religions had been given to particular nations. No conqueror, legislator, philosopher, in the extravagance of ambition, had ever dreamed of subjecting all nations to a common faith.

This conception of a universal religion, intended alike for Jew and Gentile, for all nations and climes, is wholly inexplicable by the circumstances of Jesus. He was a Jew, and the first and deepest and most constant impression on a Jew's mind, was that of the superiority conferred on his people and himself by the national religion introduced by Moses. The wall between the Jew and the Gentile seemed to reach to heaven. The abolition of the peculiarity of Moses, the prostration of the temple on Mount Zion, the erection of a new religion, in which all men would meet as brethren, and which would be the common and equal property of Jew and Gentile, these were of all ideas the last to spring up in Judea, the last for enthusiasm or imposture to originate.

Compare next these views of Christ with his station in life. He was of humble birth and education, with nothing in his lot, with no extensive means, no rank, or wealth, or patronage, to infuse vast thoughts and extravagant plans. The shop of a carpenter, the village of Nazareth, were not spots for ripening a scheme more aspiring and extensive than had ever been formed. It is a principle of human nature, that, except in case of insanity, some proportion is observed between the power of an individual, and his plans and hopes. The purpose, to which Jesus devoted himself, was as ill suited to his condition as an attempt to change the seasons, or to make the sun rise in the west. That a young man, in obscure life, belonging to an oppressed nation, should seriously think of subverting the time-hallowed and deep-rooted religions of the world, is a strange fact; but with this purpose we see the mind of Jesus thoroughly imbued; and, sublime as it is, he never falls below it in his language or conduct, but speaks and acts with a consciousness of superiority, with a dignity and authority, becoming this unparalleled destination.

In this connexion, I cannot but add another striking circumstance in Jesus, and that is, the calm confidence with which he always looked forward to the accomplishment of his design. He fully knew the strength of the passions and powers which were arrayed against him, and was perfectly aware that his life was to be shortened by violence; yet not a word escapes him implying a doubt of the ultimate triumphs of his religion. One of the beauties of the Gospels, and one of the proofs of their genuineness, is found in our Saviour's indirect and obscure allusions to his approaching sufferings, and to the glory which was to follow; allusions showing us the workings of a mind, thoroughly conscious of being appointed to accomplish infinite good through great calamity. This entire and patient relinquishment of immediate success, this ever present persuasion, that he was to perish before his religion would advance, and this calm, unshaken anticipation of distant and unbounded triumphs, are remarkable traits, throwing a tender and solemn grandeur over our Lord, and wholly inexplicable by human principles, or by the circumstances in which he was placed.

The views hitherto taken of Christ relate to his public character and office. If we pass to what may be called his private character, we shall receive the same impression of inexplicable excellence. The most striking trait in Jesus was, undoubtedly, benevolence; and, although this virtue had existed before, yet it had not been manifested in the same form and extent. Christ's benevolence was distinguished first by its expansiveness. At that age, an unconfined philanthropy, proposing and toiling to do good without distinction of country or rank, was unknown. Love to man as man, love comprehending the hated Samaritan and the despised publican, was a feature which separated Jesus from the best men of his nation and of the world. Another characteristic of the benevolence of Jesus, was its gentleness and tenderness, forming a strong contrast with the hardness and ferocity of the spirit and manners which then prevailed, and with that sternness and inflexibility, which the purest philosophy of Greece and Rome inculcated as the perfection of virtue. But its most distinguishing trait was its superiority to injury. Revenge was one of the recognised rights of the age in which he lived; and though a few sages, who had seen its inconsistency with man's dignity, had condemned it, yet none had inculcated the duty of regarding one's worst enemies with that kindness which God manifests to sinful men, and of returning curses with blessings and prayers. This form of benevolence, the most disinterested and divine form, was, as you well know, manifested by Jesus Christ in infinite strength, amidst injuries and indignities which cannot be surpassed. Now this singular eminence of goodness, this superiority to the degrading influences of the age, under which all other men suffered, needs to be explained; and one thing it demonstrates, that Jesus Christ was not an unprincipled deceiver, exposing not only his own life but the lives of confiding friends, in an enterprise next to desperate.

I cannot enlarge on other traits of the character of Christ. I will only observe, that it had one distinction, which more than any thing, forms a perfect character. It was made up of contrasts; in other words, it was a union of excellences which are not easily reconciled, which seem at first sight incongruous, but which, when blended and duly proportioned, constitute moral harmony, and attract, with equal power, love and veneration. For example, we discover in Jesus Christ an unparalleled dignity of character, a consciousness of greatness, never discovered or approached by any other individual in history; and yet this was blended with a condescension, lowliness, and unostentatious simplicity, which had never before been thought consistent with greatness. In like manner, he united an utter superiority to the world, to its pleasures and ordinary interests, with suavity of manners and freedom from austerity. He joined strong feeling and self-possession; an indignant sensibility to sin, and compassion to the sinner; an intense devotion to his work, and calmness under opposition and ill success; a universal philanthropy, and a susceptibility of private attachments; the authority which became the Saviour of the world, and the tenderness and gratitude of a son. Such was the author of our religion. And is his character to be explained by imposture or insane enthusiasm? Does it not bear the unambiguous marks of a heavenly origin?

Perhaps it may be said, this character never existed. Then the invention of it is to be explained, and the reception which this fiction met with; and these perhaps are as difficult of explanation on natural principles, as its real existence. Christ's history bears all the marks of reality; a more frank, simple, unlabored, unostentatious narrative was never penned. Besides, his character, if invented, must have been an invention of singular difficulty, because no models existed on which to frame it. He stands alone in the records of time. The conception of a being, proposing such new and exalted ends, and governed by higher principles than the progress of society had developed, implies singular intellectual power. That several individuals should join in equally vivid conceptions of this character; and should not merely describe in general terms the fictitious being to whom it was attributed, but should introduce him into real life, should place him in a great variety of circumstances, in connexion with various ranks of men, with friends and foes, and should in all preserve his identity, show the same great and singular mind always acting in harmony with itself; this is a supposition hardly credible, and, when the circumstances of the writers of the New Testament are considered, seems to be as inexplicable on human principles, as what I before suggested, the composition of Newton's "Principia" by a savage. The character of Christ, though delineated in an age of great moral darkness, has stood the scrutiny of ages; and, in proportion as men's moral sentiments have been refined, its beauty has been more seen and felt. To suppose it invented, is to suppose that its authors, outstripping their age, had attained to a singular delicacy and elevation of moral perception and feeling. But these attainments are not very reconcilable with the character of its authors, supposing it to be a fiction; that is, with the character of habitual liars and impious deceivers.

But we are not only unable to discover powers adequate to this invention. There must have been motives for it ; for men do not make great efforts, without strong motives ; and, in the whole compass of human incitements, we challenge the infidel to suggest any, which could have prompted to the work now to be explained.

Once more, it must be recollected, that this invention, if it were one, was received as real, at a period so near to the time ascribed to Christ's appearance, that the means of detecting it were infinite. That men should send out such a forgery, and that it should prevail and triumph, are circumstances not easily reconcilable with the principles of our nature.

The character of Christ, then, was real. Its reality is the only explanation of the mighty revolution produced by his religion. And how can you account for it, but by that cause to which he always referred it, — a mission from the Father ?

Next to the character of Christ, his religion might be shown to abound in circumstances which contradict and repel the idea of a human origin. For example, its representations of the paternal character of God ; its inculcation of a universal charity ; the stress which it lays on inward purity ; its substitution of a spiritual worship for the forms and ceremonies, which everywhere had usurped the name and extinguished the life of religion ; its preference of humility, and of the mild, unostentatious, passive virtues, to the dazzling qualities which had monopolized men's admiration ; its consistent and bright discoveries of immortality ; its adaptation to the wants of man as a sinner ; its adaptation to all the conditions, capacities, and sufferings of human nature ; its pure, sublime, yet practicable morality ; its high and generous motives ; and its fitness to form a character, which plainly prepares for a higher life than the present; these are peculiarities of Christianity, which will strike us more and more, in proportion as we understand distinctly the circumstances of the age and country in which this religion appeared, and for which no adequate human cause has been or can be assigned.

Passing over these topics, each of which might be enlarged into a discourse, I will make but one remark on this religion, which strikes my own mind very forcibly. Since its introduction, human nature has made great progress, and society experienced great changes; and in this advanced condition of the world, Christianity, instead of losing its application and importance, is found to be more and more congenial and adapted to man's nature and wants. Men have outgrown the other institutions of that period when Christianity appeared, its philosophy, its modes of warfare, its policy, its public and private economy; but Christianity has never shrunk as intellect has opened, but has always kept in advance of men's faculties, and unfolded nobler views in proportion as they have ascended. The highest powers and affections, which our nature has developed, find more than adequate objects in this religion. Christianity is indeed peculiarly fitted to the more improved stages of society, to the more delicate sensibilities of refined minds, and especially to that dissatisfaction with the present state, which always grows with the growth of our moral powers and affections. As men advance in civilization, they become susceptible of mental sufferings, to which ruder ages are strangers; and these Christianity is fitted to assuage. Imagination and intellect become more restless; and Christianity brings them tranquillity, by the eternal and magnificent truths, the solemn and unbounded prospects, which it unfolds. This fitness of our religion to more advanced stages of society than that in which it was introduced, to wants of human nature not then developed, seems to me very striking. The religion bears the marks of having come from a being who perfectly understood the human mind, and had power to provide for its progress. This feature of Christianity is of the nature of prophecy. It was an anticipation of future and distant ages; and, when we consider among whom our religion sprung, where, but in God, can we find an explanation of this peculiarity?

I have now offered a few hints on the character of Christ, and on the character of his religion; and, before quitting these topics, I would observe, that they form a strong presumption in favor of the miraculous facts of the Christian history. These miracles were not wrought by a man, whose character, in other respects, was ordinary. They were acts of a being, whose mind was as singular as his works, who spoke and acted with more than human authority, whose moral qualities and sublime purposes were in accordance with superhuman powers. Christ's miracles are in unison with his whole character, and bear a proportion to it, like that which we observe in the most harmonious productions of nature; and in this way they receive from it great confirmation. And the same presumption in their favor arises from his religion. That a religion, carrying in itself such marks of divinity, and so inexplicable on human principles, should receive outward confirmations from Omnipotence, is not surprising. The extraordinary character of the religion accords with and seems to demand extraordinary interpositions in its behalf. Its miracles are not solitary, naked, unexplained, disconnected events, but are bound up with a system, which is worthy of God, and impressed with God; which occupies a large space, and is operating, with great and increasing energy, in human affairs.

As yet I have not touched on what seem to many writers the strongest proofs of Christianity, I mean the direct evidences of its miracles; by which we mean the testimony borne to them, including the character, conduct, and condition of the witnesses. These I have not time to unfold; nor is this labor needed; for Paley's inestimable work, which is one of your classical books, has stated these proofs with great clearness and power. I would only observe, that they may all be resolved into this single principle, namely, that the Christian miracles were originally believed under such circumstances, that this belief can only be explained by their actual occurrence. That Christianity was received at first on the ground of miracles, and that its first preachers and converts proved the depth and strength of their conviction of these facts, by attesting them in sufferings and in death, we know from the most ancient records which relate to this religion, both Christian and Heathen; and, in fact, this conviction can alone explain their adherence to Christianity. Now, that this conviction could only have sprung from the reality of the miracles, we infer from the known circumstances of these witnesses, whose passions, interests, and strongest prejudices were originally hostile to the new religion; whose motives for examining with care the facts on which it rested, were as urgent and solemn, and whose means and opportunities of ascertaining their truth were as ample and unfailing, as can be conceived to conspire; so that the supposition of their falsehood cannot be admitted, without subverting our trust in human judgment and human testimony under the most favorable circumstances for discovering truth; that is, without introducing universal skepticism.

There is one class of Christian evidences, to which I have but slightly referred, but which has struck with peculiar force men of reflecting minds. I refer to the marks of truth and reality, which are found in the Christian Records; to the internal proofs, which the books of the New Testament carry with them, of having been written by men who lived in the first age of Christianity, who believed and felt its truth, who bore a part in the labors and conflicts which attended its establishment, and who wrote from personal knowledge and deep conviction. A few remarks to illustrate the nature and power of these internal proofs, which are furnished by the books of the New Testament, I will now subjoin.

The New Testament consists of histories and epistles. The historical books, namely, the Gospels and the Acts, are a continued narrative, embracing many years, and professing to give the history of the rise and progress of the religion. Now it is worthy of observation, that these writings completely answer their end; that they completely solve the problem, how this peculiar religion grew up and established itself in the world; that they furnish precise and adequate causes for this stupendous revolution in human affairs. It is also worthy of remark, that they relate a series of facts, which are not only connected with one another, but are intimately linked with the long series which has followed them, and agree accurately with subsequent history, so as to account for and sustain it. Now, that a collection of fictitious narratives, coming from different hands, comprehending many years, and spreading over many countries, should not only form a consistent whole, when taken by themselves ; but should also connect and interweave themselves with real history so naturally and intimately, as to furnish no clue for detection, as to exclude the appearance of incongruity and discordance, and as to give an adequate explanation and the only explanation of acknowledged events, of the most important revolution in society ; this is a supposition from which an intelligent man at once revolts, and which, if admitted, would shake a principal foundation of history.

I have before spoken of the unity and consistency of Christ's character as developed in the Gospels, and of the agreement of the different writers in giving us the singular features of his mind. Now there are the same marks of truth running through the whole of these narratives. For example, the effects produced by Jesus on the various classes of society ; the different feelings of admiration, attachment, and envy, which he called forth ; the various expressions of these feelings ; the prejudices, mistakes, and gradual illumination of his disciples ; these are all given to us with such marks of truth and reality as could not easily be counterfeited. The whole history is precisely such, as might be expected from the actual appearance of such a person as Jesus Christ, in such a state of society as then existed.

The Epistles, if possible, abound in marks of truth and reality even more than the Gospels. They are imbued thoroughly with the spirit of the first age of Christianity. They bear all the marks of having come from men plunged in the conflicts which the new religion excited, alive to its interests, identified with its fortunes. They betray the very state of mind which must have been generated by the peculiar condition of the first propagators of the religion. They are letters written on real business, intended for immediate effects, designed to meet prejudices and passions, which such a religion must at first have awakened. They contain not a trace of the circumstances of a later age, or of the feelings, impressions, and modes of thinking by which later times were characterized, and from which later writers could not easily have escaped. The letters of Paul have a remarkable agreement with his history. They are precisely such as might be expected from a man of a vehement mind, who had been brought up in the schools of Jewish literature, who had been converted by a sudden, overwhelming miracle, who had been intrusted with the preaching of the new religion to the Gentiles, and who was everywhere met by the prejudices and persecuting spirit of his own nation. They are full of obscurities growing out of these points of Paul's history and character, and out of the circumstances of the infant church, and which nothing but an intimate acquaintance with that early period can illustrate. This remarkable infusion of the spirit of the first age into the Christian Records, cannot easily be explained but by the fact, that they were written in that age by the real and zealous propagators of Christianity, and that they are records of real convictions and of actual events.

There is another evidence of Christianity, still more nternal than any on which I have yet dwelt, an evidence to be felt rather than described, but not less real because founded on feeling. I refer to that conviction of the divine original of our religion, which springs up and continually gains strength, in those who apply it habitually to their tempers and lives, and who imbibe its spirit and hopes. In such men, there is a consciousness of the adaptation of Christianity to their noblest faculties; a consciousness of its exalting and consoling influences, of its power to confer the true happiness of human nature, to give that peace which the world cannot give; which assures them, that it is not of earthly origin, but a ray from the Everlasting Light, a stream from the Fountain of Heavenly Wisdom and Love. This is the evidence which sustains the faith of thousands, who never read and cannot understand the learned books of Christian apologists, who want, perhaps, words to explain the ground of their belief, but whose faith is of adamantine firmness, who hold the Gospel with a conviction more intimate and unwavering than mere argument ever produced.

But I must tear myself from a subject, which opens upon me continually as I proceed. — Imperfect as this discussion is, the conclusion, I trust, is placed beyond doubt, that Christianity is true. And, my hearers, if true, it is the greatest of all truths, deserving and demanding our reverent attention and fervent gratitude. This religion must never be confounded with our common blessings. It is a revelation of pardon, which, as sinners, we all need. Still more, it is a revelation of human immortality; a doctrine, which, however undervalued amidst the bright anticipations of inexperienced youth, is found to be our strength and consolation, and the only effectual spring of persevering and victorious virtue, when the realities of life have scattered our visionary hopes; when pain, disappointment, and temptation press upon us; when this world's enjoyments are found unable to quench that deep thirst of happiness which burns in every breast; when friends, whom we love as our own souls, die; and our own graves open before us. — To all who hear me, and especially to my young hearers, I would say, let the truth of this religion be the strongest conviction of your understandings; let its motives and precepts sway with an absolute power your characters and lives.

EVIDENCES OF CHRISTIANITY.

ROMANS i. 16: "I am not ashamed of the Gospel of Christ."

PART I.

THESE words of Paul are worthy of his resolute and disinterested spirit. In uttering them he was not an echo of the multitude, a servile repeater of established doctrines. The vast majority around him were ashamed of Jesus. The cross was then coupled with infamy. Christ's name was scorned as a malefactor's, and to profess his religion was to share his disgrace. Since that time what striking changes have occurred! The cross now hangs as an ornament from the neck of beauty. It blazes on the flags of navies, and the standards of armies. Millions bow before it in adoration, as if it were a shrine of the divinity. Of course, the temptation to be ashamed of Jesus is very much diminished. Still it is not wholly removed. Much of the homage now paid to Christianity is outward, political, worldly, and paid to its corruptions much more than to its pure and lofty spirit; and accordingly its conscientious and intrepid friends must not think it a strange thing to be encountered with occasional coldness or reproach. We may still be tempted to be ashamed of our religion, by being thrown among skeptics, who deny and deride it. We may be tempted to be ashamed of the simple and rational doctrines of Christ, by being brought into connexion with narrow zealots, who enforce their dark and perhaps degrading peculiarities as essential to salvation. We may be tempted to be ashamed of his pure, meek, and disinterested precepts, by being thrown among the licentious, self-seeking, and vindictive. Against these perils we should all go armed. To be loyal to truth and conscience under such trials, is one of the signal proofs of virtue. No man deserves the name of Christian, but he who adheres to his principles amidst the unbelieving, the intolerant, and the depraved.

"I am not ashamed of the gospel of Christ." So said Paul. So would I say. Would to God that I could catch the spirit as well as the language of the Apostle, and bear my testimony to Christianity with the same heroic resolution. Do any ask, why I join in this attestation to the gospel? Some of my reasons I propose now to set before you; and in doing so, I ask the privilege of speaking, as the Apostle has done, in the first person; of speaking in my own name, and of laying open my own mind in the most direct language. There are cases, in which the ends of public discourse may be best answered by the frank expression of individual feeling; and this mode of address, when adopted with such views, ought not to be set down to the account of egotism.

I proceed to state the reasons why I am not ashamed of the gospel of Christ; and I begin with one so important, that it will occupy the present discourse.

I am not ashamed of the gospel of Christ, because it is *true*. This is my first reason. The religion is *true*, and no consideration but this could induce me to defend it. I adopt it, not because it is popular, for false and ruinous systems have enjoyed equal reputation; nor because it is thought to uphold the order of society, for I believe that nothing but truth can be permanently useful. It is *true*; and I say this not lightly, but after deliberate examination. I am not repeating the accents of the nursery. I do not affirm the truth of Christianity, because I was so taught before I could inquire, or because I was brought up in a community pledged to this belief. It is not unlikely, that my faith and zeal will be traced by some to these sources; and believing such imputations to be groundless, fidelity to the cause of truth binds me to repel them. The circumstance of having been born and educated under Christianity, so far from disposing me to implicit faith, has often been to me the occasion of serious distrust of our religion. On observing how common it is for men of all countries and names, whether Christians, Jews, or Mahometans, to receive the religion of their fathers, I have again and again asked myself, whether I too was not a slave, whether I too was not blindly walking in the path of tradition, and yielding myself as passively as others to an hereditary faith. I distrust and fear the power of numbers and of general opinion over my judgment; and few things incite me more to repel a doctrine than intolerant attempts to force it on my understanding. Perhaps my Christian education and connexions have inclined me to skepticism, rather than bowed my mind to authority.

It may still be said, that the pride and prejudices

and motives of interest, which belong to my profession as a Christian minister, throw a suspiciousness over my reasoning and judgment on the present subject. I reply, that to myself I seem as free from biases of this kind, as the most indifferent person. I have no priestly prepossessions. I know and acknowledge the corruptions and perversions of the ministerial office from the earliest age of the church. I reprobate the tyranny which it exercises so often over the human mind. I recognise no peculiar sanctity in those who sustain it. I think, then, that I come to the examination of Christianity with as few blinding partialities as any man. I indeed claim no exemption from error; I ask no implicit faith in my conclusions; I care not how jealously and thoroughly my arguments are sifted. I only ask, that I may not be prejudged as a servile or interested partisan of Christianity. I ask that I may be heard as a friend of truth, desirous to aid my fellow-creatures in determining a question of great and universal concern. I appear as the advocate of Christianity, solely because it approves itself to my calmest reason as a revelation from God, and as the purest, brightest light which He has shed on the human mind. I disclaim all other motives. No policy, no vassalage to opinion, no dread of reproach even from the good, no private interest, no desire to uphold a useful superstition, nothing in short but a deliberate conviction of the truth of Christianity, induces me to appear in its ranks. I should be ashamed of it, did I not believe it true.

In discussing this subject, I shall express my convictions strongly; I shall speak of infidelity as a gross and perilous error. But in so doing, I beg not to be understood as passing sentence on the character of individual unbelievers. I shall show that the Christian religion is true, is from God; but I do not therefore conclude, that all who reject it are the enemies of God, and are to be loaded with reproach. I would uphold the truth without ministering to uncharitableness. The criminality, the damnable guilt of unbelief in all imaginable circumstances, is a position which I think untenable; and persuaded as I am, that it prejudices the cause of Christianity, by creating an antipathy between its friends and opposers, which injures both, and drives the latter into more determined hostility to the truth, I think it worthy of a brief consideration in this stage of the discussion.

I lay it down as a principle, that unbelief, considered in itself, has no moral quality, is neither a virtue nor a vice, but must receive its character, whether good or bad, from the dispositions or motives which produce or pervade it. Mere acts of the understanding are neither right nor wrong. When I speak of faith as a holy or virtuous principle, I extend the term beyond its primitive meaning, and include in it not merely the assent of the intellect, but the disposition or temper by which this assent is determined, and which it is suited to confirm; and I attach as broad a signification to unbelief, when I pronounce it a crime. The truth is, that the human mind, though divided by our philosophy into many distinct capacities, seldom or never exerts them separately, but generally blends them in one act. Thus in forming a judgment, it exerts the will and affections, or the moral principles of our nature, as really as the power of thought. Men's passions and interests mix with, and are expressed in, the decisions of the intellect. In the Scriptures, which use language freely, and not with philosophical strictness, faith and unbelief are mental acts of this complex character, or joint products of the understanding and heart; and on this account alone, they are objects of approbation or reproof. In these views, I presume, reflecting Christians of every name agree.

According to these views, opinions cannot be laid down as unerring and immutable signs of virtue and vice. The very same opinion may be virtuous in one man and vicious in another, supposing it, as is very possible, to have originated in different states of mind. For example, if through envy and malignity I should rashly seize on the slightest proofs of guilt in my neighbour, my judgment of his criminality would be morally wrong. Let another man arrive at the same conclusion, in consequence of impartial inquiry and love of truth, and his decision would be morally right. Still more, according to these views, it is possible for the belief of Christianity to be as criminal as unbelief. Undoubtedly the reception of a system, so pure in spirit and tendency as the gospel, is to be regarded in general as a favorable sign. But let a man adopt this religion, because it will serve his interest and popularity; let him shut his mind against objections to it, lest they should shake his faith in a gainful system; let him tamper with his intellect, and for base and selfish ends exhaust its strength in defence of the prevalent faith, and he is just as criminal in believing, as another would be in rejecting Christianity under the same bad impulses. Our religion is at this moment adopted, and passionately defended by vast multitudes, on the ground of the very same pride, worldliness, love of popularity, and blind devotion to hereditary prejudices, which led the Jews and Heathens to reject it in the primitive age; and the faith of the first is as wanting in virtue, as was the infidelity of the last.

To judge of the character of faith and unbelief, we must examine the times and the circumstances in which they exist. At the first preaching of the gospel, to believe on Christ was a strong proof of an upright mind; to enlist among his followers, was to forsake ease, honor, and wordly success; to confess him was an act of signal loyalty to truth, virtue, and God. To believe in Christ at the present moment has no such significance. To confess him argues no moral courage. It may even betray a servility and worldliness of mind. These remarks apply in their spirit to unbelief. At different periods, and in different conditions of society, unbelief may express very different states of mind. Before we pronounce it a crime, and doom it to perdition, we ought to know the circumstances under which it has sprung up, and to inquire with candor whether they afford no palliation or defence. When Jesus Christ was on earth, when his miracles were wrought before men's eyes, when his voice sounded in their ears, when not a shade of doubt could be thrown over the reality of his supernatural works, and not a human corruption had mingled with his doctrine, there was the strongest presumption against the uprightness and the love of truth of those who rejected him. He knew too the hearts and the lives of those who surrounded him, and saw distinctly in their envy, ambition, worldliness, sensuality, the springs of their unbelief; and accordingly he pronounced it a crime. Since that period, what changes have taken place! Jesus Christ has left the world. His miracles are events of a remote age, and the proofs of them though abundant, are to many perfectly unknown; and, what is incomparably more important, his religion has undergone corruption, adulteration, disastrous change, and its likeness to its Founder is in no small degree effaced. The clear, consistent, quickening truth, which came from the lips of Jesus, has been exchanged for a hoarse jargon and vain babblings. The stream, so pure at the fountain, has been polluted and poisoned through its whole course. Not only has Christianity been overwhelmed by absurdities, but by impious doctrines, which have made the Universal Father, now a weak and vain despot, to be propitiated by forms and flatteries, and now an almighty torturer, foreordaining multitudes of his creatures to guilt, and then glorifying his justice by their everlasting woe. When I think what Christianity has become in the hands of politicians and priests, how it has been shaped into a weapon of power, how it has crushed the human soul for ages, how it has struck the intellect with palsy and haunted the imagination with superstitious phantoms, how it has broken whole nations to the yoke, and frowned on every free thought; when I think how, under almost every form of this religion, its ministers have taken it into their own keeping, have hewn and compressed it into the shape of rigid creeds, and have then pursued by menaces of everlasting woe whoever should question the divinity of these works of their hands; when I consider, in a word, how, under such influences, Christianity has been and still is exhibited, in forms which shock alike the reason, conscience, and heart, I feel deeply, painfully, what a different system it is from that which Jesus taught, and I dare not apply to unbelief the terms of condemnation which belonged to the infidelity of the primitive age.

Perhaps I ought to go further. Perhaps I ought to say, that to reject Christianity under some of its corruptions is rather a virtue than a crime. At the present moment, I would ask, whether it is a vice to doubt the truth of Christianity, as it is manifested in Spain and Portugal? When a patriot in those benighted countries, who knows Christianity only as a bulwark of despotism, as a rearer of inquisitions, as a stern jailer immuring wretched women in the convent, as an executioner stained and reeking with the blood of the friends of freedom; I say, when the patriot, who sees in our religion the instrument of these crimes and woes, believes and affirms that it is not from God, are we authorized to charge his unbelief on dishonesty and corruption of mind, and to brand him as a culprit? May it not be that the spirit of Christianity in his heart emboldens him to protest with his lips against what bears the name? And if he thus protest, through a deep sympathy with the oppression and sufferings of his race, is he not nearer the kingdom of God than the priest and inquisitor who boastingly and exclusively assume the Christian name? Jesus Christ has told us, that "this is the condemnation" of the unbelieving, "that they love darkness rather than light;" and who does not see, that this ground of condemnation is removed, just in proportion as the light is quenched, or Christian truth is buried in darkness and debasing error?

I know I shall be told that a man in the circumstances now supposed, would still be culpable for his unbelief, because the Scriptures are within his reach, and these are sufficient to guide him to the true doctrines of Christ. But in the countries of which I have spoken, the Scriptures are not common; and if they were, I apprehend that we should task human strength too severely, in requiring it, under every possible disadvantage, to gain the truth from this source alone. A man, born and brought up in the thickest darkness, and amidst the grossest corruptions of Christianity, accustomed to hear the Scriptures disparaged, accustomed to connect false ideas with their principal terms, and wanting our most common helps of criticism, can hardly be expected to detach from the mass of error which bears the name of the Gospel, the simple principles of the primitive faith. Let us not exact too much of our fellow-creatures. In our zeal for Christianity, let us not forget its spirit of equity and mercy. — In these remarks I have taken an extreme case. I have supposed a man subjected to the greatest disadvantages in regard to the knowledge of Christianity. But obstacles less serious may exculpate the unbeliever. In truth, none of us can draw the line which separates between innocence and guilt in this particular. To measure the responsibility of a man, who doubts or denies Christianity, we must know the history of his mind, his capacity of judgment, the early influences and prejudices to which he was exposed, the forms under which the religion and its proofs first fixed his thoughts, and the opportunities since enjoyed of eradicating errors, which struck root before the power of trying them was unfolded. We are not his judges. At another and an unerring tribunal he must give account.

I cannot, then, join in the common cry against infidelity as the sure mark of a corrupt mind. That unbelief often has its origin in evil dispositions, I cannot doubt. The character of the unbeliever often forces us to acknowledge, that he rejects Christianity to escape its rebukes; that its purity is its chief offence; that he seeks infidelity as a refuge from fear and virtuous restraint. But to impute these unholy motives to a man of pure life, is to judge rashly, and it may be unrighteously. I cannot look upon unbelief as essentially and unfailingly a crime. But I do look upon it as among the greatest of calamities. It is the loss of the chief aid of virtue, of the mightiest power over temptation, of the most quickening knowledge of God, of the only unfailing light, of the only sure hope. The unbeliever would gain unspeakably by parting with every possession for the truth which he doubts or rejects. And how shall we win him to the faith? Not by reproach, by scorn, by tones of superiority; but by paying due respect to his understanding, his virtues, and his right of private judgment; by setting before him Christianity in its simple majesty, its reasonableness, and wonderful adaptation to the wants of our spiritual nature; by exhibiting its proofs without exaggeration, yet in their full strength; and, above all, by showing in our own characters and lives, that there is in Christianity a power to purify, elevate, and console, which can be found in no human teaching. These are the true instruments of conversion. The ignorant and superstitious may indeed be driven into a religion by menace and reproach. But the reflecting unbeliever cannot but distrust a cause which admits such weapons. He must be reasoned with as a man, an equal, and a brother. Perhaps we may silence him for a time, by spreading through the community a fanatical excitement, and a persecuting hatred of infidelity. But as by such processes Christianity would be made to take a more unlovely and irrational form, its secret foes would be multiplied; its brightest evidence would be dimmed, its foundation sapped, its energy impaired; and whenever the time should arrive for throwing off the mask (and that time would come), we should learn, that in the very ranks of its nominal disciples, there had been trained a host of foes, who would burn to prostrate the intolerant faith, which had so long sealed their lips, and trampled on the rights and freedom of the human mind.

According to these views, I do not condemn the unbeliever, unless he bear witness against himself by an immoral and irreligious life. It is not given me to search his heart. But this power is given to himself, and as a friend, I call upon him to exert it; I ask him to look honestly into his own mind, to question his past life, and to pronounce impartial sentence on the causes of his unbelief. Let him ask himself, whether he has inquired into the principles and proofs of Christianity deliberately and in the love of truth; whether the desire to discover and fulfil his duties to God and his fellow-creatures has governed his examination; whether he has surrendered himself to no passions or pursuits which religion and conscience rebuke, and which bar the mind and sear the heart against the truth. If, thus self-questioned, his heart acquit him, let no man condemn him, and let him heed no man's condemnation. But if conscience bear witness against him, he has cause to suspect and dread his unbelief. He has reason to fear, that it is the fruit of a depraved mind, and that it will ripen and confirm the depravity from which it sprung.

I know that there are those, who will construe what they will call my lenity towards unbelief, into treachery towards Christianity. There are those who think, that unless skepticism be ranked among the worst crimes, and the infidel be marked out for abhorrence and dread, the multitude of men will lose their hold on the gospel. An opinion more discreditable to Christianity cannot easily be advanced by its friends. It virtually admits, that the proofs of our religion, unless examined under the influence of terror, cannot work conviction; that the gospel cannot be left, like other subjects, to the calm and unbiassed judgment of mankind. It discovers a distrust of Christianity, with which I have no sympathy. And here I would remark, that the worst abuses of our religion have sprung from this cowardly want of confidence in its power. Its friends have feared, that it could not stand without a variety of artificial buttresses. They have imagined, that men must now be bribed into faith by annexing to it temporal privileges, now driven into it by menaces and inquisitions, now attracted by gorgeous forms, now awed by mysteries and superstitions; in a word, that the multitude must be imposed upon, or the religion will fall. I have no such distrust of Christianity; I believe in its invincible powers. It is founded in our nature. It meets our deepest wants. Its proofs as well as principles are adapted to the common understandings of men, and need not to be aided by appeals to fear or any other passion, which would discourage inquiry or disturb the judgment. I fear nothing for Christianity, if left to speak in its own tones, to approach men with its unveiled, benignant countenance. I do fear much from the weapons of policy and intimidation, which are framed to uphold the imagined weakness of Christian truth.

I now come to the great object of this discourse, — an exhibition of the proofs of Christianity; — and I begin with a topic which is needed to prepare some, if not many, to estimate these proofs fairly, and according to their true weight. I begin with the position, That there is nothing in the general idea of Revelation at which Reason ought to take offence, nothing inconsistent with any established truth, or with our best views of God and Nature. This topic meets a prejudice not very rare. I repeat it then, Revelation is nothing incredible, nothing which carries contradiction on its face, nothing at war with any great principles of reason or experience. On hearing of God's teaching us by some other means than the fixed order of nature, we ought not to be surprised, nor ought the suggestion to awaken resistance in our minds.

Revelation is not at war with nature. From the necessity of the case, the earliest instruction must have come to human beings from this source. If our race had a beginning (and nothing but the insanity of Atheism can doubt this), then its first members, created as they were without human parentage, and having no resource in the experience of fellow-creatures who had preceded them, required an immediate teaching from their Creator; they would have perished without it. Revelation was the very commencement of human history, the foundation of all later knowledge and improvement. It was an essential part of the course of Providence, and must not then be regarded as a discord in God's general system.

Revelation is not at war with nature. Nature prompts us to expect it from the relation which God bears to the human race. The relation of Creator is the most intimate which can subsist; and it leads us to anticipate a free and affectionate intercourse with the creature.

That the Universal Father should be bound by a parental interest to his offspring, that he should watch over and assist the progress of beings whom he has enriched with the divine gifts of reason and conscience, is so natural a doctrine, so accordant with his character, that various sects, both philosophical and religious, both anterior and subsequent to Christianity, have believed, not only in general revelation, but that God reveals himself to every human soul. When I think of the vast capacities of the human mind, of God's nearness to it, and unbounded love towards it, I am disposed to wonder, not that revelations have been made, but that they have not been more variously vouchsafed to the wants of mankind.

Revelation has a striking agreement with the chief method which God has instituted for carrying forward individuals and the race, and is thus in harmony with his ordinary operations. Whence is it, that we all acquire our chief knowledge? Not from the outward universe; not from the fixed laws of material nature; but from intelligent beings, more advanced than ourselves. The teachings of the wise and good are our chief aids. Were our connexion with superior minds broken off, had we no teacher but nature with its fixed laws, its unvarying revolutions of night and day and seasons, we should remain for ever in the ignorance of childhood. Nature is a volume, which we can read only by the help of an intelligent interpreter. The great law under which man is placed, is, that he shall receive illumination and impulse from beings more improved than himself. Now revelation is only an extension of this universal method of carrying forward mankind. In this case, God takes on himself the office to which all rational beings are called. He becomes an immediate teacher to a few, communicating to them a higher order of truths than had before been attained, which they in turn are to teach to their race. Here is no new power or element introduced into the system, but simply an enlargement of that agency on which the progress of man chiefly depends.

Let me next ask you to consider, Why or for what end God has ordained, as the chief means of human improvement, the communication of light from superior to inferior minds; and if it shall then appear, that revelation is strikingly adapted to promote a similar though more important end, you will have another mark of agreement between revelation and his ordinary Providence. Why is it that God has made men's progress dependent on instruction from their fellow-beings? Why are the more advanced commissioned to teach the less informed? A great purpose, I believe the chief purpose, is, to establish interesting relations among men, to bind them to one another by generous sentiments, to promote affectionate intercourse, to call forth a purer love than could spring from a communication of mere outward gifts. Now it is rational to believe, that the Creator designs to bind his creatures to Himself as truly as to one another, and to awaken towards himself even stronger gratitude, confidence, and love; for these sentiments towards God are more happy and ennobling than towards any other being; and it is plain that revelation, or immediate divine teaching, serves as effectually to establish these ties between God and man, as human teaching to attach men to one another. We see, then, in revelation an end corresponding to what the Supreme Being adopts in his common providence.

That the end here affirmed is worthy of his interposition, who can doubt? His benevolence can propose no higher purpose, than that of raising the minds and hearts of his creatures to himself. His parental character is a pledge that he must intend this ineffable happiness for his rational offspring; and Revelation is suited to this end, not only by unfolding new doctrines in relation to God, but by the touching proof which it carries in itself of the special interest which he takes in his human family. There is plainly an expression of deeper concern, a more affectionate character, in this mode of instruction, than in teaching us by the fixed order of nature. Revelation is God speaking to us in our own language, in the accents which human friendship employs. It shows a love, breaking through the reserve and distance, which we all feel to belong to the method of teaching us by his works alone. It fastens our minds on him. We can look on nature, and not think of the Being whose glory it declares; but God is indissolubly connected with, and indeed is a part of, the idea of revelation. How much nearer does this direct intercourse bring him to the mass of mankind! On this account revelation would seem to me important, were it simply to repeat the teachings of nature. This reiteration of great truths in a less formal style, in kinder, more familiar tones, is peculiarly fitted to awaken the soul to the presence and benignity of its heavenly Parent. I see, then, in revelation a purpose corresponding with that for which human teaching was instituted. Both are designed to bring together the teacher and the taught in pure affections.

Let me next ask you to consider, what is the kind of instruction which the higher minds among men are chiefly called to impart to the inferior. You will here see another agreement between revelation and that ordinary human teaching, which is the great instrument of improving the race. What kind of instruction is it, which parents, which the aged and experienced, are most anxious to give to the young, and on which the safety of this class mainly depends? It is instruction in relation to the Future, to their adult years, such as is suited to prepare them fcr the life that is opening before them. It is God's will, when he gives us birth, that we should be forewarned of the future stages of our being, of approaching manhood or womanhood, of the scenes, duties, labors, through which we are to pass; and for this end he connects us with beings, who have traversed the paths on which we are entering, and whose duty it is to train us for a more advanced age. Instruction in regard to Futurity is the great means of improvement. Now the Christian revelation has for its aim to teach us on this very subject; to disclose the life which is before us, and to fit us for it. A Future state is its constant burden. That God should give us light in regard to that state, if he designs us for it, is what we should expect from his solicitude to teach us in regard to what is future in our earthly existence. Nature thirsts for, and analogy almost promises, some illumination on the subject of human destiny. This topic I shall insist on more largely hereafter. I wish now simply to show you the agreement of revelation, in this particular, with the ordinary providence of God.

I proceed to another order of reflections, which to my own mind is particularly suited to meet the vague idea, that revelation is at war with nature. To judge of nature, we should look at its highest ranks of beings. We should inquire of the human soul, which we all feel to be a higher existence than matter. Now I maintain, that there are in the human soul wants, deep wants, which are not met by the influences and teachings, which the ordinary course of things affords. I am aware that this is a topic to provoke distrust, if not derision, in the low-minded and sensual; but I speak what I do know; and nothing moves me so little as the scoffs of men who despise their own nature. One of the most striking views of human nature, is the disproportion between what it conceives and thirsts for, and what it finds or can secure in the range of the present state. It is prone to stretch beyond its present bounds. Ideas of excellence and happiness spring up, which it cannot realize now. It carries within itself a standard, of which it daily and hourly falls short. This self-contradiction is the source of many sharp pains. There is, in most men, a dim consciousness, at least, of being made for something higher than they have gained, a feeling of internal discord, a want of some stable good, a disappointment in merely outward acquisitions; and in proportion as these convictions and wants become distinct, they break out in desires of illumination and aids from God not found in nature. I am aware, that the wants of which I have spoken are but faintly developed in the majority of men. Accustomed to give their thoughts and strength to the outward world, multitudes do not penetrate and cannot interpret their own souls. They impute to outward causes the miseries which spring from an internal fountain. They do not detain, and are scarcely conscious of the better thoughts and feelings, which sometimes dart through their minds. Still there are few, who are not sometimes dissatisfied with themselves, who do not feel the wrong which they have done to themselves, and who do not desire a purer and nobler state of mind. The suddenness, with which the multitude are thrilled by the voice of fervent eloquence, when it speaks to them of the spiritual world in tones of reality, shows the deep wants of human nature even amidst ignorance and degradation. But all men do not give themselves wholly to outward things. There are those, and not a few, who are more true to their nature, and ought therefore to be regarded as its more faithful representatives; and in such, the wants, of which I have spoken, are unfolded with energy. There are those, who feel painfully the weight of their present imperfection; who are fired by rare examples of magnanimity and devotion; who desire nothing so intensely as power over temptation, as elevation above selfish passions, as conformity of will to the inward law of duty, as the peace of conscious rectitude and religious trust; who would rejoice to lay down the present life for that spotless, bright, disinterested virtue, of which they have the type or germ in their own minds. Such men can find no resource but in God, and are prepared to welcome a revelation of his merciful purposes as an unspeakable gift. I say, then, that the human mind has wants which nature does not answer. And these are not accidental feelings, unaccountable caprices, but are deep, enduring, and reproduced in all ages under one or another form. They breathe through the works of genius; they burn in the loftiest souls. Here are principles implanted by God in the highest order of his creatures on earth, to which revelation is adapted; and I say, then, that revelation is any thing but hostility to nature.

I will offer but one more view in illustration of this topic. I ask you to consider, on what Principle of human nature the Christian revelation is intended to bear and to exert influence, and then to inquire whether the peculiar importance of this principle be not a foundation for peculiar interposition in its behalf. If so, revelation may be said to be a demand of the human soul, and its imagined incongruity with nature will disappear. For what principle or faculty of the mind, then, was Christianity intended? It was plainly not given to enrich the intellect by teaching philosophy, or to perfect the imagination and taste by furnishing sublime and beautiful models of composition. It was not meant to give sagacity in public life, or skill and invention in common affairs. It was undoubtedly designed to develope all these faculties, but secondarily, and through its influence on a higher principle. It addresses itself primarily, and is especially adapted, to the Moral power in man. It regards and is designed for man as a moral being, endued with conscience or the principle of duty, who is capable of that peculiar form of excellence which we call righteousness or virtue, and exposed to that peculiar evil, guilt. Now the question offers itself, Why does God employ such extraordinary means for promoting virtue rather than science, for aiding conscience rather than intellect and our other powers? Is there a foundation in the moral principle for peculiar interpositions in its behalf? I affirm that there is. I affirm that a broad distinction exists between our moral nature and our other capacities. Conscience is the Supreme power within us. Its essence, its grand characteristic, is Sovereignty. It speaks with a divine authority. Its office is to command, to rebuke, to reward; and happiness and honor depend on the reverence with which we listen to it. All our other powers become useless and worse than useless, unless controlled by the principle of duty. Virtue is the supreme good, the supreme beauty, the divinest of God's gifts, the healthy and harmonious unfolding of the soul, and the germ of immortality. It is worth every sacrifice, and has power to transmute sacrifices and sufferings into crowns of glory and rejoicing. Sin, vice, is an evil of its own kind, and not to be confounded with any other. Who does not feel at once the broad distinction between misfortune and crime, between disease of body and turpitude of soul? Sin, vice, is war with the highest power in our own breasts, and in the universe. It makes a being odious to himself, and arms against him the principle of rectitude in God and in all pure beings. It poisons or dries up the fountains of enjoyment, and adds unspeakable weight to the necessary pains of life. It is not a foreign evil, but a blight and curse in the very centre of our being. Its natural associates are fear, shame, and self-torture; and, whilst it robs the present of consolation, it leaves the future without hope. Now I say, that in this peculiar ruin wrought by moral evil and in this peculiar worth of moral goodness, we see reasons for special interpositions of God in behalf of virtue, in resistance of sin. It becomes the Infinite Father to manifest peculiar interest in the moral condition and wants of his creatures. Their great and continued corruption is an occasion for peculiar methods of relief; and a revelation given to restore them, and carry them forward to perfection, has an end which justifies, if it does not demand, this signal expression of parental love.

The preceding views have been offered, not as sufficient to prove that a revelation has been given, but for the purpose of removing the vague notion that it is at war with nature, and of showing its consistency with the spirit and principles of the divine administration. I proceed now to consider the direct and positive proofs of Christianity, beginning with some remarks on the nature and sufficiency of the evidence on which it chiefly relies.

Christianity sprung up about eighteen hundred years ago. Of course its evidences are to be sought in history. We must go back to the time of its birth, and understand the condition in which it found the world, as well as the circumstances of its origin, progress, and establishment; and happily, on these points, we have all the light necessary to a just judgment. We must not imagine, that a religion, which bears the date of so distant an age, must therefore be involved in obscurity. We know enough of the earliest times of Christianity to place the question of its truth within our reach. The past may be known as truly as the present; and I deem this principle so important in the present discussion that I ask your attention to it.

The past, I have said, may be known; nor is this all; we derive from it our most important knowledge. Former times are our chief instructors. Our political, as well as religious institutions, our laws, customs, modes of thinking, arts of life, have come down from earlier ages, and most of them are unintelligible without a light borrowed from history.

Not only are we able to know the nearest of past ages, or those which touch on our own times, but those which are remote. No educated man doubts any more of the victories of Alexander or Cæsar, before Christ, than of Napoleon's conquests in our own day. So open is our communication with some ages of antiquity, so many are the records which they have transmitted, that we know them even better than nearer times ; and a religion which grew up eighteen hundred years ago, may be more intelligible and accompanied with more decisive proofs of truth or falsehood, than one which is not separated from us by a fourth part of that duration.

From the nature of things, we may and must know much of the past ; for the present has grown out of the past, is its legacy, fruit, representative, and is deeply impressed with it. Events do not expire at the moment of their occurrence. Nothing takes place without leaving traces behind it ; and these are in many cases so distinct and various, as to leave not a doubt of their cause. We all understand, how, in the material world, events testify of themselves to future ages. Should we visit an unknown region, and behold masses of lava covered with soil of different degrees of thickness, and surrounding a blackened crater, we should have as firm a persuasion of the occurrence of remote and successive volcanic eruptions, as if we had lived through the ages in which they took place. The chasms of the earth would report how terribly it had been shaken, and the awful might of long-extinguished fires would be written in desolations which ages had failed to efface. Now conquest, and civil and religious revolutions, leave equally their impressions on society, leave institutions, manners, and a variety of monuments, which are inexplicable without them, and which, taken together, admit not a doubt of their occurrence. The past stretches into the future, the present is crowded with it, and can be interpreted only by the light of history.

But besides these effects and remains of earlier times, we have other and more distinct memorials of the past, which, when joined with the former, place it clearly within our knowledge. I refer to books. A book is more than a monument of a preceding age. It is a voice coming to us over the interval of centuries. Language, when written, as truly conveys to us another's mind as when spoken. It is a species of personal intercourse. By it the wise of former times give us their minds as really, as if by some miracle they were to rise from the dead and communicate with us by speech.

From these remarks we learn that Christianity is not placed beyond the reach of our investigations by the remoteness of its origin; and they are particularly applicable to the age in which the gospel was first given to the world. Our religion did not spring up before the date of authentic history. Its birth is not hidden in the obscurity of early and fabulous times. We have abundant means of access to its earliest stages; and, what is very important, the deep and peculiar interest which Christianity has awakened, has fixed the earnest attention of the most learned and sagacious men on the period of its original publication, so that no age of antiquity is so thoroughly understood. Christianity sprung up at a time, when the literature and philosophy of Greece was spread far and wide, and had given a great impulse to the human mind; and when Rome by unexampled conquests had become a centre and bond of union to the civilized world and to many half civilized regions, and had established a degree of communication between distant countries before unknown. We are not, then, left to grope our way by an unsteady light. Our means of information are various and great. We have incontestable facts in relation to the origin of our religion, from which its truth may be easily deduced. A few of these facts, which form the first steps of our reasoning on this subject, I will now lay before you.

1. First, then, we know with certainty the *time* when Christianity was founded. As to this fact, there is and can be no doubt. Heathen and Christian historians speak on this point with one voice. Christianity was first preached in the age of Tiberius. Not a trace of it exists before that period, and afterwards the marks and proofs of its existence are so obvious and acknowledged as to need no mention. Here is one important fact placed beyond doubt.

2. In the next place, we know the *place* where Christianity sprung up. No one can dispute the country of its birth. Its Jewish origin is not only testified by all history, but is stamped on its front and woven into its frame. The language in which it is conveyed, carries us at once to Judea. Its name is derived from Jewish prophecy. None but Jews could have written the New Testament. So natural, undesigned, and perpetual are the references and allusions of the writers to the opinions and manners of that people, so accustomed are they to borrow from the same source the metaphors, smilitudes, types, by which they illustrate their doctrines, that Christianity, as to its outward form, may be said to be steeped in Judaism. We have, then, another established fact. We know where it was born.

3. Again, we know the individual by whom Christianity was founded. We know its Author, and from the nature of the case this fact cannot but be known. The founder of a religion is naturally and necessarily the object of general inquiry. Wherever the new faith

is carried, the first and most eager questions are, "From whom does it come? On whose authority does it rest?" Curiosity is never more intense, than in regard to the individual, who claims a divine commission and sends forth a new religion. He is the last man to be overlooked or mistaken. In the case of Christianity especially, its founder may be said to have been forced on men's notice, for his history forms an essential part of his religion. Christianity is not an abstract doctrine, which keeps its author out of sight. He is its very soul. It rests on him, and finds its best illustration in his life. These reflections however may be spared. The simple consideration, that Christianity must have had an author, and that it has been always ascribed to Jesus, and to no one else, places the great fact, which I would establish, beyond doubt.

4. I next observe, that we not only know the founder of Christianity, but the ministers by whom he published and spread it through the world. A new religion must have propagators, first teachers, and with these it must become intimately associated. A community can no more be ignorant as to the teachers who converted it to a new faith, than as to the conqueror who subjected it to a new government; and where the art of writing is known and used for recording events, the latter fact will not more certainly be transmitted to posterity than the former. We have the testimony of all ages, that the men called Apostles were the first propagators of Christianity, nor have any others been named as sustaining this office; and it is impossible that, on such a point, such testimony should be false.

5. Again; we know not only when, and where, and by whom Christianity was introduced; — we know, from

a great variety of sources, what in the main this religion was, as it came from the hands of its founder. To assure ourselves on this point, we need not recur to any sacred books. From the age following that of Christ and the Apostles, down to the present day, we have a series, and an almost numberless host, of writers on the subject of Christianity; and whilst we discover in them a great diversity of opinions, and opposite interpretations of some of Christ's teachings, yet on the whole they so far agree in the great facts of his history, and in certain great principles of his religion, that we cannot mistake as to the general character of the system which he taught. There is not a shadow of reason for the opinion that the original system which Jesus taught was lost, and a new one substituted and fastened on the world in his name. The many and great corruptions of Christianity did not and could not hide its principal features. The greatest corruptions took place in the century which followed the death of the Apostles, when certain wild and visionary sects endeavoured to establish a union between the new religion and the false philosophy to which they had been wedded in their heathen state. You may judge of their character and claims, when I tell you, that they generally agreed in believing, that the God who made the world, and who was worshipped by the Jews, was not the supreme God, but an inferior and imperfect Deity, and that matter had existed from eternity, and was essentially and unchangeably evil. Yet these sects endeavoured to sustain themselves on the writings which the great body of Christians received and honored as the works of the Apostles; and, amidst their delusions they recognised and taught the miracles of Christ, his resurrection, and the most important principles of his religion; so that the general nature of Christianity, as it came from its Founder, may be ascertained beyond a doubt. Here another great point is fixed.

6. I have now stated to you several particulars relating to Christianity, which admit no doubt; and these indisputable facts are of great weight in a discussion of the Christian evidences. There is one point more, of importance, which cannot be settled so expeditiously as these. I hope, however, enough may be said to place it beyond doubt, without exceeding the limits of a discourse; and I invite to it your serious attention. I say, then, that we not only know in general what Christianity was at its first promulgation; but we know precisely what its first propagators taught, for we have their writings. We have their religion under their own hands. We have particularly four narratives of the life, works, and words of their Master, which put us in possession of his most private as well as public teaching. It is true, that without those writings we should still have strong arguments for the truth of Christianity; but we should be left in doubt as to some of its important principles; and its internal evidence, which corroborates, and, as some think, exceeds the external, would be very much impaired. The possession of the writings of the first propagators of the gospel, must plainly render us great aid in judging of its claims. These writings, I say, we have, and this point I would now establish.

I am aware that the question, to which I now ask your attention, is generally confined to professed students. But it is one on which men of good sense are competent to judge, and its great importance gives it a claim to the serious consideration of every Christian.

The question is, whether the four Gospels are genuine, that is, whether they were written by those to whom they are ascribed. To answer it, let us consider how we determine the genuineness of books in general. I begin with the obvious remark, that to know the author of a work, it is not necessary that we should be eye-witnesses of its composition. Perhaps of the numberless publications of the present day, we have not seen one growing under the pen of the writer. By far the greater number come to us across the ocean, and yet we are as confident in regard to their authors as if we had actually seen them first committed to paper. The ascription of a book to an individual, during his life, by those whe are interested in him, and who have the best means of knowing the truth, removes all doubts as to its author. A strong and wide-spread conviction of this kind must have a cause, and can only be explained by the actual production of the work by the reputed writer. It should here be remembered that there is a strong disposition in men to ascertain the author of an important and interesting work. We have had a remarkable illustration of this in our own times. The author of "Waverley" saw fit to wrap himself for a time in mystery; and what was the consequence? No subject in politics or science was agitated more generally than the question to whom the work belonged. It was not only made a topic in almost every periodical publication, but one book was expressly written to solve the problem. The instance, I know, was remarkable; but this inquisitiveness in regard to books is a principle of our nature, and is particularly active, when the book in debate is a work of singular authority.

I have spoken of the confidence which we feel as to

the authors of books published in our own times. But our certainty is not confined to these. Every reading man is as sure that Hume and Robertson wrote the histories which bear their names, as that Scott has in our own time sent out the "Life of Bonaparte." Those eminent men were born more than a hundred years ago, and they died before the birth of most to whom I speak. But the communication between their times and our own is so open and various, that we know their literary labors as well as those of the present day. Not a few persons now living have had intercourse with some of the contemporaries of these historians; and through this channel in particular, we of this generation have the freest access to the preceding, and know its convictions in regard to the authors of interesting books as fully as if we had lived in it ourselves. That the next age will have the same communication with the present as the present has with the past, and that these convictions of our predecessors will be transmitted by us to our immediate successors, you will easily comprehend; and you will thus learn the respect which is due to the testimony of the third generation on such a subject.

In what has now been said, we see with what confidence and certainty we determine the authors of writings published in our own age or in the times nearest our own. These remarks may be easily applied to the productions of antiquity. When the question arises, whether an ancient book was written by the individual whose name it bears, we must inquire into the opinion of his contemporaries, or of those who succeeded his contemporaries so nearly as to have intimate communication with them. The competency of these to a just judgment on the subject, we have seen; and if they have transmitted their convictions to us in undisputed writings, it ought to be decisive. On this testimony, we ascribe many ancient books to their authors with the firmest faith; and, in truth, we receive as genuine many works of antiquity on far inferior proofs. There are many books of which no notice can be found for several ages after the time of their reputed authors. Still the fact, that, as soon as they are named, they are ascribed undoubtingly, and by general consent, to certain authors, is esteemed a sufficient reason for regarding them as their productions, unless some opposite proof can be adduced. This general reception of a work as having come from a particular writer, is an effect which requires a cause; and the most natural and obvious explanation of his being named, rather than any other man, is, that he actually composed it.

I now proceed to apply these principles to the four histories of Christ, commonly called Gospels. The question is, what testimony respecting their authors has come down to us from the age of their reputed authors, or from times so near it and so connected with it, as to be faithful representatives of its convictions. By this testimony, as we have seen, the genuineness of the books must be decided. And I begin with admitting that no evidence on the subject is to be derived from contemporary writers. No author, living in the age of the first propagators of Christianity, has named the Gospels. The truth is, that no undisputed writings of their immediate converts have been preserved. A few tracts, bearing the name of men acquainted with the Apostles, have indeed come down to us; but so much uncertainty hangs over their origin, that I am unwilling to ground on them any reasoning. Nor ought we to wonder that the works of private Christians of the primitive age are wanting to us; for that was an age of persecution, when men were called to *die* rather than *write* for their religion. I suppose too, that during the times of the Apostles, little importance was attached to any books but such as were published or authorized by these eminent men; and, of course, what was written by others was little circulated, and soon passed away.

The undisputed writings of the early Christians begin about seventy years after the times of the Apostles. At that period there probably remained none of the first converts or contemporaries of the Apostles. But there were living not a few, who had been acquainted with the last survivors of that honored generation. When the Apostles died, they must have left behind a multitude who had known them; and of these not a few must have continued many years, and must have had intercourse with the new generation which sprung up after the apostolic age. Now in the times of this generation, the series of Christian authors begins. Although, then, we have no productions of the apostolic age to bear witness to the Gospels, we have writings from the ages which immediately followed it, and which, from their connexion with it, ought, as we have seen, to be regarded as most credible witnesses on such a subject. What, then, do these writings teach? I answer, Their testimony is clear and full. We learn from them, not only that the Gospels existed in those times, but that they were widely diffused, that they were received as the writings of the men whose names they bear, and that they were regarded with a confidence and veneration yielded to no other books. They are quoted as books given by their revered authors to the Christian community, to be public and enduring records of the religion; and they are spoken of as read in the assemblies which were held for the inculcation and extension of the faith. I ask you to weigh this testimony. It comes to us from times connected intimately with the first age. Had the Gospels been invented and first circulated among the generation which succeeded the Apostles, could that generation have received them, as books known and honored before their time, and as the most authoritative and precious records transmitted to them from their fathers and predecessors? The case may seem too plain to require explanation; but as many are unaccustomed to inquiries of this kind, I will offer an example. You well know, that nearly a century ago a great religious excitement was spread through this country chiefly by the ministry of Whitefield. Suppose now that four books were at this moment to come forth, bearing the names of four of the most distinguished men of that period, of Whitefield, of the venerable Edwards, and of two others intimately associated with them in their religious labors; and suppose these books not only to furnish narratives of what then took place, but to contain principles and rules urged with all possible earnestness and authority on the disciples or admirers of these religious leaders. Do you think it possible that their followers of the present day, and the public, could be made to believe, that these books had been published by their pretended authors, had been given as standards to a religious community, and had been handed down as venerated books, when no such works had been heard of before? This is but a faint illustration; for Whitefield and Edwards are names of little weight or authority, compared with what the Apostles possessed in the primitive church.

We have, then, strong and sufficient reasons for believing that the histories called Gospels were received, in the times of the Apostles, as works of those whose names they bear; and were handed down as theirs with veneration by their contemporaries. Will any say that all this may be true, but that, during the lives of the Apostles, books forged in their names may have obtained general currency? To this extravagant supposition it would be sufficient to reply, according to my previous remarks, that the general ascription of a book to an author during his life, is the ground on which the genuineness of the most unquestioned works depends. But I would add, that this evidence is singularly conclusive in the present case. The original propagators of Christianity, to whom the Gospels were ascribed, were, from their office, among the public men of their age. They must have travelled extensively. They must have been consulted by inhabitants of various countries on the subject of the new religion. They must have been objects of deep interest to the first converts. They lived in the world's eye. Their movements, visits, actions, words, and writings, must have awakened attention. Books from their hands must have produced a great sensation. We cannot conceive a harder task, than to impose writings, forged in their name, on Christians and Christian communities, thus intimately connected with them, and so alive to their efforts for the general cause. The opportunities of detecting the falsehood were abundant; and to imagine falsehood to prosper under such circumstances, argues a strange ignorance of literary history and of human nature.

Let me add, that the motives of the first Christians, to ascertain distinctly whether writings ascribed to the

Apostles were truly theirs, were the strongest which can be conceived. I have mentioned, in my previous remarks, the solicitude of the world to learn the author of "Waverley." The motive was mere curiosity; and yet to what earnest inquiries were multitudes impelled. The name of the author was of little or no moment. The book was the same, its portraits equally vivid, its developements of the human heart equally true and powerful, whether the author were known or not. So it is with most works. Books of science, philosophy, morals, and polite literature, owe their importance and authority, not to their writers, but to their contents. Now, the four Gospels were different in this respect. They were not the same to the first converts, come from whom they might. If written by Apostles or by their associates, they had an authority and sacredness, which could belong to them on no other condition. They became books of laws to the Christian community, became binding on their consciences and lives. To suppose such books received blindly and without inquiry, by great numbers who had all the means of ascertaining their true origin, is to suppose the first converts insane or idiots, a charge which I believe their worst enemies will not think of urging against them, and which the vast superiority of their religious and moral system to all the philosophical systems of the times abundantly disproves.

I have now finished what is called the historical or external evidence of the genuineness of the four Gospels; that is, the evidence drawn from their being received and revered as the writings of the Apostles in the first and succeeding ages of Christianity. But before leaving this head, I would notice a difficulty which may press on some minds. I suppose, that many of you have heard, that very early, probably about the beginning of the second century, writings were forged in the name of the Apostles ; and some may ask why the four Gospels may not belong to this description. The answer is, that the Gospels, as we have seen, were received and honored by the great body of Christians, in the first and succeeding ages of Christianity, as writings of Apostles or their associates. The forgeries are known to be forgeries, because they were not so received, because they were held in no veneration, but were rejected as fictitious by the Christian community. Here is a broad line of distinction. It must not surprise us, that in the great excitement produced by the first publication and triumphs of Christianity, a variety of extravagant notions should spring up, and that attempts should be made to blend the new religion with established systems ; and as the names of the first propagators of the Gospel were held in peculiar reverence, we cannot wonder that the leaders of sects should strive to attach an apostolic sanction to their opinions, by sending abroad partly true and partly false accounts of the preaching of these eminent men. Whether these writings were sent forth as compositions of the Apostles, or only as records of their teaching, made by their hearers, is a question open to debate ; but as to their origin there can be little doubt. We can account for their existence, and for the degree of favor which they obtained. They were generally written to give authority to the dreams or speculations of some extravagant sects, to which they were very much confined, and with which most of them passed away. There is not a shadow of reason for confounding with these our Gospels, which were spread from the beginning through the Christian world, and were honored and transmitted as the works of the venerated men by whose names they were called.

Having now given the historical argument in favor of the genuineness of the Gospels, that is, in favor of their being written by their reputed authors, I now add, that there are several presumptive and internal proofs of the same truth, which, taken alone, have great weight, and, when connected with the preceding, form an amount of evidence not easily withstood. I have time to glance at only a few of these.

It is a presumption in favor of the claims of an author, that the book ascribed to him has never been assigned to any other individual. Now I am not aware, that unbelief has in any age named any individuals, to whom the Gospels may be traced rather than to those whose names they bear. We are not called upon to choose between different writers. In common cases, this absence of rival claims is considered as decisive in favor of the reputed author, unless the books themselves give ground to suspect another hand. Why shall not this principle be applied to the Gospels as well as to all other works?

Another presumption in favor of the belief that these histories were written by the first propagators of Christianity, arises from the consideration, that such books were to be expected from them. It is hardly conceivable that the Apostles, whose zeal carried abroad their system through so many nations, and who lived in an age of reading and writing, should leave their doctrines to tradition, should neglect the ordinary precaution of embodying them in the only permanent form, the only one in which they could be accurately transmitted, and by which all other systems were preserved. It is reasonable to suppose that they wro e what they taught; and if so, it is hardly possible that their writings should be lost. Their accounts must have been received and treasured up just as we know the Gospels were cherished; and hence arises a strong presumption in favor of the genuineness of these books.

Again; these books carry one strong mark of having been written in the time of the Apostles. They contain no trace of later times, nothing to indicate that the authors belonged to another age. Now to those of you, who are acquainted with such subjects, it is hardly necessary to observe, how difficult it is for a writer to avoid betraying the period in which he lives; and the cause is very obvious. Every age has its peculiarities, has manners, events, feelings, words, phrases of its own; and a man brought up among these falls so naturally under their influence, and incorporates them so fully with his own mind, that they break out and manifest themselves, almost necessarily and without his consciousness, in his words and writings. The present makes an impression incomparably more vivid than the past, and accordingly traces of the real age of a writer may almost always be discovered by a critical eye, however anxious he may be to assume the style and character of a preceding age. Now the Gospels betray no marks of the feelings, manners, contentions, events of a period later than that in which the Apostles lived; and when we consider, that, with the exception of Luke's history, they have all the appearance of having come from plain men, unused to composition, this argument applies to them with peculiar force. Under this head, I might place before you the evidence of the genuineness of these books derived from the language, dialect, idiom, in which they are written. You can easily understand, that by these helps the country and age of a writing may often be traced; but the argument belongs to the learned. It may however be satisfactory to know, that the profoundest scholars see in the dialect and idiom of the Gospels, a precise accordance with what might be expected of Jews, writing in the age of the Apostles.

Another internal proof, and one within the reach of all, may be gathered from the style and character of the evangelical narratives. They are written with the simplicity, minuteness, and ease, which are the natural tones of truth, which belong to writers thoroughly acquainted with their subjects, and writing from reality. You discover in them nothing of the labor, caution, and indistinctness, which can scarcely be escaped by men who are assuming a character not their own, and aiming to impose on the world. There is a difference which we have all discerned and felt, though we cannot describe it, between an honest, simple-hearted witness, who tells what he has seen or is intimately acquainted with, and the false witness, who affects an intimate knowledge of events and individuals, which are in whole or in part his own fabrication. Truth has a native frankness, an unaffected freedom, a style and air of its own, and never were narratives more strongly characterized by these than the Gospels. It is a striking circumstance in these books, that whilst the life and character which they portray, are the most extraordinary in history, the style is the most artless. There is no straining for epithets or for elevation of language to suit the dignity of the great personage who is the subject. You hear plain men telling you what they know, of a character which they venerated too much to think of adorning or extolling. It is also worthy of remark, that the character of Jesus, though the most peculiar and exalted in history, though the last to be invented and the hardest to be sustained, is yet unfolded through a great variety of details and conditions, with perfect unity and consistency. The strength of this proof can only be understood by those who are sufficiently acquainted with literary history, to appreciate the difficulty of accomplishing a consistent and successful forgery Such consistency is, in the present case, an almost infallible test. Suppose four writers, of a later age, to have leagued together in the scheme of personating the first propagators of Christianity, and of weaving, in their name, the histories of their Master's life. Removed as these men would have been from the original, and having no model or type of his character in the elevation of their own minds, they must have portrayed him with an unsteady hand, must have marred their work with incongruous features, must have brought down their hero on some occasion to the ordinary views and feelings of men, and in particular must have been warped in their selection and representation of incidents by the private purpose which led them to this singular coöperation. That four writers, under such circumstances, should sustain throughout so peculiar and elevated a character as Jesus, and should harmonize with each other in the delineation, would be a prodigy which no genius, however preëminent, could achieve. I say, then, that the narratives bear strong internal marks of having been drawn from the living original, by those who had the best means of knowing his character and life.

So various, strong, sufficient are the proofs that the four Gospels are the works of the first preachers of Christianity, whose name they bear. I will only add, that the genuineness of few ancient books is supported by proofs equally strong. Most of the works, which have come down to us from antiquity, and which are ascribed to their reputed writers with undoubting confidence, are so ascribed on evidence inferior to that on which the claims of the Evangelists rest. On this point therefore not a doubt should remain.

Here I pause. The proofs of Christianity, which are involved in or founded on the facts now established, will be the subjects of future discussion.

PART II.

I HAVE now stated some of the great facts relating to the origin of Christianity, of which we have clear and full proof. We know when and where this religion sprung up. We know its Author, and the men whom he employed as the first propagators of his doctrine. We know the great features of the religion as it was originally taught; and still more, we have the writings of its first teachers, by which its precise character is placed beyond doubt. I now proceed to lay before you some of the arguments in support of Christianity, which are involved in or are founded on these facts. I must confine myself to a few, and will select those to which some justice may be done in the compass of a discourse.

I. I believe Christianity to be true, or to have come from God, because it seems to me impossible to trace it to any other origin. It must have had a cause, and no other adequate cause can be assigned. The incongruity between this religion and all the circumstances amidst which it grew up, is so remarkable, that we are compelled to look beyond and above this world for its explanation. When I go back to the origin of Christianity, and place myself in the age and country of its birth, I can find nothing in the opinions of men, or in the state of society, which can account for its beginning or diffusion. There was no power on earth to create or uphold such a system. There was nothing congenial with it in Judaism, in heathenism, or in the state of society among the most cultivated communities. If you study the religions, governments, and philosophical systems of that age, you will discover in them not even a leaning towards Christianity. It sprung up in opposition to all, making no compromise with human prejudice or passion; and it sprung up, not only superior to all, but possessing at its very beginning a perfection, which has been the admiration of ages, and which, instead of being dimmed by time, has come forth more brightly, in proportion to the progress of the human mind.

I know, indeed, that, at the origin of our religion, the old heathen worship had fallen into disrepute among the enlightened classes through the Roman Empire, and was gradually losing its hold on the populace. Accordingly some have pretended that Christianity grew from the ruins of the ancient faith. But this is not true; for the decline of the heathen systems was the product of causes singularly adverse to the origination of such a system as Christianity. One cause was the monstrous depravity of the age, which led multitudes to an utter scorn of religion in all its forms and restraints, and which prepared others to exchange their old worship for still grosser and more licentious superstitions, particularly for the magical arts of Egypt. Surely this corruption of manners, this wide-wasting moral pestilence, will not be considered by any as a germ of the Christian religion. Another principal agent in loosening the foundations of the old systems, was Philosophy, a noble effort indeed of the human intellect, but one which did nothing to prepare the way for Christianity.

The most popular systems of philosophy at the birth of Christianity were the Skeptical and the Epicurean, the former of which turned religion into a jest, denied the possibility of arriving at truth, and cast the mind on an ocean of doubt in regard to every subject of inquiry; whilst the latter placed happiness in ease, inculcated a calm indifference both as to this world and the next, and would have set down the Christian doctrine of self-sacrifice, of suffering for truth and duty, as absolute insanity. Now I ask in what single point do these systems touch Christianity, or what impulse could they have given to its invention. There was indeed another philosophical sect of a nobler character; I mean the Stoical. This maintained that virtue was the supreme good, and it certainly nurtured some firm and lofty spirits amidst the despotism which then ground all classes in the dust. But the self-reliance, sternness, apathy, and pride of the Stoic, his defiance and scorn of mankind, his want of sympathy with human suffering, and his extravagant exaggerations of his own virtue, placed this sect in singular opposition to Christianity; so that our religion might as soon have sprung from Skepticism and Epicureanism, as from Stoicism. There was another system, if it be worthy of the name, which prevailed in Asia, and was not unknown to the Jews, often called the Oriental philosophy. But this, though certainly an improvement on the common heathenism, was visionary and mystical, and placed happiness in an intuition or immediate perception of God, which was to be gained by contemplation and ecstasies, by emaciation of the body, and desertion of the world. I need not tell you how infinitely removed was the practical, benevolent spirit of Christianity, from this spurious sanctity and profitless enthusiasm. I repeat it, then, that the various causes which were silently operating against the established heathen systems in the time of Christ, had no tendency to suggest and spread such a religion as he brought, but were as truly hostile to it as the worst forms of heathenism.

We cannot find, then, the origin of Christianity in the heathen world. Shall we look for it in the Jewish? This topic is too familiar to need much exposition. You know the character, feelings, expectations of the descendants of Abraham at the appearing of Jesus; and you need not be told, that a system, more opposed to the Jewish mind than that which he taught, cannot be imagined. There was nothing friendly to it in the soil or climate of Judea. As easily might the luxuriant trees of our forest spring from the sands of an Arabian desert. There was never perhaps a national character so deeply stamped as the Jewish. Ages after ages of unparalleled suffering have done little to wear away its indelible features. In the time of Jesus the whole influence of education and religion was employed to fix it in every member of the state. In the bosom of this community, and among its humblest classes, sprung up Christianity, a religion as unfettered by Jewish prejudices, as untainted by the earthly, narrow views of the age, as if it had come from another world. Judaism was all around it, but did not mar it by one trace, or sully its brightness by a single breath. Can we find, then, the cause of Christianity in the Jewish any more than in the heathen world?

Christianity, I maintain, was not the growth of any of the circumstances, principles, or feelings of the age in which it appeared. In truth, one of the great distinctions of the Gospel is, that it did not *grow*. The conception, which filled the mind of Jesus, of a religion more spiritual, generous, comprehensive, and unworldly than Judaism, and destined to take its place, was not of gradual formation. We detect no signs of it, and no efforts to realize it, before his time; nor is there an appearance of its having been gradually matured by Jesus himself. Christianity was delivered from the first in its full proportions, in a style of singular freedom and boldness, and without a mark of painful elaboration. This suddenness with which this religion broke forth, this maturity of the system at the very moment of its birth, this absence of gradual developement, seems to me a strong mark of its divine original. If Christianity be a human invention, then I can be pointed to something in the history of the age which impelled and fitted the mind of its author to its production; then I shall be able to find some germ of it, some approximation to it, in the state of things amidst which it first appeared. How was it, that from thick darkness there burst forth at once meridian light? Were I told that the sciences of the civilized world had sprung up to perfection at once, amidst a barbarous horde, I should pronounce it incredible. Nor can I easily believe, that Christianity, the religion of unbounded love, a religion which broke down the barrier between Jew and Gentile, and the barriers between nations, which proclaimed one Universal Father, which abolished forms and substituted the worship of the soul, which condemned alike the false greatness of the Roman and the false holiness of the Jew, and which taught an elevation of virtue, that the growing knowledge of succeeding ages has made more admirable;— I say, I cannot easily believe that such a religion was suddenly, immediately struck out by human ingenuity, among a people distinguished by bigotry and narrowness of spirit, by superstitious reliance on outward worship, by hatred and scorn of other nations, and by the proud, impatient hope of soon bending all nations to their sway.

Christianity, I repeat it, was not the growth of the age in which it appeared. It had no sympathy with that age. It was the echo of no sect or people. It stood alone at the moment of its birth. It used not a word of conciliation. It stooped to no error or passion. It had its own tone, the tone of authority and superiority to the world. It struck at the root of what was everywhere called glory, reversed the judgments of all former ages, passed a condemning sentence on the idols of this world's admiration, and held forth, as the perfection of human nature, a spirit of love, so pure and divine, so free and full, so mild and forgiving, so invincible in fortitude yet so tender in its sympathies, that even now few comprehend it in its extent and elevation. Such a religion had not its origin in this world.

I have thus sought to unfold one of the evidences of Christianity. Its incongruity with the age of its birth, its freedom from earthly mixtures, its original, unborrowed, solitary greatness, and the suddenness with which it broke forth amidst the general gloom, these are to me strong indications of its divine descent. I cannot reconcile them with a human origin.

II. Having stated the argument in favor of Christianity, derived from the impossibility of accounting for it by the state of the world at the time of its birth, I proceed, in the second place, to observe, that it cannot be accounted for by any of the motives which instigate men to the fabrication of religions. Its aims and objects are utterly irreconcilable with imposture. They are pure, lofty, and worthy of the most illustrious delegate of heaven. This argument deserves to be unfolded with some particularity.

Men act from Motives. The inventors of religions have purposes to answer by them. Some systems have been framed by legislators to procure reverence to their laws, to bow the minds of the people to the civil power ; and some have been forged by priests, to establish their sway over the multitude, to form themselves into a dominant caste, and to extort the wealth of the industrious. Now I affirm, that Christianity cannot be ascribed to any selfish, ambitious, earthly motive. It is suited to no private end. Its purpose is generous and elevated, and thus bears witness to its heavenly origin.

The great object which has seduced men to pretend to inspiration, and to spread false religions, has been Power, in one form or another, sometimes political power, sometimes spiritual, sometimes both. Is Christianity to be explained by this selfish aim ? I answer, No. I affirm that the love of power is the last principle to be charged on the Founder of our religion. Christianity is distinguished by nothing more than by its earnest enforcement of a meek and humble spirit, and by its uncompromising reprobation of that passion for dominion, which had in all ages made the many the prey of the few, and had been worshipped as the attribute and impulse of the greatest minds. Its tone on this subject was original, and altogether its own. Jesus felt, as none had felt before, and as few feel now, the baseness of selfish ambition, and the grandeur of that benevolence which waves every mark of superiority, that it may more effectually bless mankind. He taught this lesson, not only in the boldest language, but, accommodating himself to the emblematical mode of religious instruction prevalent in the East, he set before his disciples a little child as their pattern, and himself washed their feet. His whole life was a commentary on his teaching. Not a trace of the passion for distinction and sway can be detected in the artless narratives of his historians. He wore no badge of superiority, exacted no signs of homage, coveted no attentions, resented no neglect. He discouraged the ruler who prostrated himself before him with flattering salutations, but received with affectionate sensibility the penitent who bathed his feet with her tears. He lived with his obscure disciples as a friend, and mixed freely with all ranks of the community. He placed himself in the way of scorn, and advanced to meet a death, more suited than any other imaginable event, to entail infamy on his name. Stronger marks of an infinite superiority to what the world calls glory, cannot be conceived than we meet in the history of Jesus.

I have named two kinds of power, Political and Spiritual, as the ordinary objects of false religions. I wish to show you more particularly the elevation of Christianity above these aims. That the Gospel was not framed for political purposes, is too plain to require proof; but its peculiarity in this respect is not sufficiently considered. In ancient times, religion was everywhere a national concern. In Judea the union between religion and government was singularly close, and political sovereignty was one of the chief splendors, with which the Jewish imagination had surrounded the expected Messiah. That in such an age and country, a religion should arise, which hardly seems to know that government exists; which makes no reference to it except in a few general inculcations of obedience to the civil powers; which says not a word nor throws out a hint of allying itself with the state; which assumes to itself no control of political affairs, and intermeddles with no public concerns; which has no tendency, however indirect, to accumulate power in particular hands; which provides no form of national worship as a substitute for those which it was intended to destroy; and which treats the distinctions of rank and office as worthless in comparison with moral influence and an unostentatious charity; — that such a religion should spring up in such a state of the world is a remarkable fact. We here see a broad line between Christianity and other systems, and a striking proof of its originality and elevation. Other systems were framed for communities; Christianity approached men as Individuals. It proposed, not the glory of the state, but the perfection of the individual mind. So far from being contrived to build up political power, Christianity tends to reduce and gradually to supplant it, by teaching men to substitute the sway of truth and love for menace and force, by spreading through all ranks a feeling of brotherhood altogether opposed to the spirit of domination, and by establishing principles which nourish self-respect in every human being, and teach the obscurest to look with an undazzled eye on the most powerful of their race.

Christianity bears no mark of the hands of a politician. One of its main purposes is to extinguish the very spirit which the ambitious statesman most anxiously cherishes, and on which he founds his success. It proscribes a narrow patriotism, shows no mercy to the spirit of conquest, requires its disciples to love other countries as truly as their own, and enjoins a spirit of peace and forbearance in language so broad and earnest, that not a few of its professors consider war in every shape and under all circumstances as a crime. The hostility between Christianity and all the political maxims of that age, cannot easily be comprehended at the present day. No doctrines were then so rooted, as, that conquest was the chief interest of a nation, and that an exclusive patriotism was the first and noblest of social virtues. Christianity, in loosening the tie which bound man to the state, that it might connect him with his race, opposed itself to what was deemed the vital principle of national safety and grandeur, and commenced a political revolution as original and unsparing as the religious and moral reform at which it aimed.

Christianity, then, was not framed for political purposes. But I shall be asked, whether it stands equally clear of the charge of being intended to accumulate Spiritual power. Some may ask, whether its founder was not instigated by the passion for religious domination, whether he did not aim to subdue men's minds, to dictate to the faith of the world, to make himself the leader of a spreading sect, to stamp his name as a prophet on human history, and thus to secure the prostration of multitudes to his will, more abject and entire than kings and conquerors can achieve.

To this I might reply by what I have said of the character of Jesus, and of the spirit of his religion. It is plain, that the founder of Christianity had a perception, quite peculiar to himself, of the moral beauty and greatness of a disinterested, meek, and self-sacrificing spirit, and such a person was not likely to meditate the subjugation of the world to himself. But, leaving this topic, I observe, that on examining Christianity we discover none of the features of a religion framed for spiritual domination. One of the infallible marks of such a system is, that it makes some terms with the passions and prejudices of men. It does not, cannot provoke and ally against itself all the powers, whether civil or religious, of the world. Christianity was throughout uncompromising and exasperating, and threw itself in the way of hatred and scorn. Such a system was any thing but a scheme for seizing the spiritual empire of the world.

There is another mark of a religion which springs from the love of spiritual domination. It infuses a servile spirit. Its author, desirous to stamp his name and image on his followers, has an interest in curbing the free action of their minds, imposes on them arbitrary doctrines, fastens on them badges which may separate them from others, and besets them with rules, forms, and distinctive observances, which may perpetually remind them of their relation to their chief. Now I see nothing in Christianity of this enslaving legislation. It has but one aim, which is, not to exalt its teacher, but to improve the disciple; not to fasten Christ's name on mankind, but to breathe into them his spirit of universal love. Christianity is not a religion of forms. It has but two ceremonies, as simple as they are expressive; and these hold so subordinate a place in the New Testament, that some of the best Christians question or deny their permanent obligation.

Neither is it a narrow creed, or a mass of doctrines which find no support in our rational nature. It may be summed up in a few great, universal, immutable principles, which reason and conscience, as far as they are unfolded, adopt and rejoice in, as their own everlasting laws, and which open perpetually enlarging views to the mind. As far as I am a Christian, I am free. My religion lays on me not one chain. It does not prescribe a certain range for my mind, beyond which nothing can be learned. It speaks of God as the Universal Father, and sends me to all his works for instruction. It does not hem me round with a mechanical ritual, does not enjoin forms, attitudes, and hours of prayer, does not descend to details of dress and food, does not put on me one outward badge. It teaches and enkindles love to God, but commands no precise expressions of this sentiment. It prescribes prayer; but lays the chief stress on the prayer of the closet, and treats all worship as worthless but that of the mind and heart. It teaches us to do good, but leaves us to devise for ourselves the means by which we may best serve mankind. In a word, the whole religion of Christ may be summed up in the love of God and of mankind, and it leaves the individual to cherish and express this spirit by the methods most accordant with his own condition and peculiar mind. Christianity is eminently the religion of freedom. The views which it gives of the parental, impartial, universal goodness of God, and of the equal right of every human being to inquire into his will, and its inculcations of candor, forbearance, and mutual respect, contribute alike to freedom of thought and enlargement of the heart. I repeat it, Christianity lays on me no chains. It is any thing but a contrivance for spiritual domination.

I am aware that I shall be told, that Christianity, if judged by its history, has no claim to the honorable title of a religion of liberty. I shall be told, that no system of heathenism ever weighed more oppressively on men's souls; that the Christian ministry has trained tyrants, who have tortured, now the body with material fire, and now the mind with the dread of fiercer flames, and who have proscribed and punished free thought and free speech as the worst of crimes. I have no disposition to soften the features of priestly oppression; but I say, let not Christianity be made to answer for it. Christianity gives its ministers no such power. They have usurped it in the face of the sternest prohibitions, and in opposition to the whole spirit of their Master. Christianity institutes no priesthood, in the original and proper sense of that word. It has not the name of priest among its officers; nor does it confer a shadow of priestly power. It invests no class of men with peculiar sanctity, ascribing to their intercessions a special influence over God, or suspending the salvation of the private Christian on ceremonies which they alone can administer. Jesus indeed appointed twelve of his immediate disciples to be the great instruments of propagating his religion; but nothing can be simpler than their office. They went forth to make known through all nations the life, death, resurrection, and teachings of Jesus Christ; and this truth they spread freely and without reserve. They did not give it as a mystery to a few who were to succeed them in their office, and according to whose direction it was to be imparted to others. They communicated it to the whole body of converts, to be their equal and common property, thus securing to all the invaluable rights of the mind. It is true, they appointed ministers or teachers in the various congregations which they formed; and in that early age, when the religion was new and unknown, and when oral teaching was the only mode of communicating it, there seems to have been no way for its diffusion but this appointment of the most enlightened disciples to the work of instruction. But the New Testament nowhere intimates, that these men were to monopolize the privilege of studying their religion, or of teaching it to others. Not a single man can claim under Christianity the right to interpret it exclusively, or to impose his interpretation on his brethren. The Christian minister enjoys no nearer access to God, and no promise of more immediate illumination, than other men. He is not intrusted with the Christian records more than they, and by these records it is both their right and duty to try his instructions. I have here pointed out a noble peculiarity of Christianity. It is the religion of liberty. It is in no degree tainted with the passion for spiritual power. "Call no man master, for ye are all brethren," is its free and generous inculcation, and to every form of freedom it is a friend and defence.

We have seen that Christianity is not to be traced to the love of power, that master passion in the authors of false religions. I add, that no other object of a selfish nature could have led to its invention. The Gospel is not of this world. At the time of its origin no ingenuity could have brought it to bear on any private or worldly interest. Its spirit is self-denial. Wealth, ease, and honor, it counts among the chief perils of life, and it insists on no duty more earnestly than on that of putting them to hazard and casting them from us, if the cause of truth and humanity so require. And these maxims were not mere speculations or rhetorical commonplaces in the times of Christ and his Apostles The first propagators of Christianity were called upon to practise what they preached, to forego every interest on its account. They could not but foreknow, that a religion so uncompromising and pure would array against them the world. They did not merely take the chance of suffering, but were sure that the whole weight of scorn, pain, and worldly persecution would descend on their heads. How inexplicable, then, is Christianity by any selfish object, or any low aim ?

The Gospel has but one object, and that too plain to be mistaken. In reading the New Testament, we see the greatest simplicity of aim. There is no lurking purpose, no by-end, betraying itself through attempts to disguise it. A perfect singleness of design runs through the records of the religion, and is no mean evidence of their truth. This end of Christianity is the moral perfection of the human soul. It aims and it tends, in all its doctrines, precepts, and promises, to rescue men from the power of moral evil ; to unite them to God by filial love, and to one another in the bonds of brotherhood ; to inspire them with a philanthropy as meek and unconquerable as that of Christ ; and to kindle intense desire, hope, and pursuit of celestial and immortal virtue.

And now, I ask, what is the plain inference from these views ? If Christianity can be traced to no selfish or worldly motive, if it was framed, not for dominion, not to compass any private purpose, but to raise men above themselves, and to conform them to God, can we help pronouncing it worthy of God ? And to whom but to God can we refer its origin ? Ought we not to recognise in the first propagators of such a faith the holiest of men, the friends of their race, and the messengers of Heaven? Christianity, from its very nature, repels the charge of imposture. It carries in itself the proof of pure intention. Bad men could not have conceived it, much less have adopted it as the great object of their lives. The supposition of selfish men giving up every private interest to spread a system which condemned themselves, and which tended only to purify mankind, is an absurdity as gross as can be found in the most irrational faith. Christianity, therefore, when tried by its Motives, approves itself to be of God.

III. I now proceed to another and very important ground of my belief in the divine origin of Christianity. Its truth was attested by miracles. Its first teachers proved themselves the ministers of God by supernatural works. They did what man cannot do, what bore the impress of a divine power, and what thus sealed the divinity of their mission. A religion so attested must be true. This topic is a great one, and I ask your patient attention to it.

I am aware that a strong prejudice exists in some minds against the kind of evidence which I have now adduced. Miracles seem to them to carry a confutation in themselves. The presumption against them seems next to infinite. In this respect, the present times differ from the past. There have been ages, when men believed any thing and every thing; and the more monstrous the story, the more eagerly was it received by the credulous multitude. In the progress of knowledge men have come to see, that most of the prodigies and supernatural events in which their forefathers believed, were fictions of fancy, or fear, or imposture. The light of knowledge has put to flight the ghosts and witches which struck terror into earlier times. We now know, that not a few of the appearances in the heavens, which appalled nations, and were interpreted as precursors of divine vengeance, were natural effects. We have learned, too, that a highly excited imagination can work some of the cures once ascribed to magic; and the lesson taught us by these natural solutions of apparent miracles, is, that accounts of supernatural events are to be sifted with great jealousy and received with peculiar care.

But the result of this new light thrown on nature and history is, that some are disposed to discredit all miracles indiscriminately. So many having proved groundless, a sweeping sentence of condemnation is passed on all. The human mind, by a natural reaction, has passed from extreme credulousness, to the excess of incredulity. Some persons are even hardy enough to deride the very idea of a miracle. They pronounce the order of nature something fixed and immutable, and all suspensions of it incredible. This prejudice, for such it is, seems to deserve particular attention; for, until it is removed, the evidences of Christian miracles will have little weight. Let us examine it patiently and impartially.

The skeptic tells me, that the order of nature is fixed. I ask him, By whom or by what is it fixed? By an iron fate? By an inflexible necessity? Does not nature bear the signatures of an intelligent Cause? Does not the very idea of its order imply an ordaining or disposing Mind? Does not the universe, the more it is explored, bear increasing testimony to a Being superior to itself? Then the order of nature is fixed by a Will which can reverse it. Then a power equal to miracles exists. Then miracles are not incredible.

It may be replied, that God indeed *can* work miracles, but that he *will* not. He will not? And how does the skeptic know this? Has God so told him? This language does not become a being of our limited faculties; and the presumptuousness which thus makes laws for the Creator, and restricts his agency to particular modes, is as little the spirit of true philosophy as of religion.

The skeptic sees nothing in miracles, but ground of offence. To me, they seem to involve in their very nature a truth so great, so vital, that I am not only reconciled to them, but am disposed to receive joyfully any sufficient proofs of their having been performed. To the skeptic, no principle is so important as the uniformity of nature, the constancy of its laws. To me, there is a vastly higher truth, to which miracles bear witness, and to which I welcome their aid. What I wish chiefly to know is, that Mind is the supreme power in the universe; that matter is its instrument and slave; that there is a Will to which nature can offer no obstruction; that God is unshackled by the laws of the universe, and controls them at his pleasure. This absolute sovereignty of the Divine Mind over the universe, is the only foundation of hope for the triumph of the human mind over matter, over physical influences, over imperfection and death. Now it is plain, that the strong impressions which we receive through the senses from the material creation, joined to our experience of its regularity, and to our instinctive trust in its future uniformity, do obscure this supremacy of God, do tempt us to ascribe a kind of omnipotence to nature's laws, and to limit our hopes to the good which is promised by these. There is a strong tendency in men to attach the idea of necessity to an unchanging regularity of operation, and to imagine bounds to a being who keeps one undeviating path, or who repeats himself perpetually. Hence, I say that I rejoice in miracles. They show and assert the supremacy of Mind in the universe. They manifest a spiritual power, which is in no degree enthralled by the laws of matter. I rejoice in these witnesses to so great a truth. I rejoice in whatever proves, that this order of nature, which so often weighs on me as a chain, and which contains no promise of my perfection, is not supreme and immutable, and that the Creator is not restricted to the narrow modes of operation with which I am most familiar.

Perhaps the form in which the objection to miracles is most frequently expressed, is the following; "It is derogatory," says the skeptic, "to the perfect wisdom of God, to suppose him to break in upon the order of his own works. It is only the unskilful artist who is obliged to thrust his hand into the machine for the purpose of supplying its defects, and of giving it a new impulse by an immediate agency." To this objection I reply, that it proceeds on false ideas of God and of the creation. God is not an artist, but a Moral Parent and Governor; nor is the creation a machine. If it were, it might be urged with greater speciousness, that miracles cannot be needed or required. One of the most striking views of the creation, is the contrast or opposition of the elements of which it consists. It includes not only matter but mind, not only lifeless and unconscious masses, but rational beings, free agents; and these are its noblest parts and ultimate objects. The material universe was framed not for itself, but for these. Its order was not appointed for its own sake, but to instruct and improve a higher rank of beings, the intelligent offspring of God; and whenever a departure from this order, that is, whenever miraculous agency can contribute to the growth and perfection of his intelligent creatures, it is demanded by his wisdom, goodness, and all his attributes. If the Supreme Being proposed only such ends as mechanism can produce, then he might have framed a machinery so perfect and sure as to need no suspension of its ordinary movements. But he has an incomparably nobler end. His great purpose is to educate, to rescue from evil, to carry forward for ever the free, rational mind or soul; and who that understands what a free mind is, and what a variety of teaching and discipline it requires, will presume to affirm, that no lights or aids, but such as come to it through an invariable order of nature, are necessary to unfold it?

Much of the difficulty in regard to miracles, as I apprehend, would be removed, if we were to consider more particularly, that the chief distinction of intelligent beings is Moral Freedom, the power of determining themselves to evil as well as good, and consequently the power of involving themselves in great misery. When God made man, he framed not a machine, but a free being, who was to rise or fall according to his use or abuse of his powers. This capacity, at once the most glorious and the most fearful which we can conceive, shows us how the human race may have come into a condition, to which the illumination of nature was inadequate. In truth, the more we consider the freedom of intelligent beings, the more we shall question the possibility of establishing an unchangeable order which will meet fully all their wants; for such beings, having of necessity a wide range of action, may bring themselves into a vast variety of conditions, and of course may come to need a relief not contained in the resources of nature. The history of the human race illustrates these truths. At the introduction of Christianity, the human family were plunged into gross and debasing error, and the light of nature had not served for ages to guide them back to truth. Philosophy had done its best, and failed. A new element, a new power seems to have been wanting to the progress of the race. That in such an exigence miraculous aid should be imparted, accords with our best views of God. I repeat it; were men mechanical beings, an undeviating order of nature might meet all their wants. They are free beings, who bear a moral relation to God, and as such may need, and are worthy of, a more various and special care than is extended over the irrational creation.

When I examine nature, I see reasons for believing that it was not intended by God to be the only method of instructing and improving mankind. I see reasons, as I think, why its order or regular course should be occasionally suspended, and why revelation should be joined to it in the work of carrying forward the race. I can offer only a few considerations on this point, but they seem to me worthy of serious attention. — The first is, that a fixed, invariable order of nature does not give us some views of God which are of great interest and importance, or at least it does not give them with that distinctness which we all desire. It reveals him as the Universal Sovereign who provides for the whole or for the general weal, but not, with sufficient clearness, as a tender father, interested in the Individual. I see, in this fixed order, his care of the race, but not his constant, boundless concern for myself. Nature speaks of a general Divinity, not of the friend and benefactor of each living soul. This is a necessary defect attending an inflexible, unvarying administration by general laws; and it seems to require that God, to carry forward the race, should reveal himself by some other manner than by general laws. No conviction is more important to human improvement than that of God's paternal interest in every human being; and how can he communicate this persuasion so effectually, as by suspending nature's order, to teach, through an inspired messenger, his paternal love?

My second remark is, that, whilst nature teaches many important lessons, it is not a direct, urgent teacher. Its truths are not prominent, and consequently men may neglect it, and place themselves beyond its influence. For example, nature holds out the doctrine of One God, but does not compel attention to it. God's name is not written in the sky in letters of light, which all nations must read, nor sounded abroad in a voice, deep and awful as thunders, so that all must hear. Nature is a gentle, I had almost said, a reserved teacher, demanding patient thought in the learner, and may therefore be unheeded. Men may easily shut their ears and harden their hearts against its testimony to God. Accordingly we learn, that, at Christ's coming, almost all nations had lost the knowledge of the true glory of the Creator, and given themselves up to gross superstitions.

To such a condition of the world, nature's indirect and unimposing mode of instruction is not fitted, and thus it furnishes a reason for a more immediate and impressive teaching. In such a season of moral darkness, was it not worthy of God to kindle another and more quickening beam? When the long repeated and almost monotonous language of creation was not heard, was it unworthy of God to speak with a new and more startling voice? What fitter method was there for rousing those whom nature's quiet regularity could not teach, than to interrupt its usual course?

I proceed to another reason for expecting revelation to be added to the light of nature. Nature, I have said, is not a direct or urgent teacher, and men may place themselves beyond its voice. I say, thirdly, that there is one great point, on which we are deeply concerned to know the truth, and which is yet taught so indistinctly by nature, that men, however disposed to learn, cannot by that light alone obtain full conviction. What, let me ask, is the question in which each man has the deepest interest? It is this, Are we to live again; or is this life all? Does the principle of thought perish with the body; or does it survive? And if it survive, where? how? in what condition? under what law? There is an inward voice which speaks of judgment to come. Will judgment indeed come? and if so, what award may we hope or fear? The Future state of man, this is the great question forced on us by our changing life, and by approaching death. I will not say, that on this topic nature throws no light. I think it does; and this light continually grows brighter to them whose eyes revelation has couched and made strong to see. But nature alone does not meet our wants. I might prove this by referring you to the ages preceding Christ, when the anxious spirit of man constantly sought to penetrate the gloom beyond the grave, when imagination and philosophy alike plunged into the future, but found no resting-place. But every man must feel, that, left to nature as his only guide, he must wander in doubt as to the life to come. Where, but from God himself, can I learn my destination? I ask at the mouth of the tomb for intelligence of the departed, and the tomb gives me no reply. I examine the various regions of nature, but I can discover no process for restoring the mouldering body, and no sign or track of the spirit's ascent to another sphere. I see the need of a power above nature to restore or perpetuate life after death; and if God intended to give assurance of this life, I see not how he can do it but by supernatural teaching, by a miraculous revelation. Miracles are the appropriate, and would seem to be the only mode of placing beyond doubt man's future and immortal being; and no miracles can be conceived so peculiarly adapted to this end as the very ones which hold the highest place in Christianity, — I mean the resurrection of Lazarus, and, still more, the resurrection of Jesus. No man will deny, that, of all truths, a future state is most strengthening to virtue and consoling to humanity. Is it then unworthy of God to employ miracles for the awakening or the confirmation of this hope? May they not even be expected, if nature, as we have seen, sheds but a faint light on this most interesting of all verities?

I add one more consideration in support of the position, that nature was not intended to be God's only method of teaching mankind. In surveying the human mind, we discover a principle which singularly fits it to be wrought upon and benefited by miraculous agency, and which might therefore lead us to expect such interposition. I refer to that principle of our nature, by which we become in a measure insensible or indifferent to what is familiar, but are roused to attention and deep interest by what is singular, strange, supernatural. This principle of wonder is an important part of our constitution; and that God should employ it in the work of our education, is what reason might anticipate. I see, then, a foundation for miracles in the human mind; and, when I consider that the mind is God's noblest work, I ought to look to this as the interpreter of his designs. We are plainly so constituted, that the order of nature, the more it is fixed, excites us the less. Our interest is blunted by its ceaseless uniformity. On the contrary, departures from this order powerfully stir the soul, break up its old and slumbering habits of thought, turn it with a new solicitude to the Almighty Interposer, and prepare it to receive with awe the communications of his will. Was it unworthy of God, who gave us this sensibility to the wonderful, to appeal to it for the recovery of his creatures to himself?

I here close my remarks on the great objection of skepticism, that miracles are inconsistent with the divine perfections; that the Supreme Being, having established an order of operation, cannot be expected to depart from it. To me, such reasoning, if reasoning it may be called, is of no weight. When I consider God's paternal and moral relation to mankind, and his interest in their progress; when I consider how accordant it is with his character that he should make himself known to them by methods most fitted to awaken the mind and heart to his goodness; when I consider the need we have of illumination in regard to the future life, more distinct and full than the creation affords ; when I consider the constitution and condition of man, his free agency, and the corruption into which he had fallen ; when I consider how little benefit a being so depraved was likely to derive from an order of nature to which he had grown familiar, and how plainly the mind is fitted to be quickened by miraculous interposition ; — I say, when I take all these things into view, I see, as I think, a foundation in nature for supernatural light and aid, and I discern in a miraculous revelation, such as Christianity, a provision suited at once to the frame and wants of the human soul, and to the perfections of its Author.

There are other objections to miracles, though less avowed, than that which I have now considered, yet perhaps not less influential, and probably operating on many minds so secretly as to be unperceived. At two of these I will just glance. Not a few, I am confident, have doubts of the Christian miracles, because they see none *now*. Were their skepticism to clothe itself in language, it would say, "Show us miracles, and we will believe them. We suspect them, because they are confined to the past." Now this objection is a childish one. It may be resolved into the principle, that nothing in the past is worthy of belief, which is not repeated in the present. Admit this, and where will incredulity stop ? How many forms and institutions of society, recorded in ancient history, have passed away. Has history, then, no title to respect ? If indeed the human race were standing still, if one age were merely a copy of preceding ones, if each had precisely the same wants, then the miracles required at one period would be reproduced in all. But who does not know that there is a progress in human affairs? that formerly mankind were in a different stage from that through which they are now passing? that of course the education of the race must be varied? and that miracles, important once, may be superfluous now? Shall we bind the Creator to invariable modes of teaching and training a race whose capacities and wants are undergoing a perpetual change? Because in periods of thick darkness God introduced a new religion by supernatural works, shall we expect these works to be repeated, when the darkness is scattered and their end attained? Who does not see that miracles, from their very nature, must be rare, occasional, limited? Would not their power be impaired by frequency? and would it not wholly cease, were they so far multiplied as to seem a part of the order of nature?

The objection I am now considering, shows us the true character of skepticism. Skepticism is essentially a narrowness of mind, which makes the present moment the measure of the past and future. It is the creature of sense. In the midst of a boundless universe, it can conceive no mode of operation but what falls under its immediate observation. The visible, the present, is every thing to the unbeliever. Let him but enlarge his views; let him look round on the immensity of the universe; let him consider the infinity of resources which are comprehended in omnipotence; let him represent to himself the manifold stages through which the human race is appointed to pass; let him remember that the education of the ever-growing mind must require a great variety of discipline; and especially let him admit the sublime thought, of which the germ is found in nature, that man was created to be trained for, and to ascend to, an incomparably higher order of existence than the present, — and he will see the childishness of making his narrow experience the standard of all that is past and is to come in human history.

It is strange, indeed, that men of science should fall into this error. The improved science of the present day teaches them, that this globe of ours, which seems so unchangeable, is not now what it was a few thousand years ago. They find proofs by digging into the earth, that this globe was inhabited before the existence of the human race, by classes of animals which have perished, and the ocean peopled by races now unknown, and that the human race are occupying a ruined and restored world. Men of science should learn to free themselves from the vulgar narrowness which sees nothing in the past but the present, and should learn the stupendous and infinite variety of the dispensations of God.

There is another objection to miracles, and the last to be now considered, which is drawn from the well-known fact, that pretended miracles crowd the pages of ancient history. No falsehoods, we are told, have been more common than accounts of prodigies, and therefore the miraculous character of Christianity is a presumption against its truth. I acknowledge that this argument has its weight; and I am ready to say, that, did I know nothing of Christianity, but that it was a religion full of miracles; did I know nothing of its doctrines, its purpose, its influences, and whole history, I should suspect it as much as the unbeliever. There is a strong presumption against miracles, considered nakedly, or separated from their design and from all circumstances which explain and support them. There s a like presumption against events not miraculous, but of an extraordinary character. But this is only a reason for severe scrutiny and slow belief, not for resisting strong and multiplied proofs. I blame no man for doubting a report of miracles when first brought to his ears. Thousands of absurd prodigies have been created by ignorance and fanaticism, and thousands more been forged by imposture. I invite you, then, to try scrupulously the miracles of Christianity; and, if they bear the marks of the superstitious legends of false religions, do not spare them. I only ask for them a fair hearing and calm investigation.

It is plainly no sufficient argument for rejecting all miracles, that men have believed in many which are false. If you go back to the times when miraculous stories were swallowed most greedily, and read the books then written on history, geography, and natural science, you will find all of them crowded with error; but do they therefore contain nothing worthy your trust? Is there not a vein of truth running through the prevalent falsehood? And cannot a sagacious mind very often detach the real from the fictitious, explain the origin of many mistakes, distinguish the judicious and honest from the credulous or interested narrator, and by a comparison of testimonies detect the latent truth? Where will you stop, if you start with believing nothing on points where former ages have gone astray? You must pronounce all religion and all morality to be delusion, for on both topics men have grossly erred. Nothing is more unworthy of a philosopher, than to found a universal censure on a limited number of unfavorable facts. This is much like the reasoning of the misanthrope, who, because he sees much vice, infers that there is no virtue, and, because he has sometimes been deceived, pronounces all men hypocrites.

I maintain that the multiplicity of false miracles, far from disproving, gives support to those on which Christianity rests; for, first, there is generally some foundation for falsehood, especially when it obtains general belief. The love of truth is an essential principle of human nature; men generally embrace error on account of some precious ingredient of truth mixed with it, and for the time inseparable from it. The universal belief of past ages in miraculous interpositions, is to me a presumption that miracles have entered into human history. Will the unbeliever say, that it only shows the insatiable thirst of the human mind for the supernatural? I reply, that, in this reasoning, he furnishes a weapon against himself; for a strong principle in the human mind, impelling men to seek for and to cling to miraculous agency, affords a presumption that the Author of our being, by whom this thirst for the supernatural was given, intended to furnish objects for it, and to assign it a place in the education of the race.

But I observe, in the next place, and it is an observation of great importance, that the exploded miracles of ancient times, if carefully examined, not only furnish a general presumption in favor of the existence of genuine ones, but yield strong proof of the truth of those in particular upon which Christianity rests. I say to the skeptic, You affirm nothing but truth in declaring history to abound in false miracles; I agree with you in exploding by far the greater part of the supernatural accounts of which ancient religions boast. But how do we know these to be false? We do not so judge without proofs. We discern in them the marks of delusion. Now I ask you to examine these marks, and then to answer me honestly, whether you find them in the miracles of Christianity. Is there not a broad line between Christ's works and those which we both agree in rejecting? I maintain that there is, and that nothing but ignorance can confound the Christian miracles with the prodigies of heathenism. The contrast between them is so strong as to forbid us to refer them to a common origin. The miracles of superstition carry the brand of falsehood in their own nature, and are disproved by the circumstances under which they were imposed on the multitude. The objects, for which they are said to have been wrought, are such as do not require or justify a divine interposition. Many of them are absurd, childish, or extravagant, and betray a weak intellect or diseased imagination. Many can be explained by natural causes. Many are attested by persons who lived in different countries and ages, and enjoyed no opportunities of inquiring into their truth. We can see the origin of many in the self-interest of those who forged them, and can account for their reception by the condition of the world. In other words, these spurious miracles were the natural growth of the ignorance, passions, prejudices, and corruptions of the times, and tended to confirm them. Now it is not enough to say, that these various marks of falsehood cannot be found in the Christian miracles. We find in them characters directly the reverse. They were wrought for an end worthy of God; they were wrought in an age of improvement; they are marked by a majesty, beneficence, unostentatious simplicity, and wisdom, which separate them immeasurably from the dreams of a disordered fancy or the contrivances of imposture.

They can be explained by no interests, passions, or prejudices of men. They are parts of a religion, which was singularly at variance with established ideas and expectations, which breathes purity and benevolence, which transcended the improvements of the age, and which thus carries with it the presumption of a divine original. Whence this immense distance between the two classes of miracles? Will you trace both to one source, and that a polluted one? Will you ascribe to one spirit, works as different as light and darkness, as earth and heaven? I am not, then, shaken in my faith by the false miracles of other religions. I have no desire to keep them out of sight; I summon them as my witnesses. They show me how naturally imposture and superstition leave the stamp of themselves on their fictions. They show how man, when he aspires to counterfeit God's agency, betrays more signally his impotence and folly. When I place side by side the mighty works of Jesus and the prodigies of heathenism, I see that they can no more be compared with one another, than the machinery and mock thunders of the theatre can be likened to the awful and beneficent powers of the universe.

In the preceding remarks on miracles, I have aimed chiefly to meet those general objections by which many are prejudiced against supernatural interpositions universally, and are disinclined to weigh any proof in their support. Hoping that this weak skepticism has been shown to want foundation in nature and reason, I proceed now to state more particularly the principal grounds on which I believe that the miracles ascribed to Jesus and the first propagators of Christianity, were actually wrought in attestation of its truth.

The evidences of facts are of two kinds, presumptive

and direct, and both meet in support of Christian miracles. First, there are strong presumptions in its favor. To this class of proofs, belong the views already given of the accordance of revelation and miracles with the wants and principles of human nature, with the perfections of God, with his relations to his human family, and with his ordinary providence. These I need not repeat. I will only observe, that a strong presumption in support of the miracles arises from the importance of the religion to which they belong. If I were told of supernatural works performed to prove, that three are more than one, or that human life requires food for its support, I should know that they were false. The presumption against them would be invincible. The author of nature could never supersede its wise and stupendous order to teach what falls within the knowledge of every child. Extraordinary interpositions of God suppose that truths of extraordinary dignity and beneficence are to be imparted. Now, in Christianity, I find truths of transcendent importance, which throw into shade all the discoveries of science, and which give a new character, aim, and interest, to our existence. Here is a fit occasion for supernatural interposition. A presumption exists in favor of miracles, by which a religion so worthy of God is sustained.

But a presumption in favor of facts, is not enough. It indeed adds much force to the direct proofs; still these are needed, nor are they wanting to Christianity. The direct proofs of facts are chiefly of two kinds; they consist of testimony, oral or written, and of effects, traces, monuments, which the facts have left behind them. The Christian miracles are supported by both. —We have first the most unexceptionable Testimony, nothing less than that of contemporaries and eye-witnesses, of the companions of Jesus and the first propagators of his religion. We have the testimony of men who could not have been deceived as to the facts which they report; who bore their witness amidst perils and persecutions; who bore it on the very spot where their Master lived and died; who had nothing to gain, and every thing to lose, if their testimony were false; whose writings breathe the sincerest love of virtue and of mankind; and who at last sealed their attestations with their blood. More unexceptionable witnesses to facts cannot be produced or conceived.

Do you say, "These witnesses lived ages ago; could we hear these accounts from their own lips, we should be satisfied"? I answer, You have something better than their own lips, or than their own word taken alone. You have, as has been proved, their writings. Perhaps you hear with some surprise that a book may be a better witness than its author; but nothing is more true, and I will illustrate it by an imaginary case in our own times.

Suppose, then, that a man claiming to be an eye-witness should relate to me the events of the three memorable days of July, in which the last revolution of France was achieved; suppose next, that a book, a history of that revolution, published and received as true in France, should be sent to me from that country. Which is the best evidence of the facts? I say the last. A single witness may deceive; but that a writer should publish in France the history of a revolution, which never occurred there, or which differed essentially from the true one, is, in the highest degree, improbable; and that such a history should obtain currency, that it should not be instantly branded as a lie, is utterly impossible. A history received by a people as true, not only gives us the testimony of the writer, but the testimony of the nation among whom it obtains credit. It is a concentration of thousands of voices, of many thousand witnesses. I say, then, that the writings of the first teachers of Christianity, received as they were by the multitude of Christians in their own times and in those which immediately followed, are the testimonies of that multitude as well as of the writers. Thousands, nearest to the events, join in bearing testimony to the Christian miracles.

But there is another class of evidence, sometimes more powerful than direct witnesses, and this belongs to Christianity. Facts are often placed beyond doubt by the effects which they leave behind them. This is the case with the miracles of Christ. Let me explain this branch of evidence. I am told, when absent and distant from your city, that on a certain day, a tide, such as had never been known, rose in your harbour, overflowed your wharves, and rushed into your streets; I doubt the fact; but hastening here, I see what were once streets, strewed with sea-weed, and shells, and the ruins of houses, and I cease to doubt. A witness may deceive, but such effects cannot lie. All great events leave effects, and these speak directly of the cause. What, I ask, are the proofs of the American revolution? Have we none but written or oral testimony? Our free constitution, the whole form of our society, the language and spirit of our laws, all these bear witness to our English origin, and to our successful conflict for independence. Now the miracles of Christianity have left effects, which equally attest their reality, and cannot be explained without them. I go back to the age of Jesus Christ, and I am immediately struck with the commencement and rapid progress of the most remarkable revolution in the annals of the world. I see a new religion, of a character altogether its own, which bore no likeness to any past or existing faith, spreading in a few years through all civilized nations, and introducing a new era, a new state of society, a change of the human mind, which has broadly distinguished all following ages. Here is a plain fact, which the skeptic will not deny, however he may explain it. I see this religion issuing from an obscure, despised, hated people. Its founder had died on the cross, a mode of punishment as disgraceful as the pillory or gallows of the present day. Its teachers were poor men, without rank, office, or education, taken from the fishing-boat and other occupations which had never furnished teachers to mankind. I see these men beginning their work on the spot where their Master's blood had been shed, as of a common malefactor; and I hear them summoning first his murderers, and then all nations and all ranks, the sovereign on the throne, the priest in the temple, the great and the learned, as well as the poor and the ignorant, to renounce the faith and the worship which had been hallowed by the veneration of all ages, and to take the yoke of their crucified Lord. I see passion and prejudice, the sword of the magistrate, the curse of the priest, the scorn of the philosopher, and the fury of the populace, joined to crush this common enemy; and yet, without a human weapon and in opposition to all human power, I see the humble Apostles of Jesus winning their way, overpowering prejudice, breaking the ranks of their opposers, changing enemies into friends, breathing into multitudes a calm spirit of martyrdom, and carrying to the bounds of civilization, and even into half-civilized regions, a religion which has contributed to advance society more than all other causes combined. Here is the effect. Here is a monument more durable than pillars or triumphal arches. Now I ask for an explanation of these effects. If Jesus Christ and his Apostles were indeed sent and empowered by God, and wrought miracles in attestation of their mission, then the establishment of Christianity is explained. Suppose them, on the other hand, to have been insane enthusiasts, or selfish impostors, left to meet the whole strength of human opposition, with nothing but their own power or rather their own weakness, and you have no cause for the stupendous effect I have described. Such men could no more have changed the face of the world, than they could have turned back rivers to their sources, sunk mountains into valleys, or raised valleys to the skies. Christianity, then, has not only the evidence of unexceptionable witnesses, but that of effects ; a proof which will grow stronger by comparing its progress with that of other religions, such as Mahometanism, which sprung from human passions, and were advanced by human power.

IV. Having given my views on the subject of Christian miracles, I now pass to the last topic of this discourse. Its extent and importance will lead me to enlarge upon it in a subsequent discourse ; but a discussion of Christian evidences, in which it should find no place, would be essentially defective. I refer to the proof of Christianity derived from the Character of its Author.

The character of Jesus was Original. He formed a new era in the moral history of the human race. His perfection was not that of his age, nor a copy of the greatness which had long engrossed the world's admiration. Jesus stood apart from other men. He borrowed from none and leaned on none. Surrounded by men of low thoughts, he rose to the conception of a higher form of human virtue than had yet been realized or imagined, and deliberately devoted himself to its promotion, as the supreme object of his life and death. Conscious of being dedicated to this great work, he spoke with a calm dignity, an unaffected elevation, which separated him from all other teachers. Unsupported, he never wavered; sufficient to himself, he refused alliance with wealth or power. Yet, with all this self-subsistence and uncompromising energy, his character was the mildest, the gentlest, the most attractive, ever manifested among men. It could not have been a fiction, for who could have conceived it, or who could have embodied the conception in such a life as Jesus is said to have led, in actions, words, manners, so natural and unstudied, so imbued with reality, so worthy of the Son of God?

The great distinction of Jesus was a philanthropy without mixture and without bounds; a philanthropy, uniting grandeur and meekness in beautiful proportions; a philanthropy, as wise as it was fervent, which comprehended the true wants and the true good of man, which compassionated, indeed, his sufferings from abroad, but which saw in the soul the deep fountain of his miseries, and labored, by regenerating this, to bring him to a pure and enduring happiness. So peculiar, so unparalleled was the benevolence of Jesus, that it has impressed itself on all future times. There went forth a virtue, a beneficent influence from his character, which operates even now. Since the death of Christ, a spirit of humanity, unknown before, has silently diffused itself over a considerable portion of the earth. A new standard of virtue has gradually possessed itself of the veneration of men. A new power has been acting on society, which has done more than all other causes combined, to disarm the selfish passions, and to bind men strongly to one another and to God. What a monument have we here to the virtue of Jesus! and if Christianity has such a Founder, it must have come from Heaven.

There are other remarkable proofs of the power and elevation of the character of Christ. It has touched and conciliated not a few of the determined adversaries of his religion. Infidelity, whilst it has laid unsparing hands on the system, has generally shrunk from offering violence to its Author. In truth, unbelievers have occasionally borne eloquent testimony to the benignant and celestial virtues of Jesus; and I record this with pleasure, not only as honorable to Christianity, but as snowing that unbelief does not universally sear the moral feelings, or breathe hostility to goodness. Nor is this all. The character of Christ has withstood the most deadly and irresistible foe of error and unfounded claims, I mean, Time. It has lost nothing of its elevation by the improvements of ages. Since he appeared, society has gone forward, men's views have become enlarged, and philosophy has risen to conceptions of far purer virtues than were the boast of antiquity. But, however the human mind may have advanced, it must still look upward, if it would see and understand Christ. He is still above it. Nothing purer, nobler, has yet dawned on human thoughts. Then Christianity is true. The delineation of Jesus in the Gospels, so warm with life, and so unrivalled in loveliness and grandeur, required the existence of an original. To suppose that this character was invented by unprincipled men, amidst Jewish and heathen darkness, and was then imposed as a reality in the very age of the founder of Christianity, argues an excess of credulity, and a strange ignorance of the powers and principles of human nature. The character of Jesus was real; and if so, Jesus must have been what he professed to be, the Son of God and the revealer of his mercy and his will to mankind.

I have now completed what I proposed in this discourse. I have laid before you some of the principal evidences of Christianity. I have aimed to state them without exaggeration. That an honest mind, which thoroughly comprehends them, can deny their force, seems to me hardly possible. Stronger proofs may indeed be conceived; but it is doubtful, whether these could be given in consistency with our moral nature, and with the moral government of God. Such a government requires, that truth should not be forced on the mind, but that we should be left to gain it, by an upright use of our understandings, and by conforming ourselves to what we have already learned. God might indeed shed on us an overpowering light, so that it would be impossible for us to lose our way; but in so doing, he would annihilate an important part of our present probation. It is then no objection to Christianity, that its evidences are not the very strongest which might be given, and that they do not extort universal assent. In this respect, it accords with other great truths. These are not forced on our belief. Whoever will, may shut his eyes on their proofs, and array against them objections. In the measure of evidence with which Christianity is accompanied, I see a just respect for the freedom of the mind, and a wise adaptation to that moral nature, which it is the great aim of this religion to carry forward to perfection.

I close as I began. I am not ashamed of the gospel of Christ; for it is True. It is true; and its truth is to break forth more and more gloriously. Of this I have not a doubt. I know indeed that our religion has been questioned even by intelligent and good men; but this does not shake my faith in its divine original or in its ultimate triumphs. Such men have questioned it, because they have known it chiefly by its corruptions. In proportion as its original simplicity shall be restored, the doubts of the well-disposed will yield. I have no fears from infidelity; especially from that form of it, which some are at this moment laboring to spread through our country; I mean, that insane, desperate unbelief, which strives to quench the light of nature as well as of revelation, and to leave us, not only without Christ, but without God. This I dread no more than I should fear the efforts of men to pluck the sun from his sphere, or to storm the skies with the artillery of the earth. We were made for religion; and unless the enemies of our faith can change our nature, they will leave the foundation of religion unshaken The human soul was created to look above material nature. It wants a Deity for its love and trust, an Immortality for its hope. It wants consolations not found in philosophy, wants strength in temptation, sorrow, and death, which human wisdom cannot minister; and knowing as I do, that Christianity meets these deep wants of men, I have no fear or doubt as to its triumphs. Men cannot long live without religion. In France there is a spreading dissatisfaction with the skeptical spirit of the past generation. A philosopher in that country would now blush to quote Voltaire as an authority in religion. Already Atheism is dumb where once it seemed to bear sway. The greatest minds in France are working back their way to the light of truth. Many of them indeed cannot yet be called Christians; but their path, like that of the wise men of old who came star-guided from the East, is towards Christ. I am not ashamed of the Gospel of Christ. It has an immortal life, and will gather strength from the violence of its foes. It is equal to all the wants of men. The greatest minds have found in it the light which they most anxiously desired. The most sorrowful and broken spirits have found in it a healing balm for their woes. It has inspired the sublimest virtues and the loftiest hopes. For the corruptions of such a religion I weep, and I should blush to be their advocate; but of the Gospel itself, I can never be ashamed.

UNITARIAN CHRISTIANITY.

DISCOURSE

AT THE

ORDINATION OF THE REV. JARED SPARKS.

BALTIMORE, 1819.

---

1 THES. v. 21: "Prove all things; hold fast that which is good."

THE peculiar circumstances of this occasion not only justify, but seem to demand a departure from the course generally followed by preachers at the introduction of a brother into the sacred office. It is usual to speak of the nature, design, duties, and advantages of the Christian ministry; and on these topics I should now be happy to insist, did I not remember that a minister is to be given this day to a religious society, whose peculiarities of opinion have drawn upon them much remark, and may I not add, much reproach. Many good minds, many sincere Christians, I am aware, are apprehensive that the solemnities of this day are to give a degree of influence to principles which they deem false and injurious. The fears and anxieties of such men I respect; and, believing that they are grounded in part on mistake, I have thought it my duty to lay before you, as clearly as I can, some of the distinguishing opinions of that class of Christians in our country, who are known to sympathize with this religious society. I must ask your patience, for such a subject is not to be despatched in a narrow compass. I must also ask you to remember, that it is impossible to exhibit, in a single discourse, our views of every doctrine of Revelation, much less the differences of opinion which are known to subsist among ourselves. I shall confine myself to topics, on which our sentiments have been mis represented, or which distinguish us most widely from others. May I not hope to be heard with candor? God deliver us all from prejudice and unkindness, and fill us with the love of truth and virtue.

There are two natural divisions under which my thoughts will be arranged. I shall endeavour to unfold, 1st, The principles which we adopt in interpreting the Scriptures. And 2dly, Some of the doctrines, which the Scriptures, so interpreted, seem to us clearly to express.

I. We regard the Scriptures as the records of God's successive revelations to mankind, and particularly of the last and most perfect revelation of his will by Jesus Christ. Whatever doctrines seem to us to be clearly taught in the Scriptures, we receive without reserve or exception. We do not, however, attach equal importance to all the books in this collection. Our religion, we believe, lies chiefly in the New Testament. The dispensation of Moses, compared with that of Jesus, we consider as adapted to the childhood of the human race, a preparation for a nobler system, and chiefly useful now as serving to confirm and illustrate the

Christian Scriptures. Jesus Christ is the only master of Christians, and whatever he taught, either during his personal ministry, or by his inspired Apostles, we regard as of divine authority, and profess to make the rule of our lives.

This authority, which we give to the Scriptures, is a reason, we conceive, for studying them with peculiar care, and for inquiring anxiously into the principles of interpretation, by which their true meaning may be ascertained. The principles adopted by the class of Christians in whose name I speak, need to be explained, because they are often misunderstood. We are particularly accused of making an unwarrantable use of reason in the interpretation of Scripture. We are said to exalt reason above revelation, to prefer our own wisdom to God's. Loose and undefined charges of this kind are circulated so freely, that we think it due to ourselves, and to the cause of truth, to express our views with some particularity.

Our leading principle in interpreting Scripture is this, that the Bible is a book written for men, in the language of men, and that its meaning is to be sought in the same manner as that of other books. We believe that God, when he speaks to the human race, conforms, if we may so say, to the established rules of speaking and writing. How else would the Scriptures avail us more, than if communicated in an unknown tongue?

Now all books, and all conversation, require in the reader or hearer the constant exercise of reason; or their true import is only to be obtained by continual comparison and inference. Human language, you well know, admits various interpretations; and every word and every sentence must be modified and explained according to the subject which is discussed, according to the purposes, feelings, circumstances, and principles of the writer, and according to the genius and idioms of the language which he uses. These are acknowledged principles in the interpretation of human writings; and a man, whose words we should explain without reference to these principles, would reproach us justly with a criminal want of candor, and an intention of obscuring or distorting his meaning.

Were the Bible written in a language and style of its own, did it consist of words, which admit but a single sense, and of sentences wholly detached from each other, there would be no place for the principles now laid down. We could not reason about it, as about other writings. But such a book would be of little worth; and perhaps, of all books, the Scriptures correspond least to this description. The Word of God bears the stamp of the same hand, which we see in his works. It has infinite connexions and dependences. Every proposition is linked with others, and is to be compared with others; that its full and precise import may be understood. Nothing stands alone. The New Testament is built on the Old. The Christian dispensation is a continuation of the Jewish, the completion of a vast scheme of providence, requiring great extent of view in the reader. Still more, the Bible treats of subjects on which we receive ideas from other sources besides itself; such subjects as the nature, passions, relations, and duties of man; and it expects us to restrain and modify its language by the known truths, which observation and experience furnish on these topics.

We profess not to know a book, which demands a

more frequent exercise of reason than the Bible. In addition to the remarks now made on its infinite connexions, we may observe, that its style nowhere affects the precision of science, or the accuracy of definition. Its language is singularly glowing, bold, and figurative, demanding more frequent departures from the literal sense, than that of our own age and country, and consequently demanding more continual exercise of judgment. — We find, too, that the different portions of this book, instead of being confined to general truths, refer perpetually to the times when they were written, to states of society, to modes of thinking, to controversies in the church, to feelings and usages which have passed away, and without the knowledge of which we are constantly in danger of extending to all times, and places, what was of temporary and local application. — We find, too, that some of these books are strongly marked by the genius and character of their respective writers, that the Holy Spirit did not so guide the Apostles as to suspend the peculiarities of their minds, and that a knowledge of their feelings, and of the influences under which they were placed, is one of the preparations for understanding their writings. With these views of the Bible, we feel it our bounden duty to exercise our reason upon it perpetually, to compare, to infer, to look beyond the letter to the spirit, to seek in the nature of the subject, and the aim of the writer, his true meaning; and, in general, to make use of what is known, for explaining what is difficult, and for discovering new truths.

Need I descend to particulars, to prove that the Scriptures demand the exercise of reason? Take, for example, the style in which they generally speak of

God, and observe how habitually they apply to him human passions and organs. Recollect the declarations of Christ, that he came not to send peace, but a sword; that unless we eat his flesh, and drink his blood, we have no life in us; that we must hate father and mother, and pluck out the right eye; and a vast number of passages equally bold and unlimited. Recollect the unqualified manner in which it is said of Christians, that they possess all things, know all things, and can do all things. Recollect the verbal contradiction between Paul and James, and the apparent clashing of some parts of Paul's writings with the general doctrines and end of Christianity. I might extend the enumeration indefinitely; and who does not see, that we must limit all these passages by the known attributes of God, of Jesus Christ, and of human nature, and by the circumstances under which they were written, so as to give the language a quite different import from what it would require, had it been applied to different beings, or used in different connexions.

Enough has been said to show, in what sense we make use of reason in interpreting Scripture. From a variety of possible interpretations, we select that which accords with the nature of the subject and the state of the writer, with the connexion of the passage, with the general strain of Scripture, with the known character and will of God, and with the obvious and acknowledged laws of nature. In other words, we believe that God never contradicts, in one part of Scripture, what he teaches in another; and never contradicts, in revelation, what he teaches in his works and providence. And we therefore distrust every interpretation, which, after deliberate attention, seems repugnant to any established truth. We reason about the Bible precisely as civilians do about the constitution under which we live; who, you know, are accustomed to limit one provision of that venerable instrument by others, and to fix the precise import of its parts, by inquiring into its general spirit, into the intentions of its authors, and into the prevalent feelings, impressions, and circumstances of the time when it was framed. Without these principles of interpretation, we frankly acknowledge, that we cannot defend the divine authority of the Scriptures. Deny us this latitude, and we must abandon this book to its enemies.

We do not announce these principles as original, or peculiar to ourselves. All Christians occasionally adopt them, not excepting those who most vehemently decry them, when they happen to menace some favorite article of their creed. All Christians are compelled to use them in their controversies with infidels. All sects employ them in their warfare with one another. All willingly avail themselves of reason, when it can be pressed into the service of their own party, and only complain of it, when its weapons wound themselves. None reason more frequently than those from whom we differ. It is astonishing what a fabric they rear from a few slight hints about the fall of our first parents; and how ingeniously they extract, from detached passages, mysterious doctrines about the divine nature. We do not blame them for reasoning so abundantly, but for violating the fundamental rules of reasoning, for sacrificing the plain to the obscure, and the general strain of Scripture to a scanty number of insulated texts.

We object strongly to the contemptuous manner in which human reason is often spoken of by our adversaries, because it leads, we believe, to universal skepticism. If reason be so dreadfully darkened by the fall, that its most decisive judgments on religion are unworthy of trust, then Christianity, and even natural theology, must be abandoned ; for the existence and veracity of God, and the divine original of Christianity, are conclusions of reason, and must stand or fall with it. If revelation be at war with this faculty, it subverts itself, for the great question of its truth is left by God to be decided at the bar of reason. It is worthy of remark, how nearly the bigot and the skeptic approach. Both would annihilate our confidence in our faculties, and both throw doubt and confusion over every truth. We honor revelation too highly to make it the antagonist of reason, or to believe that it calls us to renounce our highest powers.

We indeed grant, that the use of reason in religion is accompanied with danger. But we ask any honest man to look back on the history of the church, and say, whether the renunciation of it be not still more dangerous. Besides, it is a plain fact, that men reason as erroneously on all subjects, as on religion. Who does not know the wild and groundless theories, which have been framed in physical and political science ? But who ever supposed, that we must cease to exercise reason on nature and society, because men have erred for ages in explaining them ? We grant, that the passions continually, and sometimes fatally, disturb the rational faculty in its inquiries into revelation. The ambitious contrive to find doctrines in the Bible, which favor their love of dominion. The timid and dejected discover there a gloomy system, and the mystical and fanatical, a visionary theology. The vicious can find examples or assertions on which to build the hope of a late repentance, or of acceptance on easy terms. The falsely refined contrive to light on doctrines which have not been soiled by vulgar handling. But the passions do not distract the reason in religious, any more than in other inquiries, which excite strong and general interest; and this faculty, of consequence, is not to be renounced in religion, unless we are prepared to discard it universally. The true inference from the almost endless errors, which have darkened theology, is, not that we are to neglect and disparage our powers, but to exert them more patiently, circumspectly, uprightly. The worst errors, after all, having sprung up in that church, which proscribes reason, and demands from its members implicit faith. The most pernicious doctrines have been the growth of the darkest times, when the general credulity encouraged bad men and enthusiasts to broach their dreams and inventions, and to stifle the faint remonstrances of reason, by the menaces of everlasting perdition. Say what we may, God has given us a rational nature, and will call us to account for it. We may let it sleep, but we do so at our peril. Revelation is addressed to us as rational beings. We may wish, in our sloth, that God had given us a system, demanding no labor of comparing, limiting, and inferring. But such a system would be at variance with the whole character of our present existence; and it is the part of wisdom to take revelation as it is given to us, and to interpret it by the help of the faculties, which it everywhere supposes, and on which it is founded.

To the views now given, an objection is commonly urged from the character of God. We are told, that God being infinitely wiser than men, his discoveries will surpass human reason. In a revelation from such a teacher, we ought to expect propositions, which we cannot reconcile with one another, and which may seem to contradict established truths ; and it becomes us not to question or explain them away, but to believe, and adore, and to submit our weak and carnal reason to the Divine Word. To this objection, we have two short answers. We say, first, that it is impossible that a teacher of infinite wisdom should expose those, whom he would teach, to infinite error. But if once we admit, that propositions, which in their literal sense appear plainly repugnant to one another, or to any known truth, are still to be literally understood and received, what possible limit can we set to the belief of contradictions ? What shelter have we from the wildest fanaticism, which can always quote passages, that, in their literal and obvious sense, give support to its extravagances ? How can the Protestant escape from transubstantiation, a doctrine most clearly taught us, if the submission of reason, now contended for, be a duty ? How can we even hold fast the truth of revelation, for if one apparent contradiction may be true, so may another, and the proposition, that Christianity is false, though involving inconsistency, may still be a verity ?

We answer again, that, if God be infinitely wise, he cannot sport with the understandings of his creatures. A wise teacher discovers his wisdom in adapting himself to the capacities of his pupils, not in perplexing them with what is unintelligible, not in distressing them with apparent contradictions, not in filling them with a skeptical distrust of their own powers. An infinitely wise teacher, who knows the precise extent of our minds, and the best method of enlightening them, will surpass all other instructors in bringing down truth to our apprehension, and in showing its loveliness and harmony. We ought, indeed, to expect occasional obscurity in such a book as the Bible, which was written for past and future ages, as well as for the present. But God's wisdom is a pledge, that whatever is necessary for *us*, and necessary for salvation, is revealed too plainly to be mistaken, and too consistently to be questioned, by a sound and upright mind. It is not the mark of wisdom, to use an unintelligible phraseology, to communicate what is above our capacities, to confuse and unsettle the intellect by appearances of contradiction. We honor our Heavenly Teacher too much to ascribe to him such a revelation. A revelation is a gift of light. It cannot thicken our darkness, and multiply our perplexities.

II. Having thus stated the principles according to which we interpret Scripture, I now proceed to the second great head of this discourse, which is, to state some of the views which we derive from that sacred book, particularly those which distinguish us from other Christians.

1. In the first place, we believe in the doctrine of God's UNITY, or that there is one God, and one only. To this truth we give infinite importance, and we feel ourselves bound to take heed, lest any man spoil us of it by vain philosophy. The proposition, that there is one God, seems to us exceedingly plain. We understand by it, that there is one being, one mind, one person, one intelligent agent, and one only, to whom underived and infinite perfection and dominion belong. We conceive, that these words could have conveyed no

other meaning to the simple and uncultivated people, who were set apart to be the depositaries of this great truth, and who were utterly incapable of understanding those hair-breadth distinctions between being and person, which the sagacity of later ages has discovered. We find no intimation, that this language was to be taken in an unusual sense, or that God's unity was a quite different thing from the oneness of other intelligent beings.

We object to the doctrine of the Trinity, that, whilst acknowledging in words, it subverts in effect, the unity of God. According to this doctrine, there are three infinite and equal persons, possessing supreme divinity, called the Father, Son, and Holy Ghost. Each of these persons, as described by theologians, has his own particular consciousness, will, and perceptions. They love each other, converse with each other, and delight in each other's society. They perform different parts in man's redemption, each having his appropriate office, and neither doing the work of the other. The Son is mediator and not the Father. The Father sends the Son, and is not himself sent; nor is he conscious, like the Son, of taking flesh. Here, then, we have three intelligent agents, possessed of different consciousnesses, different wills, and different perceptions, performing different acts, and sustaining different relations; and if these things do not imply and constitute three minds or beings, we are utterly at a loss to know how three minds or beings are to be formed. It is difference of properties, and acts, and consciousness, which leads us to the belief of different intelligent beings, and, if this mark fails us, our whole knowledge falls; we have no proof, that all the agents and persons in the universe are not one and the same mind. When we attempt to conceive of three Gods, we can do nothing more than represent to ourselves three agents, distinguished from each other by similar marks and peculiarities to those which separate the persons of the Trinity; and when common Christians hear these persons spoken of as conversing with each other, loving each other, and performing different acts, how can they help regarding them as different beings, different minds?

We do, then, with all earnestness, though without reproaching our brethren, protest against the irrational and unscriptural doctrine of the Trinity. "To us," as to the Apostle and the primitive Christians, "there is one God, even the Father." With Jesus, we worship the Father, as the only living and true God. We are astonished, that any man can read the New Testament, and avoid the conviction, that the Father alone is God. We hear our Saviour continually appropriating this character to the Father. We find the Father continually distinguished from Jesus by this title. "God sent his Son." "God anointed Jesus." Now, how singular and inexplicable is this phraseology, which fills the New Testament, if this title belong equally to Jesus, and if a principal object of this book is to reveal him as God, as partaking equally with the Father in supreme divinity! We challenge our opponents to adduce one passage in the New Testament, where the word God means three persons, where it is not limited to one person, and where, unless turned from its usual sense by the connexion, it does not mean the Father. Can stronger proof be given, that the doctrine of three persons in the Godhead is not a fundamental doctrine of Christianity?

This doctrine, were it true, must, from its difficulty, singularity, and importance, have been laid down with great clearness, guarded with great care, and stated with all possible precision. But where does this statement appear? From the many passages which treat of God, we ask for one, one only, in which we are told, that he is a threefold being, or that he is three persons, or that he is Father, Son, and Holy Ghost. On the contrary, in the New Testament, where, at least, we might expect many express assertions of this nature, God is declared to be one, without the least attempt to prevent the acceptation of the words in their common sense; and he is always spoken of and addressed in the singular number, that is, in language which was universally understood to intend a single person, and to which no other idea could have been attached, without an express admonition. So entirely do the Scriptures abstain from stating the Trinity, that when our opponents would insert it into their creeds and doxologies, they are compelled to leave the Bible, and to invent forms of words altogether unsanctioned by Scriptural phraseology. That a doctrine so strange, so liable to misapprehension, so fundamental as this is said to be, and requiring such careful exposition, should be left so undefined and unprotected, to be made out by inference, and to be hunted through distant and detached parts of Scripture, this is a difficulty, which, we think, no ingenuity can explain.

We have another difficulty. Christianity, it must be remembered, was planted and grew up amidst sharp-sighted enemies, who overlooked no objectionable part of the system, and who must have fastened with great earnestness on a doctrine involving such apparent contradictions as the Trinity. We cannot conceive an opinion, against which the Jews, who prided themselves on an adherence to God's unity, would have raised an equal clamor. Now, how happens it, that in the apostolic writings, which relate so much to objections against Christianity, and to the controversies which grew out of this religion, not one word is said, implying that objections were brought against the Gospel from the doctrine of the Trinity, not one word is uttered in its defence and explanation, not a word to rescue it from reproach and mistake? This argument has almost the force of demonstration. We are persuaded, that had three divine persons been announced by the first preachers of Christianity, all equal, and all infinite, one of whom was the very Jesus who had lately died on a cross, this peculiarity of Christianity would have almost absorbed every other, and the great labor of the Apostles would have been to repel the continual assaults, which it would have awakened. But the fact is, that not a whisper of objection to Christianity, on that account, reaches our ears from the apostolic age. In the Epistles we see not a trace of controversy called forth by the Trinity.

We have further objections to this doctrine, drawn from its practical influence. We regard it as unfavorable to devotion, by dividing and distracting the mind in its communion with God. It is a great excellence of the doctrine of God's unity, that it offers to us ONE OBJECT of supreme homage, adoration, and love, One Infinite Father, one Being of beings, one original and fountain, to whom we may refer all good, in whom all our powers and affections may be concentrated, and whose lovely and venerable nature may pervade all our thoughts. True piety, when directed to an undivided

Deity, has a chasteness, a singleness, most favorable to religious awe and love. Now, the Trinity sets before us three distinct objects of supreme adoration, three infinite persons, having equal claims on our hearts; three divine agents, performing different offices, and to be acknowledged and worshipped in different relations. And is it possible, we ask, that the weak and limited mind of man can attach itself to these with the same power and joy, as to One Infinite Father, the only First Cause, in whom all the blessings of nature and redemption meet as their centre and source? Must not devotion be distracted by the equal and rival claims of three equal persons, and must not the worship of the conscientious, consistent Christian, be disturbed by an apprehension, lest he withhold from one or another of these, his due proportion of homage?

We also think, that the doctrine of the Trinity injures devotion, not only by joining to the Father other objects of worship, but by taking from the Father the supreme affection, which is his due, and transferring it to the Son. This is a most important view. That Jesus Christ, if exalted into the infinite Divinity, should be more interesting than the Father, is precisely what might be expected from history, and from the principles of human nature. Men want an object of worship like themselves, and the great secret of idolatry lies in this propensity. A God, clothed in our form, and feeling our wants and sorrows, speaks to our weak nature more strongly, than a Father in heaven, a pure spirit, invisible and unapproachable, save by the reflecting and purified mind.—We think, too, that the peculiar offices ascribed to Jesus by the popular theology, make him the most attractive person in the Godhead. The Father is the depositary of the justice, the vindicator of the rights, the avenger of the laws of the Divinity. On the other hand, the Son, the brightness of the divine mercy, stands between the incensed Deity and guilty humanity, exposes his meek head to the storms, and his compassionate breast to the sword of the divine justice, bears our whole load of punishment, and purchases with his blood every blessing which descends from heaven. Need we state the effect of these representations, especially on common minds, for whom Christianity was chiefly designed, and whom it seeks to bring to the Father as the loveliest being? We do believe, that the worship of a bleeding, suffering God, tends strongly to absorb the mind, and to draw it from other objects, just as the human tenderness of the Virgin Mary has given her so conspicuous a place in the devotions of the Church of Rome. We believe, too, that this worship, though attractive, is not most fitted to spiritualize the mind, that it awakens human transport, rather than that deep veneration of the moral perfections of God, which is the essence of piety.

2. Having thus given our views of the unity of God, I proceed in the second place to observe, that we believe in the unity of Jesus Christ. We believe that Jesus is one mind, one soul, one being, as truly one as we are, and equally distinct from the one God. We complain of the doctrine of the Trinity, that, not satisfied with making God three beings, it makes Jesus Christ two beings, and thus introduces infinite confusion into our conceptions of his character. This corruption of Christianity, alike repugnant to common sense and to the general strain of Scripture, is a remarkable proof of the power of a false philosophy in disfiguring the simple truth of Jesus.

According to this doctrine, Jesus Christ, instead of being one mind, one conscious intelligent principle, whom we can understand, consists of two souls, two minds; the one divine, the other human; the one weak, the other almighty; the one ignorant, the other omniscient. Now we maintain, that this is to make Christ two beings. To denominate him one person, one being, and yet to suppose him made up of two minds, infinitely different from each other, is to abuse and confound language, and to throw darkness over all our conceptions of intelligent natures. According to the common doctrine, each of these two minds in Christ has its own consciousness, its own will, its own perceptions. They have, in fact, no common properties. The divine mind feels none of the wants and sorrows of the human, and the human is infinitely removed from the perfection and happiness of the divine. Can you conceive of two beings in the universe more distinct? We have always thought that one person was constituted and distinguished by one consciousness. The doctrine, that one and the same person should have two consciousnesses, two wills, two souls, infinitely different from each other, this we think an enormous tax on human credulity.

We say, that if a doctrine, so strange, so difficult, so remote from all the previous conceptions of men, be indeed a part and an essential part of revelation, it must be taught with great distinctness, and we ask our brethren to point to some plain, direct passage, where Christ is said to be composed of two minds infinitely different, yet constituting one person. We find none. Other Christians, indeed, tell us, that this doctrine is necessary to the harmony of the Scriptures, that some texts ascribe to Jesus Christ human, and others divine properties, and that to reconcile these, we must suppose two minds, to which these properties may be referred. In other words, for the purpose of reconciling certain difficult passages, which a just criticism can in a great degree, if not wholly, explain, we must invent an hypothesis vastly more difficult, and involving gross absurdity. We are to find our way out of a labyrinth, by a clue which conducts us into mazes infinitely more inextricable.

Surely, if Jesus Christ felt that he consisted of two minds, and that this was a leading feature of his religion, his phraseology respecting himself would have been colored by this peculiarity. The universal language of men is framed upon the idea, that one person is one person, is one mind, and one soul; and when the multitude heard this language from the lips of Jesus, they must have taken it in its usual sense, and must have referred to a single soul all which he spoke, unless expressly instructed to interpret it differently. But where do we find this instruction? Where do you meet, in the New Testament, the phraseology which abounds in Trinitarian books, and which necessarily grows from the doctrine of two natures in Jesus? Where does this divine teacher say, "This I speak as God, and this as man; this is true only of my human mind, this only of my divine"? Where do we find in the Epistles a trace of this strange phraseology? Nowhere. It was not needed in that day. It was demanded by the errors of a later age.

We believe, then, that Christ is one mind, one being, and, I add, a being distinct from the one God. That Christ is not the one God, not the same being with the Father, is a necessary inference from our former head, in which we saw that the doctrine of three persons in God is a fiction. But on so important a subject, I would add a few remarks. We wish, that those from whom we differ, would weigh one striking fact. Jesus, in his preaching, continually spoke of God. The word was always in his mouth. We ask, does he, by this word, ever mean himself? We say, never. On the contrary, he most plainly distinguishes between God and himself, and so do his disciples. How this is to be reconciled with the idea, that the manifestation of Christ, as God, was a primary object of Christianity, our adversaries must determine.

If we examine the passages in which Jesus is distinguished from God, we shall see, that they not only speak of him as another being, but seem to labor to express his inferiority. He is continually spoken of as the Son of God, sent of God, receiving all his powers from God, working miracles because God was with him, judging justly because God taught him, having claims on our belief, because he was anointed and sealed by God, and as able of himself to do nothing. The New Testament is filled with this language. Now we ask, what impression this language was fitted and intended to make? Could any, who heard it, have imagined that Jesus was the very God to whom he was so industriously declared to be inferior; the very Being by whom he was sent, and from whom he professed to have received his message and power? Let it here be remembered, that the human birth, and bodily form, and humble circumstances, and mortal sufferings of Jesus, must all have prepared men to interpret, in the most unqualified manner, the language in which his inferiority to God was declared. Why, then, was this language used so continually, and without limitation, if Jesus were the Supreme Deity, and if this truth were an essential part of his religion? I repeat it, the human condition and sufferings of Christ tended strongly to exclude from men's minds the idea of his proper Godhead; and, of course, we should expect to find in the New Testament perpetual care and effort to counteract this tendency, to hold him forth as the same being with his Father, if this doctrine were, as is pretended, the soul and centre of his religion. We should expect to find the phraseology of Scripture cast into the mould of this doctrine, to hear familiarly of God the Son, of our Lord God Jesus, and to be told, that to us there is one God, even Jesus. But, instead of this, the inferiority of Christ pervades the New Testament. It is not only implied in the general phraseology, but repeatedly and decidedly expressed, and unaccompanied with any admonition to prevent its application to his whole nature. Could it, then, have been the great design of the sacred writers to exhibit Jesus as the Supreme God?

I am aware that these remarks will be met by two or three texts, in which Christ is called God, and by a class of passages, not very numerous, in which divine properties are said to be ascribed to him. To these we offer one plain answer. We say, that it is one of the most established and obvious principles of criticism, that language is to be explained according to the known properties of the subject to which it is applied. Every man knows, that the same words convey very different ideas, when used in relation to different beings. Thus, Solomon *built* the temple in a different manner from the architect whom he employed; and God *repents* differently from man. Now we maintain, that the known properties and circumstances of Christ, his birth, sufferings, and death, his constant habit of speaking of God as a distinct being from himself, his praying to God, his ascribing to God all his power and offices, these acknowledged properties of Christ, we say, oblige us to interpret the comparatively few passages which are thought to make him the Supreme God, in a manner consistent with his distinct and inferior nature. It is our duty to explain such texts by the rule which we apply to other texts, in which human beings are called gods, and are said to be partakers of the divine nature, to know and possess all things, and to be filled with all God's fulness. These latter passages we do not hesitate to modify, and restrain, and turn from the most obvious sense, because this sense is opposed to the known properties of the beings to whom they relate; and we maintain, that we adhere to the same principle, and use no greater latitude, in explaining, as we do, the passages which are thought to support the Godhead of Christ.

Trinitarians profess to derive some important advantages from their mode of viewing Christ. It furnishes them, they tell us, with an infinite atonement, for it shows them an infinite being suffering for their sins. The confidence with which this fallacy is repeated astonishes us. When pressed with the question, whether they really believe, that the infinite and unchangeable God suffered and died on the cross, they acknowledge that this is not true, but that Christ's human mind alone sustained the pains of death. How have we, then, an infinite sufferer? This language seems to us an imposition on common minds, and very derogatory to God's justice, as if this attribute could be satisfied by a sophism and a fiction.

We are also told, that Christ is a more interesting object, that his love and mercy are more felt, when he is viewed as the Supreme God, who left his glory to take humanity and to suffer for men. That Trinitarians are strongly moved by this representation, we do not mean to deny; but we think their emotions altogether founded on a misapprehension of their own doctrines. They talk of the second person of the Trinity's leaving his glory and his Father's bosom, to visit and save the world. But this second person, being the unchangeable and infinite God, was evidently incapable of parting with the least degree of his perfection and felicity. At the moment of his taking flesh, he was as intimately present with his Father as before, and equally with his Father filled heaven, and earth, and immensity. This Trinitarians acknowledge; and still they profess to be touched and overwhelmed by the amazing humiliation of this immutable being! But not only does their doctrine, when fully explained, reduce Christ's humiliation to a fiction, it almost wholly destroys the impressions with which his cross ought to be viewed. According to their doctrine, Christ was comparatively no sufferer at all. It is true, his human mind suffered; but this, they tell us, was an infinitely small part of Jesus, bearing no more proportion to his whole nature, than a single hair of our heads to the whole body, or than a drop to the ocean. The divine mind of Christ, that which was most properly himself, was infinitely happy, at the very moment of the suffering of his humanity. Whilst hanging on the cross, he was the happiest being in the universe, as happy as the infinite Father; so that his pains, compared with his felicity, were nothing. This Trinitarians do, and must, acknowledge. It follows necessarily from the immutableness of the divine nature, which they ascribe to Christ; so that their system, justly viewed, robs his death of interest, weakens our sympathy with his sufferings, and is, of all others, most unfavorable to a love of Christ, founded on a sense of his sacrifices for mankind. We esteem our own views to be vastly more affecting. It is our belief, that Christ's humiliation was real and entire, that the whole Saviour, and not a part of him, suffered, that his crucifixion was a scene of deep and unmixed agony. As we stand round his cross, our minds are not distracted, nor our sensibility weakened, by contemplating him as composed of incongruous and infinitely differing minds, and as having a balance of infinite felicity. We recognise in the dying Jesus but one mind. This, we think, renders his sufferings, and his patience and love in bearing them, incomparably more impressive and affecting than the system we oppose.

3. Having thus given our belief on two great points, namely, that there is one God, and that Jesus Christ is a being distinct from, and inferior to, God, I now proceed to another point, on which we lay still greater stress. We believe in the *moral perfection of God*. We consider no part of theology so important as that which treats of God's moral character; and we value our views of Christianity chiefly as they assert his amiable and venerable attributes.

It may be said, that, in regard to this subject, all Christians agree, that all ascribe to the Supreme Being infinite justice, goodness, and holiness. We reply, that it is very possible to speak of God magnificently, and to think of him meanly; to apply to his person high-sounding epithets, and to his government, principles which make him odious. The Heathens called Jupiter the greatest and the best; but his history was black with cruelty and lust. We cannot judge of men's real ideas of God by their general language, for in all ages they have hoped to soothe the Deity by adulation. We must inquire into their particular views of his purposes, of the principles of his administration, and of his disposition towards his creatures.

We conceive that Christians have generally leaned towards a very injurious view of the Supreme Being. They have too often felt, as if he were raised, by his greatness and sovereignty, above the principles of morality, above those eternal laws of equity and rectitude, to which all other beings are subjected. We believe, that in no being is the sense of right so strong, so omnipotent, as in God. We believe that his almighty power is entirely submitted to his perceptions of rectitude; and this is the ground of our piety. It is not because he is our Creator merely, but because he created us for good and holy purposes; it is not because his will is irresistible, but because his will is the perfection of virtue, that we pay him allegiance. We cannot bow before a being, however great and powerful, who governs tyrannically. We respect nothing but excellence, whether on earth or in heaven. We venerate not the loftiness of God's throne, but the equity and goodness in which it is established.

We believe that God is infinitely good, kind, benevolent, in the proper sense of these words; good in disposition, as well as in act; good, not to a few, but to all; good to every individual, as well as to the general system.

We believe, too, that God is just; but we never

forget, that his justice is the justice of a good being, dwelling in the same mind, and acting in harmony, with perfect benevolence. By this attribute, we understand God's infinite regard to virtue or moral worth expressed in a moral government; that is, in giving excellent and equitable laws, and in conferring such rewards, and inflicting such punishments, as are best fitted to secure their observance. God's justice has for its end the highest virtue of the creation, and it punishes for this end alone, and thus it coincides with benevolence; for virtue and happiness, though not the same, are inseparably conjoined.

God's justice thus viewed, appears to us to be in perfect harmony with his mercy. According to the prevalent systems of theology, these attributes are so discordant and jarring, that to reconcile them is the hardest task, and the most wonderful achievement, of infinite wisdom. To us they seem to be intimate friends, always at peace, breathing the same spirit, and seeking the same end. By God's mercy, we understand not a blind instinctive compassion, which forgives without reflection, and without regard to the interests of virtue. This, we acknowledge, would be incompatible with justice, and also with enlightened benevolence. God's mercy, as we understand it, desires strongly the happiness of the guilty, but only through their penitence. It has a regard to character as truly as his justice. It defers punishment, and suffers long, that the sinner may return to his duty, but leaves the impenitent and unyielding, to the fearful retribution threatened in God's Word.

To give our views of God in one word, we believe in his Parental character. We ascribe to him, not only the name, but the dispositions and principles of a father. We believe that he has a father's concern for his creatures, a father's desire for their improvement, a father's equity in proportioning his commands to their powers, a father's joy in their progress, a father's readiness to receive the penitent, and a father's justice for the incorrigible. We look upon this world as a place of education, in which he is training men by prosperity and adversity, by aids and obstructions, by conflicts of reason and passion, by motives to duty and temptations to sin, by a various discipline suited to free and moral beings, for union with himself, and for a sublime and ever-growing virtue in heaven.

Now, we object to the systems of religion, which prevail among us, that they are adverse, in a greater or less degree, to these purifying, comforting, and honorable views of God; that they take from us our Father in heaven, and substitute for him a being, whom we cannot love if we would, and whom we ought not to love if we could. We object, particularly on this ground, to that system, which arrogates to itself the name of Orthodoxy, and which is now industriously propagated through our country. This system indeed takes various shapes, but in all it casts dishonor on the Creator. According to its old and genuine form, it teaches, that God brings us into life wholly depraved, so that under the innocent features of our childhood is hidden a nature averse to all good and propense to all evil, a nature which exposes us to God's displeasure and wrath, even before we have acquired power to understand our duties, or to reflect upon our actions. According to a more modern exposition, it teaches, that we came from the hands of our Maker with such a constitution, and are placed under such influences and circumstances, as to render certain and infallible the total depravity of every human being, from the first moment of his moral agency; and it also teaches, that the offence of the child, who brings into life this ceaseless tendency to unmingled crime, exposes him to the sentence of everlasting damnation. Now, according to the plainest principles of morality, we maintain, that a natural constitution of the mind, unfailingly disposing it to evil and to evil alone, would absolve it from guilt; that to give existence under this condition would argue unspeakable cruelty; and that to punish the sin of this unhappily constituted child with endless ruin, would be a wrong unparalleled by the most merciless despotism.

This system also teaches, that God selects from this corrupt mass a number to be saved, and plucks them, by a special influence, from the common ruin; that the rest of mankind, though left without that special grace which their conversion requires, are commanded to repent, under penalty of aggravated woe; and that forgiveness is promised them, on terms which their very constitution infallibly disposes them to reject, and in rejecting which they awfully enhance the punishments of hell. These proffers of forgiveness and exhortations of amendment, to beings born under a blighting curse, fill our minds with a horror which we want words to express.

That this religious system does not produce all the effects on character, which might be anticipated, we most joyfully admit. It is often, very often, counteracted by nature, conscience, common sense, by the general strain of Scripture, by the mild example and precepts of Christ, and by the many positive declarations of God's universal kindness and perfect equity. But still we think that we see its unhappy influence. It tends to discourage the timid, to give excuses to the bad, to feed the vanity of the fanatical, and to offer shelter to the bad feelings of the malignant. By shocking, as it does, the fundamental principles of morality, and by exhibiting a severe and partial Deity, it tends strongly to pervert the moral faculty, to form a gloomy, forbidding, and servile religion, and to lead men to substitute censoriousness, bitterness, and persecution, for a tender and impartial charity. We think, too, that this system, which begins with degrading human nature, may be expected to end in pride; for pride grows out of a consciousness of high distinctions, however obtained, and no distinction is so great as that which is made between the elected and abandoned of God.

The false and dishonorable views of God, which have now been stated, we feel ourselves bound to resist unceasingly. Other errors we can pass over with comparative indifference. But we ask our opponents to leave to us a God, worthy of our love and trust, in whom our moral sentiments may delight, in whom our weaknesses and sorrows may find refuge. We cling to the Divine perfections. We meet them everywhere in creation, we read them in the Scriptures, we see a lovely image of them in Jesus Christ; and gratitude, love, and veneration call on us to assert them. Reproached, as we often are, by men, it is our consolation and happiness, that one of our chief offences is the zeal with which we vindicate the dishonored goodness and rectitude of God.

4. Having thus spoken of the unity of God; of the unity of Jesus, and his inferiority to God; and of the

perfections of the Divine character; I now proceed to give our views of the mediation of Christ, and of the purposes of his mission. With regard to the great object which Jesus came to accomplish, there seems to be no possibility of mistake. We believe, that he was sent by the Father to effect a moral, or spiritual deliverance of mankind; that is, to rescue men from sin and its consequences, and to bring them to a state of everlasting purity and happiness. We believe, too, that he accomplishes this sublime purpose by a variety of methods; by his instructions respecting God's unity, parental character, and moral government, which are admirably fitted to reclaim the world from idolatry and impiety, to the knowledge, love, and obedience of the Creator; by his promises of pardon to the penitent, and of divine assistance to those who labor for progress in moral excellence; by the light which he has thrown on the path of duty; by his own spotless example, in which the loveliness and sublimity of virtue shine forth to warm and quicken, as well as guide us to perfection; by his threatenings against incorrigible guilt; by his glorious discoveries of immortality; by his sufferings and death; by that signal event, the resurrection, which powerfully bore witness to his divine mission, and brought down to men's senses a future life; by his continual intercession, which obtains for us spiritual aid and blessings; and by the power with which he is invested of raising the dead, judging the world, and conferring the everlasting rewards promised to the faithful.

We have no desire to conceal the fact, that a difference of opinion exists among us, in regard to an interesting part of Christ's mediation; I mean, in regard to the precise influence of his death on our forgiveness.

Many suppose, that this event contributes to our pardon, as it was a principal means of confirming his religion, and of giving it a power over the mind; in other words, that it procures forgiveness by leading to that repentance and virtue, which is the great and only condition on which forgiveness is bestowed. Many of us are dissatisfied with this explanation, and think that the Scriptures ascribe the remission of sins to Christ's death, with an emphasis so peculiar, that we ought to consider this event as having a special influence in removing punishment, though the Scriptures may not reveal the way in which it contributes to this end.

Whilst, however, we differ in explaining the connexion between Christ's death and human forgiveness, a connexion which we all gratefully acknowledge, we agree in rejecting many sentiments which prevail in regard to his mediation. The idea, which is conveyed to common minds by the popular system, that Christ's death has an influence in making God placable, or merciful, in awakening his kindness towards men, we reject with strong disapprobation. We are happy to find, that this very dishonorable notion is disowned by intelligent Christians of that class from which we differ. We recollect, however, that, not long ago, it was common to hear of Christ, as having died to appease God's wrath, and to pay the debt of sinners to his inflexible justice; and we have a strong persuasion, that the language of popular religious books, and the common mode of stating the doctrine of Christ's mediation, still communicate very degrading views of God's character. They give to multitudes the impression, that the death of Jesus produces a change in the mind of God towards man, and that in this its efficacy chiefly consists.

No error seems to us more pernicious. We can endure no shade over the pure goodness of God. We earnestly maintain, that Jesus, instead of calling forth, in any way or degree, the mercy of the Father, was sent by that mercy, to be our Saviour; that he is nothing to the human race, but what he is by God's appointment; that he communicates nothing but what God empowers him to bestow; that our Father in heaven is originally, essentially, and eternally placable, and disposed to forgive; and that his unborrowed, underived, and unchangeable love is the only fountain of what flows to us through his Son. We conceive, that Jesus is dishonored, not glorified, by ascribing to him an influence, which clouds the splendor of Divine benevolence.

We farther agree in rejecting, as unscriptural and absurd, the explanation given by the popular system, of the manner in which Christ's death procures forgiveness for men. This system used to teach as its fundamental principle, that man, having sinned against an infinite Being, has contracted infinite guilt, and is consequently exposed to an infinite penalty. We believe, however, that this reasoning, if reasoning it may be called, which overlooks the obvious maxim, that the guilt of a being must be proportioned to his nature and powers, has fallen into disuse. Still the system teaches, that sin, of whatever degree, exposes to endless punishment, and that the whole human race, being infallibly involved by their nature in sin, owe this awful penalty to the justice of their Creator. It teaches, that this penalty cannot be remitted, in consistency with the honor of the divine law, unless a substitute be found to endure it or to suffer an equivalent. It also teaches, that, from the nature of the case, no substitute is adequate to this work, save the infinite God himself; and accordingly, God, in his second person, took on him human nature, that he might pay to his own justice the debt of punishment incurred by men, and might thus reconcile forgiveness with the claims and threatenings of his law. Such is the prevalent system. Now, to us, this doctrine seems to carry on its front strong marks of absurdity; and we maintain that Christianity ought not to be encumbered with it, unless it be laid down in the New Testament fully and expressly. We ask our adversaries, then, to point to some plain passages where it is taught. We ask for one text, in which we are told, that God took human nature that he might make an infinite satisfaction to his own justice; for one text, which tells us, that human guilt requires an infinite substitute; that Christ's sufferings owe their efficacy to their being borne by an infinite being; or that his divine nature gives infinite value to the sufferings of the human. Not *one word* of this description can we find in the Scriptures; not a text, which even hints at these strange doctrines. They are altogether, we believe, the fictions of theologians. Christianity is in no degree responsible for them. We are astonished at their prevalence. What can be plainer, than that God cannot, in any sense, be a sufferer, or bear a penalty in the room of his creatures? How dishonorable to him is the supposition, that his justice is now so severe, as to exact infinite punishment for the sins of frail and feeble men, and now so easy and yielding, as to accept the limited pains of Christ's human soul, as a full equivalent for the endless woes due from the world? How plain is it also, according to this doctrine, that God, instead of being plenteous in forgiveness, never forgives; for it seems absurd to speak of men as forgiven, when their whole punishment, or an equivalent to it, is borne by a substitute? A scheme more fitted to obscure the brightness of Christianity and the mercy of God, or less suited to give comfort to a guilty and troubled mind, could not, we think, be easily framed.

We believe, too, that this system is unfavorable to the character. It naturally leads men to think, that Christ came to change God's mind rather than their own; that the highest object of his mission was to avert punishment, rather than to communicate holiness; and that a large part of religion consists in disparaging good works and human virtue, for the purpose of magnifying the value of Christ's vicarious sufferings. In this way, a sense of the infinite importance and indispensable necessity of personal improvement is weakened, and high-sounding praises of Christ's cross seem often to be substituted for obedience to his precepts. For ourselves, we have not so learned Jesus. Whilst we gratefully acknowledge, that he came to rescue us from punishment, we believe, that he was sent on a still nobler errand, namely, to deliver us from sin itself, and to form us to a sublime and heavenly virtue. We regard him as a Saviour, chiefly as he is the light, physician, and guide of the dark, diseased, and wandering mind. No influence in the universe seems to us so glorious, as that over the character; and no redemption so worthy of thankfulness, as the restoration of the soul to purity. Without this, pardon, were it possible, would be of little value. Why pluck the sinner from hell, if a hell be left to burn in his own breast? Why raise him to heaven, if he remain a stranger to its sanctity and love? With these impressions, we are accustomed to value the Gospel chiefly as it abounds in effectual aids, motives, excitements to a generous and divine virtue. In this virtue, as in a common centre, we see all its doctrines, precepts, promises meet; and we believe, that faith in this religion is of no worth, and contributes nothing to salvation, any farther than as it uses these doctrines, precepts, promises, and the whole life, character, sufferings, and triumphs of Jesus, as the means of purifying the mind, of changing it into the likeness of his celestial excellence.

5. Having thus stated our views of the highest object of Christ's mission, that it is the recovery of men to virtue, or holiness, I shall now, in the last place, give our views of the nature of Christian virtue, or true holiness. We believe that all virtue has its foundation in the moral nature of man, that is, in conscience, or his sense of duty, and in the power of forming his temper and life according to conscience. We believe that these moral faculties are the grounds of responsibility, and the highest distinctions of human nature, and that no act is praiseworthy, any farther than it springs from their exertion. We believe, that no dispositions infused into us without our own moral activity, are of the nature of virtue, and therefore, we reject the doctrine of irresistible divine influence on the human mind, moulding it into goodness, as marble is hewn into a statue. Such goodness, if this word may be used, would not be the object of moral approbation, any more than the instinctive affections of inferior animals, or the constitutional amiableness of human beings.

By these remarks, we do not mean to deny the importance of God's aid or Spirit; but by his Spirit, we mean a moral, illuminating, and persuasive influence, not physical, not compulsory, not involving a necessity of virtue. We object, strongly, to the idea of many Christians respecting man's impotence and God's irresistible agency on the heart, believing that they subvert our responsibility and the laws of our moral nature, that they make men machines, that they cast on God the blame of all evil deeds, that they discourage good minds, and inflate the fanatical with wild conceits of immediate and sensible inspiration.

Among the virtues, we give the first place to the love of God. We believe, that this principle is the true end and happiness of our being, that we were made for union with our Creator, that his infinite perfection is the only sufficient object and true resting-place for the insatiable desires and unlimited capacities of the human mind, and that, without him, our noblest sentiments, admiration, veneration, hope, and love, would wither and decay. We believe, too, that the love of God is not only essential to happiness, but to the strength and perfection of all the virtues; that conscience, without the sanction of God's authority and retributive justice, would be a weak director; that benevolence, unless nourished by communion with his goodness, and encouraged by his smile, could not thrive amidst the selfishness and thanklessness of the world; and that self-government, without a sense of the divine inspection, would hardly extend beyond an outward and partial purity. God, as he is essentially goodness, holiness, justice, and virtue, so he is the life, motive, and sustainer of virtue in the human soul.

But, whilst we earnestly inculcate the love of God, we believe that great care is necessary to distinguish it from counterfeits. We think that much which is called piety is worthless. Many have fallen into the error, that there can be no excess in feelings which have God for their object; and, distrusting as coldness that self-possession, without which virtue and devotion lose all their dignity, they have abandoned themselves to extravagances, which have brought contempt on piety. Most certainly, if the love of God be that which often bears its name, the less we have of it the better. If religion be the shipwreck of understanding, we cannot keep too far from it. On this subject, we always speak plainly. We cannot sacrifice our reason to the reputation of zeal. We owe it to truth and religion to maintain, that fanaticism, partial insanity, sudden impressions, and ungovernable transports, are any thing rather than piety.

We conceive, that the true love of God is a moral sentiment, founded on a clear perception, and consisting in a high esteem and veneration, of his moral perfections. Thus, it perfectly coincides, and is in fact the same thing, with the love of virtue, rectitude, and goodness. You will easily judge, then, what we esteem the surest and only decisive signs of piety. We lay no stress on strong excitements. We esteem him, and him only a pious man, who practically conforms to God's moral perfections and government; who shows his delight in God's benevolence, by loving and serving his neighbour; his delight in God's justice, by being resolutely upright; his sense of God's purity, by regulating his thoughts, imagination, and desires; and whose conversation, business, and domestic life are swayed by a regard to God's presence and authority. In all things else men may deceive themselves. Disordered nerves may give them strange sights, and sounds, and impressions. Texts of Scripture may come to them as from Heaven. Their whole souls may be moved, and their confidence in God's favor be undoubting. But in all this there is no religion. The question is, Do they love God's commands, in which his character is fully expressed, and give up to these their habits and passions? Without this, ecstasy is a mockery. One surrender of desire to God's will, is worth a thousand transports. We do not judge of the bent of men's minds by their raptures, any more than we judge of the natural direction of a tree during a storm. We rather suspect loud profession, for we have observed, that deep feeling is generally noiseless, and least seeks display.

We would not, by these remarks, be understood as wishing to exclude from religion warmth, and even transport. We honor, and highly value, true religious sensibility. We believe, that Christianity is intended to act powerfully on our whole nature, on the heart as well as the understanding and the conscience. We conceive of heaven as a state where the love of God will be exalted into an unbounded fervor and joy; and we desire, in our pilgrimage here, to drink into the spirit of that better world. But we think, that religious warmth is only to be valued, when it springs naturally from an improved character, when it comes unforced, when it is the recompense of obedience, when it is the warmth of a mind which understands God by being like him, and when, instead of disordering, it exalts the understanding, invigorates conscience, gives a pleasure to common duties, and is seen to exist in connexion with cheerfulness, judiciousness, and a reasonable frame of mind. When we observe a fervor, called religious, in men whose general character expresses little refinement and elevation, and whose piety seems at war with reason, we pay it little respect. We honor religion too much to give its sacred name to a feverish, forced, fluctuating zeal, which has little power over the life.

Another important branch of virtue, we believe to be love to Christ. The greatness of the work of Jesus, the spirit with which he executed it, and the sufferings which he bore for our salvation, we feel to be strong claims on our gratitude and veneration. We see in nature no beauty to be compared with the loveliness of his character, nor do we find on earth a benefactor to whom we owe an equal debt. We read his history with delight, and learn from it the perfection of our nature. We are particularly touched by his death, which was endured for our redemption, and by that strength of charity which triumphed over his pains. His resurrection is the foundation of our hope of immortality. His intercession gives us boldness to draw nigh to the throne of grace, and we look up to heaven with new desire, when we think, that, if we follow him here, we shall there see his benignant countenance, and enjoy his friendship for ever.

I need not express to you our views on the subject of the benevolent virtues. We attach such importance to these, that we are sometimes reproached with exalting them above piety. We regard the spirit of love, charity, meekness, forgiveness, liberality, and beneficence, as the badge and distinction of Christians, as the brightest image we can bear of God, as the best proof of piety. On this subject, I need not, and cannot enlarge ; but there is one branch of benevolence which I ought not to pass over in silence, because we think that we conceive of it more highly and justly than many of our brethren. I refer to the duty of candor, charitable judgment, especially towards those who differ in religious opinion. We think, that in nothing have Christians so widely departed from their religion, as in this particular. We read with astonishment and horror, the history of the church ; and sometimes when we look back on the fires of persecution, and on the zeal of Christians, in building up walls of separation, and in giving up one another to perdition, we feel as if we were reading the records of an infernal, rather than a heavenly kingdom. An enemy to every religion, if asked to describe a Christian, would, with some show of reason, depict him as an idolater of his own distinguishing opinions, covered with badges of party, shutting his eyes on the virtues, and his ears on the arguments, of his opponents, arrogating all excellence to his own sect and all saving power to his own creed, sheltering under the name of pious zeal the love of domination, the conceit of infallibility, and the spirit of intolerance, and trampling on men's rights under the pretence of saving their souls.

We can hardly conceive of a plainer obligation on beings of our frail and fallible nature, who are instructed in the duty of candid judgment, than to abstain from condemning men of apparent conscientiousness and sincerity, who are chargeable with no crime but that of differing from us in the interpretation of the Scriptures, and differing, too, on topics of great and acknowledged obscurity. We are astonished at the hardihood of those, who, with Christ's warnings sounding in their ears, take on them the responsibility of making creeds for his church, and cast out professors of virtuous lives for imagined errors, for the guilt of thinking for themselves.

We know that zeal for truth is the cover for this usurpation of Christ's prerogative ; but we think that zeal for truth, as it is called, is very suspicious, except in men, whose capacities and advantages, whose patient deliberation, and whose improvements in humility, mildness, and candor, give them a right to hope that their views are more just than those of their neighbours. Much of what passes for a zeal for truth, we look upon with little respect, for it often appears to thrive most luxuriantly where other virtues shoot up thinly and feebly ; and we have no gratitude for those reformers, who would force upon us a doctrine which has not sweetened their own tempers, or made them better men than their neighbours.

We are accustomed to think much of the difficulties attending religious inquiries ; difficulties springing from the slow developement of our minds, from the power of early impressions, from the state of society, from human authority, from the general neglect of the reasoning powers, from the want of just principles of criticism and of important helps in interpreting Scripture, and from various other causes. We find, that on no subject have men, and even good men, ingrafted so many strange conceits, wild theories, and fictions of fancy, as on religion ; and remembering, as we do, that we ourselves are sharers of the common frailty, we dare not assume infallibility in the treatment of our fellow-Christians, or encourage in common Christians, who have little time for investigation, the habit of denouncing and contemning other denominations, perhaps more enlightened and virtuous than their own. Charity, forbearance, a delight in the virtues of different sects, a backwardness to censure and condemn, these are virtues, which, however poorly practised by us, we admire and recommend; and we would rather join ourselves to the church in which they abound, than to any other communion, however elated with the belief of its own orthodoxy, however strict in guarding its creed, however burning with zeal against imagined error.

I have thus given the distinguishing views of those Christians in whose names I have spoken. We have embraced this system, not hastily or lightly, but after much deliberation; and we hold it fast, not merely because we believe it to be true, but because we regard it as purifying truth, as a doctrine according to godliness, as able to "work mightily" and to "bring forth fruit" in them who believe. That we wish to spread it, we have no desire to conceal; but we think, that we wish its diffusion, because we regard it as more friendly to practical piety and pure morals than the opposite doctrines, because it gives clearer and nobler views of duty, and stronger motives to its performance, because it recommends religion at once to the understanding and the heart, because it asserts the lovely and venerable attributes of God, because it tends to restore the benevolent spirit of Jesus to his divided and afflicted church, and because it cuts off every hope of God's favor, except that which springs from practical conformity to the life and precepts of Christ. We see nothing in our views to give offence, save their purity, and it is their purity, which makes us seek and hope their extension through the world.

My friend and brother;—You are this day to take upon you important duties; to be clothed with an office, which the Son of God did not disdain; to devote yourself to that religion, which the most hallowed lips have preached, and the most precious blood sealed. We trust that you will bring to this work a willing mind, a firm purpose, a martyr's spirit, a readiness to toil and suffer for the truth, a devotion of your best powers to the interests of piety and virtue. I have spoken of the doctrines which you will probably preach ; but I do not mean, that you are to give yourself to controversy. You will remember, that good practice is the end of preaching, and will labor to make your people holy livers, rather than skilful disputants. Be careful, lest the desire of defending what you deem truth, and of repelling reproach and misrepresentation, turn you aside from your great business, which is to fix in men's minds a living conviction of the obligation, sublimity, and happiness of Christian virtue. The best way to vindicate your sentiments, is to show, in your preaching and life, their intimate connexion with Christian morals, with a high and delicate sense of duty, with candor towards your opposers, with inflexible integrity, and with an habitual reverence for God. If any light can pierce and scatter the clouds of prejudice, it is that of a pure example. My brother, may your life preach more loudly than your lips. Be to this people a pattern of all good works, and may your instructions derive authority from a well-grounded belief in your hearers, that you speak from the heart, that you preach from experience, that the truth which you dispense has wrought powerfully in your own heart, that God, and Jesus, and heaven, are not merely words on your lips, but most affecting realities to your mind, and springs of hope and consolation, and strength, in all your trials. Thus laboring, may you reap abundantly, and have a testimony of your faithfulness, not only in your own conscience, but in the esteem, love, virtues, and improvements of your people.

To all who hear me, I would say, with the Apostle, Prove all things, hold fast that which is good. Do not, brethren, shrink from the duty of searching God's Word for yourselves, through fear of human censure and denunciation. Do not think, that you may innocently follow the opinions which prevail around you, without investigation, on the ground, that Christianity is now so purified from errors, as to need no laborious research. There is much reason to believe, that Christianity is at this moment dishonored by gross and cherished corruptions. If you remember the darkness which hung over the Gospel for ages; if you consider the impure union, which still subsists in almost every Christian country, between the church and state, and which enlists men's selfishness and ambition on the side of established error; if you recollect in what degree the spirit of intolerance has checked free inquiry, not only before, but since the Reformation; you will see that Christianity cannot have freed itself from all the human inventions, which disfigured it under the Papal tyranny. No. Much stubble is yet to be burned; much rubbish to be removed; many gaudy decorations, which a false taste has hung around Christianity, must be swept away; and the earth-born fogs, which have long shrouded it, must be scattered, before this divine fabric will rise before us in its native and awful majesty, in its harmonious proportions, in its mild and celestial splendors. This glorious reformation in the church, we hope, under God's blessing, from the progress of the human intellect, from the moral progress of society, from the consequent decline of prejudice and bigotry, and, though last not least, from the subversion of human authority in matters of religion, from the fall of those hierarchies, and other human institutions, by which the minds of individuals are oppressed under the weight of numbers, and a Papal dominion is perpetuated in the Protestant church. Our earnest prayer to God is, that he will overturn, and overturn, and overturn the strong-holds of spiritual usurpation, until HE shall come, whose right it is to rule the minds of men ; that the conspiracy of ages against the liberty of Christians may be brought to an end ; that the servile assent, so long yielded to human creeds, may give place to honest and devout inquiry into the Scriptures ; and that Christianity, thus purified from error, may put forth its almighty energy, and prove itself, by its ennobling influence on the mind, to be indeed "the power of God unto salvation."

UNITARIAN CHRISTIANITY

MOST FAVORABLE TO PIETY.

DISCOURSE

AT THE

DEDICATION OF THE SECOND CONGREGATIONAL UNITARIAN CHURCH.

New York, 1826.

Mark xii. 29, 30: "And Jesus answered him, The first of all the commandments is, Hear, O Israel; The Lord our God is one Lord. And thou shalt love the Lord thy God with all thy heart, and with all thy soul, and with all thy mind, and with all thy strength. This is the first commandment."

We have assembled to dedicate this building to the worship of the only living and true God, and to the teaching of the religion of his son, Jesus Christ. By this act we do not expect to confer on this spot of ground and these walls any peculiar sanctity or any mysterious properties. We do not suppose, that, in consequence of rites now performed, the worship offered here will be more acceptable than prayer uttered in the closet, or breathed from the soul in the midst of business; or that the instructions delivered from this pulpit will be more effectual, than if they were uttered in a private dwelling or the open air. By dedication we understand only a solemn expression of the purpose for which this building is reared, joined with prayer to Him, who alone can crown our enterprise with success, that our design may be accepted and fulfilled. For this religious act, we find indeed no precept in the New Testament, and on this account some have scrupled as to its propriety. But we are not among those who consider the written Word as a statute-book, by the letter of which every step in life must be governed. We believe, on the other hand, that one of the great excellences of Christianity is, that it does not deal in minute regulation, but that, having given broad views of duty, and enjoined a pure and disinterested spirit, it leaves us to apply these rules and express this spirit according to the promptings of the divine monitor within us, and according to the claims and exigencies of the ever varying conditions in which we are placed. We believe, too, that revelation is not intended to supersede God's other modes of instruction; that it is not intended to drown, but to make more audible, the voice of nature. Now, nature dictates the propriety of such an act as we are this day assembled to perform. Nature has always taught men, on the completion of an important structure, designed for public and lasting good, to solemnize its first appropriation to the purpose for which it was reared, by some special service. To us there is a sacredness in this moral instinct, in this law written on the heart; and in listening reverently to God's dictates, however conveyed, we doubt not that we shall enjoy his acceptance and blessing.

I have said, we dedicate this building to the teaching of the Gospel of Christ. But in the present state of the Christian church, these words are not as definite as they one day will be. This Gospel is variously interpreted. It is preached in various forms. Christendom is parcelled out into various sects. When, therefore, we see a new house of worship reared, the question immediately arises, To what mode of teaching Christianity is it to be devoted ? I need not tell you, my hearers, that this house has been built by that class of Christians, who are called Unitarians, and that the Gospel will here be taught, as interpreted by that body of believers. This you all know ; but perhaps all present have not attached a very precise meaning to the word, by which our particular views of Christianity are designated. Unitarianism has been made a term of so much reproach, and has been uttered in so many tones of alarm, horror, indignation, and scorn, that to many it gives only a vague impression of something monstrous, impious, unutterably perilous. To such, I would say, that this doctrine, which is considered by some as the last and most perfect invention of Satan, the consummation of his blasphemies, the most cunning weapon ever forged in the fires of hell, amounts to this, — That there is One God, even the Father ; and that Jesus Christ is not this One God, but his son and messenger, who derived all his powers and glories from the Universal Parent, and who came into the world not to claim supreme homage for himself, but to carry up the soul to his Father as the Only Divine Person, the Only Ultimate Object of religious worship. To us, this doctrine seems not to have sprung from hell, but to have descended from the throne of God, and to invite and attract us thither. To us it seems to come from the Scriptures, with a voice loud as the sound of many waters, and as articulate and clear as if Jesus, in a bodily form, were pronouncing it distinctly in our ears. To this doctrine, and to Christianity interpreted in consistency with it, we dedicate this building.

That we desire to propagate this doctrine, we do not conceal. It is a treasure, which we wish not to confine to ourselves, which we dare not lock up in our own breasts. We regard it as given to us for others, as well as for ourselves. We should rejoice to spread it through this great city, to carry it into every dwelling, and to send it far and wide to the remotest settlements of our country. Am I asked, why we wish this diffusion? We dare not say, that we are in no degree influenced by sectarian feeling; for we see it raging around us, and we should be more than men, were we wholly to escape an epidemic passion. We do hope, however, that our main purpose and aim is not sectarian, but to promote a purer and nobler piety than now prevails. We are not induced to spread our opinions by the mere conviction that they are true; for there are many truths, historical, metaphysical, scientific, literary, which we have no anxiety to propagate. We regard them as the highest, most important, most efficient truths, and therefore demanding a firm testimony, and earnest efforts to make them known. In thus speaking, we do not mean, that we regard our peculiar views as essential to salvation. Far from us be this spirit of exclusion, the very spirit of antichrist, the worst of all the delusions of Popery and of Protestantism. We hold nothing to be essential, but the simple and supreme dedication of the mind, heart, and life to God and to his will. This inward and practical devotedness to the Supreme Being, we are assured, is attained and accepted under all the forms of Christianity. We believe, however, that it is favored by that truth which we maintain, as by no other system of faith. We regard Unitarianism as peculiarly the friend of inward, living, practical religion. For this we value it. For this we would spread it; and we desire none to embrace it, but such as shall seek and derive from it this celestial influence.

This character and property of Unitarian Christianity, its fitness to promote true, deep, and living piety, being our chief ground of attachment to it, and our chief motive for dedicating this house to its inculcation, I have thought proper to make this the topic of my present discourse. I do not propose to prove the truth of Unitarianism by Scriptural authorities, for this argument would exceed the limits of a sermon, but to show its superior tendency to form an elevated religious character. If, however, this position can be sustained, I shall have contributed no weak argument in support of the truth of our views; for the chief purpose of Christianity undoubtedly is, to promote piety, to bring us to God, to fill our souls with that Great Being, to make us alive to him; and a religious system can carry no more authentic mark of a divine original, than its obvious, direct, and peculiar adaptation to quicken and raise the mind to its Creator. — In speaking thus of Unitarian Christianity as promoting piety, I ought to observe, that I use this word in its proper and highest sense. I mean not every thing which bears the name of piety, for under this title superstition, fanaticism, and formality are walking abroad and claiming respect. I mean not an anxious frame of mind, not abject and slavish fear, not a dread of hell, not a repetition of forms, not church-going, not loud profession, not severe censure of others' irreligion; but filial love and reverence towards God, habitual gratitude, cheerful trust, ready obedience, and, though last not least, an imitation of the ever-active and unbounded benevolence of the Creator.

The object of this discourse requires me to speak with great freedom of different systems of religion. But let me not be misunderstood. Let not the uncharitableness, which I condemn, be lightly laid to my charge. Let it be remembered, that I speak only of systems, not of those who embrace them. In setting forth with all simplicity what seem to me the good or bad tendencies of doctrines, I have not a thought of giving standards or measures by which to estimate the virtue or vice of their professors. Nothing would be more unjust, than to decide on men's characters from their peculiarities of faith; and the reason is plain. Such peculiarities are not the only causes which impress and determine the mind. Our nature is exposed to innumerable other influences. If indeed a man were to know nothing but his creed, were to meet with no human beings but those who adopt it, were to see no example and to hear no conversation, but such as were formed by it; if his creed were to meet him everywhere, and to exclude every other object of thought; then his character might be expected to answer to it with great precision. But our Creator has not shut us up in so narrow a school. The mind is exposed to an infinite variety of influences, and these are multiplying with the progress of society. Education, friendship, neighbourhood, public opinion, the state of society, "the genius of the place" where we live, books, events, the pleasures and business of life, the outward creation, our physical temperament, and innumerable other causes, are perpetually pouring in upon the soul thoughts, views, and emotions; and these influences are so complicated, so peculiarly combined in the case of every individual, and so modified by the original susceptibilities and constitution of every mind, that on no subject is there greater uncertainty, than on the formation of character. To determine the precise operation of a religious opinion amidst this host of influences, surpasses human power. A great truth may be completely neutralized by the countless impressions and excitements, which the mind receives from other sources ; and so a great error may be disarmed of much of its power, by the superior energy of other and better views, of early habits, and of virtuous examples. Nothing is more common than to see a doctrine believed without swaying the will. Its efficacy depends, not on the assent of the intellect, but on the place which it occupies in the thoughts, on the distinctness and vividness with which it is conceived, on its association with our common ideas, on its frequency of recurrence, and on its command of the attention, without which it has no life. Accordingly, pernicious opinions are not seldom held by men of the most illustrious virtue. I mean not, then, in commending or condemning systems, to pass sentence on their professors. I know the power of the mind to select from a multifarious system, for its habitual use, those features or principles which are generous, pure, and ennobling, and by these, to sustain its spiritual life amidst the nominal profession of many errors. I know that a creed is one thing, as written in a book, and another, as it exists in the minds of its advocates. In the book, all the doctrines appear in equally strong and legible lines. In the mind, many are faintly traced and seldom recurred to, whilst others are inscribed as with sunbeams, and are the chosen, constant lights of the soul. Hence, in good men of opposing denominations, a real agreement may subsist as to their vital principles of faith; and amidst the division of tongues, there may be unity of soul, and the same internal worship of God. By these remarks, I do not mean that error is not evil, or that it bears no pernicious fruit. Its tendencies are always bad. But I mean, that these tendencies exert themselves amidst so many counteracting influences; and that injurious opinions so often lie dead, through the want of mixture with the common thoughts, through the mind's not absorbing them, and changing them into its own substance; that the highest respect may, and ought to be cherished for men, in whose creed we find much to disapprove. In this discourse I shall speak freely, and some may say severely, of Trinitarianism; but I love and honor not a few of its advocates; and in opposing what I deem their error, I would on no account detract from their worth. After these remarks, I hope that the language of earnest discussion and strong conviction will not be construed into the want of that charity, which I acknowledge as the first grace of our religion.

I now proceed to illustrate and prove the superiority of Unitarian Christianity, as a means of promoting a deep and noble piety.

I. Unitarianism is a system most favorable to piety, because it presents to the mind One, and only one, Infinite Person, to whom supreme homage is to be paid. It does not weaken the energy of religious sentiment by dividing it among various objects. It collects and concentrates the soul on One Father of unbounded, undivided, unrivalled glory. To Him it teaches the mind to rise through all beings. Around Him it gathers all the splendors of the universe. To Him it teaches us to ascribe whatever good we receive or behold, the beauty and magnificence of nature, the liberal gifts of Providence, the capacities of the soul, the bonds of society, and especially the riches of grace and redemption, the mission, and powers, and beneficent influences of Jesus Christ. All happiness it traces up to the Father, as the sole source; and the mind, which these views have penetrated, through this intimate association of every thing exciting and exalting in the universe with One Infinite Parent, can and does offer itself up to him with the intensest and profoundest love, of which human nature is susceptible. The Trinitarian indeed professes to believe in one God, and means to hold fast this truth. But three persons, having distinctive qualities and relations, of whom one is sent and another the sender, one is given and another the giver, of whom one intercedes and another hears the intercession, of whom one takes flesh and another never becomes incarnate,—three persons, thus discriminated, are as truly three objects of the mind, as if they were acknowledged to be separate divinities; and, from the principles of our nature, they cannot act on the mind as deeply and powerfully as one Infinite Person, to whose sole goodness all happiness is ascribed. To multiply infinite objects for the heart, is to distract it. To scatter the attention among three equal persons, is to impair the power of each. The more strict and absolute the unity of God, the more easily and intimately all the impressions and emotions of piety flow together, and are condensed into one glowing thought, one thrilling love. No language can express the absorbing energy of the thought of one Infinite Father. When vitally implanted in the soul, it grows and gains strength for ever. It enriches itself by every new view of God's word and works; gathers tribute from all regions and all ages; and attracts into itself all the rays of beauty, glory, and joy, in the material and spiritual creation.

My hearers, as you would feel the full influence of God upon your souls, guard sacredly, keep unobscured and unsullied, that fundamental and glorious truth, that there is One, and only One Almighty Agent in the universe, one Infinite Father. Let this truth dwell in me in its uncorrupted simplicity, and I have the spring and nutriment of an ever-growing piety. I have an object for my mind towards which all things bear me. I know whither to go in all trial, whom to bless in all joy, whom to adore in all I behold. But let three persons claim from me supreme homage, and claim it on different grounds, one for sending and another for coming to my relief, and I am divided, distracted, perplexed. My frail intellect is overborne. Instead of One Father, on whose arm I can rest, my mind is torn from object to object, and I tremble, lest among so many claimants of supreme love, I should withhold from one or another his due.

II. Unitarianism is the system most favorable to piety, because it holds forth and preserves inviolate the spirituality of God. "God is a spirit, and they that worship him must worship him in spirit and in truth." It is of great importance to the progress and elevation of the religious principle, that we should refine more and more our conceptions of God; that we should separate from him all material properties, and whatever is limited or imperfect in our own nature; that we should regard him as a pure intelligence, an unmixed and infinite Mind. When it pleased God to select the Jewish people and place them under miraculous interpositions, one of the first precepts given them was, that they should not represent God under any bodily form, any graven image, or the likeness of any creature. Next came Christianity, which had this as one of its great objects, to render religion still more spiritual, by abolishing the ceremonial and outward worship of former times, and by discarding those grosser modes of describing God, through which the ancient prophets had sought to impress an unrefined people.

Now, Unitarianism concurs with this sublime moral purpose of God. It asserts his spirituality. It approaches him under no bodily form, but as a pure spirit, as the infinite and the universal Mind. On the other hand, it is the direct influence of Trinitarianism to materialize men's conceptions of God ; and, in truth, this system is a relapse into the error of the rudest and earliest ages, into the worship of a corporeal God. Its leading feature is, the doctrine of a God clothed with a body, and acting and speaking through a material frame, — of the Infinite Divinity dying on a cross ; a doctrine, which in earthliness reminds us of the mythology of the rudest pagans, and which a pious Jew, in the twilight of the Mosaic religion, would have shrunk from with horror. It seems to me no small objection to the Trinity, that it supposes God to take a body in the later and more improved ages of the world, when it is plain, that such a manifestation, if needed at all, was peculiarly required in the infancy of the race. The effect of such a system in debasing the idea of God, in associating with the Divinity human passions and infirmities, is too obvious to need much elucidation. On the supposition that the second person of the Trinity became incarnate, God may be said to be a material being, on the same general ground, on which this is affirmed of man ; for man is material only by the union of the mind with the body ; and the very meaning of incarnation is, that God took a body, through which he acted and spoke, as the human soul operates through its corporeal organs. Every bodily affection may thus be ascribed to God. Accordingly the Trinitarian, in his most solemn act of adoration, is heard to pray in these appalling words : "Good Lord, deliver us ; by the mystery of thy holy incarnation, by thy holy nativity and circumcision, by thy baptism, fasting, and temptation, by thine agony and bloody sweat, by thy cross and passion, good Lord, deliver us." Now I ask you to judge, from the principles of human nature, whether to worshippers, who adore their God for his wounds and tears, his agony, and blood, and sweat, the ideas of corporeal existence and human suffering will not predominate over the conceptions of a purely spiritual essence ; whether the mind, in clinging to the man, will not lose the God ; whether a surer method for depressing and adulterating the pure thought of the Divinity could have been devised. That the Trinitarian is unconscious of this influence of his faith, I know, nor do I charge it on him as a crime. Still it exists, and cannot be too much deplored.

The Roman Catholics, true to human nature and their creed, have sought, by painting and statuary, to bring their imagined God before their eyes ; and have thus obtained almost as vivid impressions of him, as if they had lived with him on the earth. The Protestant condemns them for using these similitudes and representations in their worship ; but, if a Trinitarian, he does so to his own condemnation. For if, as he believes, it was once a duty to bow in adoration before the living body of his incarnate God, what possible guilt can there be in worshipping before the pictured or sculptured memorial of the same being ? Christ's body may as truly be represented by the artist, as any other human form ; and its image may be used as effectually and properly, as that of an ancient sage or hero, to recall him with vividness to the mind. — Is it said, that God has expressly forbidden the use of images in our worship ? But why was that prohibition laid on the Jews ? For this express reason, that God had not presented himself to them in any form, which admitted of representation. Hear the language of Moses : "Take good heed lest ye make you a graven image, for ye saw no manner of similitude on the day that the Lord spake unto you in Horeb out of the midst of the fire."* If, since that period, God has taken a body, then the reason of the prohibition has ceased ; and if he took a body, among other purposes, that he might assist the weakness of the intellect, which needs a material form, then a statue, which lends so great an aid to the conception of an absent friend, is not only justified, but seems to be required.

This materializing and embodying of the Supreme Being, which is the essence of Trinitarianism, cannot but be adverse to a growing and exalted piety. Human and divine properties, being confounded in one being, lose their distinctness. The splendors of the Godhead are dimmed. The worshippers of an incarnate Deity, through the frailty of their nature, are strongly tempted

* Deut. iv. 15, 16. — The arrangement of the text is a little changed, to put the reader immediately in possession of the meaning.

to fasten chiefly on his human attributes ; and their devotion, instead of rising to the Infinite God, and taking the peculiar character which infinity inspires, becomes rather a human affection, borrowing much of its fervor from the ideas of suffering, blood, and death. It is indeed possible, that this God-man (to use the strange phraseology of Trinitarians) may excite the mind more easily, than a purely spiritual divinity ; just as a tragedy, addressed to the eye and ear, will interest the multitude more than the contemplation of the most exalted character. But the emotions, which are the most easily roused, are not the profoundest or most enduring. This human love, inspired by a human God, though at first more fervid, cannot grow and spread through the soul, like the reverential attachment, which an infinite, spiritual Father awakens. Refined conceptions of God, though more slowly attained, have a more quickening and all-pervading energy, and admit of perpetual accessions of brightness, life, and strength.

True, we shall be told, that Trinitarianism has converted only one of its three persons into a human Deity, and that the other two remain purely spiritual beings. But who does not know, that man will attach himself most strongly to the God who has become a man ? Is not this even a duty, if the Divinity has taken a body to place himself within the reach of human comprehension and sympathy ? That the Trinitarian's views of the Divinity will be colored more by his visible, tangible, corporeal God, than by those persons of the Trinity, who remain comparatively hidden in their invisible and spiritual essence, is so accordant with the principles of our nature, as to need no labored proof.

My friends, hold fast the doctrine of a purely spiritual

Divinity. It is one of the great supports and instruments of a vital piety. It brings God near, as no other doctrine can. One of the leading purposes of Christianity is, to give us an ever-growing sense of God's immediate presence, a consciousness of him in our souls. Now, just as far as corporeal or limited attributes enter into our conception of him, we remove him from us. He becomes an outward, distant being, instead of being viewed and felt as dwelling in the soul itself. It is an unspeakable benefit of the doctrine of a purely spiritual God, that he can be regarded as inhabiting, filling our spiritual nature ; and, through this union with our minds, he can and does become the object of an intimacy and friendship, such as no embodied being can call forth.

III. Unitarianism is the system most favorable to piety, because it presents a distinct and intelligible object of worship, a being, whose nature, whilst inexpressibly sublime, is yet simple and suited to human apprehension. An infinite Father is the most exalted of all conceptions, and yet the least perplexing. It involves no incongruous ideas. It is illustrated by analogies from our own nature. It coincides with that fundamental law of the intellect, through which we demand a cause proportioned to effects. It is also as interesting as it is rational ; so that it is peculiarly congenial with the improved mind. The sublime simplicity of God, as he is taught in Unitarianism, by relieving the understanding from perplexity, and by placing him within the reach of thought and affection, gives him peculiar power over the soul. Trinitarianism, on the other hand, is a riddle. Men call it a mystery ; but it is mysterious, not like the great truths of religion, by its vastness and grandeur, but by the irreconcilable ideas which it involves. One God, consisting of three persons or agents, is so strange a being, so unlike our own minds, and all others with which we hold intercourse, is so misty, so incongruous, so contradictory, that he cannot be apprehended with that distinctness and that feeling of reality, which belong to the opposite system. Such a heterogeneous being, who is at the same moment one and many; who includes in his own nature the relations of Father and Son, or, in other words, is Father and Son to himself; who, in one of his persons, is at the same moment the Supreme God and a mortal man, omniscient and ignorant, almighty and impotent; such a being is certainly the most puzzling and distracting object ever presented to human thought. Trinitarianism, instead of teaching an intelligible God, offers to the mind a strange compound of hostile attributes, bearing plain marks of those ages of darkness, when Christianity shed but a faint ray, and the diseased fancy teemed with prodigies and unnatural creations. In contemplating a being, who presents such different and inconsistent aspects, the mind finds nothing to rest upon; and, instead of receiving distinct and harmonious impressions, is disturbed by shifting, unsettled images. To commune with such a being must be as hard, as to converse with a man of three different countenances, speaking with three different tongues. The believer in this system must forget it, when he prays, or he could find no repose in devotion. Who can compare it, in distinctness, reality, and power, with the simple doctrine of One Infinite Father?

IV. Unitarianism promotes a fervent and enlightened piety, by asserting the absolute and unbounded perfection of God's character. This is the highest service which can be rendered to mankind. Just and generous conceptions of the Divinity are the soul's true wealth. To spread these is to contribute more effectually, than by any other agency, to the progress and happiness of the intelligent creation. To obscure God's glory is to do greater wrong, than to blot out the sun. The character and influence of a religion must answer to the views which it gives of the Divinity; and there is a plain tendency in that system, which manifests the divine perfections most resplendently, to awaken the sublimest and most blessed piety.

Now, Trinitarianism has a fatal tendency to degrade the character of the Supreme Being, though its advocates, I am sure, intend no such wrong. By multiplying divine persons, it takes from each the glory of independent, all-sufficient, absolute perfection. This may be shown in various particulars. And in the first place, the very idea, that three persons in the Divinity are in any degree important, implies and involves the imperfection of each; for it is plain, that if one divine person possesses all possible power, wisdom, love, and happiness, nothing will be gained to himself or to the creation by joining with him two, or two hundred other persons. To say that he needs others for any purpose or in any degree, is to strip him of independent and all-sufficient majesty. If our Father in heaven, the God and Father of our Lord Jesus Christ, is not of himself sufficient to all the wants of his creation; if, by his union with other persons, he can accomplish any good to which he is not of himself equal; or if he thus acquires a claim to the least degree of trust or hope, to which he is not of himself entitled by his own independent attributes; then it is plain, he is not a being of infinite and absolute perfection. Now Trinitarianism teaches, that the highest good accrues to the human race from the existence of three divine persons, sustaining different offices and relations to the world; and it regards the Unitarian, as subverting the foundation of human hope, by asserting that the God and Father of our Lord Jesus is alone and singly God. Thus it derogates from his infinite glory.

In the next place, Trinitarianism degrades the character of the Supreme Being, by laying its disciples under the necessity of making such a distribution of offices and relations among the three persons, as will serve to designate and distinguish them; for in this way it interferes with the sublime conceptions of One Infinite Person, in whom all glories are concentred. If we are required to worship three persons, we must view them in different lights, or they will be mere repetitions of each other, mere names and sounds, presenting no objects, conveying no meaning to the mind. Some appropriate character, some peculiar acts, feelings, and relations must be ascribed to each. In other words, the glory of all must be shorn, that some special distinguishing lustre may be thrown on each. Accordingly, creation is associated peculiarly with the conception of the Father; satisfaction for human guilt with that of the Son; whilst sanctification, the noblest work of all, is given to the Holy Spirit as his more particular work. By a still more fatal distribution, the work of justice, the office of vindicating the rights of the Divinity, falls peculiarly to the Father, whilst the loveliness of interposing mercy clothes peculiarly the person of the Son. By this unhappy influence of Trinitarianism, from which common minds at least cannot escape, the splendors of the Godhead, being scattered among three objects, instead of being united in One Infinite Father, are dimmed; and he, whose mind is thoroughly and practically possessed by this system, can hardly conceive the effulgence of glory in which the One God offers himself to a pious believer in his strict unity.

But the worst has not been told. I observe, then, in the third place, that if Three Divine Persons are believed in, such an administration or government of the world must be ascribed to them, as will furnish them with a sphere of operation. No man will admit three persons into his creed, without finding a use for them. Now it is an obvious remark, that a system of the universe, which involves and demands more than one Infinite Agent, must be wild, extravagant, and unworthy the perfect God; because there is no possible or conceivable good, to which such an Agent is not adequate. Accordingly we find Trinitarianism connecting itself with a scheme of administration, exceedingly derogatory to the Divine character. It teaches, that the Infinite Father saw fit to put into the hands of our first parents the character and condition of their whole progeny; and that, through one act of disobedience, the whole race bring with them into being a corrupt nature, or are born depraved. It teaches, that the offences of a short life, though begun and spent under this disastrous influence, merit endless punishment, and that God's law threatens this infinite penalty; and that man is thus burdened with a guilt, which no sufferings of the created universe can expiate, which nothing but the sufferings of an Infinite Being can purge away. In this condition of human nature, Trinitarianism finds a sphere of action for its different persons. I am aware that some Trinitarians, on hearing this statement of their system, may reproach me with ascribing to them the errors of Calvinism, a system which they abhor as much as ourselves. But none of the peculiarities of Calvinism enter into this exposition. I have given what I understand to be the leading features of Trinitarianism all the world over; and the benevolent professors of that faith, who recoil from this statement, must blame not the preacher, but the creeds and establishments by which these doctrines are diffused. For ourselves, we look with horror and grief on the views of God's government, which are naturally and intimately united with Trinitarianism. They take from us our Father in heaven, and substitute a stern and unjust lord. Our filial love and reverence rise up against them. We say to the Trinitarian, touch any thing but the perfections of God. Cast no stain on that spotless purity and loveliness. We can endure any errors but those, which subvert or unsettle the conviction of God's paternal goodness. Urge not upon us a system, which makes existence a curse, and wraps the universe in gloom. Leave us the cheerful light, the free and healthful atmosphere, of a liberal and rational faith; the ennobling and consoling influences of the doctrine, which nature and revelation in blessed concord teach us, of One Father of unbounded and inexhaustible love.

V. Unitarianism is peculiarly favorable to piety, because it accords with nature, with the world around and the world within us; and through this accordance it gives aid to nature, and receives aid from it, in impressing the mind with God. We live in the midst of a glorious universe, which was meant to be a witness and a preacher of the Divinity; and a revelation from God may be expected to be in harmony with this system, and to carry on a common ministry with it in lifting the soul to God. Now, Unitarianism is in accordance with nature. It teaches One Father, and so does creation, the more it is explored. Philosophy, in proportion as it extends its views of the universe, sees in it, more and more, a sublime and beautiful unity, and multiplies proofs, that all things have sprung from one intelligence, one power, one love. The whole outward creation proclaims to the Unitarian the truth in which he delights. So does his own soul. But neither nature nor the soul bears one trace of Three Divine Persons. Nature is no Trinitarian. It gives not a hint, not a glimpse of a tri-personal author. Trinitarianism is a confined system, shut up in a few texts, a few written lines, where many of the wisest minds have failed to discover it. It is not inscribed on the heavens and the earth, not borne on every wind, not resounding and reëchoing through the universe. The sun and stars say nothing of a God of three persons. They all speak of the One Father whom *we* adore. To *our* ears, one and the same voice comes from God's word and works, a full and swelling strain, growing clearer, louder, more thrilling as we listen, and with one blessed influence lifting up our souls to the Almighty Father.

This accordance between nature and revelation increases the power of both over the mind. Concurring as they do in one impression, they make that impression deeper. To men of reflection, the conviction of the reality of religion is exceedingly heightened, by a perception of harmony in the views of it which they derive from various sources. Revelation is never received with so intimate a persuasion of its truth, as when it is seen to conspire to the same ends and impressions, for which all other things are made. It is no small objection to Trinitarianism, that it is an insulated doctrine, that it reveals a God whom we meet nowhere in the universe. Three Divine Persons, I repeat it, are found only in a few texts, and those so dark, that the gifted minds of Milton, Newton, and Locke, could not find them there. Nature gives them not a whisper of evidence. And can they be as real and powerful to the mind, as that One Father, whom the general strain and common voice of Scripture, and the universal voice of nature call us to adore?

VI. Unitarianism favors piety by opening the mind to new and ever-enlarging views of God. Teaching, as it does, the same God with nature, it leads us to seek him in nature. It does not shut us up in the written word, precious as that manifestation of the Divinity is. It considers revelation, not as independent of his other means of instruction; not as a separate agent; but as a part of the great system of God for enlightening and elevating the human soul; as intimately joined with creation and providence, and intended to concur with them; and as given to assist us in reading the volume of the universe. Thus Unitarianism, where its genuine influence is experienced, tends to enrich and fertilize the mind; opens it to new lights, wherever they spring up; and, by combining, makes more efficient, the means of religious knowledge. Trinitarianism, on the other hand, is a system which tends to confine the mind; to shut it up in what is written; to diminish its interest in the universe; and to disincline it to bright and enlarged views of God's works. — This effect will be explained, in the first place, if we consider, that the peculiarities of Trinitarianism differ so much from the teachings of the universe, that he who attaches himself to the one, will be in danger of losing his interest in the other. The ideas of Three Divine Persons, of God clothing himself in flesh, of the infinite Creator saving the guilty by transferring their punishment to an innocent being, these ideas cannot easily be made to coalesce in the mind with that which nature gives, of One Almighty Father and Unbounded Spirit, whom no worlds can contain, and whose vicegerent in the human breast pronounces it a crime, to lay the penalties of vice on the pure and unoffending.

But Trinitarianism has a still more positive influence in shutting the mind against improving views from the universe. It tends to throw gloom over God's works. Imagining that Christ is to be exalted, by giving him an exclusive agency in enlightening and recovering mankind, it is tempted to disparage other lights and influences ; and, for the purpose of magnifying his salvation, it inclines to exaggerate the darkness and desperateness of man's present condition. The mind thus impressed, naturally leans to those views of nature and of society, which will strengthen the ideas of desolation and guilt. It is tempted to aggravate the miseries of life, and to see in them only the marks of divine displeasure and punishing justice ; and overlooks their obvious fitness and design to awaken our powers, exercise our virtues, and strengthen our social ties. In like manner, it exaggerates the sins of men, that the need of an Infinite atonement may be maintained. Some of the most affecting tokens of God's love within and around us are obscured by this gloomy theology. The glorious faculties of the soul, its high aspirations, its sensibility to the great and good in character, its sympathy with disinterested and suffering virtue, its benevolent and religious instincts, its thirst for a happiness not found on earth, these are overlooked or thrown into the shade, that they may not disturb the persuasion of man's natural corruption. Ingenuity is employed to disparage what is interesting in the human character. Whilst the bursts of passion in the newborn child are gravely urged as indications of a native, rooted corruption; its bursts of affection, its sweet smile, its innocent and irrepressible joy, its loveliness and beauty, are not listened to, though they plead more eloquently its alliance with higher natures. The sacred and tender affections of home; the unwearied watchings and cheerful sacrifices of parents; the reverential, grateful assiduity of children, smoothing an aged father's or mother's descent to the grave; woman's love, stronger than death; the friendship of brothers and sisters; the anxious affection, which tends around the bed of sickness; the subdued voice, which breathes comfort into the mourner's heart; all the endearing offices, which shed a serene light through our dwellings; these are explained away by the thorough advocates of this system, so as to include no real virtue, so as to consist with a natural aversion to goodness. Even the higher efforts of disinterested benevolence, and the most unaffected expressions of piety, if not connected with what is called "the true faith," are, by the most rigid disciples of the doctrine which I oppose, resolved into the passion for distinction, or some other working of "unsanctified nature." Thus, Trinitarianism and its kindred doctrines have a tendency to veil God's goodness, to sully his fairest works, to dim the lustre of those innocent and pure affections, which a divine breath kindles in the soul, to blight the beauty and freshness of creation, and in this way to consume the very nutriment of piety. We know, and rejoice to know, that in multitudes this tendency is counteracted by a cheerful temperament, a benevolent nature, and a strength of gratitude, which bursts the shackles of a melancholy system. But from the nature of the doctrine, the tendency exists and is strong ; and an impartial observer will often discern it resulting in gloomy, depressing views of life and the universe.

Trinitarianism, by thus tending to exclude bright and enlarged views of the creation, seems to me not only to chill the heart, but to injure the understanding, as far as moral and religious truth is concerned. It does not send the mind far and wide for new and elevating objects ; and we have here one explanation of the barrenness and feebleness, by which theological writings are so generally marked. It is not wonderful, that the prevalent theology should want vitality and enlargement of thought, for it does not accord with the perfections of God and the spirit of the universe. It has not its root in eternal truth ; but is a narrow, technical, artificial system, the fabrication of unrefined ages, and consequently incapable of being blended with the new lights which are spreading over the most interesting subjects, and of being incorporated with the results and anticipations of original and progressive minds. It stands apart in the mind, instead of seizing upon new truths, and converting them into its own nutriment. With few exceptions, the Trinitarian theology of the present day is greatly deficient in freshness of thought, and in power to awaken the interest and to meet the intellectual and spiritual wants of thinking men. I see indeed superior minds and great minds among the adherents of the prevalent system; but they seem to me to move in chains, and to fulfil poorly their high function of adding to the wealth of the human intellect. In theological discussion, they remind me more of Samson grinding in the narrow mill of the Philistines, than of that undaunted champion achieving victories for God's people, and enlarging the bounds of their inheritance. Now, a system which has a tendency to confine the mind, and to impair its sensibility to the manifestations of God in the universe, is so far unfriendly to piety, to a bright, joyous, hopeful, evergrowing love of the Creator. It tends to generate and nourish a religion of a melancholy tone, such, I apprehend, as now predominates in the Christian world.

VII. Unitarianism promotes piety, by the high place which it assigns to piety in the character and work of Jesus Christ. What is it which the Unitarian regards as the chief glory of the character of Christ? I answer, his filial devotion, the entireness with which he surrendered himself to the will and benevolent purposes of God. The piety of Jesus, which, on the supposition of his Supreme Divinity, is a subordinate and incongruous, is, to us, his prominent and crowning, attribute. We place his "oneness with God," not in an unintelligible unity of essence, but in unity of mind and heart, in the strength of his love, through which he renounced every separate interest, and identified himself with his Father's designs. In other words, filial piety, the consecration of his whole being to the benevolent will of his Father, this is the mild glory in which he always offers himself to our minds; and, of consequence, all our sympathies with him, all our love and veneration towards him, are so many forms of delight in a pious character, and our whole knowledge of him incites us to a like surrender of our whole nature and existence to God.

In the next place, Unitarianism teaches, that the highest work or office of Christ is, to call forth and strengthen piety in the human breast; and thus it sets before us this character as the chief acquisition and end of our being. To us, the great glory of Christ's mission consists in the power with which he "reveals the Father," and establishes the "kingdom or reign of God within" the soul. By the crown which he wears, we understand the eminence which he enjoys in the most beneficent work in the universe, that of bringing back the lost mind to the knowledge, love, and likeness of its Creator. With these views of Christ's office, nothing can seem to us so important as an enlightened and profound piety, and we are quickened to seek it, as the perfection and happiness to which nature and redemption jointly summon us.

Now we maintain, that Trinitarianism obscures and weakens these views of Christ's character and work; and this it does, by insisting perpetually on others of an incongruous, discordant nature. It diminishes the power of his piety. Making him, as it does, the Supreme Being, and placing him as an equal on his Father's throne, it turns the mind from him as the meekest worshipper of God; throws into the shade, as of very inferior worth, his self-denying obedience; and gives us other grounds for revering him, than his entire homage, his fervent love, his cheerful self-sacrifice to the Universal Parent. There is a plain incongruity in the belief of his Supreme Godhead with the ideas of filial piety and exemplary devotion. The mind, which has been taught to regard him as of equal majesty and authority with the Father, cannot easily feel the power of his character as the affectionate son, whose meat it was to do his Father's will. The mind, accustomed to make him the ultimate object of worship, cannot easily recognise in him the pattern of that worship, the guide to the Most High. The characters are incongruous, and their union perplexing, so that neither exerts its full energy on the mind.

Trinitarianism also exhibits the work as well as character of Christ, in lights less favorable to piety. It does not make the promotion of piety his chief end. It teaches, that the highest purpose of his mission was to reconcile God to man, not man to God. It teaches, that the most formidable obstacle to human happiness lies in the claims and threatenings of divine justice. Hence, it leads men to prize Christ more for answering these claims and averting these threatenings, than for awakening in the human soul sentiments of love towards its Father in heaven. Accordingly, multitudes seem to prize pardon more than piety, and think it a greater boon to escape, through Christ's sufferings, the fire of hell, than to receive, through his influence, the spirit of heaven, the spirit of devotion. Is such a system propitious to a generous and ever-growing piety?

If I may be allowed a short digression, I would conclude this head with the general observation, that we deem our views of Jesus Christ more interesting than those of Trinitarianism. We feel that we should lose much, by exchanging the distinct character and mild radiance with which he offers himself to our minds, for the confused and irreconcilable glories with which that system labors to invest him. According to Unitarianism, he is a being who may be understood, for he is one mind, one conscious nature. According to the opposite faith, he is an inconceivable compound of two most dissimilar minds, joining in one person a finite and infinite nature, a soul weak and ignorant, and a soul almighty and omniscient. And is such a being a proper object for human thought and affection?—I add, as another important consideration, that to us Jesus, instead of being the second of three obscure unintelligible persons, is first and preëminent in the sphere in which he acts, and is thus the object of a distinct attachment, which he shares with no equals or rivals. To us, he is first of the sons of God, the Son by peculiar nearness and likeness to the Father. He is first of all the ministers of God's mercy and beneficence, and through him the largest stream of bounty flows to the creation. He is first in God's favor and love, the most accepted of worshippers, the most prevalent of intercessors. In this mighty universe, framed to be a mirror of its Author, we turn to Jesus as the brightest image of God, and gratefully yield him a place in our souls, second only to the Infinite Father, to whom he himself directs our supreme affection.

VIII. I now proceed to a great topic. Unitarianism promotes piety, by meeting the wants of man as a sinner. The wants of the sinner may be expressed almost in one word. He wants assurances of mercy in his Creator. He wants pledges, that God is Love in its purest form, that is, that He has a goodness so disinterested, free, full, strong, and immutable, that the ingratitude and disobedience of his creatures cannot overcome it. This unconquerable love, which in Scripture is denominated grace, and which waits not for merit to call it forth, but flows out to the most guilty, is the sinner's only hope, and it is fitted to call forth the most devoted gratitude. Now, this grace or mercy of God, which seeks the lost, and receives and blesses the returning child, is proclaimed by that faith which we advocate, with a clearness and energy, which cannot be surpassed. Unitarianism will not listen for a moment to the common errors, by which this bright attribute is obscured. It will not hear of a vindictive wrath in God, which must be quenched by blood ; or of a justice, which binds his mercy with an iron chain, until its demands are satisfied to the full. It will not hear that God needs any foreign influence to awaken his mercy ; but teaches, that the yearnings of the tenderest human parent towards a lost child, are but a faint image of God's deep and overflowing compassion towards erring man. This essential and unchangeable propensity of the Divine Mind to forgiveness, the Unitarian beholds shining forth through the whole Word of God, and especially in the mission and revelation of Jesus Christ, who lived and died to make manifest the inexhaustible plenitude of divine grace ; and, aided by revelation, he sees this attribute of God everywhere, both around him and within him. He sees it in the sun which shines, and the rain which descends on the evil and unthankful ; in the peace, which returns to the mind in proportion to its return to God and duty ; in the sentiment of compassion, which springs up spontaneously in the human breast towards the fallen and lost ; and in the moral instinct, which teaches us to cherish this compassion as a sacred principle, as an emanation of God's infinite love. In truth, Unitarianism asserts so strongly the mercy of God, that the reproach thrown upon it is, that it takes from the sinner the dread of punishment, — a reproach wholly without foundation; for our system teaches that God's mercy is not an instinctive tenderness, which cannot inflict pain; but an all-wise love, which desires the true and lasting good of its object, and consequently desires first for the sinner that restoration to purity, without which, shame, and suffering, and exile from God and heaven are of necessity and unalterably his doom. Thus Unitarianism holds forth God's grace and forgiving goodness most resplendently; and, by this manifestation of him, it tends to awaken a tender and confiding piety; an ingenuous love, which mourns that it has offended; an ingenuous aversion to sin, not because sin brings punishment, but because it separates the mind from this merciful Father.

Now we object to Trinitarianism, that it obscures the mercy of God. It does so in various ways. We have already seen, that it gives such views of God's government, that we can hardly conceive of this attribute as entering into his character. Mercy to the sinner is the principle of love or benevolence in its highest form; and surely this cannot be expected from a being who brings us into existence burdened with hereditary guilt, and who threatens with endless punishment and woe the heirs of so frail and feeble a nature. With such a Creator, the idea of mercy cannot coalesce; and I will say more, that, under such a government, man would need no mercy; for he would owe no allegiance to such a maker, and could not of course contract the guilt of violating it; and, without guilt, no grace or pardon would be wanted. The severity of this system would place him on the ground of an injured being. The wrong would lie on the side of the Creator.

In the next place, Trinitarianism obscures God's mercy, by the manner in which it supposes pardon to be communicated. It teaches, that God remits the punishment of the offender, in consequence of receiving an equivalent from an innocent person; that the sufferings of the sinner are removed by a full satisfaction made to divine justice, in the sufferings of a substitute. And is this "the quality of mercy"? What means forgiveness, but the reception of the returning child through the strength of parental love? This doctrine invests the Saviour with a claim of merit, with a right to the remission of the sins of his followers; and represents God's reception of the penitent as a recompense due to the worth of his Son. And is mercy, which means free and undeserved love, made more manifest, more resplendent, by the introduction of merit and right as the ground of our salvation? Could a surer expedient be invented for obscuring its freeness, and for turning the sinner's gratitude from the sovereign who demands, to the sufferer who offers, full satisfaction for his guilt?

I know it is said, that Trinitarianism magnifies God's mercy, because it teaches, that he himself provided the substitute for the guilty. But I reply, that the work here ascribed to mercy is not the most appropriate, nor most fitted to manifest it and impress it on the heart. This may be made apparent by familiar illustrations. Suppose that a creditor, through compassion to certain debtors, should persuade a benevolent and opulent man to pay him in their stead. Would not the debtors see a greater mercy, and feel a weightier obligation, if they were to receive a free, gratuitous release? And will not their chief gratitude stray beyond the creditor to the benevolent substitute? Or, suppose that a parent, unwilling to inflict a penalty on a disobedient but feeble child, should persuade a stronger child to bear it. Would not the offender see a more touching mercy in a free forgiveness, springing immediately from a parent's heart, than in this circuitous remission? And will he not be tempted to turn with his strongest love to the generous sufferer? In this process of substitution, of which Trinitarianism boasts so loudly, the mercy of God becomes complicated with the rights and merits of the substitute, and is a more distant cause of our salvation. These rights and merits are nearer, more visible, and more than divide the glory with grace and mercy in our rescue. They turn the mind from Divine Goodness, as the only spring of its happiness, and only rock of its hope. Now this is to deprive piety of one of its chief means of growth and joy. Nothing should stand between the soul and God's mercy. Nothing should share with mercy the work of our salvation. Christ's intercession should ever be regarded as an application to love and mercy, not as a demand of justice, not as a claim of merit. I grieve to say, that Christ, as now viewed by multitudes, hides the lustre of that very attribute which it is his great purpose to display. I fear, that, to many, Jesus wears the glory of a more winning, tender mercy, than his Father, and that he is regarded as the sinner's chief resource. Is this the way to invigorate piety?

Trinitarians imagine, that there is one view of their system peculiarly fitted to give peace and hope to the sinner, and consequently to promote gratitude and love. It is this. They say, it provides an Infinite substitute for the sinner, than which nothing can give greater relief to the burdened conscience. Jesus, being the second person of the Trinity, was able to make infinite satisfaction for sin; and what, they ask, in Unitarianism, can compare with this? I have time only for two brief replies. And first, this doctrine of an Infinite satisfaction, or, as it is improperly called, of an Infinite atonement, subverts, instead of building up, hope; because it argues infinite severity in the government which requires it. Did I believe, what Trinitarianism teaches, that not the least transgression, not even the first sin of the dawning mind of the child, could be remitted without an infinite expiation, I should feel myself living under a legislation unspeakably dreadful, under laws written, like Draco's, in blood; and, instead of thanking the Sovereign for providing an infinite substitute, I should shudder at the attributes which render this expedient necessary. It is commonly said, that an infinite atonement is needed to make due and deep impressions of the evil of sin. But He who framed all souls, and gave them their susceptibilities, ought not to be thought so wanting in goodness and wisdom, as to have constituted a universe, which demands so dreadful and degrading a method of enforcing obedience, as the penal sufferings of a God. This doctrine, of an Infinite substitute suffering the penalty of sin, to manifest God's wrath against sin, and thus to support his government, is, I fear, so familiar to us all, that its severe character is overlooked. Let me, then, set it before you, in new terms, and by a new illustration; and if, in so doing, I may wound the feelings of some who hear me, I beg them to believe, that I do it with pain, and from no impulse but a desire to serve the cause of truth. —

Suppose, then, that a teacher should come among you, and should tell you, that the Creator, in order to pardon his own children, had erected a gallows in the centre of the universe, and had publicly executed upon it, in room of the offenders, an Infinite Being, the partaker of his own Supreme Divinity; suppose him to declare, that this execution was appointed, as a most conspicuous and terrible manifestation of God's justice, and of the infinite woe denounced by his law; and suppose him to add, that all beings in heaven and earth are required to fix their eyes on this fearful sight, as the most powerful enforcement of obedience and virtue. Would you not tell him, that he calumniated his Maker? Would you not say to him, that this central gallows threw gloom over the universe; that the spirit of a government, whose very acts of pardon were written in such blood, was terror, not paternal love; and that the obedience which needed to be upheld by this horrid spectacle, was nothing worth? Would you not say to him, that even you, in this infancy and imperfection of your being, were capable of being wrought upon by nobler motives, and of hating sin through more generous views; and that much more the angels, those pure flames of love, need not the gallows and an executed God to confirm their loyalty? You would all so feel, at such teaching as I have supposed; and yet how does this differ from the popular doctrine of atonement? According to this doctrine, we have an Infinite Being sentenced to suffer, as a substitute, the death of the cross, a punishment more ignominious and agonizing than the gallows, a punishment reserved for slaves and the vilest malefactors; and he suffers this punishment, that he may show forth the terrors of God's law, and strike a dread of sin through the universe. — I am indeed aware, that multitudes, who profess this doctrine, are not accustomed to bring it to their minds distinctly in this light; that they do not ordinarily regard the death of Christ as a criminal execution, as an infinitely dreadful infliction of justice, as intended to show, that, without an infinite satisfaction, they must hope nothing from God. Their minds turn, by a generous instinct, from these appalling views, to the love, the disinterestedness, the moral grandeur and beauty of the sufferer; and through such thoughts they make the cross a source of peace, gratitude, love, and hope; thus affording a delightful exemplification of the power of the human mind, to attach itself to what is good and purifying in the most irrational system. Not a few may shudder at the illustration which I have here given; but in what respects it is unjust to the popular doctrine of atonement, I cannot discern. I grieve to shock sincere Christians, of whatever name; but I grieve more for the corruption of our common faith, which I have now felt myself bound to expose.

I have a second objection to this doctrine of Infinite atonement. When examined minutely, and freed from ambiguous language, it vanishes into air. It is wholly delusion. The Trinitarian tells me, that, according to his system, we have an infinite substitute; that the Infinite God was pleased to bear our punishment, and consequently, that pardon is made sure. But I ask him, Do I understand you? Do you mean, that the Great God, who never changes, whose happiness is the same yesterday, to-day, and for ever, that this Eternal Being really bore the penalty of my sins, really suffered and died? Every pious man, when pressed by this question, answers, No. What, then, does the doctrine of Infinite atonement mean ? Why, this ; that God took into union with himself our nature, that is, a human body and soul ; and these bore the suffering for our sins ; and, through his union with these, God may be said to have borne it himself. Thus, this vaunted system goes out, — in words. The Infinite victim proves to be frail man, and God's share in the sacrifice is a mere fiction. I ask with solemnity, Can this doctrine give one moment's ease to the conscience of an unbiassed, thinking man ? Does it not unsettle all hope, by making the whole religion suspicious and unsure ? I am compelled to say, that I see in it no impression of majesty, or wisdom, or love, nothing worthy of a God ; and when I compare it with that nobler faith, which directs our eyes and hearts to God's essential mercy, as our only hope, I am amazed that any should ascribe to it superior efficacy, as a religion for sinners, as a means of filling the soul with pious trust and love. I know, indeed, that some will say, that, in giving up an infinite atonement, I deprive myself of all hope of divine favor. To such, I would say, You do wrong to God's mercy. On that mercy I cast myself without a fear. I indeed desire Christ to intercede for me. I regard his relation to me as God's kindest appointment. Through him, "grace and truth come" to me from Heaven, and I look forward to his friendship, as among the highest blessings of my whole future being. But I cannot, and dare not ask him, to offer an infinite satisfaction for my sins ; to appease the wrath of God ; to reconcile the Universal Father to his own offspring ; to open to me those arms of Divine mercy, which have encircled and borne me from the first moment of my being. The essential and unbounded mercy of my Creator, is the foundation of my hope, and a broader and surer the universe cannot give me.

IX. I now proceed to the last consideration, which the limits of this discourse will permit me to urge. It has been more than once suggested, but deserves to be distinctly stated. I observe, then, that Unitarianism promotes piety, because it is a rational religion. By this, I do not mean that its truths can be fully comprehended ; for there is not an object in nature or religion, which has not innumerable connexions and relations beyond our grasp of thought. I mean, that its doctrines are consistent with one another, and with all established truth. Unitarianism is in harmony with the great and clear principles of revelation ; with the laws and powers of human nature ; with the dictates of the moral sense ; with the noblest instincts and highest aspirations of the soul ; and with the lights which the universe throws on the character of its author. We can hold this doctrine without self-contradiction, without rebelling against our rational and moral powers, without putting to silence the divine monitor in the breast. And this is an unspeakable benefit ; for a religion thus coincident with reason, conscience, and our whole spiritual being, has the foundations of universal empire in the breast ; and the heart, finding no resistance in the intellect, yields itself wholly, cheerfully, without doubts or misgivings, to the love of its Creator.

To Trinitarianism we object, what has always been objected to it, that it contradicts and degrades reason, and thus exposes the mind to the worst delusions. Some of its advocates, more courageous than prudent, have even recommended "the prostration of the understanding," as preparatory to its reception. Its chief doctrine is an outrage on our rational nature. Its three persons who constitute its God, must either be frittered away into three unmeaning distinctions, into sounds signifying nothing ; or they are three conscious agents, who cannot, by any human art or metaphysical device, be made to coalesce into one being ; who cannot be really viewed as one mind, having one consciousness and one will. Now a religious system, the cardinal principle of which offends the understanding, very naturally conforms itself throughout to this prominent feature, and becomes prevalently irrational. He who is compelled to defend his faith in any particular, by the plea, that human reason is so depraved through the fall, as to be an inadequate judge of religion, and that God is honored by our reception of what shocks the intellect, seems to have no defence left against accumulated absurdities. According to these principles, the fanatic who exclaimed, "I believe, because it is impossible," had a fair title to canonization. Reason is too godlike a faculty, to be insulted with impunity. Accordingly, Trinitarianism, as we have seen, links itself with several degrading errors ; and its most natural alliance is with Calvinism, that cruel faith, which, stripping God of mercy and man of power, has made Christianity an instrument of torture to the timid, and an object of doubt or scorn to hardier spirits. I repeat it, a doctrine which violates reason like the Trinity, prepares its advocates, in proportion as it is incorporated into the mind, for worse and worse delusions. It breaks down the distinctions and barriers between truth and falsehood. It creates a diseased taste for prodigies, fictions, and exaggerations, for startling mysteries, and wild dreams of enthusiasm. It destroys the relish for the simple, chaste, serene beauties of truth. Especially when the prostration of understanding is taught as an act of piety, we cannot wonder, that the grossest superstitions should be devoured, and that the credulity of the multitude should keep pace with the forgeries of imposture and fanaticism. The history of the Church is the best comment on the effects of divorcing reason from religion ; and if the present age is disburdened of many of the superstitions under which Christianity and human nature groaned for ages, it owes its relief in no small degree to the reinstating of reason in her long-violated rights.

The injury to religion, from irrational doctrines when thoroughly believed, is immense. The human soul has a unity. Its various faculties are adapted to one another. One life pervades it ; and its beauty, strength, and growth depend on nothing so much, as on the harmony and joint action of all its principles. To wound and degrade it in any of its powers, and especially in the noble and distinguishing power of reason, is to inflict on it universal injury. No notion is more false, than that the heart is to thrive by dwarfing the intellect; that perplexing doctrines are the best food of piety ; that religion flourishes most luxuriantly in mist and darkness. Reason was given for God as its great object ; and for him it should be kept sacred, invigorated, clarified, protected from human usurpation, and inspired with a meek self-reverence.

The soul never acts so effectually or joyfully, as when all its powers and affections conspire ; as when thought and feeling, reason and sensibility, are called forth together by one great and kindling object. It will never devote itself to God with its whole energy, whilst its guiding faculty sees in him a being to shock and confound it. We want a harmony in our inward nature. We want a piety, which will join light and fervor, and on which the intellectual power will look benignantly. We want religion to be so exhibited, that, in the clearest moments of the intellect, its signatures of truth will grow brighter ; that, instead of tottering, it will gather strength and stability from the progress of the human mind. These wants we believe to be met by Unitarian Christianity, and therefore we prize it as the best friend of piety.

I have thus stated the chief grounds, on which I rest the claim of Unitarianism to the honor of promoting an enlightened, profound, and happy piety.

Am I now asked, why we prize our system, and why we build churches for its inculcation ? If I may be allowed to express myself in the name of conscientious Unitarians, who apply their doctrine to their own hearts and lives, I would reply thus : We prize and would spread our views, because we believe that they reveal God to us in greater glory, and bring us nearer to him, than any other. We are conscious of a deep want, which the creation cannot supply, the want of a Perfect Being, on whom the strength of our love may be centred, and of an Almighty Father, in whom our weaknesses, imperfections, and sorrows may find resource ; and such a Being and Father, Unitarian Christianity sets before us. For this we prize it above all price. We can part with every other good. We can endure the darkening of life's fairest prospects. But this bright, consoling doctrine of One God, even the Father, is dearer than life, and we cannot let it go. — Through this faith, every thing grows brighter to our view. Born of such a Parent, we esteem our existence an inestimable gift. We meet everywhere our Father, and his presence is as a sun shining on our path. We see him in his works, and hear his praise rising from every spot which we tread. We feel him near in our solitudes, and sometimes enjoy communion with him more tender than human friendship. We see him in our duties, and perform them more gladly, because they are the best tribute we can offer our Heavenly Benefactor. Even the consciousness of sin, mournful as it is, does not subvert our peace; for, in the mercy of God, as made manifest in Jesus Christ, we see an inexhaustible fountain of strength, purity, and pardon, for all who, in filial reliance, seek these heavenly gifts. — Through this faith, we are conscious of a new benevolence springing up to our fellow-creatures, purer and more enlarged than natural affection. Towards all mankind we see a rich and free love flowing from the common Parent, and, touched by this love, we are the friends of all. We compassionate the most guilty, and would win them back to God. — Through this faith, we receive the happiness of an ever-enlarging hope. There is no good too vast for us to anticipate for the universe or for ourselves, from such a Father as we believe in. We hope from him, what we deem his greatest gift, even the gift of his own Spirit, and the happiness of advancing for ever in truth and virtue, in power and love, in union of mind with the Father and the Son. — We are told, indeed, that our faith will not prove an anchor in the last hour. But we have known those, whose departure it has brightened; and our experience of its power, in trial and peril, has proved it to be equal to all the wants of human nature.

We doubt not, that, to its sincere followers, death will be a transition to the calm, pure, joyful mansions, prepared by Christ for his disciples. There we expect to meet that great and good Deliverer. With the eye of faith, we already see him looking round him with celestial love on all of every name, who have imbibed his spirit. His spirit; his loyal and entire devotion to the will of his Heavenly Father; his universal, unconquerable benevolence, through which he freely gave from his pierced side his blood, his life for the salvation of the world; this divine love, and not creeds, and names, and forms, will then be found to attract his supreme regard. This spirit we trust to see in multitudes of every sect and name; and we trust, too, that they, who now reproach us, will at that day recognise, in the dreaded Unitarian, this only badge of Christ, and will bid him welcome to the joy of our common Lord.—I have thus stated the views with which we have reared this building. We desire to glorify God, to promote a purer, nobler, happier piety. Even if we err in doctrine, we think that these motives should shield us from reproach; should disarm that intolerance, which would exclude us from the church on earth, and from our Father's house in heaven.

We end, as we began, by offering up this building to the Only Living and True God. We have erected it amidst our private habitations, as a remembrancer of our Creator. We have reared it in this busy city, as a retreat for pious meditation and prayer. We dedicate it to the King and Father Eternal, the King of kings and Lord of lords. We dedicate it to his Unity, to his unrivalled and undivided Majesty. We dedicate it to the praise of his free, unbought, unmerited grace.

We dedicate it to Jesus Christ, to the memory of his love, to the celebration of his divine virtue, to the preaching of that truth, which he sealed with blood. We dedicate it to the Holy Spirit, to the sanctifying influence of God, to those celestial emanations of light and strength, which visit and refresh the devout mind. We dedicate it to prayers and praises, which, we trust, will be continued and perfected in heaven. We dedicate it to social worship, to Christian intercourse, to the communion of saints. We dedicate it to the cause of pure morals, of public order, of temperance, uprightness, and general good will. We dedicate it to Christian admonition, to those warnings, remonstrances, and earnest and tender persuasions, by which the sinner may be arrested, and brought back to God. We dedicate it to Christian consolation, to those truths which assuage sorrow, animate penitence, and lighten the load of human anxiety and fear. We dedicate it to the doctrine of Immortality, to sublime and joyful hopes which reach beyond the grave. In a word, we dedicate it to the great work of perfecting the human soul, and fitting it for nearer approach to its Author. Here may heart meet heart. Here may man meet God. From this place may the song of praise, the ascription of gratitude, the sigh of penitence, the prayer for grace, and the holy resolve, ascend as fragrant incense to Heaven; and, through many generations, may parents bequeath to their children this house, as a sacred spot, where God had "lifted upon them his countenance," and given them pledges of his everlasting love.

OBJECTIONS TO UNITARIAN CHRISTIANITY CONSIDERED.

1819.

It is due to truth, and a just deference to our fellow-Christians, to take notice of objections which are currently made to our particular views of religion ; nor ought we to dismiss such objections as unworthy of attention, on account of their supposed lightness ; because what is light to us, may weigh much with our neighbour, and truth may suffer from obstructions which a few explanations might remove. It is to be feared that those Christians, who are called Unitarian, have been wanting in this duty. Whilst they have met the labored arguments of their opponents fully and fairly, they have overlooked the loose, vague, indefinite objections, which float through the community, and operate more on common minds than formal reasoning. On some of these objections, remarks will now be offered ; and it is hoped that our plainness of speech will not be construed into severity, nor our strictures on different systems be ascribed to a desire of retaliation. It cannot be expected, that we shall repel with indifference, what seem to us reproaches on some of the most important and consoling views of Christianity. Believing that the truths, which through God's good providence we are called to maintain, are necessary to the vindication of the Divine character, and to the prevalence of a more enlightened and exalted piety, we are bound to assert them earnestly, and to speak freely of the opposite errors which now disfigure Christianity. — What, then, are the principal objections to Unitarian Christianity ?

I. It is objected to us, that we deny the Divinity of Jesus Christ. Now what does this objection mean ? What are we to understand by the Divinity of Christ ? In the sense in which many Christians, and perhaps a majority, interpret it, we do not deny it, but believe it as firmly as themselves. We believe firmly in the Divinity of Christ's mission and office, that he spoke with Divine authority, and was a bright image of the Divine perfections. We believe that God dwelt in him, manifested himself through him, taught men by him, and communicated to him his spirit without measure. We believe that Jesus Christ was the most glorious display, expression, and representative of God to mankind, so that in seeing and knowing him, we see and know the invisible Father ; so that when Christ came, God visited the world and dwelt with men more conspicuously than at any former period. In Christ's words, we hear God speaking ; in his miracles, we behold God acting ; in his character and life, we see an unsullied image of God's purity and love. We believe, then, in the Divinity of Christ, as this term is often and properly used. — How, then, it may be asked, do we differ from other Christians ? We differ in this important respect. Whilst we honor Christ as the Son, representative, and image of the Supreme God, we do not believe him to be the Supreme God himself. We maintain, that Christ and God are *distinct beings*, two beings, not one and the same being. On this point a little repetition may be pardoned, for many good Christians, after the controversies of ages, misunderstand the precise difference between us and themselves. Trinitarianism teaches, that Jesus Christ is the supreme and Infinite God, and that he and his Father are not only one in affection, counsel, and will, but are strictly and literally one and the same being. Now to us this doctrine is most unscriptural and irrational. We say that the Son cannot be the same being with his own Father ; that he, who was sent into the world to save it, cannot be the living God who sent him. The language of Jesus is explicit and unqualified. "I came not to do mine own will." — "I came not from myself." — "I came from God." Now we affirm, and this is our chief heresy, that Jesus was not and could not be the God from whom he came, but was another being ; and it amazes us that any can resist this simple truth. The doctrine, that Jesus, who was born at Bethlehem ; who ate and drank and slept ; who suffered and was crucified ; who came from God ; who prayed to God ; who did God's will ; and who said, on leaving the world, "I ascend to my Father and your Father, to my God and your God" ; the doctrine that this Jesus was the Supreme God himself, and the same being with his Father, this seems to us a contradiction to reason and Scripture so flagrant, that the simple statement of it is a sufficient refutation. We are often charged with degrading Christ ; but if this reproach belong to any Christians, it falls, we fear, on those who accuse him of teaching a doctrine so contradictory, and so subversive of the supremacy of our Heavenly Father. Certainly our humble and devout Master has given no ground for this accusation. He always expressed towards God the reverence of a son. He habitually distinguished himself from God. He referred to God all his powers. He said without limitation or reserve, "The Father is greater than I." — "Of myself I can do nothing." If to represent Christ as a being distinct from God, and as inferior to him, be to degrade him, then let our opponents lay the guilt where it belongs, not on us, but on our Master, whose language we borrow, in whose very words we express our sentiments, whose words we dare not trifle with and force from their plain sense. Our limits will not allow us to say more ; but we ask common Christians, who have taken their opinions from the Bible, rather than from human systems, to look honestly into their own minds, and to answer frankly, whether they have not understood and believed Christ's divinity, in the sense maintained by us, rather than in that for which the Trinitarians contend.

2. We proceed to another objection, and one which probably weighs more with multitudes than any other. It is this, that our doctrine respecting Christ takes from the sinner the only ground of hope. It is said by our opponents, "We and all men are sinners by our very nature, and infinitely guilty before God. The sword of divine justice hangs over us, and hell opens beneath us ; and where shall we find a refuge but in an infinite Saviour? We want an Infinite Atonement ; and in depriving us of this, you rob us of our hope, you tear from the Scriptures the only doctrine which meets our wants. We may burn our Bibles, if your interpretation be true, for our case is desperate ; we are lost for ever." In such warm and wild language, altogether unwarranted by Scripture, yet exceedingly fitted to work on common and terror-stricken minds, our doctrine is constantly assailed.

Now, to this declamation, for such we esteem it, we oppose one plain request. Show us, we say, a single passage in the Bible, in which we are told that the sin of man is infinite, and needs an infinite atonement. We find not one. Not even a whisper of this doctrine comes to us from the sacred writers. Let us stop a moment and weigh this doctrine. It teaches us that man, although created by God a frail, erring, and imperfect being, and even created with an irresistible propensity to sin, is yet regarded by the Creator as an infinite offender, meriting infinite punishment for his earliest transgressions; and that he is doomed to endless torment, unless an infinite Saviour appear for his rescue! How can any one, we ask, charge on our benevolent and righteous Parent such a government of his creatures?—We maintain, that man is not created in a condition which makes an infinite atonement necessary; nor do we believe that any creature can fall into a condition, from which God may not deliver him without this rigid expedient. Surely, if an infinite satisfaction to justice were indispensable to our salvation, if God took on him human nature for the very purpose of offering it, and if this fact constitute the peculiar glory, the life and essence, and the saving efficacy of the Gospel, we must find it expressed clearly, definitely, in at least one passage in the Bible. But not one, we repeat it, can be found there.—We maintain, further, that this doctrine of God becoming a victim and sacrifice for his own rebellious subjects, is as irrational as it is unscriptural. We have always supposed that atonement, if necessary, was to be made *to*, not by, the sovereign who has been offended; and we cannot conceive a more unlikely method of vindicating his authority, than that he himself should bear the punishment which is due to transgressors of his laws.—We have another objection. If an infinite atonement be necessary, and if, consequently, none but God can make it, we see not but that God must become a sufferer, must take upon himself our pain and woe; a thought from which a pious mind shrinks with horror. To escape this difficulty, we are told, that Christ suffered as man, not as God; but if man only suffered, if only a human and finite mind suffered, if Christ, as God, was perfectly happy on the cross, and bore only a short and limited pain in his human nature, where, we ask, was the infinite atonement? Where is the boasted hope which this doctrine is said to give to the sinner?

The objection, that there is no hope for the sinner, unless Christ be the infinite God, amazes us. Surely if we have a Father in heaven, of infinite goodness and power, we need no other infinite person to save us. The common doctrine disparages and dishonors the only true God, our Father, as if, without the help of a second and a third divinity, equal to himself, he could not restore his frail creature, man. We have not the courage of our brethren. With the Scriptures in our hands, with the solemn attestations which they contain to the divine Unity, and to Christ's dependence, we dare not give to the God and Father of Jesus an equal or rival in the glory of originating our redemption, or of accomplishing it by underived and infinite power. — Are we asked, as we sometimes are, what is our hope, if Christ be not the supreme God? We answer, it is the boundless and almighty goodness of his Father and our Father; a goodness which cannot require an infinite atonement for the sins of a frail and limited creature. God's essential and unchangeable mercy, not Christ's infinity, is the Scriptural foundation of a sinner's hope. In the Scriptures, our heavenly Father is always represented as the sole original, spring, and first cause of our salvation; and let no one presume to divide His glory with another. That Jesus came to save us, we owe entirely to the Father's benevolent appointment. That Jesus is perfectly adequate to the work of our salvation, is to be believed, not because he is himself the supreme God, but because the supreme and unerring God selected, commissioned, and empowered him for this office.—That his death is an important means of our salvation, we gratefully acknowledge; but ascribe its efficacy to the merciful disposition of God towards the human race. To build the hope of pardon on the independent and infinite sufficiency of Jesus Christ, is to build on an unscriptural and false foundation; for Jesus teaches us, that of himself he can do nothing; that all power is given to him by his Father; and that he is a proper object of trust, because he came not of himself, or to do his own will, but because the Father sent him. We indeed lean on Christ, but it is because he is "a corner-stone, chosen by God and laid by God in Zion." God's forgiving love, declared to mankind by Jesus Christ, and exercised through him, is the foundation of hope to the penitent, on which we primarily rest, and a firmer the universe cannot furnish us.

3. We now proceed to another objection. We are charged with expecting to be saved by Works, and not by Grace. This charge may be easily despatched, and a more groundless one cannot easily be imagined. We indeed attach great importance to Christian works, or Christian obedience, believing that a practice or life conformed to the precepts and example of Jesus, is the great end for which faith in him is required, and is the great condition on which everlasting life is bestowed. We are accustomed to speak highly of the virtues and improvements of a true Christian, rejecting with abhorrence the idea, that they are no better than the outward Jewish righteousness, which the Prophet called "filthy rags"; and maintaining with the Apostle, that they are "in the sight of God, of great price." We believe that holiness or virtue is the very image of God in the human soul, a ray of his brightness, the best gift which he communicates to his creatures, the highest benefit which Christ came to confer, the only important and lasting distinction between man and man. Still we always and earnestly maintain, that no human virtue, no human obedience, can give a legal claim, a right by merit, to the life and immortality brought to light by Christ. We see and mourn over the

deficiencies, broken resolutions, and mixed motives of the best men. We always affirm, that God's grace, benignity, free kindness, is needed by the most advanced Christians, and that to this alone we owe the promise in the Gospel, of full remission, and everlasting happiness to the penitent. None speak of mercy more constantly than we. One of our distinctions is, that we magnify this lovely attribute of the Deity. So accustomed are we to insist on the infinity of God's grace and mercy, that our adversaries often charge us with forgetting his justice; and yet it is objected to us, that, renouncing grace, we appeal to justice, and build our hope on the abundance of our merit!

4. We now proceed to another objection often urged against our views, or rather against those who preach them; and it is this, that we preach morality. To meet this objection, we beg to know what is intended by morality. Are we to understand by it, what it properly signifies, our whole duty, however made known to us, whether by nature or revelation? Does it mean the whole extent of those obligations which belong to us as moral beings? Does it mean that "sober, righteous, godly life," which our moral Governor has prescribed to us by his Son, as the great preparation for heaven? If this be morality, we cheerfully plead guilty to the charge of preaching it, and of laboring chiefly and constantly to enforce it; and believing, as we do, that all the doctrines, precepts, threatenings, and promises of the Gospel, are revealed for no other end than to make men moral, in this true and generous sense, we hope to continue to merit this reproach.

We fear, however, that this is not the meaning of the morality, which is said to be the burden of our preaching. Some, at least, who thus reproach us, mean that we are accustomed to enjoin only a worldly and social morality, consisting in common honesty, common kindness, and freedom from gross vices ; neglecting to inculcate inward purity, devotion, heavenly-mindedness, and love to Jesus Christ. We hope that the persons who thus accuse us speak from rumor, and have never heard our instructions for themselves ; for the charge is false ; and no one who ever sat under our ministry can urge it, without branding himself a slanderer. The first and great commandment, which is to love God supremely, is recognised and enforced habitually in our preaching; and our obligations to Jesus Christ, the friend who died for us, are urged, we hope, not wholly without tenderness and effect.

It is but justice, however, to observe of many, that when they reproach us with moral preaching, they do not mean that we teach only outward decencies, but that we do not inculcate certain favorite doctrines, which are to them the very marrow and richness of the Gospel. When such persons hear a sermon, be the subject what it may, which is not seasoned with recognitions of the Trinity, total depravity, and similar articles of faith, they call it moral. According to this strange and unwarrantable use of the term, we rejoice to say that we are "moral preachers" ; and it comforts us that we have for our pattern, "him who spake as man never spake," and who, in his longest discourse, has dropped not a word about a Trinity, or inborn corruption, or special and electing grace ; and still more, we seriously doubt whether our preaching could with propriety be called moral, did we urge these doctrines, especially the two last ; for, however warmly they may be defended by honest men, they seem to us to border on immorality ; that is, to dishonor God, to weaken the sense of responsibility, to break the spirit, and to loosen the restraints on guilty passion.

5. Another objection urged against us, is, that our system does not produce as much zeal, seriousness, and piety as other views of religion. The objection it is difficult

to repel, except by language which will seem to be a boasting of ourselves. When expressed in plain language, it amounts to this ; — "We Trinitarians and Calvinists are better and more pious than you Unitarians, and consequently our system is more Scriptural than yours." Now assertions of this kind do not strike us as very modest and humble, and we believe that truth does not require us to defend it by setting up our piety above that of our neighbours. — This, however, we would say, that if our zeal and devotion are faint, the fault is our own, not that of our doctrine. We are sure that our views of the Supreme Being are incomparably more affecting and attractive than those which we oppose. It is the great excellence of our system, that it exalts God, vindicates his parental attributes, and appeals powerfully to the ingenuous principles of love, gratitude, and veneration ; and when we compare it with the doctrines which are spread around us, we feel that of all men we are most inexcusable, if a filial piety do not spring up and grow strong in our hearts.

Perhaps it may not be difficult to suggest some causes for the charge, that our views do not favor seriousness and zeal. One reason probably is, that we interpret with much rigor those precepts of Christ, which forbid ostentation, and enjoin modesty and retirement in devotion. We dread a showy religion. We are disgusted with pretensions to superior sanctity, that stale and vulgar way of building up a sect. We believe that true religion speaks in actions more than in words, and manifests itself chiefly in the common temper and life ; in giving up the passions to God's authority, in inflexible uprightness and truth, in active and modest charity, in candid judgment, and in patience under trials and injuries. We think it no part of piety to publish its fervors, but prefer a delicacy in regard to these secrets of the soul ; and hence, to those persons who think religion is to be worn conspicuously and spoken of passionately, we may seem cold and dead, when perhaps, were the heart uncovered, it might be seen to be "alive to God," as truly as their own.

Again, it is one of our principles, flowing necessarily from our views of God, that religion is cheerful; that where its natural tendency is not obstructed by false theology, or a melancholy temperament, it opens the heart to every pure and innocent pleasure. We do not think that piety disfigures its face, or wraps itself in a funeral pall as its appropriate garb Now, too many conceive of religion as something gloomy, and never to be named but with an altered tone and countenance; and where they miss these imagined signs of piety, they can hardly believe that a sense of God dwells in the heart.

Another cause of the error in question, we believe to be this. Our religious system excludes, or at least does not favor, those overwhelming terrors and transports which many think essential to piety. We do not believe in shaking and disordering men's understandings, by excessive fear, as a preparation for supernatural grace and immediate conversion. This we regard as a dreadful corruption and degradation of religion. Religion, we believe, is a gradual and rational work, beginning sometimes in sudden impressions, but confirmed by reflection, growing by the regular use of Christian means, and advancing silently to perfection. Now, because we specify no time when we were overpowered and created anew by irresistible impulse; because we relate no agonies of despair succeeded by miraculous light and joy, we are thought by some to be strangers to piety; — how reasonably, let the judicious determine.

Once more; we are thought to want zeal, because our principles forbid us to use many methods for spreading them, which are common with other Christians. Whilst we value highly our peculiar views, and look to them for the best fruits of piety, we still consider ourselves as bound to think charitably of those who doubt or deny them; and with this conviction, we cannot enforce them with that vehemence, positiveness, and style of menace, which constitute much of the zeal of certain denominations; — and we freely confess that we would on no account exchange our charity for their zeal; and we trust that the time is near, when he who holds what he deems truth with lenity and forbearance, will be accounted more pious than he who compasseth sea and land to make proselytes to his sect, and "shuts the gates of mercy" on all who will not bow their understandings to his creed. — We fear, that in these remarks we may have been unconsciously betrayed into a self-exalting spirit. Nothing could have drawn them from us, but the fact that a very common method of opposing our sentiments, is to decry the piety of those who adopt them. After all, we mean not to deny our great deficiencies. We have nothing to boast before God, although the cause of truth forbids us to submit to the censoriousness of our brethren.

6. Another objection to our views, is, that they lead to a rejection of revelation. Unitarianism has been called "a half-way house to infidelity." — Now, to this objection we need not oppose general reasonings. We will state a plain fact. It is this. A large proportion of the most able and illustrious defenders of the truth of Christianity have been Unitarians; and our religion has received from them, to say the least, as important service in its conflicts with infidelity, as from any class of Christians whatever. From the long catalogue of advocates of Christianity among Unitarians, we can select now but a few; but these few are a host. The name of John Locke is familiar to every scholar. He rendered distinguished service to

the philosophy of the human mind ; nor is this his highest praise. His writings on government and toleration contributed more than those of any other individual, to the diffusion of free and generous sentiments through Europe and America ; and perhaps Bishop Watson was not guilty of great exaggeration, when he said, "This great man has done more for the establishment of pure Christianity than any author I am acquainted with." He was a laborious and successful student of the Scriptures. His works on the "Epistles of Paul," and on the "Reasonableness of Christianity," formed an era in sacred literature ; and he has the honor of having shed a new and bright light on the darkest parts of the New Testament, and in general on the Christian system. Now Locke, be it remembered, was a Unitarian.—We pass to another intellectual prodigy,—to Newton, a name which every man of learning pronounces with reverence ; for it reminds him of faculties so exalted above those of ordinary men, that they seem designed to help our conceptions of superior orders of being. This great man, who gained by intuition what others reap from laborious research, after exploring the laws of the universe, turned for light and hope to the Bible ; and although his theological works cannot be compared with Locke's, yet in his illustrations of the prophecies, and of Scripture chronology, and in his criticisms on two doubtful passages,* which are among the chief supports of the doctrine of the Trinity, he is considered as having rendered valuable services to the Christian cause. Newton, too, was a Unitarian.—We are not accustomed to boast of men, or to prop our faith by great names ; for Christ, and He only, is our Master ; but it is with pleasure, that we find in our ranks the most gifted, sagacious, and exalted minds ; and we cannot but smile, when we sometimes hear from men and women of

* 1 John v. 7 ; 1 Tim. iii. 16.

very limited culture, and with no advantages for enlarged inquiry, reproachful and contemptuous remarks on a doctrine which the vast intelligence of Locke and Newton, after much study of the Scriptures, and in opposition to a prejudiced and intolerant age, received as the truth of God. It is proper to state, that doubts have lately been raised as to the religious opinions of Locke and Newton, and for a very obvious reason. In these times of growing light, their names have been found too useful to the Unitarian cause. But the long and general belief of the Unitarianism of these illustrious men can hardly be accounted for, but by admitting the fact; and we know of no serious attempts to set aside the proofs on which this belief is founded.

We pass to another writer, who was one of the brightest ornaments of the Church of England and of the age in which he lived, Dr. Samuel Clarke. In classical literature, and in metaphysical speculation, Dr. Clarke has a reputation which needs no tribute at our hands. His sermons are an invaluable repository of Scriptural criticism; and his work on the evidences of natural and revealed religion, has ever been considered as one of the ablest vindications of our common faith. This great man was a Unitarian. He believed firmly that Jesus was a distinct being from his Father, and a derived and dependent being; and he desired to bring the liturgy of his church into a correspondence with these doctrines.

To those who are acquainted with the memorable infidel controversy in the early part of the last century, excited by the writings of Bolingbroke, Tindal, Morgan, Collins, and Chubb, it will be unnecessary to speak of the zeal and power with which the Christian cause was maintained by learned Unitarians. But we must pass over these, to recall a man whose memory is precious to enlightened believers; we mean Lardner, that most patient and successful advocate of Christianity; who has written, we believe, more largely than any other author on the evidences of the Gospel; from whose works later authors have drawn as from a treasure-house; and whose purity and mildness have disarmed the severity and conciliated the respect of men of very different views from his own. Lardner was a Unitarian. — Next to Lardner, the most laborious advocate of Christianity against the attacks of infidels, in our own day, was Priestley; and whatever we may think of some of his opinions, we believe that none of his opposers ever questioned the importance of his vindications of our common faith. We certainly do not say too much, when we affirm that Unitarians have not been surpassed by any denomination in zealous, substantial service to the Christian cause. Yet we are told that Unitarianism leads to infidelity! We are reproached with defection from that religion, round which we have gathered in the day of its danger, and from which, we trust, persecution and death cannot divorce us.

It is indeed said, that instances have occurred of persons, who, having given up the Trinitarian doctrine, have not stopped there, but have resigned one part of Christianity after another, until they have become thorough infidels. To this we answer, that such instances we have never known; but that such should occur is not improbable, and is what we should even expect; for it is natural that when the mind has detected one error in its creed, it should distrust every other article, and should exchange its blind and hereditary assent for a sweeping skepticism. We have examples of this truth at the present moment, both in France and Spain, where multitudes have proceeded from rejecting Popery to absolute Atheism. Now, who of us will argue that the Catholic faith is true, because multitudes who relinquished it have also cast away every religious principle and restraint; and if the argument be not sound on the side of Popery, how can it be pressed into the service of Trinitarianism? The fact is, that false and absurd doctrines, when exposed, have a natural tendency to beget skepticism in those who received them without reflection. None are so likely to believe too little as those who have begun with believing too much; and hence we charge upon Trinitarianism whatever tendency may exist in those who forsake it, to sink gradually into infidelity.

Unitarianism does not lead to infidelity. On the contrary, its excellence is, that it fortifies faith. Unitarianism is Christianity stripped of those corrupt additions which shock reason and our moral feelings. It is a rational and amiable system, against which no man's understanding or conscience, or charity, or piety revolts. Can the same be said of that system, which teaches the doctrines of three equal persons in one God, of natural and total depravity, of infinite atonement, of special and electing grace, and of the everlasting misery of the non-elected part of mankind? We believe that unless Christianity be purified from these corruptions, it will not be able to bear the unsparing scrutiny to which the progress of society is exposing it. We believe that it must be reformed, or intelligent men will abandon it. As the friends of Christianity, and the foes of infidelity, we are therefore solicitous to diffuse what seem to us nobler and juster views of this divine system.

7. It was our purpose to consider one more objection to our views; namely, that they give no consolation in sickness and death. But we have only time to express amazement at such a charge. What! a system which insists with a peculiar energy on the pardoning mercy of God, on his universal and parental love, and on the doctrine of a resurrection and immortality, — such a system

unable to give comfort? It unlocks infinite springs of consolation and joy, and gives to him who practically receives it, a living, overflowing, and unspeakable hope. Its power to sustain the soul in death has been often tried; and did we believe dying men to be inspired, or that peace and hope in the last hours were God's seal to the truth of doctrines, we should be able to settle at once the controversy about Unitarianism. A striking example of the power of this system in disarming death, was lately given by a young minister in a neighbouring town,* known to many of our readers, and singularly endeared to his friends by eminent Christian virtue. He was smitten by sickness in the midst of a useful and happy life, and sunk slowly to the grave. His religion, and it was that which has now been defended, gave habitual peace to his mind, and spread a sweet smile over his pale countenance. He retained his faculties to his last hour; and when death came, having left pious counsel to the younger members of his family, and expressions of gratitude to his parents, he breathed out life in the language of Jesus, — "Father, into thy hands I commend my spirit." Such was the end of one who held, with an unwavering faith, the great principles which we have here advanced; and yet our doctrine has no consolation, we are told, for sickness and death!

We have thus endeavoured to meet objections commonly urged against our views of religion; and we have done this, not to build up a party, but to promote views of Christianity, which seem to us particularly suited to strengthen men's faith in it, and to make it fruitful of good works and holy lives. Christian virtue, Christian holiness, love to God and man, these are all which we

* Rev. John E. Abbot, of Salem. This tract was first published in 1819 in the "Christian Disciple."

think worth contending for; and these we believe to be intimately connected with the system now maintained. If in this we err, may God discover our error, and disappoint our efforts. We ask no success, but what he may approve, — no proselytes but such as will be made better, purer, happier by the adoption of our views.

THE MORAL ARGUMENT AGAINST

CALVINISM,

Illustrated in a Review of a Work entitled "A GENERAL VIEW OF THE DOCTRINES OF CHRISTIANITY, designed more especially for the Edification and Instruction of Families. Boston, 1809."

THE work, of which we have prefixed the title to this article, was published several years ago, and has been read by many among us with pleasure and profit. But it is not known as widely as it should be, and we wish to call to it the notice which it merits. It is not an original work, but was compiled chiefly from the writings of the Rev. Robert Fellowes, whose name is probably known to most of our readers. The title we think not altogether happy, because it raises an expectation which the book does not answer. We should expect from it a regular statement of the great truths of our religion ; but we find, what at present is perhaps as useful, a vindication of Christianity from the gross errors, which Calvinism has labored to identify with this divine system. This may easily be supposed from the table of contents. The book professes to treat of the following subjects : — The nature of religion and the mistakes that occur on that subject ; the free-agency and accountableness of man ; the fall of Adam, and original sin ; the doctrine of faith in general, and of religious faith in particular ; the doctrine of works ; the doctrine of regeneration ; the doctrine of repentance ; the doctrine of grace ; the doctrine of election and reprobation ; the doctrine of perseverance ; the visiting of the iniquities of the fathers upon the children ; and the sin against the Holy Ghost. — By those, who are acquainted with the five thorny points of Calvinism, the design of this compilation will be sufficiently understood from the enumeration of topics now given ; and few designs are more praiseworthy, than to free Christianity from the reproach brought upon it by that system.

The work under review is professedly popular in its style and mode of discussion. It has little refined and elaborate reasoning, but appeals to the great moral principles of human nature, and to the general strain of the Scriptures. It expresses strongly and without circumlocution the abhorrence with which every mind, uncorrupted by false theology, must look on Calvinism ; and although some of its delineations may be overcharged, yet they are substantially correct, and their strength is their excellence. The truth is, that nothing is so necessary on this subject as to awaken moral feeling in men's breasts. Calvinism owes its perpetuity to the influence of fear in palsying the moral nature. Men's minds and consciences are subdued by terror, so that they dare not confess, even to themselves, the shrinking, which they feel, from the unworthy views which this system gives of God ; and, by thus smothering their just abhorrence, they gradually extinguish it, and even come to vindicate in God what would disgrace his creatures. A voice of power and solemn warning is needed to rouse them from this lethargy, to give them a new and a juster dread, the dread of incurring God's displeasure, by making him odious, and exposing religion to insult and aversion. — In the present article, we intend to treat this subject with great freedom. But we beg that it may be understood that by Calvinism we intend only the peculiarities or distinguishing features of that system. We would also have it remembered, that these peculiarities form a small part of the religious faith of a Calvinist. He joins with them the general, fundamental, and most important truths of Christianity, by which they are always neutralized in a greater or less degree, and in some cases nullified. Accordingly it has been our happiness to see in the numerous body by which they are professed, some of the brightest examples of Christian virtue. Our hostility to the doctrine does not extend to its advocates. In bearing our strongest testimony against error, we do not the less honor the moral and religious worth, with which it is often connected.

The book under review will probably be objected to by theologians, because it takes no notice of a distinction, invented by Calvinistic metaphysicians, for rescuing their doctrines from the charge of aspersing God's equity and goodness. We refer to the distinction between *natural* and *moral inability*, a subtilty which may be thought to deserve some attention, because it makes such a show in some of the principal books of this sect. But, with due deference to its defenders, it seems to us groundless and idle, a distinction without a difference. An inability to do our duty, which is *born* with us, is to all intents and according to the established meaning of the word, *natural*. Call it moral, or what you please, it is still a part of the nature which our Creator gave us, and to suppose that he punishes us for it, because it is an inability seated in the will, is just as absurd, as to suppose him to punish us for a weakness of sight or of a limb. Common people cannot understand this distinction, cannot split this hair; and it is no small objection to Calvinism, that, according to its ablest defenders, it can only be reconciled to God's perfections, by a metaphysical subtilty, which the mass of people cannot comprehend.

If we were to speak as critics of the style of this book, we should say, that, whilst generally clear, and sometimes striking, it has the faults of the style which was very current not many years ago in this country, and which, we rejoice to say, is giving place to a better. The style to which we refer, and which threatened to supplant good writing in this country, intended to be elegant, but fell into jejuneness and insipidity. It delighted in words and arrangements of words, which were little soiled by common use, and mistook a spruce neatness for grace. We had a Procrustes' bed for sentences, and there seemed to be a settled war between the style of writing and the free style of conversation. Times we think have changed. Men have learned more to write as they speak, and are ashamed to dress up familiar thoughts, as if they were just arrived from a far country, and could not appear in public without a foreign and studied attire. They have learned that common words are common, precisely because most fitted to express real feeling and strong conception, and that the circuitous, measured phraseology, which was called elegance, was but the parade of weakness. They have learned that words are the signs of thought, and worthless counterfeits without it, and that style is good, when, instead of being anxiously cast into a mould, it seems a free and natural expression of thought, and gives to us with power the workings of the author's mind.

We have been led to make these remarks on the style which in a degree marks the book before us, from a persuasion, that this mode of writing has been particularly injurious to religion, and to rational religion. It has crept into sermons perhaps more than into any other compositions, and has imbued them with that soporific quality, which they have sometimes been found to possess in an eminent degree. How many hearers have been soothed by a smooth, watery flow of words, a regular chime of sentences, and elegantly rocked into repose! We are aware, that preachers, above all writers, are excusable for this style, because it is the easiest; and, having too much work to do, they must do it of course in the readiest way. But we mourn the necessity, and mourn still more the effect.—It gives us great pleasure to say, that, in this particular, we think we perceive an improvement taking place in this region. Preaching is becoming more direct, aims more at impression, and seeks the nearest way to men's hearts and consciences. We often hear from the pulpit strong thought in plain and strong language. It is hoped, from the state of society, that we shall not fly from one extreme to another, and degenerate into coarseness; but perhaps even this is a less evil than tameness and insipidity.

To return; the principal argument against Calvinism, in the General View of Christian Doctrines, is the *moral argument*, or that which is drawn from the inconsistency of the system with the divine perfections. It is plain, that a doctrine, which contradicts our best ideas of goodness and justice, cannot come from the just and good God, or be a true representation of his character. This moral argument has always been powerful to the pulling down of the strong-holds of Calvinism. Even in the dark period, when this system was shaped and finished at Geneva, its advocates often writhed under the weight of it; and we cannot but deem it a mark of the progress of society, that Calvinists are more and more troubled with the palpable repugnance of their doctrines to God's nature, and accordingly labor to soften and explain them, until in many cases the name only is retained. If the stern reformer of Geneva could lift up his head, and hear the mitigated tone, in which some of his professed followers dispense his fearful doctrines, we fear, that he could not lie down in peace, until he had poured out his displeasure on their cowardice and degeneracy. He would tell them, with a frown, that *moderate Calvinism* was a solecism, a contradiction in terms, and would bid them in scorn to join their real friend, Arminius. Such is the power of public opinion and of an improved state of society on creeds, that naked, undisguised Calvinism is not very fond of showing itself, and many of consequence know imperfectly what it means. What then is the system against which the View of Christian Doctrines is directed?

Calvinism teaches, that, in consequence of Adam's sin in eating the forbidden fruit, God brings into life all his posterity with a nature wholly corrupt, so that they are utterly indisposed, disabled, and made opposite to all that is spiritually good, and wholly inclined to all evil, and that continually. It teaches, that all mankind, having fallen in Adam, are under God's wrath and curse, and so made liable to all miseries in this life, to death itself, and to the pains of hell for ever. It teaches, that, from this ruined race, God, out of his mere good pleasure, has elected a certain number to be saved by Christ, not induced to this choice by any foresight of their faith or good works, but wholly by his free grace and love; and that, having thus predestinated them to eternal life, he renews and sanctifies them by his almighty and special agency, and brings them into a state of grace, from which they cannot fall and perish. It teaches, that the rest of mankind he is pleased to pass over, and to ordain them to dishonor and wrath for their sins, to the honor of his justice and power; in other words, he leaves the rest to the corruption in which they were born, withholds the grace which is necessary to their recovery, and condemns them to "most grievous torments in soul and body without intermission in hell-fire for ever." Such is Calvinism, as gathered from the most authentic records of the doctrine. Whoever will consult the famous Assembly's Catechisms and Confession, will see the peculiarities of the system in all their length and breadth of deformity. A man of plain sense, whose spirit has not been broken to this creed by education or terror, will think that it is not necessary for us to travel to heathen countries, to learn how mournfully the human mind may misrepresent the Deity.

The moral argument against Calvinism, of which we have spoken, must seem irresistible to common and unperverted minds, after attending to the brief statement now given. It will be asked with astonishment, How is it possible that men can hold these doctrines and yet maintain God's goodness and equity? What principles can be more contradictory ?— To remove the objection to Calvinism, which is drawn from its repugnance to the Divine perfections, recourse has been had, as before observed, to the distinction between natural and moral inability, and to other like subtilties. But a more common reply, we conceive, has been drawn from the weakness and imperfection of the human mind, and from its incapacity of comprehending God. Calvinists will tell us, that, because a doctrine opposes our convictions of rectitude, it is not necessarily false ; that apparent are not always real inconsistencies ; that God is an infinite and incomprehensible being, and not to be tried by *our* ideas of fitness and morality ; that we bring their system to an incompetent tribunal, when we submit it to the decision of human reason and conscience ; that we are weak judges of what is right and wrong, good and evil, in the Deity ; that the happiness of the universe may require an administration of human affairs which is very offensive to limited understandings ; that we must follow revelation, not reason or moral feeling, and must consider doctrines, which shock us in revelation, as awful mysteries, which are dark through our ignorance, and which time will enlighten. How little, it is added, can man explain or understand God's ways. How inconsistent the miseries of life appear with goodness in the Creator. How prone, too, have men always been to confound good and evil, to call the just, unjust. How presumptuous is it in such a being, to sit in judgment upon God, and to question the rectitude of the divine administration, because it shocks *his* sense of rectitude. Such we conceive to be a fair statement of the manner in which the Calvinist frequently meets the objection, that his system is at war with God's attributes. Such the reasoning by which the voice of conscience and nature is stifled, and men are reconciled to doctrines, which, if tried by the established principles of morality, would be rejected with horror. On this reasoning we purpose to offer some remarks; and we shall avail ourselves of the opportunity, to give our views of *the confidence which is due to our rational and moral faculties in religion.*

That God is infinite, and that man often errs, we affirm as strongly as our Calvinistic brethren. We desire to think humbly of ourselves, and reverently of our Creator. In the strong language of Scripture, "We now see through a glass darkly." "We cannot by searching find out God unto perfection. Clouds and darkness are round about him. His judgments are a great deep." God is great and good beyond utterance or thought. We have no disposition to idolize our own powers, or to penetrate the secret counsels of the Deity. But, on the other hand, we think it ungrateful to disparage the powers which our Creator has given us, or to question the certainty or importance of the knowledge, which he has seen fit to place within our reach. There is an affected humility, we think, as dangerous as pride. We may rate our faculties too meanly, as well as too boastingly. The worst error in religion, after all, is that of the skeptic, who records triumphantly the weaknesses and wanderings of the human intellect, and maintains, that no trust is due to the decisions of this erring reason. We by no means conceive, that man's greatest danger springs from pride of understanding, though we think as badly of this vice as other Christians. The history of the church proves, that men may trust their faculties too little as well as too much, and that the timidity, which shrinks from investigation, has injured the mind, and betrayed the interests of Christianity, as much as an irreverent boldness of thought.

It is an important truth, which, we apprehend, has not been sufficiently developed, that the ultimate reliance of a human being is and must be on his own mind. To confide in God, we must first confide in the faculties by which He is apprehended, and by which the proofs of his existence are weighed. A trust in our ability to distinguish between truth and falsehood is implied in every act of belief; for to question this ability would of necessity unsettle all belief. We cannot take a step in reasoning or action without a secret reliance on our own minds. Religion in particular implies, that we have understandings endowed and qualified for the highest employments of intellect. In affirming the existence and perfections of God, we suppose and affirm the existence in ourselves of faculties which correspond to these sublime objects, and which are fitted to discern them. Religion is a conviction and an act of the human soul, so that, in denying confidence to the one, we subvert the truth and claims of the other. Nothing is gained to piety by degrading human nature, for in the competency of this nature to know and judge of God all piety has its foundation. Our proneness to err instructs us indeed to use our powers with great caution, but not to contemn and neglect them. The occasional abuse of our faculties, be it ever so enormous, does not prove them unfit for their highest end, which is, to form clear and consistent views of God. Because our eyes sometimes fail or deceive us, would a wise man pluck them out, or cover them with a bandage, and choose to walk and work in the dark? or, because they cannot distinguish distant objects, can they discern nothing clearly in their proper sphere, and is sight to be pronounced a fallacious guide? Men who, to support a creed, would shake our trust in the calm, deliberate, and distinct decisions of our rational and moral powers, endanger religion more than its open foes, and forge the deadliest weapon for the infidel.

It is true that God is an infinite being, and also true, that his powers and perfections, his purposes and operations, his ends and means, being unlimited, are *incomprehensible*. In other words, they cannot be *wholly taken in* or *embraced* by the human mind. In the strong and figurative language of Scripture, we "know nothing" of God's ways; that is, we know *very few* of them. But this is just as true of the most advanced archangel as of man. In comparison with the vastness of God's system, the range of the highest created intellect is narrow; and, in this particular, man's lot does not differ from that of his elder brethren in heaven. We are both confined in our observation and experience to a little spot in the creation. But are an angel's faculties worthy of no trust, or is his knowledge uncertain, because he learns and reasons from a small part of God's works? or are his judgments respecting the Creator to be charged with presumption, because his views do not spread through the whole extent of the universe? We grant that our understandings cannot stretch beyond a very narrow sphere. But still the lessons, which we learn within this sphere, are just as sure, as if it were indefinitely enlarged. Because much is unexplored, we are not to suspect what we have actually discovered. Knowledge is not the less real, because confined. The man, who has never set foot beyond his native village, knows its scenery and inhabitants as undoubtingly, as if he had travelled to the poles. We indeed see very little ; but that little is as true, as if every thing else were seen ; and our future discoveries must agree with and support it. Should the whole order and purposes of the universe be opened to us, it is certain that nothing would be disclosed, which would in any degree shake our persuasion, that the earth is inhabited by rational and moral beings, who are authorized to expect from their Creator the most benevolent and equitable government. No extent of observation can unsettle those primary and fundamental principles of moral truth, which we derive from our highest faculties operating in the relations in which God has fixed us. In every region and period of the universe, it will be as true as it is now on the earth, that knowledge and power are the measures of responsibility, and that natural incapacity absolves from guilt. These and other moral verities, which are among our clearest perceptions, would, if possible, be strengthened, in proportion as our powers should be enlarged ; because harmony and consistency are the characters of God's administration, and all our researches into the universe only serve to manifest its unity, and to show a wider operation of the laws which we witness and experience on earth.

We grant that God is *incomprehensible*, in the sense already given. But he is not therefore *unintelligible*, and this distinction we conceive to be important. We do not pretend to know the *whole* nature and properties of God, but still we can form some *clear ideas* of him, and can reason from these ideas as justly as from any other. The truth is, that we cannot be said to comprehend any being whatever, not the simplest plant or animal. All have hidden properties. Our knowledge of all is limited. But have we therefore no distinct ideas of the objects around us, and is all our reasoning about them unworthy of trust? Because God is infinite, his name is not therefore a mere sound. It is a representative of some distinct conceptions of our Creator; and these conceptions are as sure, and important, and as proper materials for the reasoning faculty, as they would be if our views were indefinitely enlarged. We cannot indeed trace God's goodness and rectitude through the whole field of his operations; but we know the essential nature of these attributes, and therefore can often judge what accords with and opposes them. God's goodness, because infinite, does not cease to be goodness, or essentially differ from the same attribute in man; nor does justice change its nature, so that it cannot be understood, because it is seated in an unbounded mind. There have indeed been philosophers, "falsely so called," who have argued from the unlimited nature of God, that we cannot ascribe to him justice and other moral attributes, in any proper or definite sense of those words; and the inference is plain, that all religion or worship, wanting an intelligible object, must be a misplaced, wasted offering. This doctrine from the infidel we reject with abhorrence; but something, not very different, too often reaches us from the mistaken Christian, who, to save his creed, shrouds the Creator in utter darkness. In opposition to both, we maintain that God's attributes are intelligible, and that we can conceive as truly of his goodness and justice, as of these qualities in men. In fact, these qualities are essentially the same in God and man, though differing in degree, in purity, and in extent of operation. We know not and we cannot conceive of any other justice or goodness, than we learn from our own nature; and if God have not these, he is altogether unknown to us as a moral being; he offers nothing for esteem and love to rest upon; the objection of the infidel is just, that worship is wasted; "We worship we know not what."

It is asked, On what authority do we ascribe to God goodness and rectitude, in the sense in which these attributes belong to men, or how can we judge of the nature of attributes in the mind of the Creator? We answer by asking, How is it that we become acquainted with the mind of a fellow-creature? The last is as invisible, as removed from *immediate* inspection, as the first. Still we do not hesitate to speak of the justice and goodness of a neighbour; and how do we gain our knowledge? We answer, by witnessing the effects, operations, and expressions of these attributes. It is a law of our nature to argue from the effect to the cause, from the action to the agent, from the ends proposed and from the means of pursuing them, to the character and disposition of the being in whom we observe them. By these processes, we learn the invisible mind and character of man; and by the same we ascend to the mind of God, whose works, effects, operations, and ends are as expressive and significant of justice and goodness, as the best and most decisive actions of men. If this reasoning be sound (and all religion rests upon it,) then God's justice and goodness are intelligible attributes, agreeing essentially with the same qualities in ourselves. Their operation indeed is infinitely wider, and they are employed in accomplishing not only immediate but remote and unknown ends. Of consequence, we must expect that many parts of the divine administration will be *obscure*, that is, will not produce *immediate* good, and an *immediate* distinction between virtue and vice. But still the unbounded operation of these attributes does not change their nature. They are still the same, as if they acted in the narrowest sphere. We can still determine in many cases what does not accord with them. We are particularly sure that those essential principles of justice, which enter into and even form our conception of this attribute, must pervade every province and every period of the administration of a just being, and that to suppose the Creator in any instance to forsake them, is to charge him directly with unrighteousness, however loudly the lips may compliment his equity.

"But is it not presumptuous in man," it is continually said, "to sit in judgment on God?" We answer, that to "sit in judgment on God" is an ambiguous and offensive phrase, conveying to common minds the ideas of irreverence, boldness, familiarity. The question would be better stated thus;—Is it not presumptuous in man to judge concerning God, and concerning what agrees or disagrees with his attributes? We answer confidently, No; for in many cases we are competent and even bound to judge. And we plead first in our defence the Scriptures. How continually does God in his word appeal to the understanding and moral judgment of man. "O inhabitants of Jerusalem and men of Judah, judge, I pray you, between me and my vineyard. What could have been done more to my vineyard, that I have not done in it." We observe, in the next place, that all religion supposes and is built on judgments passed by us on God and on his operations. Is it not, for example, our duty and a leading part of piety to *praise* God:

And what is praising a being, but to adjudge and ascribe to him just and generous deeds and motives? And of what value is praise, except from those, who are capable of distinguishing between actions which exalt and actions which degrade the character? Is it presumption to call God *excellent*? And what is this, but to refer his character to a standard of excellence, to try it by the established principles of rectitude, and to pronounce its conformity to them; that is, to judge of God and his operations?

We are presumptuous, we are told, in judging of our Creator. But he himself has made this our duty, in giving us a moral faculty; and to decline it, is to violate the primary law of our nature. Conscience, the sense of right, the power of perceiving moral distinctions, the power of discerning between justice and injustice, excellence and baseness, is the highest faculty given us by God, the whole foundation of our responsibility, and our sole capacity for religion. Now we are forbidden by this faculty to love a being, who wants, or who fails to discover, moral excellence. God, in giving us conscience, has implanted a principle within us, which forbids us to prostrate ourselves before mere power, or to offer praise where we do not discover worth; a principle, which challenges our supreme homage for supreme goodness, and which absolves us from guilt, when we abhor a severe and unjust administration. Our Creator has consequently waved his own claims on our veneration and obedience, any farther than he discovers himself to us in characters of benevolence, equity, and righteousness. He rests his authority on the perfect coincidence of his will and government with those great and fundamental principles of morality written on our souls. He desires no worship, but that which springs from the exercise of our moral faculties upon his character, from our discernment and persuasion of his rectitude and goodness. He asks, he accepts, no love or admiration but from those, who can understand the nature and the proofs of moral excellence.

There are two or three striking facts, which show that there is no presumption in judging of God, and of what agrees or disagrees with his attributes. The first fact is, that the most intelligent and devout men have often employed themselves in proving the existence and perfections of God, and have been honored for this service to the cause of religion. Now we ask, what is meant by the *proofs* of a divine perfection? They are certain acts, operations, and methods of government, which are proper and natural effects, signs, and expressions of this perfection, and from which, according to the established principles of reasoning, it may be inferred. To prove the divine attributes is to collect and arrange those works and ways of the Creator, which accord with these attributes, correspond to them, flow from them, and express them. Of consequence, to prove them requires and implies *the power of judging of what agrees with them*, of discerning their proper marks and expressions. All our treatises on natural theology rest on this power. Every argument in support of a divine perfection is an exercise of it. To deny it, is to overthrow all religion.

Now if such are the proofs of God's goodness and justice, and if we are capable of discerning them, then we are not necessarily presumptuous, when we say of particular measures ascribed to him, that they are inconsistent with his attributes, and cannot belong to him.

There is plainly no more presumption in affirming of certain principles of administration, that they oppose God's equity and would prove him unrighteous, than to affirm of others, that they prove him upright and good. There are signs and evidences of injustice as unequivocal as those of justice; and our faculties are as adequate to the perception of the last as of the first. If they must not be trusted in deciding what would prove God unjust, they are unworthy of confidence when they gather evidences of his rectitude; and of course, the whole structure of religion must fall.

It is no slight objection to the mode of reasoning adopted by the Calvinist, that it renders the proof of the divine attributes impossible. When we object to his representations of the divine government, that they shock our clearest ideas of goodness and justice, he replies, that still they may be true, because we know very little of God, and what seems unjust to man, may be in the Creator the perfection of rectitude. Now this weapon has a double edge. If the strongest marks and expressions of injustice do not prove God unjust, then the strongest marks of the opposite character do not prove him righteous. If the first do not deserve confidence, because of our narrow views of God, neither do the last. If, when more shall be known, the first may be found consistent with perfect rectitude, so, when more shall be known, the last may be found consistent with infinite malignity and oppression. This reasoning of our opponents casts us on an ocean of awful uncertainty. Admit it, and we have no proofs of God's goodness and equity to rely upon. What we call proofs, may be mere appearances, which a wider knowledge of God may reverse. The future may show us, that the very laws and works of the Creator, from which we now infer his kindness, are consistent with the most determined purpose to spread infinite misery and guilt, and were intended, by raising hope, to add the agony of disappointment to our other woes. Why may not these anticipations, horrible as they are, be verified by the unfolding of God's system, if our reasonings about his attributes are rendered so very uncertain, as Calvinism teaches, by the infinity of his nature?

We have mentioned one fact to show that it is not presumptuous to judge of God, and of what accords with and opposes his attributes; namely, the fact that his attributes are thought susceptible of proof. Another fact, very decisive on this point, is, that Christians of all classes have concurred in resting the truth of Christianity in a great degree on its *internal* evidence, that is, on its accordance with the perfections of God. How common is it to hear from religious teachers, that Christianity is worthy of a good and righteous being, that it bears the marks of a divine original. Volumes have been written on its internal proofs, on the coincidence of its purposes and spirit with our highest conceptions of God. How common too is it, to say of other religions, that they are at war with the divine nature, with God's rectitude and goodness, and that we want no other proofs of their falsehood. And what does all this reasoning imply? Clearly this, that we are capable of determining, in many cases, what is worthy and what is unworthy of God, what accords with and what opposes his moral attributes. Deny us this capacity, and it would be no presumption against a professed revelation, that it ascribed to the Supreme Being the most detestable practices. It might still be said in support of such a system, that it is arrogant in man to determine what kind of revelation suits the character of the Creator. Christianity then leans, at least in part, and some think chiefly, on internal evidence, or on its agreeableness to God's moral attributes; and is it probable, that this religion, having this foundation, contains representations of God's government which shock our ideas of rectitude, and that it silences our objections by telling us, that we are no judges of what suits or opposes his infinite nature?

We will name one more fact to show, that it is not presumptuous to form these judgments of the Creator. All Christians are accustomed to reason from God's attributes, and to use them as tests of doctrines. In their controversies with one another, they spare no pains to show, that their particular views accord best with the divine perfections, and every sect labors to throw on its adversaries the odium of maintaining what is unworthy of God. Theological writings are filled with such arguments; and yet *we*, it seems, are guilty of awful presumption, when we deny of God principles of administration, against which every pure and good sentiment in our breasts rises in abhorrence.

We shall conclude this discussion with an important inquiry. If God's justice and goodness are consistent with those operations and modes of government, which Calvinism ascribes to him, of what use is our belief in these perfections? What expectations can we found upon them? If it consist with divine rectitude to consign to everlasting misery, beings who have come guilty and impotent from his hand, we beg to know what interest we have in this rectitude, what pledge of good it contains, or what evil can be imagined which may not be its natural result? If justice and goodness, when stretched to infinity, take such strange forms and appear in such unexpected and apparently inconsistent operations, how are we sure, that they will not give up the best men to ruin, and leave the universe to the powers of darkness? Such results indeed seem incompatible with these attributes, but not more so than the acts attributed to God by Calvinism. Is it said, that the divine faithfulness is pledged in the Scriptures to a happier issue of things? But why should not divine faithfulness transcend our poor understandings as much as divine goodness and justice, and why may not God, consistently with this attribute, crush every hope which his word has raised? Thus all the divine perfections are lost to us as grounds of encouragement and consolation, if we maintain, that their infinity places them beyond our judgment, and that we must expect from them measures and operations entirely opposed to what seems to us most accordant with their nature.

We have thus endeavoured to show, that the testimony of our rational and moral faculties against Calvinism is worthy of trust. — We know that this reasoning will be met by the question, What then becomes of Christianity? for this religion plainly teaches the doctrines you have condemned. Our answer is ready. Christianity contains no such doctrines. Christianity, reason, and conscience are perfectly harmonious on the subject under discussion. Our religion, fairly construed, gives no countenance to that system, which has arrogated to itself the distinction of Evangelical. We cannot, however, enter this field at present. We will only say, that the general spirit of Christianity affords a very strong presumption, that its records teach no such doctrines as we have opposed. This spirit is love, charity, benevolence. Christianity, we all agree, is designed to manifest God as perfect benevolence, and to bring men to love and imitate him. Now is it probable, that a religion, having this object, gives views of the Supreme Being, from which our moral convictions and benevolent sentiments shrink with horror, and which, if made our pattern, would convert us into monsters! It is plain, that, were a human parent to form himself on the universal Father, as described by Calvinism, that is, were he to bring his children into life totally depraved, and then to pursue them with endless punishment, we should charge him with a cruelty not surpassed in the annals of the world; or, were a sovereign to incapacitate his subjects in any way whatever for obeying his laws, and then to torture them in dungeons of perpetual woe, we should say, that history records no darker crime. And is it probable, that a religion, which aims to attract and assimilate us to God, considered as love, should hold him up to us in these heart-withering characters? We may confidently expect to find in such a system the brightest views of the divine nature; and the same objections lie against interpretations of its records, which savour of cruelty and injustice, as lie against the literal sense of passages which ascribe to God bodily wants and organs. Let the Scriptures be read with a recollection of the spirit of Christianity, and with that modification of particular texts by this general spirit, which a just criticism requires, and Calvinism would no more enter the mind of the reader, than Popery, we had almost said, than Heathenism.

In the remarks now made, it will be seen, we hope,

that we have aimed to expose doctrines, not to condemn their professors. It is true, that men are apt to think themselves assailed, when their system only is called to account. But we have no foe but error. We are less and less disposed to measure the piety of others by peculiarities of faith. Men's characters are determined, not by the opinions which they profess, but by those on which their thoughts habitually fasten, which recur to them most forcibly, and which color their ordinary views of God and duty. The creed of habit, imitation, or fear, may be defended stoutly, and yet have little practical influence. The mind, when compelled by education or other circumstances to receive irrational doctrines, has yet a power of keeping them, as it were, on its surface, of excluding them from its depths, of refusing to incorporate them with its own being; and, when burdened with a mixed, incongruous system, it often discovers a sagacity, which reminds us of the instinct of inferior animals, in selecting the healthful and nutritious portions, and in making them its daily food. Accordingly the real faith often corresponds little with that which is professed. It often happens, that, through the progress of the mind in light and virtue, opinions, once central, are gradually thrown outward, lose their vitality, and cease to be principles of action, whilst through habit they are defended as articles of faith. The words of the creed survive, but its advocates sympathize with it little more than its foes. These remarks are particularly applicable to the present subject. A large number, perhaps a majority of those, who surname themselves with the name of Calvin, have little more title to it than ourselves. They keep the name, and drop the principles which it signifies. They adhere to the system as a whole, out shrink from all its parts and distinguishing points. This silent but real defection from Calvinism is spreading more and more widely. The grim features of this system are softening, and its stern spirit yielding to conciliation and charity. We beg our readers to consult for themselves the two Catechisms and the Confession of the Westminster Assembly, and to compare these standards of Calvinism, with what now bears its name. They will rejoice, we doubt not, in the triumphs of truth. With these views, we have no disposition to disparage the professors of the system which we condemn, although we believe that its influence is yet so extensive and pernicious as to bind us to oppose it.

Calvinism, we are persuaded, is giving place to better views. It has passed its meridian, and is sinking, to rise no more. It has to contend with foes more formidable than theologians, with foes, from whom it cannot shield itself in mystery and metaphysical subtilties, we mean with the progress of the human mind, and with the progress of the spirit of the Gospel. Society is going forward in intelligence and charity, and of course is leaving the theology of the sixteenth century behind it. We hail this revolution of opinion as a most auspicious event to the Christian cause. We hear much at present of efforts to spread the Gospel. But Christianity is gaining more by the removal of degrading errors, than it would by armies of missionaries who should carry with them a corrupted form of the religion. We think the decline of Calvinism one of the most encouraging facts in our passing history ; for this system, by outraging conscience and reason, tends to array these high faculties against revelation. Its errors are peculiarly mournful, because they relate to the character of

God. It darkens and stains his pure nature; spoils his character of its sacredness, loveliness, glory; and thus quenches the central light of the universe, makes existence a curse, and the extinction of it a consummation devoutly to be wished. We now speak of the *peculiarities* of this system, and of their natural influence, when not counteracted, as they always are in a greater or less degree, by better views, derived from the spirit and plain lessons of Christianity.

We have had so much to do with our subject, that we have neglected to make the usual extracts from the book which we proposed to review. We earnestly wish, that a work, answering to the title of this, which should give us "a general view of Christian doctrines," might be undertaken by a powerful hand. Next to a good commentary on the Scriptures, it would be the best service which could be rendered to Christian truth.

LETTER ON CATHOLICISM,

TO THE

EDITOR OF THE "WESTERN MESSENGER,"

LOUISVILLE, KENTUCKY.

ON CATHOLICISM.

BOSTON, *June*, 1836.

MY DEAR SIR,

I have received your letter, expressing a very earnest desire that I would make some contribution to the pages of the "Western Messenger." Your appeal is too strong to be resisted. I feel that I must send you something, though circumstances, which I cannot control, do not allow me to engage in any elaborate discussion. I have therefore resolved to write you a letter, with the same freedom which I should use, if writing not for the public, but to a friend. Perhaps it may meet the wants, and suit the frank spirit of the West, more than a regular essay. But judge for yourself, and do what you will with my hasty thoughts.

I begin with expressing my satisfaction in your having planted yourself in the West. I am glad for your own sake, as well as for the sake of the cause you have adopted. I say, your own sake. You have chosen the good part. The first question to be asked by a young man entering into active life, is, in what situation he can find the greatest scope and excitement to his powers and good affections? That sphere is the best for a man, in which he can best unfold the faculties of a Man, in which he can do justice to his whole nature; in which his intellect, heart, conscience, will be called into the most powerful life. I am always discouraged when I hear a young man asking for the easiest condition, when I see him looking out for some beaten path, in which he may move on mechanically, and with the least expense of thought or feeling. The young minister sometimes desires to become a fixture in an established congregation, which is bound to its place of worship by obstinate ties of habit, and which can therefore be kept together with little effort of his own. If the congregation happens to be what is called a respectable one, that is, if it happens so far to regard the rules of worldly decorum as never to shock him by immoralities, and never to force him into any new or strenuous exertion for its recovery, so much the better. Such a minister is among the most pitiable members of the community. Happily this extreme case is rare. But the case is not rare of those, who, wishing to do good, still desire to reconcile usefulness with all the comforts of life, who shrink from the hazards, which men take in other pursuits, who want the spirit of enterprise, who prefer to reap where others have sowed, and to linger round the places of their nativity. At a time when men of other professions pour themselves into the new parts of the country, and are seeking their fortunes with buoyant spirits, and overflowing hopes, the minister seems little inclined to seek what is better than fortune in untried fields of labor. Of all men, the minister should be first to inquire, where shall I find the circumstances most fitted to wake up my whole soul, to task all my faculties, to inspire a profound interest, to carry me out of myself? I believe *you* have asked yourself this question, and I think you have answered it wisely. You have thrown yourself into a new country, where there are admirable materials, but where a congregation is to be created by your own faithfulness and zeal. Not even a foundation is laid, on which you can build. There are no mechanical habits among the people, which the minister can use as labor-saving machines, which will do much of his work for him, which will draw people to church whether he meets their wants or not. Still more, there are no rigid rules, binding you down to specific modes of action, cramping your energies, warring with your individuality. You may preach in your own way, preach from your observation of the effects produced on a free-speaking people. Tradition does not take the place of your own reason. In addition to this, you see and feel the pressing need of religious instruction, in a region where religious institutions are in their infancy. That under such circumstances, a man who starts with the true spirit will make progress, can hardly be doubted. You have peculiar trials, but in these you find impulses, which, I trust, are to carry you forward to greater usefulness, and to a higher action of the whole soul.

Boston has sometimes been called the Paradise of ministers; and undoubtedly the respect in which the profession is held, and the intellectual helps afforded here, give some reason for the appellation. But there are disadvantages also, and one in particular, to which you are not exposed. Shall I say a word of evil of this good city of Boston? Among all its virtues it does not abound in a tolerant spirit. The yoke of opinion is a heavy one, often crushing individuality of judgment and action. A censorship, unfriendly to free exertion, is exercised over the pulpit as well as over other concerns. No city in the world is governed so little by a police, and so much by mutual inspection, and what is called public sentiment. We stand more in awe of one another, than most people. Opinion is less individual, or runs more into masses, and often rules with a rod of iron. Undoubtedly opinion, when enlightened, lofty, pure, is a useful sovereign; but in the present imperfect state of society, it has its evils as well as benefits. It suppresses the grosser vices, rather than favors the higher virtues. It favors public order, rather than originality of thought, moral energy, and spiritual life. To prescribe its due bounds, is a very difficult problem. Were its restraints wholly removed, the decorum of the pulpit would be endangered; but that these restraints are excessive in this city, and especially in our denomination, that they often weigh oppressively on the young minister, and that they often take from ministers of all ages the courage, confidence, and authority which their high mission should inspire, cannot, I fear, be denied. The minister here, on entering the pulpit, too often feels, that he is to be judged, rather than to judge; that instead of meeting sinful men, who are to be warned or saved, he is to meet critics to be propitiated or disarmed. He feels, that should he trust himself to his heart, speak without book, and consequently break some law of speech, or be hurried into some daring hyperbole, he should find little mercy. Formerly Felix trembled before Paul; now the successor of Paul more frequently trembles. Foreigners generally set down as one of our distinctions, the awe in which we stand of opinion, the want of freedom of speech, the predominance of caution and calculation over impulse. This feature of our society exempts it from some dangers; and those persons who see only ruin in the reforming spirit of the times, will prize it as our best characteristic. Be this as it may, one thing is sure, that it does not give energy to the ministry, or favor the nobler action or higher products of the mind. Your situation gives you greater freedom. You preach, I understand, wholly without notes. In this you may carry your liberty too far. Writing is one of the great means of giving precision, clearness, consistency, and energy to thought. Every other sermon, I think, should be written, if circumstances allow it. But he who only preaches from notes, will never do justice to his own powers and feelings. The deepest fountains of eloquence within him will not be unsealed. He will never know the full power given him over his fellow-creatures.

The great danger to a minister at this time is the want of life, the danger of being dead while he lives. Brought up where Christianity is established, he is in danger of receiving it as a tradition. Brought up, where a routine of duty is marked out for him, and a certain style of preaching imposed, he is in danger of preaching from tradition. Ministers are strongly tempted to say what they are expected to say. Accordingly their tones and looks too often show, that they understand but superficially what is meant by their words. You see that they are talking of that which is not *real* to them. This danger of lifelessness is great in old congregations, made up of people of steady habits and respectable characters. The minister in such a case is apt to feel as if his hearers needed no mighty change, and as if his work were accomplished, when his truisms, expressed with more or less propriety, are received with due respect. He ought to feel, that the people may be spiritually dead with their regular habits, as he may be with his regular preaching; that both may need to be made alive. It is the advantage of such a situation as you are called to fill, that you can do nothing without life. A machine in a western pulpit cannot produce even the show of an effect. The people may be less enlightened than we are, more irregular in habits, more defective in character; but they must have living men to speak to them, and must hear a voice which, whether true or erring, still comes from the soul, or they cannot be brought to hear. This is no small compensation for many disadvantages.

This Life of which I speak, though easily recognised by a congregation, cannot be easily described by them, just as the most ignorant man can distinguish a living from a dead body, but knows very little in what vitality consists. A common mistake is, that Life in the minister is strong emotion. But it consists much more in the clear perception, the deep conviction of the Reality of religion, the *reality* of virtue, of man's spiritual nature, of God, of Immortality, of Heaven. The tone which most proves a minister to be alive, is that of calm, entire confidence in the *truth* of what he says, the tone of a man who speaks of what he has seen and handled, the peculiar tone which belongs to one who has come fresh from what he describes, to whom the future world is as substantial as the present, who does not echo what others say of the human soul, but feels his own spiritual nature as others feel their bodies, and to whom God is as truly present as the nearest fellow-creature. Strong emotion in the pulpit is too often a fever caught by sympathy, or a fervor worked up for the occasion, or a sensibility belonging more to the nerves than the mind, and excited by vague views which fade away before the calm reason. Hence enthusiasts often become skeptics. The great sign of life is to see and feel, that there is something real, substantial, immortal, in Christian virtue; to be conscious of the reality and nearness of your relations to God and the invisible world. This is the life, which the minister needs, and which it is his great work to communicate. My hope is, that by sending ministers into new situations, where new wants cry to them for supply, a living power may be awakened, to which a long established routine of labors is not favorable, and which may spread beyond them to their brethren.

I pass now to another subject. We hear much of the Catholic religion in the West, and of its threatening progress. There are not a few here who look upon this alarm as a pious fraud, who consider the cry of "No Popery," as set up by a particular sect to attract to itself distinction and funds; but fear is so natural, and a panic spreads so easily, that I see no necessity of resorting to so unkind an explanation. It must be confessed that Protestantism enters on the warfare with Popery under some disadvantages, and may be expected to betray some consciousness of weakness. Most Protestant sects are built on the Papal foundation. Their creeds and excommunications embody the grand idea of Infallibility, as truly as the decrees of Trent and the Vatican; and if the people must choose between different infallibilities, there is much to incline them to that of Rome. This has age, the majority of votes, more daring assumption, and bolder denunciation on its side. The popes of our different sects are certainly less imposing to the imagination than the Pope at Rome.

I trust, however, that, with these advantages, Catholicism is still not very formidable. It has something more to do, than to fight with sects; its great foe is the progress of society. The creation of dark times, it cannot stand before the light. In this country in particular, it finds no coadjutors in any circumstances, passions, or institutions. Catholicism is immovable, and movement and innovation are the order of the day. It rejects the idea of melioration, and the passion for improvement is inflaming all minds. It takes its stand in the Past, and this generation are living in the Future. It clings to forms, which the mind has outgrown. It will not modify doctrines in which the intelligence of the age cannot but recognise the stamp of former ignorance. It forbids free inquiry, and inquiry is the spirit of the age, the boldest inquiry, stopping nowhere, invading every region of thought. Catholicism wrests from the people the right to choose their own ministers, and the right of election is the very essence of our institutions. It establishes an aristocratical priesthood, and the whole people are steeped in republicanism. It withholds the Scriptures, and the age is a reading one, and reads the more what is forbidden. Catholicism cannot comprehend that the past is not the present, cannot comprehend the revolution which the art of printing and the revival of learning have effected. Its memory seems not to come down lower than the middle ages. It aims to impose restraints on thought, which were comparatively easy before the press was set in motion, and labors to shore up institutions, in utter unconsciousness that the state of society, and the modes of thinking on which they rested, have passed away.

The political revolutions of the times are enough to seal the death-warrant of Catholicism, but it has to encounter a far more important spiritual revolution. Catholicism belongs to what may be called the dogmatical age of Christianity, the age when it was thought our religion might be distilled into a creed, which would prove an elixir of life to whoever would swallow it. We have now come to learn, that Christianity is not a dogma, but a spirit, that its essence is the spirit of its divine founder, that it is of little importance what church a man belongs to, or what formula of doctrines he subscribes, that nothing is important but the supreme love, choice, pursuit of moral perfection, shining forth in the life and teachings of Christ. This is the true Catholic doctrine, the creed of the true Church, gathering into one spiritual communion all good and holy men of all ages and regions, and destined to break down all the earthly clay-built, gloomy barriers, which now separate the good from one another. To this great idea of reason and revelation, of the understanding and heart, of experience and philosophy, to this great truth of an advanced civilization, Catholicism stands in direct hostility. How sure then is its fall!

The great foe of the Romish Church is not the theologian. *He* might be imprisoned, chained, burned. It is human nature waking up to a consciousness of its powers, catching a glimpse of the perfection for which it was made, beginning to respect itself, thirsting for free action and developement, learning through a deep consciousness that there is something diviner than forms, or churches, or creeds, recognising in Jesus Christ its own celestial model, and claiming kindred with all wno have caught any portion of his spiritual life and disinterested love; here, here is the great enemy of Catholicism. I look confidently to the ineradicable, ever-unfolding principles of human nature, for the victory over all superstitions. Reason and conscience, the powers by which we discern the true and the right, are immortal as their author. Oppressed for ages, they yet live. Like the central fires of the earth, they can heave up mountains. It is encouraging to see under what burdens and clouds they have made their way; and we must remember, that, by every new developement, they are brought more into contact with the life-giving, omnipotent truth and character of Jesus Christ. It makes me smile, to hear immortality claimed for Catholicism or Protestantism, or for any past interpretations of Christianity; as if the human soul had exhausted itself in its infant efforts, or as if the men of one or a few generations could bind the energy of human thought and affection for ever. A theology at war with the laws of physical nature would be a battle of no doubtful issue. The laws of our spiritual nature give still less chance of success to the system, which would thwart or stay them. The progress of the individual and of society, which has shaken the throne of Rome, is not an accident, not an irregular spasmodic effort, but the natural movement of the soul. Catholicism must fall before it. In truth, it is very much fallen already. It exists, and will long exist as an outward institution. But compare the Catholicism of an intelligent man of the nineteenth century with what it was in the tenth. The name, the letter remain, — how changed the spirit! The silent reform spreading in the very bosom of Catholicism, is as important as the reformation of the sixteenth century, and in truth more effectual.

Catholicism has always hoped for victory over Protestantism, on the ground of the dissensions of Protestants. But its anticipations have not approached fulfilment, and they show us how the most sagacious err, when they attempt to read futurity. I have long since learned to hear with composure the auguries of the worldy wise. The truth is, that the dissensions of Protestantism go far to constitute its strength. Through them its spirit, which is freedom, the only spirit which Rome cannot conquer, is kept alive. Had its members been organized, and bound into a single church, it would have become a despotism as unrelenting, and corrupt, and hopeless as Rome. But this is not all. Protestantism, by being broken into a great variety of sects, has adapted itself to the various modifications of human nature. Every sect has embodied religion in a form suited to some large class of minds. It has met some want, answered to some great principle of the soul, and thus every new denomination has been a new standard, under which to gather and hold fast a host against Rome. One of the great arts, by which Catholicism spread and secured its dominion, was its wonderful flexibleness, its most skilful adaptation of itself to the different tastes, passions, wants of men; and to this means of influence and dominion, Protestantism could oppose nothing, but variety of sects. I do not recollect, that I ever saw this feature of Catholicism brought out distinctly, and yet nothing in the system has impressed me more strongly. The Romish religion calls itself one, but it has a singular variety of forms and aspects. For the lover of forms and outward religion, it has a gorgeous ritual. To the mere man of the world, it shows a pope on the throne, bishops in palaces, and all the splendor of earthly dominion. At the same time, for the self-denying, ascetic, mystical, and fanatical, it has all the forms of monastic life. To him, who would scourge himself into godliness, it offers a whip. For him who would starve himself into spirituality, it provides the mendicant convents of St. Francis. For the anchorite, it prepares the death-like silence of La Trappe. To the passionate young woman, it presents the raptures of St. Theresa, and the marriage of St. Catharine with her Saviour. For the restless pilgrim, whose piety needs greater variety than the cell of the monk, it offers shrines, tombs, relics, and other holy places in Christian lands, and above all, the holy sepulchre near Calvary. To the generous, sympathizing enthusiast, it opens some fraternity or sisterhood of Charity. To him, who inclines to take heaven by violence, it gives as much penance as he can ask; and to the mass of men, who wish to reconcile the two worlds, it promises a purgatory, so far softened down by the masses of the priest and the prayers of the faithful, that its fires can be anticipated without overwhelming dread. This composition of forces in the Romish Church seems to me a wonderful monument of skill. When, in Rome, the traveller sees by the side of the purple, lackeyed cardinal, the begging friar; when, under the arches of St. Peter, he sees a coarsely dressed monk holding forth to a ragged crowd; or when, beneath a Franciscan church, adorned with the most precious works of art, he meets a charnel-house, where the bones of the dead brethren are built into walls, between which the living walk to read their mortality, he is amazed, if he gives himself time for reflection, at the infinite variety of machinery which Catholicism has brought to bear on the human mind; at the sagacity with which it has adapted itself to the various tastes and propensities of human nature. Protestantism attains this end by more simple, natural, and in the main more effectual ways. All the great principles of our nature are represented in different sects, which have on the whole a keener passion for self-aggrandizement than the various orders in the Romish Church, and thus men of all varieties of mind find something congenial, find a class to sympathize with.

And, here, I cannot but observe, that Episcopacy renders good service to the Protestant cause. Without being thoroughly Protestant, it is especially efficient against Catholicism; and this good work it does by its very proximity to Rome. From the wide diffusion and long continuance of Catholicism, we may be sure that it embodies some great idea, and answers some want, which is early and powerfully developed in the progress of civilization. There is of consequence a tendency to Catholicism in society, though more and more restrained by higher tendencies. Happily, Episcopacy is built on the same great idea, but expresses it in a more limited and rational form. It is Catholicism improved, or mother church with a lower mitre and a less royal air; and by meeting the want which carries men to the Romish Church, stops numbers on their way to it. Hence, Catholicism hates Episcopacy more than any other form of dissent. Sects are apt to hate each other in proportion to their proximity. The old proverb that two of a trade cannot agree, applies to religion as strongly as to common life. — The amount is, that Catholicism derives little aid from Protestant divisions. In an age as unimproved in Christianity as the present, these divisions are promising symptoms. They prevent men from settling down in a rude Christianity. They keep alive inquiry and zeal. They are essential to freedom and progress. Without these, Protestantism would be only a new edition of Catholicism; and the old pope would certainly beat any new one who could be arrayed against him.

Do you ask me, how I think Catholicism may be most successfully opposed? I know but one way. Spread just, natural, ennobling views of religion. Lift men above Catholicism, by showing them the great spiritual purpose of Christianity. Violence will avail nothing. Romanism cannot be burned down, like the convent at Charlestown. That outrage bound every Catholic faster to his church, and attracted to it the sympathies of the good. Neither is Popery to be subdued by virulence and abuse. The priest can call as hard names as the Protestant pastor. Neither do I think that any thing is to be gained by borrowing from the Catholic Church her forms, and similar means of influence. Borrowed forms are peculiarly formal. No sect will be benefited by forms which do not grow from its own spirit. A sect which has true life, will seize by instinct the emblems and rites, which are in accordance with itself; and, without life, it will only find in borrowed rites its winding-sheet. It is not uncommon to hear persons who visit Catholic countries, recommending the introduction of this or that usage of Romanism among ourselves. For example, they enter Catholic churches and see at all hours worshippers before one or another altar, and contrasting with this the desertion of our houses of worship during the week, doubt whether we are as pious, and wish to open the doors of our sanctuaries, that Protestants may at all hours approve themselves as devoted as the Papists. Now such recommendations show a misconception of the true foundation and spirit of Roman usages. In the case before us, nothing is more natural than that Catholics should go to churches or public places to pray. In the first place, in the southern countries of Europe, where Catholicism first took its form, the people live in public. They are an outdoor people. Their domestic occupations go on in the outward air. That they should perform their private devotions in public, is in harmony with all their habits. What a violence it would be to ours! In the next place, the Catholic believes that the church has a peculiar sanctity. A prayer offered from its floor finds its way to heaven more easily than from any other spot. The pernicious superstition of his religion carries him to do the work of his religion in one consecrated place, and therefore he does it the less elsewhere. Again: Catholic churches are attractive from the miraculous virtue ascribed to the images which are worshipped there. Strange, monstrous as the superstition is, yet nothing is more common in Catholic countries than the ascription of this or that supernatural agency to one or another shrine or statue. A saint, worshipped at one place, or under one image, will do more, than if worshipped elsewhere. I recollect asking an Italian, why a certain church of rather humble appearance, in a large city, was so much frequented. He smiled, and told me, that the Virgin, who was adored there, was thought particularly propitious to those who had bought tickets in the lottery. Once more, we can easily conceive why visiting the churches, for daily prayer, has been encouraged by the priesthood. The usage brought the multitude still more under priestly power, and taught them to associate their most secret aspirations of piety with the church. Who, that takes all these circumstances into consideration, can expect Protestants to imitate the Catholics in frequenting the church for secret devotion, or can wish it? Has not Jesus said, "When thou prayest, go into thy closet, and shut thy door, and pray to thy Father, who seeth in secret"? Catholicism says, "When thou prayest, go into the public church, and pray before the multitude." Of the little efficacy of this worship we have too painful proofs. The worship of the churches of Italy is directed chiefly to the Virgin. She is worshipped as *the Virgin.* The great idea of this Catholic deity is purity, chastity; and yet, unless all travellers deceive us, the country where she is worshipped is disfigured by licentiousness, beyond all countries of the civilized world. I return to my position. We need borrow nothing from Catholicism. Episcopacy retained (did not borrow) as much of the ritual of that church as is wanted in the present age, for those among us who have Catholic propensities. Other sects, if they need forms, must originate them, and this they must do not mechanically, but from the promptings of the spiritual life, from a thirst for new modes of manifesting their religious hopes and aspirations. Woe to that church, which looks round for forms to wake it up to spiritual life. The dying man is not to be revived by a new dress, however graceful. The disease of a languid sect is too deep to be healed by ceremonies. It needs deeper modes of cure. Let it get life, and it will naturally create the emblems or rites which it needs to express and maintain its spiritual force.

The great instrument of influence and dominion in the Catholic Church, is one which we should shudder to borrow, but which may still give important hints as to the means of promoting religion. I refer to Confession. Nothing too bad can be said of this. By laying open the secrets of all hearts to the priest, it makes the priest the master of all. Still, to a good man it gives the power of doing good, a power, which, I doubt not, is often conscientiously used. It gives to the religious teacher an access to men's minds and conscience, such as the pulpit does not furnish. Instead of scattering generalities among the crowd, he can administer to each soul the very instruction, warning, encouragement it needs. In Catholic countries there is little preaching, nor is it necessary. The confessional is far more powerful than the pulpit. And what do we learn from this? That Protestants should adopt confession? No. But the question arises, whether the great principle of confession, that on which its power rests, viz. access to the individual mind, may not be used more than it is by Protestant teachers; whether such access may not be gained by honorable and generous means, and so used as to be guarded against abuse. Preaching is now our chief reliance; but preaching is an arrow which shoots over many heads, and flies wide of the hearts of more. Its aim is too vague to do much execution. It is melancholy to think how little clear knowledge on the subject of duty and religion, is communicated by the pulpit, and how often the emotion which it excites, for want of clear views, for want of wisdom, runs into morbidness or excess. No art, no science is taught so vaguely as religion from the pulpit. No book is so read or expounded as the Bible is, that is, in minute fragments, and without those helps of method, by which all other branches are taught. Is not a freer, easier, opener communication with his pupils needed, than the minister does or can hold from the pulpit? Should not modes of teaching and intercourse be adopted, by which he can administer truth to different minds, according to their various capacities and wants. Must not he rely less on preaching, and more on more familiar communication.

This question becomes of more importance, because it is very plain that preaching is becoming less and less efficacious. Preaching is not what it was in the first age of Christianity. Then, when there was no printing, comparatively no reading, Christianity could only be spread by the living voice. Hence to preach became synonymous with teaching. It was the great means of access to the multitude. Now the press preaches incomparably more than the pulpit. Through this, all are permitted to preach. Woman, if she may not speak in the church, may speak from the printing room, and her touching expositions of religion, not learned in theological institutions, but in the schools of affection, of sorrow, of experience, of domestic change, sometimes make their way to the heart more surely than the minister's homilies. The result is, that preaching does not hold the place now, which it had in dark and unrefined ages. The minister addresses from his pulpit many as well educated as himself, and almost every parishioner has at home better sermons than he hears in public. The minister, too, has competitors in the laity, as they are called, who very wisely refuse to leave to him the monopoly of public speaking, and who are encroaching on his province more and more. In this altered condition of the world, the ministry is to undergo important changes. What they must be, I have not time now to inquire. I will only say, that the vagueness which belongs to so much religious instruction from the pulpit, must give place to a teaching which shall meet more the wants of the individual, and the wants of the present state of society. Great principles must be expounded in accommodation to different ages, capacities, stages of improvement, and an intercourse be established by which all classes may be helped to apply them to their own particular conditions. How shall Christianity be brought to bear on the individual, and on society at the present moment, in its present struggles? This is the great question to be solved, and the reply to it will determine the form which the Christian ministry is to take. I imagine, that in seeking the solution of this problem, it will be discovered, that the ministry must have greater freedom than in past times. It will be discovered, that the individual minister must not be rigidly tied down to certain established modes of operation, that he must not be required to cast his preaching into the old mould, to circumscribe himself to the old topics, to keep in motion a machinery which others have invented, but that he will do most good if left to work according to his own nature, according to the promptings of the Holy Spirit within his own breast. I imagine it will be discovered, that, as justice may be administered without a wig, and the executive function without a crown or sceptre, so Christianity may be administered in more natural and less formal ways than have prevailed, and that the minister, in growing less technical, will find religion becoming, to himself and others, a more living reality. I imagine, that our present religious organizations will silently melt away, and that hierarchies will be found no more necessary for religion than for literature, science, medicine, law, or the elegant and useful arts. But I will check these imaginings. The point from which I started was, that Catholicism might teach us one element of an effectual ministry, that the Protestant teacher needs and should seek access to the individual mind, beyond what he now possesses; and the point at which I stop is, that this access is to be so sought and so used, as not to infringe religious liberty, the rights of private judgment, the free action of the individual mind. Nothing but this liberty can secure it from the terrible abuse to which it has been exposed in the Catholic Church.

In the free remarks, which I have now made on certain denominations of Christians, I have been influenced by no unkindness or disrespect towards the individuals who compose them. In all sects I recognise joyfully true disciples of the common Master. Catholicism boasts of some of the best and greatest names in history, so does Episcopacy, so Presbyterianism, &c. I exclude none. I know that Christianity is mighty enough to accomplish its end in all. I cannot however speak of religious, any more than of political parties, without betraying the little respect I have for them as parties. There is no portion of human history more humbling than that of sects. When I meditate on the grand moral, spiritual purpose of Christianity, in which all its glory consists; when I consider how plainly Christianity attaches importance to nothing but to the moral excellence, the disinterested, divine virtue, which was embodied in the teaching and life of its founder; and when from this position I look down on the sects which have figured, and now figure in the church; when I see them making such a stir about matters generally so unessential; when I see them seizing on a disputed and disputable doctrine, making it a watch-word, a test of God's favor, a bond of communion, a ground of self-complacency, a badge of peculiar holiness, a warrant for condemning its rejectors, however imbued with the spirit of Christ; when I see them overlooking the weightier matters of the law, and laying infinite stress here on a bishop and prayer-book, there on the quantity of water applied in baptism, and there on some dark solution of an incomprehensible article of faith; when I see the mock dignity of their exclusive claims to truth, to churchship, to the promises of God's word; when I hear the mimic thunderbolts of denunciation and excommunication, which they delight to hurl; when I consider how their deep theology, in proportion as it is examined, evaporates into words, how many opposite and extravagant notions are covered by the same broad shield of mystery and tradition, and how commonly the persuasion of infallibility is proportioned to the absurdity of the creed; when I consider these things, and other matters of like import, I am lost in amazement at the amount of arrogant folly, of self-complacent intolerance, of almost incredible blindness to the end and essence of Christianity, which the history of sects reveals. I have indeed profound respect for individuals in all communions of Christians. But on sects, and on the spirit of sects, I *must* be allowed to look with grief, shame, pity, I had almost said, contempt. In passing these censures, I claim no superiority. I am sure there are thousands of all sects, who think and feel as I do in this particular, and who, far from claiming superior intelligence, are distinguished by following out the plain dictates, the natural impulses, and spontaneous judgments of conscience and common sense.

It is time for me to finish this letter, which indeed has grown under my hands beyond all reasonable bounds. But I must add a line or two in reply to your invitation to visit you. You say, that Kentucky will not exclude me for my opinions on slavery. I rejoice to hear it, not for my own sake, but for the sake of the country. I rejoice in a tolerant spirit, wherever manifested. What you say accords with what I have heard, of the frank, liberal character of Kentucky. All our accounts of the West make me desire to visit it. I desire to see nature under new aspects; but still more to see a new form of society. I hear of the defects of the West; but I learn that a man there feels himself to be a man, that he has a self-respect which is not always to be found in older communities, that he speaks his mind freely, that he acts more from generous impulses, and less from selfish calculations. These are good tidings. I rejoice that the intercourse between the East and West is increasing. Both will profit. The West may learn from us the love of order, the arts which adorn and cheer life, the institutions of education and religion, which lie at the foundation of our greatness, and may give us in return the energies and virtues which belong to and distinguish a fresher state of society. Such exchanges I regard as the most precious fruits of the Union, worth more than exchanges of products of industry, and they will do more to bind us together as one people.

You press me to come and preach in your part of the country. I should do it cheerfully if I could. It would rejoice me to bear a testimony, however feeble, to great truths in your new settlements. I confess, however, that I fear, that my education would unfit me for great usefulness among you. I fear that the habits, rules, and criticisms, under which I have grown up, and almost grown old, have not left me the freedom and courage which are needed in the style of address best suited to the Western people. I have fought against these chains. I have labored to be a free man, but in the state of the ministry and of society here, freedom is a hard acquisition. I hope the rising generation will gain it more easily and abundantly than their fathers.

I have only to add, my young brother, my best wishes for your usefulness. I do not ask for you enjoyment. I ask for you something better and greater, something which includes it, even a spirit to live and die for a cause, which is dearer than your own enjoyment. If I were called to give you one rule, which your situation demands above all others, it would be this. Live a life of faith and hope. Believe in God's great purposes towards the human race. Believe in the mighty power of truth and love. Believe in the omnipotence of Christianity. Believe that Christ lived and died to breathe into his church and into society a diviner spirit than now exists. Believe in the capacities and greatness of human nature. Believe that the celestial virtue, revealed in the life and teaching of Jesus Christ, is not a bright vision for barren admiration, but is to become a reality in your own and others' souls. Carry to your work a trustful spirit. Do not waste your breath in wailing over the times. Strive to make them better. Do not be disheartened by evils. Feel through your whole soul, that evil is not the mightiest power in the universe, that it is permitted only to call forth the energy of love, wisdom, persuasion, and prayer for its removal. Settle it in your mind, that a minister can never speak an effectual word without faith. Be strong in the Lord and the power of his might. Allow me to say, that I have a good hope of you. I learned some time ago, from one of your dear friends, that you comprehended the grandeur of your work as a Christian minister. I learned that the pulpit, from which a divinely moved teacher communicates everlasting truths, seemed to you more glorious than a throne. I learned, that you had come to understand what is the greatest power which God gives to man, the power of acting generously on the soul of his brother; of communicating to others a divine spirit, of awakening in others a heavenly life, which is to outlive the stars. I then felt that you would not labor in vain. You have indeed peculiar trials. You are dwelling far from your brethren, but there is a sense of God's presence more cheering than the dearest human society. There is a consciousness of working with God, more strengthening than all human coöperation. There is a sight, granted to the pure mind, of the cross of Christ, which makes privations and sufferings in the cause of his truth seem light, which makes us sometimes to rejoice in tribulation, like the primitive heroes of our faith. My young brother, I wish you these blessings. What else ought I to wish for you?

This letter, you will perceive, is written in great haste. The opinions indeed have been deliberately formed; but they probably might have been expressed with greater caution. If it will serve, in your judgment, the cause of truth, freedom, and religion, you are at liberty to insert it in your work.

Your sincere friend,

William E. Channing.

EXTRACTS FROM A LETTER

ON

CREEDS.

ON CREEDS.

My aversion to human creeds as bonds of Christian union, as conditions of Christian fellowship, as means of fastening chains on men's minds, constantly gains strength.

My first objection to them is, that they separate us from Jesus Christ. To whom am I to go for my knowledge of the Christian religion, but to the Great Teacher, to the Son of God, to him in whom the fulness of the divinity dwelt. This is my great privilege as a Christian, that I may sit at the feet not of a human but divine master, that I may repair to him in whom truth lived and spoke without a mixture of error; who was eminently the Wisdom of God and the light of the world. And shall man dare to interpose between me and my heavenly guide and Saviour, and prescribe to me the articles of my Christian faith? What is the state of mind in which I shall best learn the truth? It is that, in which I forsake all other teachers for Christ, in which my mind is brought nearest to him; it is that in which I lay myself open most entirely to the impressions of his mind. Let me go to Jesus with a human voice sounding in my ears, and telling me what I must hear from the Great Teacher, and how can I listen to him in singleness of heart? All Protestant sects indeed tell the learner to listen to Jesus Christ; but most of them shout around him their own articles so vehemently and imperiously, that the voice of the heavenly master is well nigh drowned. He is told to listen to Christ, but told that he will be damned, if he receives any lessons but such as are taught in the creed. He is told that Christ's word is alone infallible, but that unless it is received as interpreted by fallible men, he will be excluded from the communion of Christians. This is what shocks me in the creed-maker. He interposes himself between me and my Saviour. He dares not trust me alone with Jesus. He dares not leave me to the word of God. This I cannot endure. The nearest possible communication with the mind of Christ, is my great privilege as a Christian. I must learn Christ's truth from Christ himself, as he speaks in the records of his life, and in the men whom he trained up and supernaturally prepared to be his witnesses to the world. On what ground, I ask, do the creed-makers demand assent to their articles as condition of church membership or salvation? What has conferred on them infallibility? "Show me your proofs," I say to them, "of Christ speaking in you. Work some miracle. Utter some prophecy. Show me something divine in you, which other men do not possess. Is it possible, that you are unaided men, like myself, having no more right to interpret the New Testament than myself, and that you yet exalt your interpretations as infallible standards of truth, and the necessary conditions of salvation. Stand out of my path. I wish to go to the master. Have you words of greater power than his?

Can you speak to the human conscience or heart in a mightier voice than he? What is it which emboldens you to tell me what I must learn of Christ or be lost?"

I cannot but look on human creeds with feelings approaching contempt. When I bring them into contrast with the New Testament, into what insignificance do they sink! What are they? Skeletons, freezing abstractions, metaphysical expressions of unintelligible dogmas; and these I am to regard as the expositions of the fresh, living, infinite truth which came from Jesus! I might with equal propriety be required to hear and receive the lispings of infancy as the expressions of wisdom. Creeds are to the Scriptures, what rush-lights are to the sun. The creed-maker defines Jesus in half a dozen lines, perhaps in metaphysical terms, and calls me to assent to this account of my Saviour. I learn less of Christ by this process, than I should learn of the sun, by being told that this glorious luminary is a circle about a foot in diameter. There is but one way of knowing Christ. We must place ourselves near him, see him, hear him, follow him from his cross to the heavens, sympathize with him and obey him, and thus catch clear and bright glimpses of his divine glory.

Christian Truth is Infinite. Who can think of shutting it up in a few lines of an abstract creed? You might as well compress the boundless atmosphere, the fire, the all-pervading light, the free winds of the universe, into separate parcels, and weigh and label them, as break up Christianity into a few propositions. Christianity is freer, more illimitable, than the light or the winds. It is too mighty to be bound down by man's puny hands. It is a spirit rather than a rigid doctrine, the spirit of boundless love. The Infinite cannot be defined and measured out like a human manufacture. It cannot be reduced to a system. It cannot be comprehended in a set of precise ideas. It is to be felt rather than described. The spiritual impressions which a true Christian receives from the character and teachings of Christ, and in which the chief efficacy of the religion lies, can be poorly brought out in words. Words are but brief, rude hints of a Christian's mind. His thoughts and feelings overflow them. To those who feel as he does, he can make himself known; for such can understand the tones of the heart; but he can no more lay down his religion in a series of abstract propositions, than he can make known in a few vague terms the expressive features and inmost soul of a much-loved friend. It has been the fault of all sects, that they have been too anxious to define their religion. They have labored to circumscribe the infinite. Christianity, as it exists in the mind of the true disciple, is not made up of fragments, of separate ideas which he can express in detached propositions. It is a vast and ever-unfolding whole, pervaded by one spirit, each precept and doctrine deriving its vitality from its union with all. When I see this generous, heavenly doctrine compressed and cramped in human creeds, I feel as I should were I to see screws and chains applied to the countenance and limbs of a noble fellow-creature, deforming and destroying one of the most beautiful works of God.

From the Infinity of Christian truth, of which I have spoken, it follows that our views of it must always be very imperfect, and ought to be continually enlarged. The wisest theologians are children who have caught but faint glimpses of the religion; who have taken but their first lessons; and whose business it is "to grow in the knowledge of Jesus Christ." Need I say how hostile to this growth is a fixed creed, beyond which we must never wander? Such a religion as Christ's demands the highest possible activity and freedom of the soul. Every new gleam of light should be welcomed with joy. Every hint should be followed out with eagerness. Every whisper of the divine voice in the soul should be heard. The love of Christian truth should be so intense, as to make us willing to part with all other things for a better comprehension of it. Who does not see that human creeds, setting bounds to thought, and telling us where all inquiry must stop, tend to repress this holy zeal, to shut our eyes on new illumination, to hem us within the beaten paths of man's construction, to arrest that perpetual progress which is the life and glory of an immortal mind.

It is another and great objection to creeds, that, wherever they acquire authority, they interfere with that simplicity and godly sincerity, on which the efficacy of religious teaching very much depends. That a minister should speak with power, it is important that he should speak from his own soul, and not studiously conform himself to modes of speaking which others have adopted. It is important that he should give out the truth in the very form in which it presents itself to his mind, in the very words which offer themselves spontaneously as the clothing of his thoughts. To express our own minds frankly, directly, fearlessly, is the way to reach other minds. Now it is the effect of creeds to check this free utterance of thought. The minister must seek words which will not clash with the consecrated articles of his church. If new ideas spring up in his mind, not altogether consonant with what the creed-monger has established, he must cover them with misty language. If he happen to doubt the standard of his church, he must strain its phraseology, must force it beyond its obvious import, that he may give his assent to it without departures from truth. All these processes must have a blighting effect on the mind and heart. They impair self-respect. They cloud the intellectual eye. They accustom men to tamper with truth. In proportion as a man dilutes his thought and suppresses his conviction, to save his orthodoxy from suspicion; in proportion as he borrows his words from others, instead of speaking in his own tongue; in proportion as he distorts language from its common use, that he may stand well with his party; in that proportion he clouds and degrades his intellect, as well as undermines the manliness and integrity of his character. How deeply do I commiserate the minister, who, in the warmth and freshness of youth, is visited with glimpses of higher truth than is embodied in the creed, but who dares not be just to himself, and is made to echo what is not the simple, natural expression of his own mind! Better were it for us to beg our bread and clothe ourselves in rags, than to part with Christian simplicity and frankness. Better for a minister to preach in barns or the open air, where he may speak the truth from the fulness of his soul, than to lift up in cathedrals, amidst pomp and wealth, a voice which is not true to his inward thoughts. If they who wear the chains of creeds, once knew the happiness of breathing the air of freedom, and of moving with an unincumbered spirit, no wealth or power in the world's gift would bribe them to part with their spiritual liberty.

Another sad effect of creeds is, that they favor unbelief. It is not the object of a creed to express the simple truths of our religion, though in these its efficiency chiefly lies, but to embody and decree those mysteries about which Christians have been contending. I use the word "mysteries," not in the Scriptural but popular sense, as meaning doctrines which give a shock to the reason and seem to contradict some acknowledged truth. Such mysteries are the staples of creeds. The celestial virtues of Christ's character, these are not inserted into articles of faith. On the contrary, doctrines which from their darkness or unintelligibleness have provoked controversy, and which owe their importance very much to the circumstance of having been fought for or fought against for ages, these are thrown by the creed-makers into the foremost ranks of the religion, and made its especial representatives. Christianity as set forth in creeds is a propounder of dark sayings, of riddles, of knotty propositions, of apparent contradictions. Who, on reading these standards, would catch a glimpse of the simple, pure, benevolent, practical character of Christianity? And what is the result? Christianity becoming identified, by means of creeds, with so many dark doctrines, is looked on by many as a subject for theologians to quarrel about, but too thorny or perplexed for common minds, while it is spurned by many more as an insult on human reason, as a triumph of fanaticism over common sense.

It is a little remarkable that most creeds, whilst they abound in mysteries of human creation, have renounced the great mystery of religion. There is in religion a great mystery. I refer to the doctrine of Free-will or moral liberty. How to reconcile this with God's foreknowledge and human dependence, is a question which has perplexed the greatest minds. It is probable that much of the obscurity arises from our applying to God the same kind of foreknowledge as men possess by their acquaintance with causes, and from our supposing the Supreme Being to bear the same relation to time as man. It is probable that juster views on these subjects will relieve the freedom of the will from some of its difficulties. Still the difficulties attending it are great. It is a mystery in the popular sense of the word. Now is it not strange that theologians who have made and swallowed so many other mysteries, have generally rejected this, and rejected it on the ground of objections less formidable than those which may be urged against their own inventions? A large part of the Protestant world have sacrificed man's freedom of will to God's foreknowledge and sovereignty, thus virtually subverting all religion, all duty, all responsibility. They have made man a machine, and destroyed the great distinction between him and the brute. There seems a fatality attending creeds. After burdening Christianity with mysteries of which it is as innocent as the unborn child, they have generally renounced the real mystery of religion, of human nature. They have subverted the foundation of moral government, by taking from man the only capacity which makes him responsible, and in this way have fixed on the commands and threatenings of God the character of a cruel despotism. What a lesson against man's attempting to impose his wisdom on his fellow-creatures as the truth of God!

THE CHURCH.

A DISCOURSE

DELIVERED IN THE

FIRST CONGREGATIONAL UNITARIAN CHURCH OF PHILADELPHIA,

SUNDAY, MAY 30, 1841.

DISCOURSE ON THE CHURCH.

MATTHEW vii. 21–27: "Not every one that saith unto me, Lord, Lord, shall enter into the kingdom of heaven; but he that doeth the will of my Father which is in heaven. Many will say to me in that day, Lord, Lord, have we not prophesied in thy name? and in thy name have cast out devils? and in thy name done many wonderful works? And then will I profess unto them, I never knew you; depart from me, ye that work iniquity.

Therefore, whosoever heareth these sayings of mine, and doeth them, I will liken him unto a wise man, which built his house upon a rock; and the rain descended, and the floods came, and the winds blew, and beat upon that house, and it fell not; for it was founded upon a rock.

And every one that heareth these sayings of mine, and doeth them not, shall be likened unto a foolish man, which built his house upon the sand; and the rain descended, and the floods came, and the winds blew, and beat upon that house, and it fell; and great was the fall of it."

THESE words, which form the conclusion of Christ's Sermon on the Mount, teach a great truth, namely, that there is but one thing essential in religion, and this is, the doing of God's will, the doing of those sayings or precepts of Christ which constitute the substance of that memorable discourse. We learn that it will avail us nothing to call Christ, Lord, Lord, to profess ourselves his disciples, to hear his words, to teach in his name, to take our place in his church, or even to do wonderful works or miracles in attestation of his truth, if we neglect to cherish the spirit and virtues of his religion. God heeds not what we say, but what we are, and what we do. The subjection of our wills to the Divine, the mortification of sensual and selfish propensities, the cultivation of supreme love to God, and of universal justice and charity towards our neighbour, — this, this is the very essence of religion; this alone places us on a rock; this is the end, the supreme and ultimate good, and is to be prized and sought above all other things.

This is a truth as simple as it is grand. The child can understand it; and yet men, in all ages, have contrived to overlook it; have contrived to find substitutes for purity of heart and life; have hoped by some other means to commend themselves to God, to enter the kingdom of heaven. Forms, creeds, churches, the priesthood, the sacraments, these and other things have been exalted into supremacy. The grand and only qualification for heaven, that which in itself is heaven, the virtue and the spirit of Jesus Christ, has been obscured, depreciated; whilst assent to certain mysteries, or union with certain churches, has been thought the narrow way that leads to life. I have not time in a single discourse to expose all the delusions which have spread on this subject. I shall confine myself to one, which is not limited to the past, but too rife in our own times.

There has always existed, and still exists, a disposition to attach undue importance to "the church" which a man belongs to. To be a member of "the true church" has been insisted on as essential to human salvation. Multitudes have sought comfort, and not seldom found their ruin, in the notion, that they were embraced in the motherly arms of "the true church"; for with this they have been satisfied. Professed Christians have fought about "the church" as if it were a matter of life and death. The Roman Catholic shuts the gate of heaven on you because you will not enter his "church." Among the Protestants are those who tell you that the promises of Christianity do not belong to you, be your character what it may, unless you receive the Christian ordinances from the ministers of their "church." Salvation is made to flow through a certain priesthood, through an hereditary order, through particular rites administered by consecrated functionaries. Even among denominations in which such exclusive claims are not set up you will still meet the idea, that a man is safer in their particular "church" than elsewhere; so that something distinct from Christian purity of heart and life is made the way of salvation.

This error I wish to expose. I wish to show that Christ's spirit, Christ's virtue, or "the doing of the Sermon on the Mount," is the great end of our religion, the only essential thing, and that all other things are important only as ministering to this. I know, indeed, that very many acknowledge the doctrine now expressed. But too often their conviction is not deep and living, and it is impaired by superstitious notions of some mysterious saving influence in "the church," or in some other foreign agency. To meet these erroneous tendencies, I shall not undertake to prove in a formal way, by logical process, the supreme importance, blessedness, and glory of righteousness, of sanctity, of love towards God and man, or to prove that nothing else is indispensable. This truth shines by its own light. It runs through the whole

New Testament; and is a gospel written in the soul by a divine hand. To vindicate it against the claims set up for "the church," nothing is needed but to offer a few plain remarks in the order in which they rise up of themselves to my mind.

I begin with the remark, that in the Sermon on the Mount Jesus said nothing about the "church"; nor do we find him, or his disciples, laying down anywhere a definite plan for its organization, or a ritual for its worship. Nor ought this to surprise us. It was the very thing to be expected in such a religion as Christianity. Judaism was intended to educate a particular nation, half civilized and surrounded with the grossest idolatry, and accordingly it hedged them in by multiplied and rigid forms. But Christianity proposes, as its grand aim, to spread the inward, spiritual worship of God through all nations, in all stages of society, under all varieties of climate, government, and condition; and such a religion cannot be expected to confine itself to any particular outward shape. Especially when we consider that it is destined to endure through all ages, to act on all, to blend itself with new forms of society and with the highest improvements of the race, it cannot be expected to ordain an immutable mode of administration, but must leave its modes of worship and communion to conform themselves silently and gradually to the wants and progress of humanity. The rites and arrangements which suit one period lose their significance or efficiency in another. The forms which minister to the mind now may fetter it hereafter, and must give place to its free unfolding. A system wanting this freedom and flexibleness would carry strong proof in itself of not having been intended for universality. It is one proof of Christ's having come to "inherit all nations," that he did not institute for all nations and all times a precise machinery of forms and outward rules, that he entered into no minute legislation as to the worship and government of his church, but left these outward concerns to be swayed by the spirit and progress of successive ages. Of consequence, no particular order of the church can be essential to salvation. No church can pretend that its constitution is defined and ordained in the Scriptures so plainly and undeniably that whoever forsakes it gives palpable proof of a spirit of disobedience to God. All churches are embraced by their members with equal religious reverence, and this assures us that in all God's favor may be equally obtained.

It is worthy of remark, that, from the necessity of the case, the church assumed at first a form which it could not long retain. It was governed by the apostles who had founded it, men who had known Christ personally, and received his truth from his lips, and witnessed his resurrection, and were enriched above all men by the miraculous illuminations and aids of his Spirit. These presided over the church with an authority peculiar to themselves, and to which none after them could with any reason pretend. They understood "the mind of Christ" as none could do but those who had enjoyed so long and close an intimacy with him; and not only were they sent forth with miraculous powers, but, by imposition of their hands, similar gifts of the Spirit were conferred on others. This presence of inspired apostles and supernatural powers gave to the primitive church obvious and important distinctions, separating it widely from the form which it was afterwards to assume. Of this we have a remarkable proof in a passage of Paul, in which he sets before us the offices or functions exercised in the original church. "God hath set in the church apostles, prophets, teachers, miracles, gifts of healings, helps, governments, diversities of tongues." * Now of all these endowments or offices, one only, that of teacher, remains in our day. The apostles, the founders and heroes of the primitive church, with their peculiar powers, have vanished, leaving as their representatives their writings, to be studied alike by all. Teachers remain, not because they existed in the first age, but because their office, from its nature, and from the condition of human nature, is needed still. The office, however, has undergone an important change. At first the Christian teacher enjoyed immediate communication with the apostles, and received miraculous aids, and thus enjoyed means of knowledge possessed by none of his successors. The Christian minister now can only approach the apostles as other men do, that is, through the Gospels and Epistles which they have left us; and he has no other aid from above in interpreting them than every true Christian enjoys. The promise of the Holy Spirit, that greatest of promises, is made without distinction to every man, of every office or rank, who perseveringly implores the Divine help; and this establishes an essential equality among all. Whether teachers are to continue in the brighter ages which prophecy announces is rendered doubtful by a very striking prediction of the times of the Messiah. "After those days," saith the Lord, "I will put my law in their inward parts, and write it in their hearts, and will be their God, and they shall be my people. And they shall teach no more every man his neighbour, and every man his brother,

* 1 Cor. xii. 28.

saying, 'Know the Lord;' for they shall all know me, from the least of them unto the greatest of them." * Is it possible that any man, with a clear comprehension of the peculiarity of the primitive church, can look back to this as an immutable form and rule, can regard any church form as essential to salvation, can ascribe to outward ordinances, so necessarily fluctuating, an importance to be compared with that which belongs to the immutable, everlasting distinctions of holiness and virtue?

The church as at first constituted presents interesting and beautiful aspects. It was not a forced and arbitrary, but free, spontaneous union. It grew out of the principles and feelings of human nature. Our nature is social. We cannot live alone. We cannot shut up any great feeling in our hearts. We seek for others to partake it with us. The full soul finds at once relief and strength in sympathy. This is especially true in religion, the most social of all our sentiments, the only universal bond on earth. In this law of our nature the Christian church had its origin. Christ did not establish it in a formal way. If you consult the New Testament, you do not find Jesus or his apostles setting about the task of forming an artificial organization of the first disciples. Read in the book of Acts the simple, touching narratives of the union of the first converts. They "were of one heart and of one soul." They could not be kept asunder. The new truth melted them into one mass, knit them into one body. In their mutual love they could not withhold from one another their possessions, but had all things in common. Blessed unity! a type of that oneness and harmony which a purer Christianity is to spread through all nations. Among those

* Jeremiah, xxxi. 33, 34.

early converts the most gifted and enlightened were chosen to be teachers in public assemblies. To these assemblies the brotherhood repaired with eagerness, to hear expositions of the new faith, to strengthen one another's loyalty to Christ, and to be open witnesses of him in the world. In their meetings they were left very much to follow the usages of the synagogue, in which they had been brought up; so little did Christianity trouble itself about forms. How simple, how natural this association! It is no mystery. It grew out of the plainest wants of the human heart. The religious sentiment, the spirit of love towards God and man, awakened afresh by Christ, craved for a new union through which to find utterance and strength. And shall this church union, the growth of the Christian spirit, and so plainly subordinate to it, usurp its place, or in any way detract from its sole sufficiency, from its supreme, unrivalled glory?

The church, according to its true idea and purpose, is an association of sincere, genuine followers of Christ; and at first this idea was in a good degree realized. The primitive disciples were drawn to Christ by conviction. They met together and confessed him, not from usage, fashion, or education, but in opposition to all these. In that age, profession and practice, the form and the spirit, the reality and the outward signs of religion went together. But with the growth of the church its life declined; its great idea was obscured; the name remained, and sometimes little more than the name. It is a remarkable fact, that the very spirit to which Christianity is most hostile, the passion for power, dominion, pomp, and preëminence, struck its deepest roots in the church. The church became the very stronghold of the lusts and vices which Christianity most abhors. Accordingly its history is one of the most melancholy records of past times. It is sad enough to read the blood-stained annals of worldly empires; but when we see the spiritual kingdom of Christ a prey for ages to usurping popes, prelates, or sectarian chiefs, inflamed with bigotry and theological hate and the lust of rule, and driven by these fires of hell to grasp the temporal sword, to persecute, torture, imprison, butcher their brethren, to mix with and embitter national wars, and to convulse the whole Christian world, we experience a deeper gloom, and are more tempted to despair of our race. History has not a darker page than that which records the persecutions of the Albigenses, or the horrors of the Inquisition. And when we come to later times, the church wears any thing rather than "Holiness" inscribed on her front. How melancholy to a Christian, the history lately given us by Ranke of the reaction of Catholicism against Protestantism! Throughout we see the ecclesiastical powers resorting to force as the grand instrument of conversion; thus proving their alliance, not with heaven, but with earth and hell. If we take broad views of the church in any age or land, how seldom do we see the prevalence of true sanctity! How many of its ministers preach for lucre or display, preach what they do not believe, or deny their doctrines in their lives! How many congregations are there, made up in a great degree of worldly men and women, who repair to the house of God from usage, or for propriety's sake, or from a vague notion of being saved; not from thirst for the Divine Spirit, not from a fulness of heart which longs to pour itself forth in prayer and praise! Such is the church. We are apt, indeed, to make it an abstraction, or to separate it in our thoughts from the individuals who compose it; and thus it becomes to us a holy thing, and we ascribe to it strange powers. Theologians speak of it as a unity, a mighty whole, one and the same in all ages; and in this way the imagination is cheated into the idea of its marvellous sanctity and grandeur. But we must separate between the theory or the purpose of the church and its actual state. When we come down to facts, we see it to be, not a mysterious, immutable unity, but a collection of fluctuating, divided, warring individuals, who bring into it, too often, hearts and hands any thing but pure. Painful as it is, we must see things as they are; and so doing, we cannot but be struck with the infinite absurdity of ascribing to such a church mysterious powers, of supposing that it can confer holiness on its members, or that the circumstance of being joined to it is of the least moment in comparison with purity of heart and life.

Purity of heart and life, Christ's spirit of love towards God and man; this is all in all. This is the only essential thing. The church is important only as it ministers to this; and every church which so ministers is a good one, no matter how, when, or where it grew up, no matter whether it worship on its knees or on its feet, or whether its ministers are ordained by pope, bishop, presbyter, or people; these are secondary things, and of no comparative moment. The church which opens on heaven is that, and that only, in which the spirit of heaven dwells. The church whose worship rises to God's ear is that, and that only, where the soul ascends. No matter whether it be gathered in cathedral or barn; whether it sit in silence, or send up a hymn; whether the minister speak from carefully prepared notes, or from immediate, fervent, irrepressible suggestion. If God be loved, and Jesus Christ be welcomed to the soul, and his instructions be meekly and wisely heard, and the solemn purpose grow up to do all duty amidst all conflict, sacrifice, and temptation, then the true end of the church is answered. "This is no other than the house of God, the gate of heaven."

In these remarks I do not mean that all churches are of equal worth. Some undoubtedly correspond more than others to the spirit and purpose of Christianity, to the simple usages of the primitive disciples, and to the principles of human nature. All have their superstitions and corruptions, but some are more pure than the rest; and we are bound to seek that which is purest, which corresponds most to the Divine will. As far as we have power to select, we should go to the church where we shall be most helped to become devout, disinterested, and morally strong. Our salvation, however, does not depend on our finding the best church on earth, for this may be distant or unknown. Amidst diversities of administrations there is the same spirit. In all religious societies professing Christ as their Lord, the plainest, grandest truths of religion will almost certainly be taught, and some souls may be found touched and enlightened from above. This is a plain, undeniable fact. In all sects, various as they are, good and holy men may be found; nor can we tell in which the holiest have grown up. The church, then, answers its end in all; for its only end is, to minister to human virtue. It is delightful to read in the records of all denominations the lives of eminent Christians who have given up every thing for their religion, who have been faithful unto death, who have shed around them the sweet light and fragrance of Christian hope and love. We cannot, then, well choose amiss, if we choose the church which, as it seems to us, best represents the grand ideas of Christ, and speaks most powerfully to our consciences and hearts. This church, however, we must not choose for our brother. He differs from us, probably, in temperament, in his range of intellect, or in the impressions which education and habit have given him. Perhaps the worship which most quickens you and me may hardly keep our neighbour awake. He must be approached through the heart and imagination; we through the reason. What to him is fervor passes with us for noise. What to him is an imposing form is to us vain show. Condemn him not. If, in his warmer atmosphere, he builds up a stronger faith in God and a more steadfast choice of perfect goodness than ourselves, his church is better to him than ours to us.

One great error in regard to churches contributes to the false estimate of them as essential to salvation. We imagine that the church, the minister, the worship can do something for us mechanically; that there are certain mysterious influences in what we call a holy place, which may act on us without our own agency. It is not so. The church and the minister can do little for us in comparison with what we must do for ourselves, and nothing for us without ourselves. They become to us blessings through our own activity. Every man must be his own priest. It is his own action, not the minister's, it is the prayer issuing from his own heart, not from another's lips, which aids him in the church. The church does him good only as by its rites, prayers, hymns, and sermons it wakes up his spirit to think, feel, pray, praise, and resolve. The church is a help, not a force. It acts on us by rational and moral means, and not by mystical operations. Its influence resembles precisely that which is exerted out of church. Its efficiency depends chiefly on the clearness, simplicity, sincerity, love, and zeal with which the minister speaks to our understandings, consciences, and hearts ; just as in common life we are benefited by the clearness and energy with which our friends set before us what is good and pure. The church is adapted to our free moral nature. It acts on us as rational and responsible beings, and serves us through our own efficiency. From these views we learn that the glory of the church does not lie in any particular government or form, but in the wisdom with which it combines such influences as are fitted to awaken and purify the soul.

Am I asked to state more particularly what these influences are to which the church owes its efficacy ? I reply, that they are such as may be found in all churches, in all denominations. The first is, the character of the minister. This has an obvious, immediate, and powerful bearing on the great spiritual purpose of the church. I say, his character, not his ordination. Ordination has no end but to introduce into the sacred office men qualified for its duties, and to give an impression of its importance. It is by his personal endowments, by his intellectual, moral, and religious worth, by his faithfulness and zeal, and not through any mysterious ceremony or power, that the minister enlightens and edifies the church. What matters it how he is ordained or set apart, if he give himself to his work in the fear of God ? What matters it who has laid hands on him, or whether he stand up in surplice or drab coat ? I go to church to be benefited, not by hands or coats, but by the action of an enlightened and holy teacher on my mind and heart; not an overpowering, irresistible action, but such as becomes effectual through my own free thought and will. I go to be convinced of what is true, and to be warmed with love of what is good; and he who thus helps me is a true minister, no matter from what school, consistory, or ecclesiastical body he comes. He carries his commission in his soul. Do not say, that his ministry has no "validity," because Rome, or Geneva, or Lambeth, or Andover, or Princeton, has not laid hands on him. What! Has he not opened my eyes to see, and roused my conscience to reprove? As I have heard him has not my heart burned within me, and have I not silently given myself to God with new humility and love? Have I not been pierced by his warnings, and softened by his looks and tones of love? Has he not taught and helped me to deny myself, to conquer the world, to do good to a foe? Has he done this; and yet has his ministry no "validity"? What other validity can there be than this? If a generous friend gives me water to drink when I am parched with thirst, and I drink and am refreshed, will it do to tell me, that, because he did not buy the cup at a certain licensed shop, or draw the water at a certain antiquated cistern, therefore his act of kindness is "invalid," and I am as thirsty and weak as I was before? What more can a minister with mitre or tiara do than help me, by wise and touching manifestations of God's truth, to become a holier, nobler man? If my soul be made alive, no matter who ministers to me; and if not, the ordinances of the church, whether high or low, orthodox or heretical, are of no validity so far as I am concerned. The diseased man who is restored to health cares little whether his physician wear wig or cowl, or receive his diploma from Paris or London; and so to the regenerate man it is of little moment where or by what processes he became a temple of the Holy Spirit.

According to these views a minister deriving power from his intellectual, moral, and religious worth is one of the chief elements of a true and quickening church. Such a man will gather a true church round him; and we here learn that a Christian community is bound to do what may aid, and to abstain from what may impair, the virtue, nobleness, spiritual energy of its minister. It should especially leave him free, should wish him to wear no restraints but those of a sense of duty. His office is, to utter God's truth according to his apprehension of it, and he should be encouraged to utter it honestly, simply. He must follow his own conscience, and no other. How can he rebuke prevalent error without an unawed spirit? Better that he should hold his peace than not speak from his own soul. Better that the pulpit be prostrated than its freedom be taken away. The doctrine of "instructions" in politics is of very doubtful expediency; but that instructions should issue from the congregation to the minister we all with one voice pronounce wrong. The religious teacher compelled to stifle his convictions grows useless to his people, is shorn of his strength, loses self-respect, shrinks before his own conscience, and owes it to himself to refrain from teaching. If he be honest, upright, and pure, worthy of trust, worthy of being a minister, he has a right to freedom; and when he uses it conscientiously, though he may err in judgment, and may give pain to judicious hearers, he has still a right to respect. There are, indeed, few religious societies which would knowingly make the minister a slave. Many err on the side of submission, and receive his doctrines with blind, unquestioning faith. Still, the members of a congregation, conscious of holding the support of their teacher in their hands, are apt to expect a cautious tenderness towards their known prejudices or judgments, which, though not regarded as servility, is very hostile to that firm, bold utterance of truth on which the success of his ministry chiefly depends.

I have mentioned the first condition of the most useful church; it is the high character of its minister. The second is to be found in the spiritual character of its members. This, like the former, is, from the very principles of human nature, fitted to purify and save. It was the intention of Christ that a quickening power should be exerted in a church, not by the minister alone, but also by the members on one another. Accordingly we read of the "working of every part, every joint," in his spiritual body. We come together in our places of worship that heart may act on heart; that in the midst of the devout a more fervent flame of piety may be kindled in our own breasts; that we may hear God's word more eagerly by knowing that it is drunk in by thirsty spirits around us; that our own purpose of obedience may be confirmed by the consciousness that a holy energy of will is unfolding itself in our neighbours. To this sympathy the church is dedicated; and in this its highest influence is sometimes found. To myself the most effectual church is that in which I see the signs of Christian affection in those around me, in which warm hearts are beating on every side, in which a deep stillness speaks of the absorbed soul, in which I recognize fellow-beings who in common life have impressed me with their piety. One look from a beaming countenance, one tone in singing from a deeply moved heart, perhaps aids me more than the sermon. When nothing is said, I feel it good to be among the devout; and I wonder not that the Quakers in some of their still meetings profess to hold the most intimate union, not only with God, but with each other. It is not with the voice only that man communicates with man. Nothing is so eloquent as the deep silence of a crowd. A sigh, a low breathing, sometimes pours into us our neighbour's soul more than a volume of words. There is a communication more subtile than freemasonry between those who feel alike. How contagious is holy feeling! On the other hand, how freezing, how palsying, is the gathering of a multitude who feel nothing, who come to God's house without reverence, without love, who gaze around on each other as if they were assembled at a show, whose restlessness keeps up a slightly disturbing sound, whose countenances reveal no collectedness, no earnestness, but a frivolous or absent mind! The very sanctity of the place makes this indifference more chilling. One of the coldest spots on earth is a church without devotion. What is it to me that a costly temple is set apart, by ever so many rites, for God's service, that priests who trace their lineage to apostles have consecrated it, if I find it thronged by the worldly and undevout? This is no church to me. I go to meet, not human bodies, but souls; and if I find them in an upper room like that where the first disciples met, or in a shed, or in a street, there I find a church. There is the true altar, the sweet incense, the accepted priest. These all I find in sanctified souls.

True Christians give a sanctifying power, a glory, to the place of worship where they come together. In them Christ is present and manifested in a far higher sense than if he were revealed to the bodily eye. We are apt, indeed, to think differently. Were there a place of worship in which a glory like that which clothed Jesus on the Mount of Transfiguration were to shine forth, how should we throng to it as the chosen spot on earth ! how should we honor this as eminently his church ! But there is a more glorious presence of Christ than this. It is Christ formed in the souls of his disciples. Christ's bodily presence does not make a church. He was thus present in the thronged streets of Jerusalem, present in the synagogues and temples ; but these were not churches. It is the presence of his spirit, truth, likeness, divine love, in the souls of men which attracts and unites them into one living body. Suppose that we meet together in a place consecrated by all manner of forms, but that nothing of Christ's spirit dwells in us. With all its forms, it is a synagogue of Satan, not a church of Jesus. Christ in the hearts of men, I repeat it, is the only church bond. The Catholics, to give them a feeling of the present Saviour, adorn their temples with paintings representing him in the most affecting scenes of his life and death ; and had worship never been directed to these, I should not object to them. But there is a far higher likeness to Christ than the artist ever drew or chiselled. It exists in the heart of his true disciple. The true disciple surpasses Raphael and Michael Angelo. The latter have given us Christ's countenance from fancy, and, at best, having little likeness to the mild beauty and majestic form which moved through Judea. But the disciple who sincerely conforms himself to the disinterestedness, and purity, and filial worship, and all-sacrificing love of Christ gives us no fancied representation, but the true, divine lineaments of his soul, the very spirit which beamed in his face, which spoke in his voice, which attested his glory as the Son of God. The truest church is that which has in the highest degree this spiritual presence of our Lord, this revelation of Jesus in his followers. This is the church in which we shall find the greatest aid to our virtue which outward institution can afford us.

I have thus spoken of the two chief elements of a living and effectual church; a pure, noble-minded minister, and faithful followers of Christ. In the preceding remarks I have had chiefly in view particular churches, organized according to some particular forms; and I have maintained that these are important only as ministering to Christian holiness or virtue. There is, however, a grander church, to which I now ask your attention; and the consideration of this will peculiarly confirm the lesson on which I am insisting, namely, that there is but one essential thing, true holiness, or disinterested love to God and man. There is a grander church than all particular ones, however extensive; the Church Catholic or Universal, spread over all lands, and one with the church in heaven. That all Christ's followers form one body, one fold, is taught in various passages in the New Testament. You remember the earnestness of his last prayer, "that they might all be One, as he and his Father are one." Into this church all who partake the spirit of Christ are admitted. It asks not who has baptized us; whose passport we carry; what badge we wear. If "baptized by the Holy Ghost," its wide gates are opened to us. Within this church are joined those whom different names have severed or still sever. We hear nothing of Greek, Roman, English churches, but of Christ's church only. My friends, this is not an imaginary union. The Scriptures in speaking of it do not talk rhetorically, but utter the soberest truth. All sincere partakers of Christian virtue are essentially one. In the spirit which pervades them dwells a uniting power found in no other tie. Though separated by oceans, they have sympathies strong and indissoluble. Accordingly, the clear, strong utterance of one gifted, inspired Christian flies through the earth. It touches kindred chords in another hemisphere. The word of such a man as Fenelon, for instance, finds its way into the souls of scattered millions. Are not he and they of one church? I thrill with joy at the name of holy men who lived ages ago. Ages do not divide us. I venerate them more for their antiquity. Are we not one body? Is not this union something real? It is not men's coming together into one building which makes a church. Suppose that in a place of worship I sit so near a fellow-creature as to touch him; but that there is no common feeling between us, that the truth which moves me he inwardly smiles at as a dream of fancy, that the disinterestedness which I honor he calls weakness or wild enthusiasm. How far apart are we, though visibly so near! We belong to different worlds. How much nearer am I to some pure, generous spirit in another continent whose word has penetrated my heart, whose virtues have kindled me to emulation, whose pure thoughts are passing through my mind whilst I sit in the house of prayer! With which of these two have I church union?

Do not tell me that I surrender myself to a fiction of imagination, when I say, that distant Christians, that all Christians and myself, form one body, one church, just as far as a common love and piety possess our hearts. Nothing is more real than this spiritual union. There *is* one grand, all-comprehending church ; and if I am a Christian, I belong to it, and no man can shut me out of it. You may exclude me from your Roman church, your Episcopal church, and your Calvinistic church, on account of supposed defects in my creed or my sect, and I am content to be excluded. But I will not be severed from the great body of Christ. Who shall sunder me from such men as Fenelon, and Pascal, and Borromeo, from Archbishop Leighton, Jeremy Taylor, and John Howard ? Who can rupture the spiritual bond between these men and myself ? Do I not hold them dear ? Does not their spirit, flowing out through their writings and lives, penetrate my soul ? Are they not a portion of my being ? Am I not a different man from what I should have been, had not these and other like spirits acted on mine ? And is it in the power of synod, or conclave, or of all the ecclesiastical combinations on earth, to part me from them ? I am bound to them by thought and affection ; and can these be suppressed by the bull of a pope or the excommunication of a council ? The soul breaks scornfully these barriers, these webs of spiders, and joins itself to the great and good ; and if it possess their spirit, will the great and good, living or dead, cast it off because it has not enrolled itself in this or another sect ? A pure mind is free of the universe. It belongs to the church, the family of the pure, in all worlds. Virtue is no local thing. It is not honorable because born in this community or that, but for its own independent, everlasting beauty. This is the bond of the universal church. No man can be excommunicated from it but by himself, by the death of goodness in his own breast. All sentences of exclusion are vain, if he do not dissolve the tie of purity which binds him to all holy souls.

I honor the Roman Catholic church on one account; it clings to the idea of a Universal Church, though it has mutilated and degraded it. The word Catholic means Universal. Would to God that the church which has usurped the name had understood the reality! Still, Romanism has done something to give to its members the idea of their connexion with that vast spiritual community, or church, which has existed in all times and spread over all lands. It guards the memory of great and holy men who in all ages have toiled and suffered for religion, asserts the honors of the heroes of the faith, enshrines them in heaven as beatified saints, converts their legends into popular literature, appoints days for the celebration of their virtues, and reveals them almost as living to the eye by the pictures in which genius has immortalized their deeds. In doing this Rome has fallen, indeed, into error. She has fabricated exploits for these spiritual persons, and exalted them into objects of worship. But she has also done good. She has given to her members the feeling of intimate relation to the holiest and noblest men in all preceding ages. An interesting and often a sanctifying tie connects the present Roman Catholic with martyrs, and confessors, and a host of men whose eminent piety and genius and learning have won for them an immortality of fame. It is no mean service thus to enlarge men's ideas and affections, to awaken their veneration for departed greatness, to teach them their connexion with the grandest spirits of all times. It was this feature of Catholicism which most interested me in visiting Catholic countries. The services at the altar did not move, but rather pained me. But when I cast my eyes on the pictures on the walls, which placed before me the holy men of departed ages, now absorbed in devotion and lost in rapture, now enduring with meek courage and celestial hope the agonies of a painful death in defence of the truth, I was touched, and I hope made better. The voice of the officiating priest I did not hear; but these sainted dead spoke to my heart, and I was sometimes led to feel as if an hour on Sunday spent in this communion were as useful to me as if it had been spent in a Protestant church. These saints never rose to my thoughts as Roman Catholics. I never connected them with any particular church. They were to me living, venerable witnesses to Christ, to the power of religion, to the grandeur of the human soul. I saw what men might suffer for the truth, how they could rise above themselves, how real might become the ideas of God and a higher life. This inward reverence for the departed good helped me to feel myself a member of the church universal. I wanted no pope or priest to establish my unity with them. My own heart was witness enough to a spiritual fellowship. Is it not to be desired that all our churches should have services to teach us our union with Christ's whole body? Would not this break our sectarian chains, and awaken reverence for Christ's spirit, for true goodness, under every name and form? It is not enough, to feel that we are members of this or that narrow communion. Christianity is universal sympathy and love. I do not recommend that our churches should be lined with pictures of saints. This usage must come in, if it come at all, not by recommendation, but by gradual change of tastes and feelings. But why may not the pulpit be used occasionally to give us the lives and virtues of eminent disciples in former ages? It is customary to deliver sermons on the history of Peter, John, Paul, and of Abraham, and Elijah, and other worthies of the Old Testament; and this we do because their names are written in the Bible. But goodness owes nothing to the circumstance of its being recorded in a sacred book, nor loses its claim to grateful, reverent commemoration because not blazoned there. Moral greatness did not die out with the apostles. Their lives were reported for this, among other ends, that their virtues might be propagated to future times, and that men might spring up as worthy a place among the canonized as themselves. What I wish is, that we should learn to regard ourselves as members of a vast spiritual community, as joint heirs and fellow-worshippers with the goodly company of Christian heroes who have gone before us, instead of immuring ourselves in particular churches. Our nature delights in this consciousness of vast connexion. This tendency manifests itself in the patriotic sentiment, and in the passionate clinging of men to a great religious denomination. Its true and noblest gratification is found in the deep feeling of a vital, everlasting connexion with the universal church, with the innumerable multitude of the holy on earth and in heaven. This church we shall never make a substitute for virtue.

I have spoken of the Roman Catholic Church. My great objection to this communion is, that it has fallen peculiarly into the error which I am laboring to expose in this Discourse, that it has attached idolatrous importance to the institution of the Church, that it virtually exalts this above Christ's spirit, above inward sanctity. Its other errors are of inferior importance. It does not offend me, that the Romanist maintains that a piece of bread, a wafer, over which a priest has pronounced some magical words, is the flesh and blood of Jesus Christ. I learn, indeed, in this error, an humbling lesson of human credulity, of the weakness of human reason; but I see nothing in it which strikes at the essential principles of religion. When, however, the Roman Catholic goes farther, and tells me that God looks with abhorrence on all who will not see in the consecrated wafer Christ's flesh and blood; and when he makes the reception of this from the hands of a consecrated priest the door into Christ's fold, then I am shocked by the dishonor he casts on God and virtue, by his debasing conceptions of our moral nature and of the Divine, and by his cruel disruption of the ties of human and Christian brotherhood. How sad and strange that a man educated under Christianity should place religion in a church-connexion, in church-rites, should shut from God's family the wisest and the best because they conscientiously abstain from certain outward ordinances! Is not holiness of heart and life dear to God for its own sake, dear to him without the manipulations of a priest, without the agency of a consecrated wafer? The grand error of Roman Catholicism is, its narrow church-spirit, its blind sectarianism, its exclusion of virtuous, pious men from God's favor because they cannot eat, drink, or pray according to certain prescribed rites. Romanism has to learn that nothing but the inward life is great and good in the sight of the Omniscient, and that all who cherish this are members of Christ's body. Romanism is any thing but what it boasts to be, the Universal Church. I am too much a Catholic to enlist under its banner.

I belong to the Universal Church; nothing shall separate me from it. In saying this, however, I am no enemy to particular churches. In the present age of the world it is perhaps best that those who agree in theological opinions should worship together; and I do not object to the union of several such churches in one denomination, provided that *all* sectarian and narrow feeling be conscientiously and scrupulously resisted. I look on the various churches of Christendom with no feelings of enmity. I have expressed my abhorrence of the sectarian spirit of Rome; but in that, as in all other churches, individuals are better than their creed; and, amidst gross error and the inculcation of a narrow spirit, noble virtues spring up, and eminent Christians are formed. It is one sign of the tendency of human nature to goodness, that it grows good under a thousand bad influences. The Romish church is illustrated by great names. Her gloomy convents have often been brightened by fervent love to God and man. Her St. Louis, and Fenelon, and Massillon, and Cheverus; her missionaries who have carried Christianity to the ends of the earth; her sisters of charity who have carried relief and solace to the most hopeless want and pain; do not these teach us that in the Romish church the Spirit of God has found a home? How much, too, have other churches to boast! In the English church we meet the names of Latimer, Hooker, Barrow, Leighton, Berkeley, and Heber; in the Dissenting Calvinistic church, Baxter, Howe, Watts, Doddridge, and Robert Hall; among the Quakers, George Fox, William Penn, Robert Barclay, and our own Anthony Benezet, and John Woolman; in the Anti-trinitarian church, John Milton, John Locke, Samuel Clarke, Price, and Priestley. To repeat these names does the heart good. They breathe a fragrance through the common air. They lift up the whole race to which they belonged. With the churches of which they were pillars or chief ornaments I have many sympathies ; nor do I condemn the union of ourselves to these or any other churches whose doctrines we approve, provided that we do it without severing ourselves in the least from the universal church. On this point we cannot be too earnest. We must shun the spirit of sectarianism as from hell. We must shudder at the thought of shutting up God in any denomination. We must think no man the better for belonging to our communion ; no man the worse for belonging to another. We must look with undiminished joy on goodness, though it shine forth from the most adverse sect. Christ's spirit must be equally dear and honored, no matter where manifested. To confine God's love or his good Spirit to any party, sect, or name is to sin against the fundamental law of the kingdom of God, to break that living bond with Christ's universal church which is one of our chief helps to perfection.

I have now given what seem to me the most important views in relation to the church ; and in doing this I have not quoted much from Scripture, because quotations cannot be given fully on this or on any controverted point in the compass of a discourse. I have relied on what is vastly more important, on the general strain and tone of Scripture, on the spirit of the Christian religion, on the sum and substance of Christ's teachings, which is plainly this, that inward holiness, or goodness, or disinterested love, is all in all. I also want time to consider at large the arguments or modes of reasoning by which this or that church sets itself forth as the only true church, and by which the necessity of entering it is thought to be proved. I cannot, however, abstain from offering a few remarks on these.

The principal arguments on which exclusive churches rest their claims are drawn from Christian history and literature, in other words, from the records of the primitive ages of our faith, and from the writings of the early Fathers. These arguments, I think, may be disposed of by a single remark, that they cannot be comprehended or weighed by the mass of Christians. How very, very few in our congregations can enter into the critical study of ecclesiastical history, or wade through the folios of the Greek and Latin Fathers! Now if it were necessary to join a particular church in order to receive the blessings of Christianity, is it to be conceived that the discovery of this church should require a learning plainly denied to the mass of human beings? Would not this church shine out with the brightness of the sun? Would it be hidden in the imperfect records of distant ages, or in the voluminous writings of a body of ancient authors, more remarkable for rhetoric than for soundness of judgment? The learned cannot agree about these authorities. How can the great multitudes of believers interpret them? Would not the Scriptures guide us by simple, sure rules to the only true church, if to miss it were death? To my own mind this argument has a force akin to demonstration.

I pass to another method of defending the claims which one or another church sets up to exclusive acceptance with God. It is an unwarrantable straining of the figurative language of Scripture. Because the church is spoken of as one body, vine, or temple, theologians have argued that it is one outward organization, to which all men must be joined. But a doctrine built on metaphor is worth little. Every kind of absurdity may find a sanction in figures of speech, explained by tame, prosaic, cold-hearted commentators. The beautiful forms of speech to which I have referred were intended to express the peculiarly close and tender unions which necessarily subsist among all the enlightened and sincere disciples of such a religion as Christ's, a religion whose soul, essence, and breath of life is love, which reveals to us in Jesus the perfection of philanthropy, and which calls to us to drink spiritually of that blood of self-sacrifice which was shed for the whole human race. How infinitely exalted is the union of minds and hearts formed by such a religion above any outward connexion established by rites and forms! Yet the latter has been seized on by the earthly understanding as the chief meaning of Scripture, and magnified into supreme importance. Has not Paul taught us that there is but one perfect bond, Love?* Has not Christ taught us that the seal set on his disciples, by which all men are to know them, is Love?† Is not this the badge of the true church, the life of the true body of Christ? And is not every disciple, of every name and form, who is inspired with this, embraced indissolubly in the Christian union?

It is sometimes urged by those who maintain the necessity of connexion with what they call "the true church," that God has a right to dispense his blessings through what channels or on what terms he pleases; that, if he sees fit to communicate his Holy Spirit through a certain priesthood or certain ordinances, we are bound to seek the gift in his appointed way; and that, having actually chosen this method of imparting it, he may just-

* Colossians, iii. 14. † John, xiii. 35.

ly withhold it from those who refuse to comply with his appointment. I reply, that the right of the Infinite Father to bestow his blessings in such ways as to his infinite wisdom and love may seem best no man can be so irreverent as to deny. But is it not reasonable to expect that he will adopt such methods or conditions as will seem to accord with his perfection? And ought we not to distrust such as seem to dishonor him? Suppose, for example, that I were told that the Infinite Father had decreed to give his Holy Spirit to such as should bathe freely in the sea. Ought I not to require the most plain, undeniable proofs of a purpose apparently so unworthy of his majesty and goodness, before yielding obedience to it? The presumption against it is exceedingly strong. That the Infinite Father, who is ever present to the human soul, to whom it is unspeakably dear, who has created it for communion with himself, who desires and delights to impart to it his grace, that he should ordain sea-bathing as a condition or means of spiritual communication is so improbable that I must insist on the strongest testimony to its truth. Now I meet precisely this difficulty in the doctrine, that God bestows his Holy Spirit on those who receive bread and wine, or flesh and blood, or a form of benediction or baptism, or any other outward ministration, from the hands or lips of certain privileged ministers or priests. It is the most glorious act and manifestation of God's power and love, to impart enlightening, quickening, purifying influences to the immortal soul. To imagine that these descend in connexion with certain words, signs, or outward rites, administered by a frail fellow-creature, and are withheld or abridged in the absence of such rites, seems, at first, an insult to his wisdom and goodness; seems to bring down his pure, infinite throne, to set arbitrary limits to his highest agency, and to assimilate his worship to that of false gods. The Scriptures teach us that "God giveth grace to the humble;" that "he giveth his Holy Spirit to them that ask him." This is the great law of Divine communications; and we can see its wisdom, because the mind which hungers for Divine assistances is most prepared to use them aright. And can we really believe that the prayers and aspirations of a penitent, thirsting soul need to be seconded by the outward offices of a minister or priest? or that for want of these they find less easy entrance into the ear of the ever-present, all-loving Father? My mind recoils from this doctrine as dishonorable to God, and I ought not to receive it without clear proofs. I want something more than metaphors, or analogies, or logical inferences. I want some express Divine testimony. And where is it given? Do we not know that thousands and millions of Christians, whose lives and deaths have borne witness to their faith, have been unable to find it in the Scriptures, or anywhere else? And can we believe that the spiritual communication of such men with the Divinity has been forfeited or impaired, because they have abstained from rites which in their consciences they could not recognize as of Divine appointment? That so irrational and extravagant a doctrine should enter the mind of a man who has the capacity of reading the New Testament would seem an impossibility, did not history show us that it has been not only believed, but made the foundation of the bitterest intolerance and the bloodiest persecutions.

The notion, that, by a decree of God's sovereign will, his grace or Spirit flows through certain rites to those who are in union with a certain church, and that it is promised to none besides, has no foundation in Scripture or reason. The church, as I have previously suggested, is not an arbitrary appointment; it does not rest on Will, but is ordained on account of its obvious fitness to accomplish the spiritual improvement which is the end of Christianity. It corresponds to our nature. It is a union of means, and influences, and offices which rational and moral creatures need. It has no affinity with the magical operations so common in false religions; its agency is intelligible and level to the common mind. Its two great rites, baptism and the Lord's supper, are not meant to act as charms. When freed from the errors and superstitions which have clung to them for ages, and when administered, as they should be, with tenderness and solemnity, they are powerful means of bringing great truths to the mind and of touching the heart, and for these ends they are ordained. The adaptation of the church to the promotion of holiness among men is its grand excellence; and where it accomplishes this end its work is done, and no greater can be conceived on earth or in heaven. The moment we shut our eyes on this truth, and conceive of the church as serving us by forms and ordinances which are effectual only in the hands of privileged officials or priests, we plunge into the region of shadows and superstitions; we have no ground to tread on, no light to guide us. This mysterious power, lodged in the hands of a few fellow-creatures, tends to give a servile spirit to the mass of Christians, to impair manliness and self-respect, to subdue the intellect to the reception of the absurdest dogmas. Religion loses its simple grandeur, and degenerates into mechanism and form. The conscience is quieted by something short of true repentance; something besides purity of heart and life is made the qualification for heaven. The surest device for making the mind a coward and a slave is a wide-spread and closely cemented church the powers of which are concentrated in the hands of a "sacred order," and which has succeeded in arrogating to its rites or ministers a sway over the future world, over the soul's everlasting weal or woe. The inevitably degrading influence of such a church is demonstrative proof against its Divine original.

There is no end to the volumes written in defence of this or that church which sets itself forth as the only true church, and claims exclusive acceptance with God. But the unlettered Christian has an answer to them all. He cannot and need not seek it in libraries. He finds it, almost without seeking, in plain passages of the New Testament, and in his own heart. He reads, and he feels, that religion is an Inward Life. This he knows, not by report, but by consciousness, by the prostration of his soul in penitence, by the surrender of his will to the Divine, by overflowing gratitude, by calm trust, and by a new love to his fellow-creatures. Will it do to tell such a man that the promises of Christianity do not belong to him, that access to God is denied him, because he is not joined with this or that exclusive church? Has not this access been granted to him already? Has he not prayed in his griefs, and been consoled? in his temptations, and been strengthened? Has he not found God near in his solitudes and in the great congregation? Does he thirst for any thing so fervently as for perfect assimilation to the Divine purity? And can he question God's readiness to help him, because he is unable to find in Scripture a command to bind himself to this or another self-magnifying church? How easily does the experience of the true Christian brush away the cobwebs of theologians! He loves and reveres God, and in this spirit has a foretaste of heaven; and can heaven be barred against him by ecclesiastical censures? He has felt the power of the cross and resurrection and promises of Jesus Christ; and is there any "height or depth" of human exclusiveness and bigotry which can separate him from his Lord? He can die for truth and humanity; and is there any man so swelled by the conceit of his union with the true church as to stand apart and say, "I am holier than thou"? When, by means of the writings or conversations of Christians of various denominations, you look into their hearts, and discern the deep workings, and conflicts, and aspirations of piety, can you help seeing in them tokens of the presence and operations of God's Spirit more authentic and touching than in all the harmonies and beneficent influences of the outward universe? Who can shut up this Spirit in any place or any sect? Who will not rejoice to witness it in its fruits of justice, goodness, purity, and piety, wherever they meet the eye? Who will not hail it as the infallible sign of the accepted worshipper of God?

One word more respecting the arguments adduced in support of one or another exclusive church. They are continually, and of necessity, losing their force. Arguments owe their influence very much to the mental condition of those to whom they are addressed. What is proof to one man is no proof to another. The evidence which is triumphant in one age is sometimes thought below notice in the next. Men's reasonings on practical subjects are not cold, logical processes, standing separate in the mind, but are carried on in intimate connexion with their prevalent feelings and modes of thought. Generally speaking, that, and that only, is truth to a man which accords with the common tone of his mind, with the mass of his impressions, with the results of his experience, with his measure of intellectual development, and especially with those deep convictions and biases which constitute what we call character. Now it is the tendency of increasing civilization, refinement, and expansion of mind, to produce a tone of thought and feeling unfriendly to the church spirit, to reliance on church forms as essential to salvation. As the world advances it leaves matters of form behind. In proportion as men get into the heart of things they are less anxious about exteriors. In proportion as religion becomes a clear reality we grow tired of shows. In the progress of ages there spring up in greater numbers men of mature thought and spiritual freedom, who unite self-reverence with reverence of God, and who cannot, without a feeling approaching shame and conscious degradation, submit to a church which accumulates outward, rigid, mechanical observances towards the Infinite Father. A voice within them, which they cannot silence, protests against the perpetual repetition of the same signs, motions, words, as unworthy of their own spiritual powers, and of Him who deserves the highest homage of the reason and the heart. Their filial spirit protests against it. In common life, a refined, lofty mind expresses itself in simple, natural, unconstrained manners ; and the same tendency, though often obstructed, is manifested in religion. The progress of Christianity, which must go on, is but another name for the growing knowledge and experience of that spiritual worship of the Father which Christ proclaimed as the end of his mission ; and before this the old idolatrous reliance on ecclesiastical forms and organizations cannot stand. There is thus a perpetually swelling current which exclusive churches have to stem, and which must sooner or later sweep away their proud pretensions. What avails it, that this or another church summons to its aid fathers, traditions, venerated usages? The spirit, the genius of Christianity is stronger than all these. The great ideas of the religion must prevail over narrow, perverse interpretations of it. On this ground I have no alarm at reports of the triumphs of the Catholic church. The spirit of Christianity is stronger than popes and councils. Its venerableness and divine beauty put to shame the dignities and pomps of a hierarchy; and men must more and more recognize it as alone essential to salvation.

From the whole discussion through which I have now led you you will easily gather how I regard the Church, and what importance I attach to it. In its true idea, or regarded as the union of those who partake in the spirit of Jesus Christ, I revere it as the noblest of all associations. Our common social unions are poor by its side. In the world we form ties of interest, pleasure, and ambition. We come together as creatures of time and sense, for transient amusement or display. In the church we meet as God's children; we recognize in ourselves something higher than this animal and worldly life. We come that holy feeling may spread from heart to heart. The church, in its true idea, is a retreat from the world. We meet in it, that, by union with the holy, we may get strength to withstand our common intercourse with the impure. We meet to adore God, to open our souls to his Spirit, and, by recognition of the common Father, to forget all distinction among ourselves, to embrace all men as brothers. This spiritual union with the holy who are departed and who yet live is the beginning of that perfect fellowship which constitutes heaven. It is to survive all ties. The bonds of husband and wife, parent and child, are severed at death ; the union of the virtuous friends of God and man is as eternal as virtue, and this union is the essence of the true church.

To the church relation, in this broad, spiritual view of it, I ascribe the highest dignity and importance. But as to union with a particular denomination or with a society of Christians for public worship and instruction, this, however important, is not to be regarded as the highest means of grace. We ought, indeed, to seek help for ourselves, and to give help to others, by upholding religious institutions, by meeting together in the name of Christ. The influence of Christianity is perpetuated and extended, in no small degree, by the public offices of piety, by the visible "communion of saints." But it is still true that the public means of religion are not its chief means. Private helps to piety are the most efficacious. The great work of religion is to be done, not in society, but in secret, in the retired soul, in the silent closet. Communion with God is eminently the means of religion, the nutriment and life of the soul, and we can commune with God in solitude as nowhere else. Here his presence may be most felt. It is by the breathing of the unrestrained soul, by the opening of the whole heart to "Him who seeth in secret" ; it is by reviewing our own spiritual history, by searching deeply into ourselves, by solitary thought, and solitary solemn consecration of ourselves to a new virtue ; it is by these acts, and not by public gatherings, that we chiefly make progress in the religious life. It is common to speak of the house of public worship as a holy place ; but it has no exclusive sanctity. The holiest spot on earth is that where the soul breathes its purest vows, and forms or executes its noblest purposes ; and on this ground, were I to seek the holiest spot in your city, I should not go to your splendid sanctuaries, but to closets of private prayer. Perhaps the "Holy of Holies" among you is some dark, narrow room from which most of us would shrink as unfit for human habitation ; but God dwells there. He hears there music more grateful than the swell of all your organs, sees there a beauty such as nature, in these her robes of spring, does not unfold ; for there he meets, and sees, and hears the humblest, most thankful, most trustful worshipper ; sees the sorest trials serenely borne, the deepest injuries forgiven ; sees toils and sacrifices cheerfully sustained, and death approached through poverty and lonely illness with a triumphant faith. The consecration which such virtues shed over the obscurest spot is not and cannot be communicated by any of those outward rites by which our splendid structures are dedicated to God.

You see the rank which belongs to the church, whether gathered in one place or spread over the whole earth. It is a sacred and blessed union ; but must not be magnified above other means and helps of religion. The great aids of piety are secret, not public. The Christian cannot live without private prayer ; he may live and make progress without a particular church. Providence may place us far from the resorts of our fellow-disciples, beyond the sound of the Sabbath-bell, beyond all ordinances ; and we may find Sabbaths and ordinances in our own spirits. Illness may separate us from the outward church as well as from the living world, and the soul may yet be in health and prosper. There have been men of eminent piety who, from conscience, have separated themselves from all denominations of Christians and all outward worship. Milton, that great soul, in the latter years of his life forsook all temples made with hands, and worshipped wholly in the inward sanctuary. So did William Law, the author of that remarkable book, "The Serious Call to a Devout and Holy Life." His excess of devotion (for in him devotion ran into excess) led him to disparage all occasional acts of piety. He lived in solitude, that he might make life a perpetual prayer. These men are not named as models in this particular. They mistook the wants of the soul, and misinterpreted the Scriptures. Even they, with all their spirituality, would have found moral strength and holy impulse in religious association. But, with such examples before us, we learn not to exclude men from God's favor because severed from the outward church.

The doctrine of this Discourse is plain. Inward sanctity, pure love, disinterested attachment to God and man, obedience of heart and life, sincere excellence of character, this is the one thing needful, this the essential thing in religion ; and all things else, ministers, churches, ordinances, places of worship, all are but means, helps, secondary influences, and utterly worthless when separated from this. To imagine that God regards any thing but this, that he looks at any thing but the heart, is to dishonor him, to express a mournful insensibility to his pure character. Goodness, purity, virtue, this is the only distinction in God's sight. This is intrinsically, essentially, everlastingly, and by its own nature, lovely, beautiful, glorious, divine. It owes nothing to time, to circumstance, to outward connexions. It shines by its own light. It is the sun of the spiritual universe. It is God himself dwelling in the human soul. Can any man think lightly of it because it has not grown up in a certain church, or exalt any church above it? My friends, one of the grandest truths of religion is, the supreme importance of character, of virtue, of that divine spirit which shone out in Christ. The grand heresy is, to substitute any thing for this, whether creed, or form, or church. One of the greatest wrongs to Christ is, to despise his character, his virtue, in a disciple who happens to wear a different name from our own.

When I represent to myself true virtue or goodness; not that which is made up of outward proprieties and prudent calculations, but that which chooses duty for its own sake and as the first concern; which respects impartially the rights of every human being; which labors and suffers with patient resolution for truth and others' welfare; which blends energy and sweetness, deep humility and self-reverence; which places joyful faith in the perfection of God, communes with him intimately, and strives to subject to his pure will all thought, imagination, and desire; which lays hold on the promise of everlasting life, and in the strength of this hope endures calmly and firmly the sorest evils of the present state; when I set before me this virtue, all the distinctions on which men value themselves fade away. Wealth is poor; worldly honor is mean; outward forms are beggarly elements. Condition, country, church, all sink into unimportance. Before this simple greatness I bow, I revere. The robed priest, the gorgeous altar, the great assembly, the pealing organ, all the exteriors of religion, vanish from my sight as I look at the good and great man, the holy, disinterested soul. Even I, with vision so dim, with heart so cold, can see and feel the divinity, the grandeur of true goodness. How, then, must God regard it? To his pure eye how lovely must it be! And can any of us turn from it, because some water has not been dropped on its forehead, or some bread put into its lips by a minister or priest; or because it has not learned to repeat some mysterious creed which a church or human council has ordained?

My friends, reverence virtue, holiness, the upright will which inflexibly cleaves to duty and the pure law of God. Reverence nothing in comparison with it. Regard this as the end, and all outward services as the means. Judge of men by this. Think no man the better, no man the worse, for the church he belongs to. Try him by his fruits. Expel from your breasts the demon of sectarianism, narrowness, bigotry, intolerance. This is not, as we are apt to think, a slight sin. It is a denial of the supremacy of goodness. It sets up something, whether a form or dogma, above the virtue of the heart and the life. Sectarianism immures itself in its particular church as in a dungeon, and is there cut off from the free air, the cheerful light, the goodly prospects, the celestial beauty of the church universal.

My friends, I know that I am addressing those who hold various opinions as to the controverted points of theology. We have grown up under different influences. We bear different names. But if we purpose solemnly to do God's will, and are following the precepts and example of Christ, we are one church, and let nothing divide us. Diversities of opinion may incline us to worship under different roofs ; or diversities of tastes or habit, to worship with different forms. But these varieties are not schisms ; they do not break the unity of Christ's church. We may still honor and love and rejoice in one another's spiritual life and progress as truly as if we were cast into one and the same unyielding form. God loves variety in nature and in the human soul, nor does he reject it in Christian worship. In many great truths, in those which are most quickening, purifying, and consoling, we all, I hope, agree. There is, too, a common ground of practice, aloof from all controversy, on which we may all meet. We may all unite hearts and hands in doing good, in fulfilling God's purposes of love towards our race, in toiling and suffering for the cause of humanity, in spreading intelligence, freedom, and virtue, in making God known for the reverence, love, and imitation of his creatures, in resisting the abuses and corruptions of past ages, in exploring and drying up the sources of poverty, in rescuing the fallen from intemperance, in succouring the orphan and widow, in enlightening and elevating the depressed portions of the community, in breaking the yoke of the oppressed and enslaved, in exposing and withstanding the spirit and horrors of war, in sending God's Word to the ends of the earth, in redeeming the world from sin and woe. The angels and pure spirits who visit our earth come not to join a sect, but to do good to all. May this universal charity descend on us, and possess our hearts ; may our narrowness, exclusiveness, and bigotry melt away under this mild, celestial fire. Thus we shall not only join ourselves to Christ's Universal Church on earth, but to the Invisible Church, to the innumerable company of the just made perfect, in the mansions of everlasting purity and peace.

NOTES.

I have spoken in this Discourse of the Romish church as excluding from salvation those who do not submit to it. I know, and rejoice to know, that many Catholics are too wise and good to hold this doctrine ; but the church, interpreted by its past words and acts, is not so liberal.

I have also expressed my reverence for the illustrious names which have adorned the English church. This church sets up higher claims than any other in the Protestant world ; but by a man acquainted with its early history it will be seen to be clothed with no peculiar authority. If any Protestant church deserves to be called a creature of the state, it is this. It was shaped by the sovereign very much after his own will. It is a problem in history, how the English people, so sturdy and stout-hearted in the main, could be so tame and flexible in matters of religion, under Henry the Eighth, Edward the Sixth, Mary, and Elizabeth. They seem to have received, almost as unresistingly as the coin, the image and superscription of the king. The causes of this yieldingness are to be found in the averseness to civil broils to which the nation had been brought by the recent bloody and exhausting wars of the Roses ; in the formidable power of the Tudor sovereigns ; in the insular position of England, and her distance from Rome, which checked the domination of the papacy ; in the ignorance of the people ; in the ravenousness of the nobles for the property of the church in the first instance, and afterwards in their greediness for court favor. This strange pliancy is a stain on the annals of the country. It was in the Puritans that the old national sturdiness revived, that England became herself again. These men were rude in aspect, and forbidding in manners; but, with all their sternness, narrowness, frowning theology, and high religious pretensions, they were the master spirits of their times. To their descendants it is delightful to think of the service they rendered to the civil and religious liberties of England and the world, and to recall their deep, vital piety, a gem most rudely set, but too precious to be overvalued.

Since the preceding Discourse has been printed, the following extract from an article in the Edinburgh Review for July, 1841, entitled "The Port-Royalists," has been deemed so strikingly coincident that it is herewith appended.

"But for every labor under the sun, says the Wise Man, there is a time. There is a time for bearing testimony against the errors of Rome; why not also a time for testifying to the sublime virtues with which those errors have been so often associated? Are we for ever to admit and never to practise the duties of kindness and mutual forbearance? Does Christianity consist in a vivid perception of the faults, and an obtuse blindness to the merits of those who differ from us? Is charity a virtue only when we ourselves are the objects of it? Is there not a church as pure and more catholic than that of Oxford or Rome, — a church comprehending within its limits every human being who, according to the measure of the knowledge placed within his reach, strives habitually to be conformed to the will of the common Father of us all? To indulge hope beyond the pale of some narrow communion has, by each Christian society in its turn, been denounced as a daring presumption. Yet hope has come to all; and with her, faith and charity, her inseparable companions. Amidst the shock of contending creeds and the uproar of anathemas, they who have ears to hear and hearts to understand have listened to gentler and more kindly sounds. Good men may debate as polemics, but they will feel as Christians. On the universal mind of Christendom is indelibly engraven one image, towards which the eyes of all are more or less earnestly directed. Whoever has himself caught any resemblance, however faint and imperfect, to that divine and benignant Original, has, in his measure, learned to recognize a brother wherever he can discern the same resemblance.

"There is an essential unity in that kingdom which is not of this world. But within the provinces of that mighty state there is room for endless varieties of administration, and for local laws and customs widely differing from each other. The unity consists in the one object of worship, the one object of affiance, the one source of virtue, the one cementing principle of mutual love which pervades and animates the whole. The diversities are, and must be, as numerous and intractable as are the essential distinctions which nature, habit, and circumstances have created amongst men. Uniformity of creeds, of discipline, of ritual, and of ceremonies, in such a world as ours! a world where no two men are not as distinguishable in their mental as in their physical aspect; where every petty community has its separate system of civil government; where all that meets the eye, and all that arrests the ear has the stamp of boundless and infinite variety! What are the harmonies of tone, of color, and of form, but the result of contrasts; of contrasts held in subordination to one pervading principle, which reconciles without confounding the component elements of the music, the painting, or the structure? In the physical works of God beauty could have no existence without endless diversities. Why assume that in religious society — a work not less surely to be ascribed to the supreme Author of all things — this law is absolutely reversed? Were it possible to subdue that innate tendency of the human mind which compels men to differ in religious opinions and observances, at least as widely as on all other subjects, what would be the results of such a triumph? Where would then be the free comparison and the continual enlargement of thought; where the self-distrusts which are the springs of humility, or the mutual dependencies which are the bonds of love? He who made us with this infinite variety in our intellectual and physical constitution must have foreseen, and foreseeing, must have intended, a corresponding dissimilarity in the opinions of his creatures on all questions submitted to their judgment and proposed for their acceptance. For truth is his law; and if all will profess to think alike, all must live in the habitual violation of it.

"Zeal for uniformity attests the latent distrusts, not the firm convictions of the zealot. In proportion to the strength of our self-reliance is our indifference to the multiplication of suffrages in favor of our own judgment. Our minds are steeped in imagery; and where the visible form is not, the impalpable spirit escapes the notice of the unreflecting multitude. In common hands analysis stops at the species or the genus, and cannot rise to the order or the class. To distinguish birds from fishes, beasts from insects, limits the efforts of the vulgar observer of the face of nature. But Cuvier could trace the sublime unity, the universal type, the fontal Idea existing in the creative Intelligence, which connects as one the mammoth and the snail. So, common observers can distinguish from each other the different varieties of religious society, and can rise no higher. Where one assembly worships with harmonies of music, fumes of incense, ancient liturgies, and a gorgeous ceremonial, and another listens to the unaided voice of a single pastor, they can perceive and record the differences; but the hidden ties which unite them both escape such observation. All appears as contrast, and all ministers to antipathy and discord. It is our belief that these things may be rightly viewed in a different aspect, and yet with the most severe conformity to the Divine will, whether as intimated by natural religion, or as revealed in Holy Scripture. We believe, that, in the judgment of an enlightened charity, many Christian societies who are accustomed to denounce each other's errors will at length come to be regarded as members in common of the one great and comprehensive church, in which diversities of forms are harmonized by an all-pervading unity of spirit. For ourselves, at least, we should deeply regret to conclude that we are aliens from that great Christian commonwealth of which the nuns and recluses of the valley of Port-Royal were members, and members assuredly of no common excellence."

SELF-CULTURE.

AN ADDRESS

INTRODUCTORY TO THE FRANKLIN LECTURES,

DELIVERED AT BOSTON, SEPT., 1838.

This Address was intended to make two lectures; but the author was led to abridge it and deliver it as one, partly by the apprehension, that some passages were too abstract for a popular address, partly to secure the advantages of presenting the whole subject at once and in close connexion, and for other reasons which need not be named. Most of the passages which were omitted, are now published. The author respectfully submits the discourse to those for whom it was particularly intended, and to the public, in the hope, that it will at least bring a great subject before the minds of some, who may not as yet have given to it the attention it deserves.

ADDRESS ON SELF-CULTURE.

MY RESPECTED FRIENDS:

By the invitation of the committee of arrangements for the Franklin Lectures, I now appear before you to offer some remarks introductory to this course. My principal inducement for doing so is my deep interest in those of my fellow-citizens, for whom these lectures are principally designed. I understood that they were to be attended chiefly by those who are occupied by manual labor; and, hearing this, I did not feel myself at liberty to decline the service to which I had been invited. I wished by compliance to express my sympathy with this large portion of my race. I wished to express my sense of obligation to those, from whose industry and skill I derive almost all the comforts of life. I wished still more to express my joy in the efforts they are making for their own improvement, and my firm faith in their success. These motives will give a particular character and bearing to some of my remarks. I shall speak occasionally as among those who live by the labor of their hands. But I shall not speak as one separated from them. I belong rightfully to the great fraternity of working men. Happily in this community we all are bred and born to work ; and this honorable mark, set on us all, should bind together the various portions of the community.

I have expressed my strong interest in the mass of the people ; and this is founded, not on their usefulness to the community, so much as on what they are in themselves. Their condition is indeed obscure ; but their importance is not on this account a whit the less. The multitude of men cannot, from the nature of the case, be distinguished ; for the very idea of distinction is, that a man stands out from the multitude. They make little noise and draw little notice in their narrow spheres of action ; but still they have their full proportion of personal worth and even of greatness. Indeed every man, in every condition, is great. It is only our own diseased sight which makes him little. A man is great as a man, be he where or what he may. The grandeur of his nature turns to insignificance all outward distinctions. His powers of intellect, of conscience, of love, of knowing God, of perceiving the beautiful, of acting on his own mind, on outward nature, and on his fellow-creatures, these are glorious prerogatives. Through the vulgar error of undervaluing what is common, we are apt indeed to pass these by as of little worth. But as in the outward creation, so in the soul, the common is the most precious. Science and art may invent splendid modes of illuminating the apartments of the opulent ; but these are all poor and worthless, compared with the common light which the sun sends into all our windows, which he pours freely, impartially over hill and valley, which kindles daily the eastern and western sky ; and so the common lights of reason, and conscience, and love, are of more worth and dignity than the rare endowments which give celebrity to a few. Let us not disparage that nature which is common to all men; for no thought can measure its grandeur. It is the image of God, the image even of his infinity, for no limits can be set to its unfolding. He who possesses the divine powers of the soul is a great being, be his place what it may. You may clothe him with rags, may immure him in a dungeon, may chain him to slavish tasks. But he is still great. You may shut him out of your houses; but God opens to him heavenly mansions. He makes no show indeed in the streets of a splendid city; but a clear thought, a pure affection, a resolute act of a virtuous will, have a dignity of quite another kind and far higher than accumulations of brick and granite and plaster and stucco, however cunningly put together, or though stretching far beyond our sight. Nor is this all. If we pass over this grandeur of our common nature, and turn our thoughts to that comparative greatness, which draws chief attention, and which consists in the decided superiority of the individual to the general standard of power and character, we shall find this as free and frequent a growth among the obscure and unnoticed as in more conspicuous walks of life. The truly great are to be found everywhere, nor is it easy to say, in what condition they spring up most plentifully. Real greatness has nothing to do with a man's sphere. It does not lie in the magnitude of his outward agency, in the extent of the effects which he produces. The greatest men may do comparatively little abroad. Perhaps the greatest in our city at this moment are buried in obscurity. Grandeur of character lies wholly in force of soul, that is, in the force of thought, moral principle, and love, and this may be found in the humblest condition of life. A man brought up to an obscure trade, and hemmed in by the wants of a growing family, may, in his narrow sphere, perceive more clearly, discriminate more keenly, weigh evidence more wisely, seize on the right means more decisively, and have more presence of mind in difficulty, than another who has accumulated vast stores of knowledge by laborious study; and he has more of intellectual greatness. Many a man, who has gone but a few miles from home, understands human nature better, detects motives and weighs character more sagaciously, than another, who has travelled over the known world, and made a name by his reports of different countries. It is force of thought which measures intellectual, and so it is force of principle which measures moral greatness, that highest of human endowments, that brightest manifestation of the Divinity. The greatest man is he who chooses the Right with invincible resolution, who resists the sorest temptations from within and without, who bears the heaviest burdens cheerfully, who is calmest in storms and most fearless under menace and frowns, whose reliance on truth, on virtue, on God, is most unfaltering; and is this a greatness, which is apt to make a show, or which is most likely to abound in conspicuous station? The solemn conflicts of reason with passion; the victories of moral and religious principle over urgent and almost irresistible solicitations to self-indulgence; the hardest sacrifices of duty, those of deep-seated affection and of the heart's fondest hopes; the consolations, hopes, joys, and peace, of disappointed, persecuted, scorned, deserted virtue; these are of course unseen;

so that the true greatness of human life is almost wholly out of sight. Perhaps in our presence, the most heroic deed on earth is done in some silent spirit, the loftiest purpose cherished, the most generous sacrifice made and we do not suspect it. I believe this greatness to be most common among the multitude, whose names are never heard. Among common people will be found more of hardship borne manfully, more of unvarnished truth, more of religious trust, more of that generosity which gives what the giver needs himself, and more of a wise estimate of life and death, than among the more prosperous. — And even in regard to influence over other beings, which is thought the peculiar prerogative of distinguished station, I believe, that the difference between the conspicuous and the obscure does not amount to much. Influence is to be measured, not by the extent of surface it covers, but by its *kind*. A man may spread his mind, his feelings, and opinions, through a great extent; but if his mind be a low one, he manifests no greatness. A wretched artist may fill a city with daubs, and by a false, showy style achieve a reputation; but the man of genius, who leaves behind him one grand picture, in which immortal beauty is embodied, and which is silently to spread a true taste in his art, exerts an incomparably higher influence. Now the noblest influence on earth is that exerted on character; and he who puts forth this, does a great work, no matter how narrow or obscure his sphere. The father and mother of an unnoticed family, who, in their seclusion, awaken the mind of one child to the idea and love of perfect goodness, who awaken in him a strength of will to repel all temptation, and who send him out prepared to profit by the conflicts of life, surpass in influence a

Napoleon breaking the world to his sway. And not only is their work higher in kind; who knows, but that they are doing a greater work even as to extent of surface than the conqueror? Who knows, but that the being, whom they inspire with holy and disinterested principles, may communicate himself to others; and that, by a spreading agency, of which they were the silent origin, improvements may spread through a nation, through the world? In these remarks you will see why I feel and express a deep interest in the obscure, in the mass of men. The distinctions of society vanish before the light of these truths. I attach myself to the multitude, not because they are voters and have political power; but because they are men, and have within their reach the most glorious prizes of humanity.

In this country the mass of the people are distinguished by possessing means of improvement, of self-culture, possessed nowhere else. To incite them to the use of these, is to render them the best service they can receive. Accordingly I have chosen for the subject of this lecture, Self-culture, or the care which every man owes to himself, to the unfolding and perfecting of his nature. I consider this topic as particularly appropriate to the introduction of a course of lectures, in consequence of a common disposition to regard these and other like means of instruction, as able of themselves to carry forward the hearer. Lectures have their use. They stir up many, who, but for such outward appeals, might have slumbered to the end of life. But let it be remembered, that little is to be gained simply by coming to this place once a-week, and giving up the mind for an hour to be wrought upon by a teacher. Unless we are roused to act upon ourselves, unless we engage in the work of self-improvement, unless we purpose strenuously to form and elevate our own minds, unless what we hear is made a part of ourselves by conscientious reflection, very little permanent good is received.

Self-culture, I am aware, is a topic too extensive for a single discourse, and I shall be able to present but a few views which seem to me most important. My aim will be, to give first the Idea of self-culture, next its Means, and then to consider some objections to the leading views which I am now to lay before you.

Before entering on the discussion, let me offer one remark. Self-culture is something possible. It is not a dream. It has foundations in our nature. Without this conviction, the speaker will but declaim, and the hearer listen without profit. There are two powers of the human soul which make self-culture possible, the self-searching and the self-forming power. We have first the faculty of turning the mind on itself; of recalling its past, and watching its present operations; of learning its various capacities and susceptibilities, what it can do and bear, what it can enjoy and suffer; and of thus learning in general what our nature is, and what it was made for. It is worthy of observation, that we are able to discern not only what we already are, but what we may become, to see in ourselves germs and promises of a growth to which no bounds can be set, to dart beyond what we have actually gained to the idea of Perfection as the end of our being. It is by this self-comprehending power that we are distinguished from the brutes, which give no signs of looking into themselves Without this there would be no self-culture, for we should not know the work to be done; and one reason why self-culture is so little proposed is, that so few penetrate into their own nature. To most men, their own spirits are shadowy, unreal, compared with what is outward. When they happen to cast a glance inward, they see there only a dark, vague chaos. They distinguish perhaps some violent passion, which has driven them to injurious excess; but their highest powers hardly attract a thought; and thus multitudes live and die as truly strangers to themselves, as to countries of which they have heard the name, but which human foot has never trodden.

But self-culture is possible, not only because we can enter into and search ourselves. We have a still nobler power, that of acting on, determining and forming ourselves. This is a fearful as well as glorious endowment, for it is the ground of human responsibility. We have the power not only of tracing our powers, but of guiding and impelling them; not only of watching our passions, but of controlling them; not only of seeing our faculties grow, but of applying to them means and influences to aid their growth. We can stay or change the current of thought. We can concentrate the intellect on objects which we wish to comprehend. We can fix our eyes on perfection, and make almost everything speed us towards it. This is indeed a noble prerogative of our nature. Possessing this, it matters little what or where we are now, for we can conquer a better lot, and even be happier for starting from the lowest point. Of all the discoveries which men need to make, the most important at the present moment, is that of the self-forming power treasured up in themselves. They little suspect its extent, as little as the savage apprehends the energy which the mind is created to exert on the material world. It transcends in importance all our power over outward nature. There is more of divinity in it, than in the force which impels the outward universe; and yet how little we comprehend it! How it slumbers in most men unsuspected, unused! This makes self-culture possible, and binds it on us as a solemn duty.

I. I am first to unfold the idea of self-culture; and this, in its most general form, may easily be seized. To cultivate any thing, be it a plant, an animal, a mind, is to make grow. Growth, expansion is the end. Nothing admits culture, but that which has a principle of life, capable of being expanded. He, therefore, who does what he can to unfold all his powers and capacities, especially his nobler ones, so as to become a well proportioned, vigorous, excellent, happy being, practises self-culture.

This culture, of course, has various branches corresponding to the different capacities of human nature; but, though various, they are intimately united and make progress together. The soul, which our philosophy divides into various capacities, is still one essence, one life; and it exerts at the same moment, and blends in the same act, its various energies of thought, feeling, and volition. Accordingly, in a wise self-culture, all the principles of our nature grow at once by joint, harmonious action, just as all parts of the plant are unfolded together. When therefore you hear of different branches of self-improvement, you will not think of them as distinct processes going on independently of each other, and requiring each its own separate means. Still a distinct consideration of these is needed to a full comprehension of the subject, and these I shall proceed to unfold.

First, self-culture is Moral, a branch of singular importance. When a man looks into himself, he discovers two distinct orders or kinds of principles, which it behoves him especially to comprehend. He discovers desires, appetites, passions, which terminate in himself, which crave and seek his own interest, gratification, distinction; and he discovers another principle, an antagonist to these, which is Impartial, Disinterested, Universal, enjoining on him a regard to the rights and happiness of other beings, and laying on him obligations which *must* be discharged, cost what they may, or however they may clash with his particular pleasure or gain. No man, however narrowed to his own interest, however hardened by selfishness, can deny, that there springs up within him a great idea in opposition to interest, the idea of Duty, that an inward voice calls him more or less distinctly, to revere and exercise Impartial Justice, and Universal Good-will. This disinterested principle in human nature we call sometimes reason, sometimes conscience, sometimes the moral sense or faculty. But, be its name what it may, it is a real principle in each of us, and it is the supreme power within us, to be cultivated above all others, for on its culture the right developement of all others depends. The passions indeed may be stronger than the conscience, may lift up a louder voice; but their clamor differs wholly from the tone of command in which the conscience speaks. They are not clothed with its authority, its binding power. In their very triumphs they are rebuked by the moral principle, and often cower before its still, deep, menacing voice. No part of self-knowledge is more important than to discern clearly these two great principles, the self-seeking and the disinterested; and the most important part of self-culture is to depress the former, and to exalt the latter, or to enthrone the sense of duty within us. There are no limits to the growth of this moral force in man, if he will cherish it faithfully. There have been men, whom no power in the universe could turn from the Right, by whom death in its most dreadful forms has been less dreaded, than transgression of the inward law of universal justice and love.

In the next place, self-culture is Religious. When we look into ourselves, we discover powers, which link us with this outward, visible, finite, ever-changing world. We have sight and other senses to discern, and limbs and various faculties to secure and appropriate the material creation. And we have, too, a power, which cannot stop at what we see and handle, at what exists within the bounds of space and time, which seeks for the Infinite, Uncreated Cause, which cannot rest till it ascend to the Eternal, All-comprehending Mind. This we call the religious principle, and its grandeur cannot be exaggerated by human language; for it marks out a being destined for higher communion than with the visible universe. To develope this, is eminently to educate ourselves. The true idea of God, unfolded clearly and livingly within us, and moving us to adore and obey him, and to aspire after likeness to him, is the noblest growth in human, and, I may add, in celestial natures. The religious principle, and the moral, are intimately connected, and grow together. The former is indeed the perfection and highest manifestation of the latter. They are both disinterested. It is the essence of true religion to recognise and adore in God the attributes of Impartial Justice and Universal Love, and to hear him commanding us in the conscience to become what we adore.

Again. Self-culture is Intellectual. We cannot look into ourselves without discovering the intellectual principle, the power which thinks, reasons, and judges, the power of seeking and acquiring truth. This, indeed, we are in no danger of overlooking. The intellect being the great instrument by which men compass their wishes, it draws more attention than any of our other powers. When we speak to men of improving themselves, the first thought which occurs to them is, that they must cultivate their understanding, and get knowledge and skill. By education, men mean almost exclusively intellectual training. For this, schools and colleges are instituted, and to this the moral and religious discipline of the young is sacrificed. Now I reverence, as much as any man, the intellect; but let us never exalt it above the moral principle. With this it is most intimately connected. In this its culture is founded, and to exalt this is its highest aim. Whoever desires that his intellect may grow up to soundness, to healthy vigor, must begin with moral discipline. Reading and study are not enough to perfect the power of thought. One thing above all is needful, and that is, the Disinterestedness which is the very soul of virtue. To gain truth, which is the great object of the understanding, I must seek it disinterestedly. Here is the first and grand condition of intellectual progress. I must choose to receive the truth, no matter how it bears on myself. I must follow it, no matter where it leads, what interests it opposes, to what persecution or loss it lays me open, from what party it severs me, or to what party it allies. Without this fairness of mind, which is only another phrase for disinterested love of truth, great native powers of understanding are perverted and led astray; genius runs wild; "the light within us becomes darkness." The subtilest reasoners, for want of this, cheat themselves as well as others, and become entangled in the web of their own sophistry. It is a fact well known in the history of science and philosophy, that men, gifted by nature with singular intelligence, have broached the grossest errors, and even sought to undermine the grand primitive truths on which human virtue, dignity, and hope depend. And, on the other hand, I have known instances of men of naturally moderate powers of mind, who, by a disinterested love of truth and their fellow-creatures, have gradually risen to no small force and enlargement of thought. Some of the most useful teachers in the pulpit and in schools, have owed their power of enlightening others, not so much to any natural superiority, as to the simplicity, impartiality, and disinterestedness of their minds, to their readiness to live and die for the truth. A man, who rises above himself, looks from an eminence on nature and providence, on society and life. Thought expands, as by a natural elasticity, when the pressure of selfishness is removed. The moral and religious principles of the soul, generously cultivated, fertilize the intellect. Duty, faithfully performed, opens the mind to truth, both being of one family, alike immutable, universal, and everlasting.

I have enlarged on this subject, because the connexion between moral and intellectual culture is often overlooked, and because the former is often sacrificed to the latter. The exaltation of talent, as it is called, above virtue and religion, is the curse of the age. Education is now chiefly a stimulus to learning, and thus men acquire power without the principles which alone make it a good. Talent is worshipped; but, if divorced from rectitude, it will prove more of a demon than a god.

Intellectual culture consists, not chiefly, as many are apt to think, in accumulating information, though this is important, but in building up a force of thought which may be turned at will on any subjects, on which we are called to pass judgment. This force is manifested in the concentration of the attention, in accurate, penetrating observation, in reducing complex subjects to their elements, in diving beneath the effect to the cause, in detecting the more subtile differences and resemblances of things, in reading the future in the present, and especially in rising from particular facts to general laws or universal truths. This last exertion of the intellect, its rising to broad views and great principles, constitutes what is called the philosophical mind, and is especially worthy of culture. What it means, your own observation must have taught you. You must have taken note of two classes of men, the one always employed on details, on particular facts, and the other using these facts as foundations of higher, wider truths. The latter are philosophers. For example, men had for ages seen pieces of wood, stones, metals falling to the ground. Newton seized on these particular facts, and rose to the idea, that all matter tends, or is attracted, towards all matter, and then defined the law according to which this attraction or force acts at different distances, thus giving us a grand principle, which, we have reason to think, extends to and controls the whole outward creation. One man reads a history, and can tell you all its events, and there stops. Another combines these events, brings them under one view, and learns the great causes which are at work on this or another nation, and what are its great tendencies, whether to freedom or despotism, to one or another form of civilization. So, one man talks continually about the particular actions of this or another neighbour; whilst another looks beyond the acts to the inward principle from which they spring, and gathers from them larger views of human nature. In a word, one man sees all things apart and in fragments, whilst another strives to discover the harmony, connexion, unity of all. One of the great evils of society is, that men, occupied perpetually with petty details, want general truths, want broad and fixed principles. Hence many, not wicked, are unstable, habitually inconsistent, as if they were overgrown children rather than men. To build up that strength of mind, which apprehends and cleaves to great universal truths, is the highest intellectual self-culture; and here I wish you to observe how entirely this culture agrees with that of the moral and the religious principles of our nature, of which I have previously spoken. In each of these, the improvement of the soul consists in raising it above what is narrow, particular, individual, selfish, to the universal and unconfined. To improve a man, is to liberalize, enlarge him in thought, feeling, and purpose. Narrowness of intellect and heart, this is the degradation from which all culture aims to rescue the human being.

Again. Self-culture is social, or one of its great offices is to unfold and purify the affections, which spring up instinctively in the human breast, which bind together husband and wife, parent and child, brother and sister; which bind a man to friends and neighbours, to his country, and to the suffering who fall under his eye, wherever they belong. The culture of these is an important part of our work, and it consists in converting them from instincts into principles, from natural into spiritual attachments, in giving them a rational, moral, and holy character. For example, our affection for our children is at first instinctive; and if it continue such, it rises little above the brute's attachment to its young. But when a parent infuses into his natural love for his offspring, moral and religious principle, when he comes to regard his child as an intelligent, spiritual, immortal being, and honors him as such, and desires first of all to make him disinterested, noble, a worthy child of God and the friend of his race, then the instinct rises into a generous and holy sentiment. It resembles God's paternal love for his spiritual family. A like purity and dignity we must aim to give to all our affections.

Again. Self-culture is Practical, or it proposes, as one of its chief ends, to fit us for action, to make us efficient in whatever we undertake, to train us to firmness of purpose and to fruitfulness of resource in common life, and especially in emergencies, in times of difficulty, danger, and trial. But passing over this and other topics for which I have no time, I shall confine myself to two branches of self-culture which have been almost wholly overlooked in the education of the people, and which ought not to be so slighted.

In looking at our nature, we discover, among its admirable endowments, the sense or perception of Beauty. We see the germ of this in every human being, and there is no power which admits greater cultivation; and why should it not be cherished in all? It deserves remark, that the provision for this principle is infinite in the universe. There is but a very minute portion of the creation which we can turn into food and clothes, or gratification for the body; but the whole creation may be used to minister to the sense of beauty. Beauty is an all-pervading presence. It unfolds in the numberless flowers of the spring. It waves in the branches of the trees and the green blades of grass. It haunts the depths of the earth and sea, and gleams out in the hues of the shell and the precious stone. And not only these minute objects, but the ocean, the mountains, the clouds, the heavens, the stars, the rising and setting sun, all overflow with beauty. The universe is its temple; and those men, who are alive to it, cannot lift their eyes without feeling themselves encompassed with it on every side. Now this beauty is so precious, the enjoyments it gives are so refined and pure, so congenial with our tenderest and noble feelings, and so akin to worship, that it is painful to think of the multitude of men as living in the midst of it, and living almost as blind to it, as if, instead of this fair earth and glorious sky, they were tenants of a dungeon. An infinite joy is lost to the world by the want of culture of this spiritual endowment. Suppose that I were to visit a cottage, and to see its walls lined with the choicest pictures of Raphael, and every spare nook filled with statues of the most exquisite workmanship, and that I were to learn, that neither man, woman, nor child ever cast an eye at these miracles of art, how should I feel their privation; how should I want to open their eyes, and to help them to comprehend and feel the loveliness and grandeur which in vain courted their notice! But every husbandman is living in sight of the works of a diviner Artist; and how much would his existence be elevated, could he see the glory which shines forth in their forms, hues, proportions, and moral expression! I have spoken only of the beauty of nature, but how much of this mysterious charm is found in the elegant arts, and especially in literature? The best books have most beauty. The greatest truths are wronged if not linked with beauty, and they win their way most surely and deeply into the soul when arrayed in this their natural and fit attire. Now no man receives the true culture of a man, in whom the sensibility to the beautiful is not cherished; and I know of no condition in life from which it should be excluded. Of all luxuries, this is the cheapest and most at hand; and it seems to me to be most important to those conditions, where coarse labor tends to give a grossness to the mind. From the diffusion of the sense of beauty in ancient Greece, and of the taste for music in modern Germany, we learn that the people at large may partake of refined gratifications, which have hitherto been thought to be necessarily restricted to a few.

What beauty is, is a question which the most penetrating minds have not satisfactorily answered; nor, were I able, is this the place for discussing it. But one thing I would say; the beauty of the outward creation is intimately related to the lovely, grand, interesting attributes of the soul. It is the emblem or expression of these. Matter becomes beautiful to us, when it seems to lose its material aspect, its inertness, finiteness, and grossness, and by the etherial lightness of its forms and motions seems to approach spirit; when it images to us pure and gentle affections; when it spreads out into a vastness which is a shadow of the Infinite; or when in more awful shapes and movements it speaks of the Omnipotent. Thus outward beauty is akin to something deeper and unseen, is the reflection of spiritual attributes; and of consequence the way to see and feel it more and more keenly, is to cultivate those moral, religious, intellectual, and social principles of which I have already spoken, and which are the glory of the spiritual nature; and I name this, that you may see, what I am anxious to show, the harmony which subsists among all branches of human culture, or how each forwards and is aided by all.

There is another power, which each man should cultivate according to his ability, but which is very much neglected in the mass of the people, and that is, the power of Utterance. A man was not made to shut up his mind in itself; but to give it voice and to exchange it for other minds. Speech is one of our grand distinctions from the brute. Our power over others lies not so much in the amount of thought within us, as in the power of bringing it out. A man, of more than ordinary intellectual vigor, may, for want of expression, be a cipher, without significance, in society. And not only does a man influence others, but he greatly aids his own intellect, by giving distinct and forcible utterance to his thoughts. We understand ourselves better, our conceptions grow clearer, by the very effort to make them clear to another. Our social rank, too, depends a good deal on our power of utterance. The principal distinction between what are called gentlemen and the vulgar lies in this, that the latter are awkward in manners, and are especially wanting in propriety, clearness, grace, and force of utterance. A man who cannot open his lips without breaking a rule of grammar, without showing in his dialect or brogue or uncouth tones his want of cultivation, or without darkening his meaning by a confused, unskilful mode of communication, cannot take the place to which, perhaps, his native good sense entitles him. To have intercourse with respectable people, we must speak their language. On this account, I am glad that grammar and a correct pronunciation are taught in the common schools of this city. These are not trifles ; nor are they superfluous to any class of people. They give a man access to social advantages, on which his improvement very much depends. The power of utterance should be included by all in their plans of self-culture.

I have now given a few views of the culture, the improvement, which every man should propose to himself. I have all along gone on the principle, that a man has within him capacities of growth, which deserve and will reward intense, unrelaxing toil. I do not look on a human being as a machine, made to be kept in action by a foreign force, to accomplish an unvarying succession of motions, to do a fixed amount of work, and then to fall to pieces at death, but as a being of free spiritual powers ; and I place little value on any culture, but that which aims to bring out these and to give them perpetual impulse and expansion. I am aware, that this view is far from being universal. The common notion has been, that the mass of the people need no other culture than is necessary to fit them for their various trades ; and, though this error is passing away, it is far from being exploded. But the ground of a man's culture lies in his nature, not in his calling. His powers are to be unfolded on account of their inherent dignity, not their outward direction. He is to be educated, because he is a man, not because he is to make shoes, nails, or pins. A trade is plainly not the great end of his being, for his mind cannot be shut up in it; his force of thought cannot be exhausted on it. He has faculties to which it gives no action, and deep wants it cannot answer. Poems, and systems of theology and philosophy, which have made some noise in the world, have been wrought at the work-bench and amidst the toils of the field. How often, when the arms are mechanically plying a trade, does the mind, lost in reverie or day-dreams, escape to the ends of the earth! How often does the pious heart of woman mingle the greatest of all thoughts, that of God, with household drudgery! Undoubtedly a man is to perfect himself in his trade, for by it he is to earn his bread and to serve the community. But bread or subsistence is not his highest good; for, if it were, his lot would be harder than that of the inferior animals, for whom nature spreads a table and weaves a wardrobe, without a care of their own. Nor was he made chiefly to minister to the wants of the community. A rational, moral being cannot, without infinite wrong, be converted into a mere instrument of others' gratification. He is necessarily an end, not a means. A mind, in which are sown the seeds of wisdom, disinterestedness, firmness of purpose, and piety, is worth more than all the outward material interests of a world. It exists for itself, for its own perfection, and must not be enslaved to its own or others' animal wants You tell me, that a liberal culture is needed for men who are to fill high stations, but not for such as are doomed to vulgar labor. I answer, that Man is a greater name than President or King. Truth and goodness are equally precious, in whatever sphere they are found. Besides, men of all conditions sustain equally the relations, which give birth to the highest virtues and demand the highest powers. The laborer is not a mere laborer. He has close, tender, responsible connections with God and his fellow-creatures. He is a son, husband, father, friend, and Christian. He belongs to a home, a country, a church, a race ; and is such a man to be cultivated only for a trade ? Was he not sent into the world for a great work ? To educate a child perfectly requires profounder thought, greater wisdom, than to govern a state ; and for this plain reason, that the interests and wants of the latter are more superficial, coarser, and more obvious, than the spiritual capacities, the growth of thought and feeling, and the subtile laws of the mind, which must all be studied and comprehended, before the work of education can be thoroughly performed ; and yet to all conditions this greatest work on earth is equally committed by God. What plainer proof do we need that a higher culture, than has yet been dreamed of, is needed by our whole race ?

II. I now proceed to inquire into the Means, by which the self-culture, just described, may be promoted ; and here I know not where to begin. The subject is so extensive, as well as important, that I feel myself unable to do any justice to it, especially in the limits to which I am confined. I beg you to consider me as presenting but hints, and such as have offered themselves with very little research to my own mind.

And, first, the great means of self-culture, that which includes all the rest, is to fasten on this culture as our Great End, to determine deliberately and solemnly, that we will make the most and the best of the powers which God has given us. Without this resolute purpose, the best means are worth little, and with it the poorest become mighty. You may see thousands, with every opportunity of improvement which wealth can gather, with teachers, libraries, and apparatus, bringing nothing to pass, and others, with few helps, doing wonders ; and simply because the latter are in earnest, and the former not. A man in earnest finds means, or, if he cannot find, creates them. A vigorous purpose makes much out of little, breathes power into weak instruments, disarms difficulties, and even turns them into assistances. Every condition has means of progress, if we have spirit enough to use them. Some volumes have recently been published, giving examples or histories of "knowledge acquired under difficulties"; and it is most animating to see in these what a resolute man can do for himself. A great idea, like this of Self-culture, if seized on clearly and vigorously, burns like a living coal in the soul. He who deliberately adopts a great end, has, by this act, half accomplished it, has scaled the chief barrier to success.

One thing is essential to the strong purpose of self-culture now insisted on, namely, faith in the practicableness of this culture. A great object, to awaken resolute choice, must be seen to be within our reach. The truth, that progress is the very end of our being, must not be received as a tradition, but comprehended and felt as a reality. Our minds are apt to pine and starve, by being imprisoned within what we have already attained. A true faith, looking up to something better, catching glimpses of a distant perfection, prophesying to ourselves improvements proportioned to our conscientious labors, gives energy of purpose, gives wings to the soul; and this faith will continually grow, by acquainting ourselves with our own nature, and with the promises of Divine help and immortal life which abound in Revelation.

Some are discouraged from proposing to themselves improvement, by the false notion, that the study of books, which their situation denies them, is the all-important, and only sufficient means. Let such consider, that the grand volumes, of which all our books are transcripts, I mean nature, revelation, the human soul, and human life, are freely unfolded to every eye. The great sources of wisdom are experience and observation; and these are denied to none. To open and fix our eyes upon what passes without and within us, is the most fruitful study. Books are chiefly useful, as they help us to interpret what we see and experience. When they absorb men, as they sometimes do, and turn them from observation of nature and life, they generate a learned folly, for which the plain sense of the laborer could not be exchanged but at great loss. It deserves attention that the greatest men have been formed without the studies, which at present are thought by many most needful to improvement. Homer, Plato, Demosthenes, never heard the name of chemistry, and knew less of the solar system than a boy in our common schools. Not that these sciences are unimportant; but the lesson is, that human improvement never wants the means, where the purpose of it is deep and earnest in the soul.

The purpose of self-culture, this is the life and strength of all the methods we use for our own elevation. I reiterate this principle on account of its great importance; and I would add a remark to prevent its misapprehension. When I speak of the purpose of self-culture, I mean, that it should be sincere. In other words, we must make self-culture really and truly our end, or choose it for its own sake, and not merely as a means or instrument of something else. And here I touch a common and very pernicious error. Not a few persons desire to improve themselves only to get property and to rise in the world; but such do not properly choose improvement, but something outward and foreign to themselves; and so low an impulse can produce only a stinted, partial, uncertain growth. A man, as I have said, is to cultivate himself because he is a man. He is to start with the conviction, that there is something greater within him than in the whole material creation, than in all the worlds which press on the eye and ear; and that inward improvements have a worth and dignity in themselves, quite distinct from the power they give over outward things. Undoubtedly a man is to labor to better his condition, but first to better himself. If he knows no higher use of his mind than to invent and drudge for his body, his case is desperate as far as culture is concerned.

In these remarks, I do not mean to recommend to the laborer indifference to his outward lot. I hold it important, that every man in every class should possess the means of comfort, of health, of neatness in food and apparel, and of occasional retirement and leisure. These are good in themselves, to be sought for their own sakes, and still more, they are important means of the self-culture for which I am pleading. A clean, comfortable dwelling, with wholesome meals, is no small aid to intellectual and moral progress. A man living in a damp cellar or a garret open to rain and snow. breathing the foul air of a filthy room, and striving without success to appease hunger on scanty or unsavory food, is in danger of abandoning himself to a desperate, selfish recklessness. Improve then your lot. Multiply comforts, and still more get wealth if you can by honorable means, and if it do not cost too much. A true cultivation of the mind is fitted to forward you in your worldly concerns, and you ought to use it for this end. Only, beware, lest this end master you ; lest your motives sink as your condition improves; lest you fall victims to the miserable passion of vying with those around you in show, luxury, and expense. Cherish a true respect for yourselves. Feel that your nature is worth more than every thing which is foreign to you. He who has not caught a glimpse of his own rational and spiritual being, of something within himself superior to the world and allied to the divinity, wants the true spring of that purpose of self-culture, on which I have insisted as the first of all the means of improvement.

I proceed to another important means of self-culture, and this is the control of the animal appetites. To raise the moral and intellectual nature, we must put down the animal. Sensuality is the abyss in which very many souls are plunged and lost. Among the most prosperous classes, what a vast amount of intellectual life is drowned in luxurious excesses ! It is one great curse of wealth, that it is used to pamper the senses ; and among the poorer classes, though luxury is wanting, yet a gross feeding often prevails, under which the spirit is whelmed. It is a sad sight to walk through our streets, and to see how many countenances bear marks of a lethargy and a brutal coarseness, induced by unrestrained indulgence. Whoever would cultivate the soul, must restrain the appetites. I am not an advocate for the doctrine, that animal food was not meant for man; but that this is used among us to excess, that as a people we should gain much in cheerfulness, activity, and buoyancy of mind, by less gross and stimulating food, I am strongly inclined to believe. Above all, let me urge on those, who would bring out and elevate their higher nature, to abstain from the use of spirituous liquors. This bad habit is distinguished from all others by the ravages it makes on the reason, the intellect; and this effect is produced to a mournful extent, even when drunkenness is escaped. Not a few men, called temperate, and who have thought themselves such, have learned, on abstaining from the use of ardent spirits, that for years their minds had been clouded, impaired by moderate drinking, without their suspecting the injury. Multitudes in this city are bereft of half their intellectual energy, by a degree of indulgence which passes for innocent. Of all the foes of the working class, this is the deadliest. Nothing has done more to keep down this class, to destroy their self-respect, to rob them of their just influence in the community, to render profitless the means of improvement within their reach, than the use of ardent spirits as a drink. They are called on to withstand this practice, as they regard their honor, and would take their just place in society. They are under solemn obligations to give their sanction to every effort for its suppression.

They ought to regard as their worst enemies (though unintentionally such), as the enemies of their rights, dignity, and influence, the men who desire to flood city and country with distilled poison. I lately visited a flourishing village, and on expressing to one of the respected inhabitants the pleasure I felt in witnessing so many signs of progress, he replied, that one of the causes of the prosperity I witnessed, was the disuse of ardent spirits by the people. And this reformation we may be assured wrought something higher than outward prosperity. In almost every family so improved, we cannot doubt that the capacities of the parent for intellectual and moral improvement were enlarged, and the means of education made more effectual to the child. I call on working men to take hold of the cause of temperance as peculiarly *their* cause. These remarks are the more needed, in consequence of the efforts made far and wide, to annul at the present moment a recent law for the suppression of the sale of ardent spirits in such quantities as favor intemperance. I know, that there are intelligent and good men, who believe, that, in enacting this law, government transcended its limits, left its true path, and established a precedent for legislative interference with all our pursuits and pleasures. No one here looks more jealously on government than myself. But I maintain, that this is a case which stands by itself, which can be confounded with no other, and on which government from its very nature and end is peculiarly bound to act. Let it never be forgotten, that the great end of government, its highest function, is, not to make roads, grant charters, originate improvements, but to prevent or repress Crimes against individual rights and social order. For this end it ordains a penal code, erects prisons, and inflicts fearful punishments. Now if it be true, that a vast proportion of the crimes, which government is instituted to prevent and repress, have their origin in the use of ardent spirits ; if our poor-houses, work-houses, jails, and penitentiaries, are tenanted in a great degree by those whose first and chief impulse to crime came from the distillery and dram-shop ; if murder and theft, the most fearful outrages on property and life, are most frequently the issues and consummation of intemperance, is not government bound to restrain by legislation the vending of the stimulus to these terrible social wrongs ? Is government never to act as a parent, never to remove the causes or occasions of wrong-doing ? Has it but one instrument for repressing crime, namely, public, infamous punishment, an evil only inferior to crime ? Is government a usurper, does it wander beyond its sphere, by imposing restraints on an article, which does no imaginable good, which can plead no benefit conferred on body or mind, which unfits the citizen for the discharge of his duty to his country, and which, above all, stirs up men to the perpetration of most of the crimes, from which it is the highest and most solemn office of government to protect society ?

I come now to another important measure of self-culture, and this is, intercourse with superior minds. I have insisted on our own activity as essential to our progress; but we were not made to live or advance alone. Society is as needful to us as air or food. A child doomed to utter loneliness, growing up without sight or sound of human beings, would not put forth equal power with many brutes ; and a man, never brought into contact with minds superior to his own, will probably run one and the same dull round of thought and action to the end of life.

It is chiefly through books that we enjoy intercourse with superior minds, and these invaluable means of communication are in the reach of all. In the best books, great men talk to us, give us their most precious thoughts, and pour their souls into ours. God be thanked for books. They are the voices of the distant and the dead, and make us heirs of the spiritual life of past ages. Books are the true levellers. They give to all, who will faithfully use them, the society, the spiritual presence, of the best and greatest of our race. No matter how poor I am. No matter though the prosperous of my own time will not enter my obscure dwelling. If the Sacred Writers will enter and take up their abode under my roof, if Milton will cross my threshold to sing to me of Paradise, and Shakspeare to open to me the worlds of imagination and the workings of the human heart, and Franklin to enrich me with his practical wisdom, I shall not pine for want of intellectual companionship, and I may become a cultivated man though excluded from what is called the best society in the place where I live.

To make this means of culture effectual, a man must select good books, such as have been written by right-minded and strong-minded men, real thinkers, who instead of diluting by repetition what others say, have something to say for themselves, and write to give relief to full, earnest souls; and these works must not be skimmed over for amusement, but read with fixed attention and a reverential love of truth. In selecting books, we may be aided much by those who have studied more than ourselves. But, after all, it is best to be determined in this particular a good deal by our own tastes. The best books for a man are not always those which the wise recommend, but oftener those which meet the peculiar wants, the natural thirst of his mind, and therefore awaken interest and rivet thought. And here it may be well to observe, not only in regard to books but in other respects, that self-culture must vary with the individual. All means do not equally suit us all. A man must unfold himself freely, and should respect the peculiar gifts or biases by which nature has distinguished him from others. Self-culture does not demand the sacrifice of individuality. It does not regularly apply an established machinery, for the sake of torturing every man into one rigid shape, called perfection. As the human countenance, with the same features in us all, is diversified without end in the race, and is never the same in any two individuals, so the human soul, with the same grand powers and laws, expands into an infinite variety of forms, and would be wofully stinted by modes of culture requiring all men to learn the same lesson or to bend to the same rules.

I know how hard it is to some men, especially to those who spend much time in manual labor, to fix attention on books. Let them strive to overcome the difficulty, by choosing subjects of deep interest, or by reading in company with those whom they love. Nothing can supply the place of books. They are cheering or soothing companions in solitude, illness, affliction. The wealth of both continents would not compensate for the good they impart. Let every man, if possible, gather some good books under his roof, and obtain access for himself and family to some social library. Almost any luxury should be sacrificed to this.

One of the very interesting features of our times, is the multiplication of books, and their distribution through all conditions of society. At a small expense, a man can now possess himself of the most precious treasures of English literature. Books, once confined to a few by their costliness, are now accessible to the multitude; and in this way a change of habits is going on in society, highly favorable to the culture of the people. Instead of depending on casual rumor and loose conversation for most of their knowledge and objects of thought; instead of forming their judgments in crowds, and receiving their chief excitement from the voice of neighbours, men are now learning to study and reflect alone, to follow out subjects continuously, to determine for themselves what shall engage their minds, and to call to their aid the knowledge, original views, and reasonings of men of all countries and ages; and the results must be, a deliberateness and independence of judgment, and a thoroughness and extent of information, unknown in former times. The diffusion of these silent teachers, books, through the whole community, is to work greater effects than artillery, machinery, and legislation. Its peaceful agency is to supersede stormy revolutions. The culture, which it is to spread, whilst an unspeakable good to the individual, is also to become the stability of nations.

Another important means of self-culture, is to free ourselves from the power of human opinion and example, except as far as this is sanctioned by our own deliberate judgment. We are all prone to keep the level of those we live with, to repeat their words, and dress our minds as well as bodies after their fashion; and hence the spiritless tameness of our characters and lives. Our greatest danger, is not from the grossly wicked around us, but from the worldly, unreflecting multitude, who are borne along as a stream by foreign impulse, and bear us along with them. Even the influence of superior minds may harm us, by bowing us to servile acquiescence and damping our spiritual activity. The great use of intercourse with other minds, is to stir up our own, to whet our appetite for truth, to carry our thoughts beyond their old tracks. We need connexions with great thinkers to make us thinkers too. One of the chief arts of self-culture, is to unite the childlike teachableness, which gratefully welcomes light from every human being who can give it, with manly resistance of opinions however current, of influences however generally revered, which do not approve themselves to our deliberate judgment. You ought indeed patiently and conscientiously to strengthen your reason by other men's intelligence, but you must not prostrate it before them. Especially if there springs up within you any view of God's word or universe, any sentiment or aspiration which seems to you of a higher order than what you meet abroad, give reverent heed to it; inquire into it earnestly, solemnly. Do not trust it blindly, for it may be an illusion; but it may be the Divinity moving within you, a new revelation, not supernatural but still most precious, of truth or duty; and if, after inquiry, it so appear, then let no clamor, or scorn, or desertion turn you from it. Be true to your own highest convictions. Intimations from our own souls of something more perfect than others teach, if faithfully followed, give us a consciousness of spiritual force and progress, never experienced by the vulgar of high life or low life, who march, as they are drilled, to the step of their times.

Some, I know, will wonder, that I should think the mass of the people capable of such intimations and glimpses of truth, as I have just supposed. These are commonly thought to be the prerogative of men of genius, who seem to be born to give law to the minds of the multitude. Undoubtedly nature has her nobility, and sends forth a few to be eminently "lights of the world." But it is also true that a portion of the same divine fire is given to all; for the many could not receive with a loving reverence the quickening influences of the few, were there not essentially the same spiritual life in both. The minds of the multitude are not masses of passive matter, created to receive impressions unresistingly from abroad. They are not wholly shaped by foreign instruction; but have a native force, a spring of thought in themselves. Even the child's mind outruns its lessons, and overflows in questionings which bring the wisest to a stand. Even the child starts the great problems, which philosophy has labored to solve for ages. But on this subject I cannot now enlarge. Let me only say, that the power of original thought is particularly manifested in those who thirst for progress, who are bent on unfolding their whole nature. A man who wakes up to the consciousness of having been created for progress and perfection, looks with new eyes on himself and on the world in which he lives. This great truth stirs the soul from its depths, breaks up old associations of ideas, and establishes new ones, just as a mighty agent of chemistry, brought into contact with natural substances, dissolves the old affinities which had bound their particles together, and arranges them anew. This truth particularly aids us to penetrate the mysteries of human life. By revealing to us the end of our being, it helps us to comprehend more and more the wonderful, the infinite system, to which we belong. A man in the common walks of life, who has faith in perfection, in the unfolding of the human spirit, as the great purpose of God, possesses more the secret of the universe, perceives more the harmonies or mutual adaptations of the world without and the world within him, is a wiser interpreter of Providence, and reads nobler lessons of duty in the events which pass before him, than the profoundest philosopher who wants this grand central truth. Thus illuminations, inward suggestions, are not confined to a favored few, but visit all who devote themselves to a generous self-culture.

Another means of self-culture may be found by every man in his Condition or Occupation, be it what it may. Had I time, I might go through all conditions of life, from the most conspicuous to the most obscure, and might show how each furnishes continual aids to improvement. But I will take one example, and that is, of a man living by manual labor. This may be made the means of self-culture. For instance, in almost all labor, a man exchanges his strength for an equivalent in the form of wages, purchase-money, or some other product. In other words, labor is a system of contracts, bargains, imposing mutual obligations. Now the man, who, in working, no matter in what way, strives perpetually to fulfil his obligations thoroughly, to do his whole work faithfully, to be honest not because honesty is the best policy, but for the sake of justice, and that he may render to every man his due, such a laborer is continually building up in himself one of the greatest principles of morality and religion. Every blow on the anvil, on the earth, or whatever material he works upon, contributes something to the perfection of his nature.

Nor is this all. Labor is a school of benevolence as well as justice. A man to support himself must serve others: He must do or produce something for their comfort or gratification. This is one of the beautiful ordinations of Providence, that, to get a living, a man must be useful. Now this usefulness ought to be an end in his labor as truly as to earn his living. He ought to think of the benefit of those he works for, as well as of his own; and in so doing, in desiring amidst his sweat and toil to serve others as well as himself, he is exercising and growing in benevolence, as truly as if he were distributing bounty with a large hand to the poor. Such a motive hallows and dignifies the commonest pursuit. It is strange, that laboring men do not think more of the vast usefulness of their toils, and take a benevolent pleasure in them on this account. This beautiful city, with its houses, furniture, markets, public walks, and numberless accommodations, has grown up under the hands of artisans and other laborers, and ought they not to take a disinterested joy in their work? One would think, that a carpenter or mason, on passing a house which he had reared, would say to himself, "This work of mine is giving comfort and enjoyment every day and hour to a family, and will continue to be a kindly shelter, a domestic gathering-place, an abode of affection, for a century or more after I sleep in the dust;" and ought not a generous satisfaction to spring up at the thought? It is by thus interweaving goodness with common labors, that we give it strength and make it a habit of the soul.

Again. Labor may be so performed as to be a high impulse to the mind. Be a man's vocation what it may, his rule should be to do its duties perfectly, to do the best he can, and thus to make perpetual progress in his art. In other words, Perfection should be proposed; and this I urge not only for its usefulness to society, nor for the sincere pleasure which a man takes in seeing a work well done. This is an important means of self-culture. In this way the idea of Perfection takes root in the mind, and spreads far beyond the man's trade. He gets a tendency towards completeness in whatever he undertakes. Slack, slovenly performance in any department of life is more apt to offend him. His standard of action rises, and every thing is better done for his thoroughness in his common vocation.

There is one circumstance attending all conditions of life, which may and ought to be turned to the use of self-culture. Every condition, be it what it may, has hardships, hazards, pains. We try to escape them; we pine for a sheltered lot, for a smooth path, for cheering friends, and unbroken success. But Providence ordains storms, disasters, hostilities, sufferings; and the great question, whether we shall live to any purpose or not, whether we shall grow strong in mind and heart, or be weak and pitiable, depends on nothing so much as on our use of these adverse circumstances. Outward evils are designed to school our passions, and to rouse our faculties and virtues into intenser action. Sometimes they seem to create new powers. Difficulty is the element, and resistance the true work of a man. Self-culture never goes on so fast, as when embarrassed circumstances, the opposition of men or the elements, unexpected changes of the times, or other forms of suffering, instead of disheartening, throw us on our inward resources, turn us for strength to God, clear up to as the great purpose of life, and inspire calm resolution. No greatness or goodness is worth much, unless tried in these fires. Hardships are not on this account to be sought for. They come fast enough of themselves, and we are in more danger of sinking under, than of needing them. But when God sends them, they are noble means of self-culture, and as such, let us meet and bear them cheerfully. Thus all parts of our condition may be pressed into the service of self-improvement.

I have time to consider but one more means of self-culture. We find it in our Free Government, in our Political relations and duties. It is a great benefit of free institutions, that they do much to awaken and keep in action a nation's mind. We are told, that the education of the multitude is necessary to the support of a republic; but it is equally true, that a republic is a powerful means of educating the multitude. It is the people's University. In a free state, solemn responsibilities are imposed on every citizen; great subjects are to be discussed; great interests to be decided. The individual is called to determine measures affecting the well-being of millions and the destinies of posterity. He must consider not only the internal relations of his native land, but its connexion with foreign states, and judge of a policy which touches the whole civilized world. He is called by his participation in the national sovereignty, to cherish public spirit, a regard to the general weal. A man who purposes to discharge faithfully these obligations, is carrying on a generous self-culture. The great public questions, which divide opinion around him and provoke earnest discussion, of necessity invigorate his intellect, and accustom him to look beyond himself. He grows up to a robustness, force, enlargement of mind, unknown under despotic rule.

It may be said that I am describing what free institutions ought to do for the character of the individual, not their actual effects ; and the objection, I must own, is too true. Our institutions do not cultivate us, as they might and should ; and the chief cause of the failure is plain. It is the strength of party-spirit ; and so blighting is its influence, so fatal to self-culture, that I feel myself bound to warn every man against it, who has any desire of improvement. I do not tell you it will destroy your country. It wages a worse war against yourselves. Truth, justice, candor, fair dealing, sound judgment, self-control, and kind affections, are its natural and perpetual prey.

I do not say, that you must take no side in politics. The parties which prevail around you differ in character, principles, and spirit, though far less than the exaggeration of passion affirms ; and, as far as conscience allows, a man should support that which he thinks best. In one respect, however, all parties agree. They all foster that pestilent spirit, which I now condemn. In all of them, party-spirit rages. Associate men together for a common cause, be it good or bad, and array against them a body resolutely pledged to an opposite interest, and a new passion, quite distinct from the original sentiment which brought them together, a fierce, fiery zeal, consisting chiefly of aversion to those who differ from them, is roused within them into fearful activity. Human nature seems incapable of a stronger, more unrelenting passion. It is hard enough for an individual, when contending all alone for an interest or an opinion, to keep down his pride, wilfulness, love of victory, anger, and other personal feelings. But let him join a multitude in the same warfare, and, without singular self-control, he receives into his single breast, the vehemence, obstinacy, and vindictiveness of all. The triumph of his party becomes immeasurably dearer to him than the principle, true or false, which was the original ground of division. The conflict becomes a struggle, not for principle, but for power, for victory; and the desperateness, the wickedness of such struggles, is the great burden of history. In truth, it matters little what men divide about, whether it be a foot of land or precedence in a procession. Let them but begin to fight for it, and self-will, ill-will, the rage for victory, the dread of mortification and defeat, make the trifle as weighty as a matter of life and death. The Greek or Eastern empire was shaken to its foundation by parties, which differed only about the merits of charioteers at the amphitheatre. Party spirit is singularly hostile to moral independence. A man, in proportion as he drinks into it, sees, hears, judges by the senses and understandings of his party. He surrenders the freedom of a man, the right of using and speaking his own mind, and echoes the applauses or maledictions, with which the leaders or passionate partisans see fit that the country should ring. On all points, parties are to be distrusted; but on no one so much as on the character of opponents. These, if you may trust what you hear, are always men without principle and truth, devoured by selfishness, and thirsting for their own elevation, though on their country's ruin. When I was young, I was accustomed to hear pronounced with abhorrence, almost with execration, the names of men, who are now hailed by their former foes as the champions of grand principles, and as worthy of the highest public trusts. This lesson of early experience, which later years have corroborated, will never be forgotten.

Of our present political divisions I have of course nothing to say. But among the current topics of party, there are certain accusations and recriminations, grounded on differences of social condition, which seem to me so unfriendly to the improvement of individuals and the community, that I ask the privilege of giving them a moment's notice. On one side we are told, that the rich are disposed to trample on the poor; and on the other, that the poor look with evil eye and hostile purpose on the possessions of the rich. These outcries seem to me alike devoid of truth and alike demoralizing. As for the rich, who constitute but a handful of our population, who possess not one peculiar privilege, and, what is more, who possess comparatively little of the property of the country, it is wonderful, that they should be objects of alarm. The vast and ever-growing property of this country, where is it? Locked up in a few hands? hoarded in a few strong boxes? It is diffused like the atmosphere, and almost as variable, changing hands with the seasons, shifting from rich to poor, not by the violence but by the industry and skill of the latter class. The wealth of the rich is as a drop in the ocean; and it is a well-known fact, that those men among us, who are noted for their opulence, exert hardly any political power on the community. That the rich do their whole duty; that they adopt, as they should, the great object of the social state, which is the elevation of the people in intelligence, character, and condition, cannot be pretended; but that they feel for the physical sufferings of their brethren, that they stretch out liberal hands for the succour of the poor, and for the support of useful public institutions, cannot be denied. Among them are admirable specimens of humanity. There is no warrant for holding them up to suspicion as the people's foes.

Nor do I regard as less calumnious the outcry against the working classes, as if they were aiming at the subversion of property. When we think of the general condition and character of this part of our population, when we recollect, that they were born and have lived amidst schools and churches, that they have been brought up to profitable industry, that they enjoy many of the accommodations of life, that most of them hold a measure of property and are hoping for more, that they possess unprecedented means of bettering their lot, that they are bound to comfortable homes by strong domestic affections, that they are able to give their children an education which places within their reach the prizes of the social state, that they are trained to the habits, and familiarized to the advantages of a high civilization; when we recollect these things, can we imagine that they are so insanely blind to their interests, so deaf to the claims of justice and religion, so profligately thoughtless of the peace and safety of their families, as to be prepared to make a wreck of social order, for the sake of dividing among themselves the spoils of the rich, which would not support the community for a month? Undoubtedly there is insecurity in all stages of society, and so there must be, until communities shall be regenerated by a higher culture, reaching and quickening all classes of the people; but there is not, I believe, a spot on earth, where property is safer than here, because, nowhere else is it so equally and righteously diffused. In aristocracies, where wealth exists in enormous masses, which have been entailed for ages by a partial legislation on a favored few, and where the multitude, after the sleep of ages, are waking up to intelligence, to self-respect, and to a knowledge of their rights, property is exposed to shocks which are not to be dreaded among ourselves. Here indeed as elsewhere, among the less prosperous members of the community, there are disappointed, desperate men, ripe for tumult and civil strife; but it is also true, that the most striking and honorable distinction of this country is to be found in the intelligence, character, and condition of the great working class. To me it seems, that the great danger to property here is not from the laborer, but from those who are making haste to be rich. For example, in this commonwealth, no act has been thought by the alarmists or the conservatives so subversive of the rights of property, as a recent law, authorizing a company to construct a free bridge, in the immediate neighbourhood of another, which had been chartered by a former legislature, and which had been erected in the expectation of an exclusive right. And with whom did this alleged assault on property originate? With levellers? with needy laborers? with men bent on the prostration of the rich? No; but with men of business, who are anxious to push a more lucrative trade. Again, what occurrence among us has been so suited to destroy confidence, and to stir up the people against the moneyed class, as the late criminal mismanagement of some of our banking institutions? And whence came this? from the rich, or the poor? From the agrarian, or the man of business? Who, let me ask, carry on the work of spoliation most extensively in society? Is not more property wrested from its owners by rash or dishonest failures, than by professed highwaymen and thieves? Have not a few unprincipled speculators sometimes inflicted wider wrongs and sufferings, than all the tenants of a state prison? Thus property is in more danger from those who are aspiring after wealth, than from those who live by the sweat of their brow. I do not believe, however, that the institution is in serious danger from either. All the advances of society in industry, useful arts, commerce, knowledge, jurisprudence, fraternal union, and practical Christianity, are so many hedges around honestly acquired wealth, so many barriers against revolutionary violence and rapacity. Let us not torture ourselves with idle alarms, and still more, let us not inflame ourselves against one another by mutual calumnies. Let not class array itself against class, where all have a common interest. One way of provoking men to crime, is to suspect them of criminal designs. We do not secure our property against the poor, by accusing them of schemes of universal robbery; nor render the rich better friends of the community, by fixing on them the brand of hostility to the people. Of all parties, those founded on different social conditions are the most pernicious; and in no country on earth are they so groundless as in our own.

Among the best people, especially among the more religious, there are some, who, through disgust with the violence and frauds of parties, withdraw themselves from all political action. Such, I conceive, do wrong. God has placed them in the relations, and imposed on them the duties of citizens; and they are no more authorized to shrink from these duties than from those of sons, husbands, or fathers. They owe a great debt to their country, and must discharge it by giving support to what they deem the best men and the best measures. Nor let them say, that they can do nothing. Every good man, if faithful to his convictions, benefits his country. All parties are kept in check by the spirit of the better portion of people whom they contain. Leaders are always compelled to ask what their party will bear, and to modify their measures, so as not to shock the men of principle within their ranks. A good man, not tamely subservient to the body with which he acts, but judging it impartially, criticizing it freely, bearing testimony against its evils, and withholding his support from wrong, does good to those around him, and is cultivating generously his own mind.

I respectfully counsel those whom I address, to take part in the politics of their country. These are the true discipline of a people, and do much for their education. I counsel you to labor for a clear understanding of the subjects which agitate the community, to make them your study, instead of wasting your leisure in vague, passionate talk about them. The time thrown away by the mass of the people on the rumors of the day, might, if better spent, give them a good acquaintance with the constitution, laws, history, and interests of their country, and thus establish them in those great principles by which particular measures are to be determined. In proportion as the people thus improve themselves, they will cease to be the tools of designing politicians. Their intelligence, not their passions and jealousies, will be addressed by those who seek their votes. They will exert, not a nominal, but a real influence on the government and the destinies of the country, and at the same time will forward their own growth in truth and virtue.

I ought not to quit this subject of politics, considered as a means of self-culture, without speaking of newspapers; because these form the chief reading of the bulk of the people. They are the literature of multitudes. Unhappily, their importance is not understood; their bearing on the intellectual and moral cultivation of the community little thought of. A newspaper ought to be conducted by one of our most gifted men, and its income should be such as to enable him to secure the contributions of men as gifted as himself. But we must take newspapers as they are; and a man, anxious for self-culture, may turn them to account, if he will select the best within his reach. He should exclude from his house such as are venomous or scurrilous, as he would a pestilence. He should be swayed in his choice, not merely by the ability with which a paper is conducted, but still more by its spirit, by its justice, fairness, and steady adherence to great principles. Especially, if he would know the truth, let him hear both sides. Let him read the defence as well as the attack. Let him not give his ear to one party exclusively. We condemn ourselves, when we listen to reproaches thrown on an individual and turn away from his exculpation; and is it just to read continual, unsparing invective against large masses of men, and refuse them the opportunity of justifying themselves?

A new class of daily papers has sprung up in our country, sometimes called cent papers, and designed for circulation among those who cannot afford costlier publications. My interest in the working class induced me some time ago to take one of these, and I was gratified to find it not wanting in useful matter. Two things however gave me pain. The advertising columns were devoted very much to patent medicines; and when I considered that a laboring man's whole fortune is his health, I could not but lament, that so much was done to seduce him to the use of articles, more fitted, I fear, to undermine than to restore his constitution. I was also shocked by accounts of trials in the police court. These were written in a style adapted to the most uncultivated minds, and intended to turn into matters of sport the most painful and humiliating events of life. Were the newspapers of the rich to attempt to extract amusement from the vices and miseries of the poor, a cry would be raised against them, and very justly. But is it not something worse, that the poorer classes themselves should seek occasions of laughter and merriment in the degradation, the crimes, the woes, the punishments of their brethren, of those who are doomed to bear like themselves the heaviest burdens of life, and who have sunk under the temptations of poverty? Better go to the hospital, and laugh over the wounds and writhings of the sick or the ravings of the insane, than amuse ourselves with brutal excesses and infernal passions, which not only expose the criminal to the crushing penalties of human laws, but incur the displeasure of Heaven, and, if not repented of, will be followed by the fearful retribution of the life to come.

One important topic remains. That great means of self-improvement, Christianity, is yet untouched, and its greatness forbids me now to approach it. I will only say, that if you study Christianity in its original records, and not in human creeds; if you consider its clear revelations of God, its life-giving promises of pardon and spiritual strength, its correspondence to man's reason, conscience, and best affections, and its adaptation to his wants, sorrows, anxieties, and fears; if you consider the strength of its proofs, the purity of its precepts, the divine greatness of the character of its author, and the immortality which it opens before us, you will feel yourselves bound to welcome it joyfully, gratefully, as affording aids and incitements to self-culture, which would vainly be sought in all other means.

I have thus presented a few of the means of self-culture. The topics, now discussed, will I hope suggest others to those who have honored me with their attention, and create an interest which will extend beyond the present hour. I owe it however to truth to make one remark. I wish to raise no unreasonable hopes. I must say, then, that the means now recommended to you, though they will richly reward every man of every age who will faithfully use them, will yet not produce their full and happiest effect, except in cases where early education has prepared the mind for future improvement. They, whose childhood has been neglected, though they may make progress in future life, can hardly repair the loss of their first years; and I say this, that we may all be excited to save our children from this loss, that we may prepare them, to the extent of our power, for an effectual use of all the means of self-culture, which adult age may bring with it. With these views, I ask you to look with favor on the recent exertions of our legislature and of private citizens, in behalf of our public schools, the chief hope of our country. The legislature has of late appointed a board of education, with a secretary, who is to devote his whole time to the improvement of public schools. An individual more fitted to this responsible office, than the gentleman who now fills it,* cannot, I believe, be found in our community; and if his labors shall be crowned with success, he will earn a title to the gratitude of the good people of this State, unsurpassed by that of any other living citizen. Let me also recall to your minds a munificent individual, † who, by a generous donation, has encouraged the legislature to resolve on the establishment of one or more institutions called Normal Schools, the object of which is, to prepare accomplished teachers of youth, a work, on which the progress of education depends more than on any other measure. The efficient friends of education are the true benefactors of their country, and their names deserve to be handed down to that posterity, for whose highest wants they are generously providing.

There is another mode of advancing education in our whole country, to which I ask your particular attention. You are aware of the vast extent and value of the public lands of the Union. By annual sales of these, large amounts of money are brought into the national treasury, which are applied to the current expenses of the Government. For this application there is no need. In truth, the country has received detriment from the excess of its revenues. Now, I ask, why shall not the public lands be consecrated (in whole or in part, as the case may require) to the education of the people? This measure would secure at once what the country most needs, that is, able, accomplished, quickening teachers of the whole rising generation. The present poor remuneration of instructors is a dark omen, and the only real obstacle which the cause of education has to

* Horace Mann, Esq. † Edmund Dwight, Esq.

contend with. We need for our schools gifted men and women, worthy, by their intelligence and their moral power, to be intrusted with a nation's youth; and, to gain these, we must pay them liberally, as well as afford other proofs of the consideration in which we hold them. In the present state of the country, when so many paths of wealth and promotion are opened, superior men cannot be won to an office so responsible and laborious as that of teaching, without stronger inducements than are now offered, except in some of our large cities. The office of instructor ought to rank and be recompensed as one of the most honorable in society; and I see not how this is to be done, at least in our day, without appropriating to it the public domain. This is the people's property, and the only part of their property which is likely to be soon devoted to the support of a high order of institutions for public education. This object, interesting to all classes of society, has peculiar claims on those whose means of improvement are restricted by narrow circumstances. The mass of the people should devote themselves to it as one man, should toil for it with one soul. Mechanics, Farmers, Laborers! let the country echo with your united cry, "The Public Lands for Education." Send to the public councils men who will plead this cause with power. No party triumphs, no trades-unions, no associations, can so contribute to elevate you as the measure now proposed. Nothing but a higher education can raise you in influence and true dignity. The resources of the public domain, wisely applied for successive generations to the culture of society and of the individual, would create a new people, would awaken through this community intellectual and moral energies, such as the records of no country display, and as would command the respect and emulation of the civilized world. In this grand object, the working men of all parties, and in all divisions of the land, should join with an enthusiasm not to be withstood. They should separate it from all narrow and local strifes. They should not suffer it to be mixed up with the schemes of politicians. In it, they and their children have an infinite stake. May they be true to themselves, to posterity, to their country, to freedom, to the cause of mankind.

III. I am aware, that the whole doctrine of this discourse will meet with opposition. There are not a few who will say to me, "What you tell us sounds well; but it is impracticable. Men, who dream in their closets, spin beautiful theories; but actual life scatters them, as the wind snaps the cobweb. You would have all men to be cultivated; but necessity wills that most men shall work; and which of the two is likely to prevail? A weak sentimentality may shrink from the truth; still it *is* true, that most men were made, not for self-culture, but for toil."

I have put the objection into strong language, that we may all look it fairly in the face. For one I deny its validity. Reason, as well as sentiment, rises up against it. The presumption is certainly very strong, that the All-wise Father, who has given to every human being reason and conscience and affection, intended that these should be unfolded; and it is hard to believe, that He, who, by conferring this nature on all men, has made all his children, has destined the great majority to wear out a life of drudgery and unimproving toil, for the benefit of a few. God cannot have made spiritual beings to be dwarfed. In the body we see no organs created to shrivel by disuse; much less are the powers of the soul given to be locked up in perpetual lethargy.

Perhaps it will be replied, that the purpose of the Creator is to be gathered, not from theory, but from facts; and that it is a plain fact, that the order and prosperity of society, which God must be supposed to intend, require from the multitude the action of their hands, and not the improvement of their minds. I reply, that a social order, demanding the sacrifice of the mind, is very suspicious, that it cannot indeed be sanctioned by the Creator. Were I, on visiting a strange country, to see the vast majority of the people maimed, crippled, and bereft of sight, and were I told that social order required this mutilation, I should say, Perish this order. Who would not think his understanding as well as best feelings insulted, by hearing this spoken of as the intention of God? Nor ought we to look with less aversion on a social system, which can only be upheld by crippling and blinding the Minds of the people.

But to come nearer to the point. Are labor and self-culture irreconcilable to each other? In the first place, we have seen that a man, in the midst of labor, may and ought to give himself to the most important improvements, that he may cultivate his sense of justice, his benevolence, and the desire of perfection. Toil is the school for these high principles; and we have here a strong presumption, that, in other respects, it does not necessarily blight the soul. Next we have seen, that the most fruitful sources of truth and wisdom are not books, precious as they are, but experience and observation; and these belong to all conditions. It is another important consideration, that almost all labor demands intellectual activity, and is best carried on by those who invigorate their minds; so that the two interests, toil and self-culture, are friends to each other. It is Mind, after all, which does the work of the world, so that the more there is of mind, the more work will be accomplished. A man, in proportion as he is intelligent, makes a given force accomplish a greater task, makes skill take the place of muscles, and, with less labor, gives a better product. Make men intelligent, and they become inventive. They find shorter processes. Their knowledge of nature helps them to turn its laws to account, to understand the substances on which they work, and to seize on useful hints, which experience continually furnishes. It is among workmen, that some of the most useful machines have been contrived. Spread education, and, as the history of this country shows, there will be no bounds to useful inventions. You think, that a man without culture will do all the better what you call the drudgery of life. Go then to the Southern plantation. There the slave is brought up to be a mere drudge. He is robbed of the rights of a man, his whole spiritual nature is starved, that he may work, and do nothing but work; and in that slovenly agriculture, in that worn-out soil, in the rude state of the mechanic arts, you may find a comment on your doctrine, that, by degrading men, you make them more productive laborers.

But it is said, that any considerable education lifts men above their work, makes them look with disgust on their trades as mean and low, makes drudgery intolerable. I reply, that a man becomes interested in labor, just in proportion as the mind works with the hands. An enlightened farmer, who understands agricultural chemistry, the laws of vegetation, the structure of plants, the properties of manures, the influences of climate, who looks intelligently on his work, and brings his knowledge to bear on exigencies, is a much more cheerful, as well as more dignified laborer, than the peasant, whose mind is akin to the clod on which he treads, and whose whole life is the same dull, unthinking, unimproving toil. But this is not all. Why is it, I ask, that we call manual labor low, that we associate with it the idea of meanness, and think that an intelligent people must scorn it? The great reason is, that, in most countries, so few intelligent people have been engaged in it. Once let cultivated men plough, and dig, and follow the commonest labors, and ploughing, digging, and trades, will cease to be mean. It is the man who determines the dignity of the occupation, not the occupation which measures the dignity of the man. Physicians and surgeons perform operations less cleanly than fall to the lot of most mechanics. I have seen a distinguished chemist covered with dust like a laborer. Still these men were not degraded. Their intelligence gave dignity to their work, and so our laborers, once educated, will give dignity to their toils.—Let me add, that I see little difference in point of dignity, between the various vocations of men. When I see a clerk, spending his days in adding figures, perhaps merely copying, or a teller of a bank counting money, or a merchant selling shoes and hides, I cannot see in these occupations greater respectableness than in making leather, shoes, or furniture. I do not see in them greater intellectual activity than in several trades. A man in the fields seems to have more chances of improvement in his work, than a man behind the counter, or a man driving the quill. It is the sign of a narrow mind, to imagine, as many seem to do, that there is a repugnance between the plain, coarse exterior of a laborer, and mental culture, especially the more refining culture. The laborer, under his dust and sweat, carries the grand elements of humanity, and he may put forth its highest powers. I doubt not, there is as genuine enthusiasm in the contemplation of nature, and in the perusal of works of genius, under a homespun garb as under finery. We have heard of a distinguished author, who never wrote so well, as when he was full dressed for company. But profound thought, and poetical inspiration, have most generally visited men, when, from narrow circumstances or negligent habits, the rent coat and shaggy face have made them quite unfit for polished saloons. A man may see truth, and may be thrilled with beauty, in one costume or dwelling as well as another; and he should respect himself the more, for the hardships under which his intellectual force has been developed.

But it will be asked, how can the laboring classes find time for self-culture? I answer, as I have already intimated, that an earnest purpose finds time or makes time. It seizes on spare moments, and turns larger fragments of leisure to golden account. A man, who follows his calling with industry and spirit, and uses his earnings economically, will always have some portion of the day at command; and it is astonishing, how fruitful of improvement a short season becomes, when eagerly seized and faithfully used. It has often been observed, that they, who have most time at their disposal, profit by it least. A single hour in the day, steadily given to the study of an interesting subject, brings unexpected accumulations of knowledge. The improvements made by well-disposed pupils, in many of our country schools, which are open but three months in the year, and in our Sunday-schools, which are kept but one or two hours in the week, show what can be brought to pass by slender means. The affections, it is said, sometimes crowd years into moments, and the intellect has something of the same power. Volumes have not only been read, but written, in flying journeys. I have known a man of vigorous intellect, who had enjoyed few advantages of early education, and whose mind was almost engrossed by the details of an extensive business, but who composed a book of much original thought, in steam-boats and on horseback, while visiting distant customers. The succession of the seasons gives to many of the working class opportunities for intellectual improvement. The winter brings leisure to the husbandman, and winter evenings to many laborers in the city. Above all, in Christian countries, the seventh day is released from toil. The seventh part of the year, no small portion of existence, may be given by almost every one to intellectual and moral culture. Why is it that Sunday is not made a more effectual means of improvement? Undoubtedly the seventh day is to have a religious character; but religion connects itself with all the great subjects of human thought, and leads to and aids the study of all. God is in nature. God is in history. Instruction in the works of the Creator, so as to reveal his perfection in their harmony, beneficence, and grandeur; instruction in the histories of the church and the world, so as to show in all events his moral government, and to bring out the great moral lessons in which human life abounds; instruction in the lives of philanthropists, of saints, of men eminent for piety and virtue; all these branches of teaching enter into religion, and are appropriate to Sunday; and, through these, a vast amount of knowledge may be given to the people. Sunday ought not to remain the dull and fruitless season that it now is to multitudes. It may be clothed with a new interest and a new sanctity. It may give a new impulse to the nation's soul. — I have thus shown, that time may be found for improvement; and the fact is, that, among our most improved people, a considerable part consists of persons, who pass the greatest portion of every day at the desk, in the counting-room, or in some other sphere, chained to tasks which have very little tendency to expand the mind. In the progress of society, with the increase of machinery, and with other aids which intelligence and philanthropy will multiply, we may expect that more and more time will be redeemed from manual labor, for intellectual and social occupations.

But some will say, "Be it granted that the working classes may find some leisure; should they not be allowed to spend it in relaxation? Is it not cruel, to summon them from toils of the hand to toils of the mind? They have earned pleasure by the day's toil, and ought to partake it." Yes, let them have pleasure. Far be it from me to dry up the fountains, to blight the spots of verdure, where they refresh themselves after life's labors. But I maintain, that self-culture multiplies and increases their pleasures, that it creates new capacities of enjoyment, that it saves their leisure from being, what it too often is, dull and wearisome, that it saves them from rushing for excitement to indulgences destructive to body and soul. It is one of the great benefits of self-improvement, that it raises a people above the gratifications of the brute, and gives them pleasures worthy of men. In consequence of the present intellectual culture of our country, imperfect as it is, a vast amount of enjoyment is communicated to men, women, and children, of all conditions, by books, an enjoyment unknown to ruder times. At this moment, a number of gifted writers are employed in multiplying entertaining works. Walter Scott, a name conspicuous among the brightest of his day, poured out his inexhaustible mind in fictions, at once so sportive and thrilling, that they have taken their place among the delights of all civilized nations. How many millions have been chained to his pages! How many melancholy spirits has he steeped in forgtfulness of their cares and sorrows! What multitudes, wearied by their day's work, have owed some bright evening hours and balmier sleep to his magical creations! And not only do fictions give pleasure. In proportion as the mind is cultivated, it takes delight in history and biography, in descriptions of nature, in travels, in poetry, and even graver works. Is the laborer then defrauded of pleasure by improvement? There is another class of gratifications to which self-culture introduces the mass of the people. I refer to lectures, discussions, meetings of associations for benevolent and literary purposes, and to other like methods of passing the evening, which every year is multiplying among us. A popular address from an enlightened man, who has the tact to reach the minds of the people, is a high gratification, as well as a source of knowledge. The profound silence in our public halls, where these lectures are delivered to crowds, shows that cultivation is no foe to enjoyment.—I have a strong hope, that by the progress of intelligence, taste, and morals among all portions of society, a class of public amusements will grow up among us, bearing some resemblance to the theatre, but purified from the gross evils which degrade our present stage, and which, I trust, will seal its ruin. Dramatic performances and recitations are means of bringing the mass of the people into a quicker sympathy with a writer of genius, to a profounder comprehension of his grand, beautiful, touching conceptions, than can be effected by the reading of the closet. No commentary throws such a light on a great poem or any impassioned work of literature, as the voice of a reader or speaker, who brings to the task a deep feeling of his author and rich and various powers of expression. A crowd, electrified by a sublime thought, or softened into a humanizing sorrow, under such a voice, partake a pleasure at once exquisite and refined; and I cannot but believe, that this and other amusements, at which the delicacy of woman and the purity of the Christian can take no offence, are to grow up under a higher social culture. — Let me only add, that, in proportion as culture spreads among a people, the cheapest and commonest of all pleasures, conversation, increases in delight. This, after all, is the great amusement of life, cheering us round our hearths, often cheering our work, stirring our hearts gently, acting on us like the balmy air or the bright light of heaven, so silently and continually, that we hardly think of its influence. This source of happiness is too often lost to men of all classes, for want of knowledge, mental activity, and refinement of feeling; and do we defraud the laborer of his pleasure, by recommending to him improvements which will place the daily, hourly, blessings of conversation within his reach?

I have thus considered some of the common objections which start up when the culture of the mass of men is insisted on, as the great end of society. For myself, these objections seem worthy little notice. The doctrine is too shocking to need refutation, that the great majority of human beings, endowed as they are with rational and immortal powers, are placed on earth, simply to toil for their own animal subsistence, and to minister to the luxury and elevation of the few. It is monstrous, it approaches impiety, to suppose that God has placed insuperable barriers to the expansion of the free, illimitable soul. True, there are obstructions in the way of improvement. But in this country, the chief obstructions lie, not in our lot, but in ourselves, not in outward hardships, but in our worldly and sensual propensities; and one proof of this is, that a true self-culture is as little thought of on exchange as in the workshop, as little among the prosperous as among those of narrower conditions. The path to perfection is difficult to men in every lot; there is no royal road for rich or poor. But difficulties are meant to rouse, not discourage. The human spirit is to grow strong by conflict. And how much has it already overcome! Under what burdens of oppression has it made its way for ages! What mountains of difficulty has it cleared! And with all this experience, shall we say, that the progress of the mass of men is to be despaired of, that the chains of bodily necessity are too strong and ponderous to be broken by the mind, that servile, unimproving drudgery is the unalterable condition of the multitude of the human race?

I conclude with recalling to you the happiest feature of our age, and that is, the progress of the mass of the people in intelligence, self-respect, and all the comforts of life. What a contrast does the present form with past times! Not many ages ago, the nation was the property of one man, and all its interests were staked in perpetual games of war, for no end but to build up his family, or to bring new territories under his yoke. Society was divided into two classes, the high-born and the vulgar, separated from one another by a great gulf, as impassable as that between the saved and the lost. The people had no significance as individuals, but formed a mass, a machine, to be wielded at pleasure by their lords. In war, which was the great sport of the times, those brave knights, of whose prowess we hear, cased themselves and their horses in armour, so as to be almost invulnerable, whilst the common people on foot were left, without protection, to be hewn in pieces or trampled down by their betters. Who, that compares the condition of Europe a few years ago, with the present state of the world, but must bless God for the change. The grand distinction of modern times is, the emerging of the people from brutal degradation, the gradual recognition of their rights, the gradual diffusion among them of the means of improvement and happiness, the creation of a new power in the state, the power of the people. And it is worthy remark, that this revolution is due in a great degree to religion, which, in the hands of the crafty and aspiring, had bowed the multitude to the dust, but which, in the fulness of time, began to fulfil its mission of freedom. It was religion, which by teaching men their near relation to God, awakened in them the consciousness of their importance as individuals. It was the struggle for religious rights, which opened men's eyes to all their rights. It was resistance to religious usurpation, which led men to withstand political oppression. It was religious discussion, which roused the minds of all classes to free and vigorous thought. It was religion, which armed the martyr and patriot in England against arbitrary power, which braced the spirits of our fathers against the perils of the ocean and wilderness, and sent them to found here the freest and most equal state on earth.

Let us thank God for what has been gained. But let us not think every thing gained. Let the people feel that they have only started in the race. How much remains to be done! What a vast amount of ignorance, intemperance, coarseness, sensuality, may still be found in our community! What a vast amount of mind is palsied and lost! When we think, that every house might be cheered by intelligence, disinterestedness, and refinement, and then remember, in how many houses the higher powers and affections of human nature are buried as in tombs, what a darkness gathers over society! And how few of us are moved by this moral desolation? How few understand, that to raise the depressed, by a wise culture, to the dignity of men, is the highest end of the social state? Shame on us, that the worth of a fellow-creature is so little felt.

I would, that I could speak with an awakening voice to the people, of their wants, their privileges, their responsibilities. I would say to them, You cannot, without guilt and disgrace, stop where you are. The past and the present call on you to advance. Let what you have gained be an impulse to something higher. Your nature is too great to be crushed. You were not created what you are, merely to toil, eat, drink, and sleep, like the inferior animals. If you will, you can rise.

No power in society, no hardship in your condition can depress you, keep you down, in knowledge, power, virtue, influence, but by your own consent. Do not be lulled to sleep by the flatteries which you hear, as if your participation in the national sovereignty made you equal to the noblest of your race. You have many and great deficiencies to be remedied; and the remedy lies, not in the ballot-box, not in the exercise of your political powers, but in the faithful education of yourselves and your children. These truths you have often heard and slept over. Awake! Resolve earnestly on Self-culture. Make yourselves worthy of your free institutions, and strengthen and perpetuate them by your intelligence and your virtues.

THE

IMITABLENESS OF CHRIST'S CHARACTER.

---

1 PETER ii. 21: "Christ also suffered for us, leaving us an example, that ye should follow his steps."

THE example of Jesus is our topic. To incite you to follow it, is the aim of this discourse. Christ came to give us a religion, — but this is not all. By a wise and beautiful ordination of Providence, he was sent to show forth his religion in himself. He did not come to sit in a hall of legislation, and from some commanding eminence to pronounce laws and promises. He is not a mere channel through which certain communications are made from God; not a mere messenger appointed to utter the words which he had heard, and then to disappear, and to sustain no further connexion with his message. He came, not only to teach with his lips, but to be a living manifestation of his religion, — to be, in an important sense, the religion itself.

This is a peculiarity worthy of attention. Christianity is not a mere code of laws, not an abstract system such as theologians frame. It is a living, embodied religion. It comes to us in a human form; it offers itself to our eyes as well as ears; it breathes, it moves in our sight. It is more than precept; it is example and action.

The importance of example, who does not understand? How much do most of us suffer from the presence, conversation, spirit, of men of low minds by whom we are surrounded! The temptation is strong, to take as our standard, the average character of the society in which we live, and to satisfy ourselves with decencies and attainments which secure to us among the multitude the name of respectable men. On the other hand, there is a power (have you not felt it?) in the presence, conversation, and example of a man of strong principle and magnanimity, to lift us, at least for the moment, from our vulgar and tame habits of thought, and to kindle some generous aspirations after the excellence which we were made to attain. I hardly need say to you, that it is impossible to place ourselves under any influence of this nature so quickening as the example of Jesus. This introduces us to the highest order of virtues. This is fitted to awaken the whole mind. Nothing has equal power to neutralize the coarse, selfish, and sensual influences, amidst which we are plunged, to refine our conception of duty, and to reveal to us the perfection on which our hopes and most strenuous desires should habitually fasten.

There is one cause, which has done much to defeat this good influence of Christ's character and example, and which ought to be exposed. It is this. Multitudes, I am afraid great multitudes, think of Jesus as a being to be admired, rather than approached. They have some vague conceptions of a glory in his nature and character which makes it presumption to think of proposing him as their standard. He is thrown so far from them, that he does them little good. Many feel that a close resemblance of Jesus Christ is not to be expected;

that this, like many other topics, may serve for declamation in the pulpit, but is utterly incapable of being reduced to practice. I think I am touching here an error, which exerts a blighting influence on not a few minds. Until men think of the religion and character of Christ as truly applicable to them, as intended to be brought into continual operation, as what they must incorporate with their whole spiritual nature, they will derive little good from Christ. Men think indeed to honor Jesus, when they place him so high as to discourage all effort to approach him. They really degrade him. They do not understand his character; they throw a glare over it, which hides its true features. This vague admiration is the poorest tribute which they can pay him.

The manner in which Jesus Christ is conceived and spoken of by many, reminds me of what is often seen in Catholic countries, where a superstitious priesthood and people imagine that they honor the Virgin Mary by loading her image with sparkling jewels and the gaudiest attire. A Protestant of an uncorrupted taste is at first shocked, as if there was something like profanation in thus decking out, as for a theatre, the meek, modest, gentle, pure, and tender mother of Jesus. It seems to me, that something of the same superstition is seen in the indefinite epithets of admiration heaped upon Jesus; and the effect is, that the mild and simple beauty of his character is not seen. Its sublimity, which had nothing gaudy or dazzling, which was plain and unaffected, is not felt; and its suitableness as an example to mankind, is discredited or denied.

I wish, in this discourse, to prevent the discouraging influence of the greatness of Jesus Christ; to show, that, however exalted, he is not placed beyond the reach of our sympathy and imitation.

I begin with the general observation, that real greatness of character, greatness of the highest order, far from being repulsive and discouraging, is singularly accessible and imitable, and, instead of severing a being from others, fits him to be their friend and model. A man who stands apart from his race, who has few points of contact with other men, who has a style and manner which strike awe, and keep others far from him, whatever rank he may hold in his own and others' eyes, wants, after all, true grandeur of mind; and the spirit of this remark, I think, may be extended beyond men to higher orders of beings, to angels and to Jesus Christ. A great soul is known by its enlarged, strong, and tender sympathies. True elevation of mind does not take a being out of the circle of those who are below him, but binds him faster to them, and gives them advantages for a closer attachment and conformity to him.

Greatness of character is a communicable attribute; I should say, singularly communicable. It has nothing exclusive in its nature. It cannot be the monopoly of an individual, for it is the enlarged and generous action of faculties and affections which enter into and constitute all minds, I mean reason, conscience, and love, so that its elements exist in all. It is not a peculiar or exclusive knowledge, which can be shut up in one or a few understandings; but the comprehension of great and universal truths, which are the proper objects of every rational being. It is not a devotion to peculiar, exclusive objects, but the adoption of public interests, the consecration of the mind to the cause of virtue and happiness in the creation, that is, to the very cause which all intelligent beings are bound to espouse. Greatness is not a secret, solitary principle, working by itself and refusing participation, but frank and open-hearted, so large in its views, so liberal in its feelings, so expansive in its purposes, so beneficent in its labors, as naturally and necessarily to attract sympathy and coöperation. It is selfishness that repels men; and true greatness has not a stronger characteristic than its freedom from every selfish taint. So far from being imprisoned in private interests, it covets nothing which it may not impart. So far from being absorbed in its own distinctions, it discerns nothing so quickly and joyfully as the capacities and pledges of greatness in others, and counts no labor so noble as to call forth noble sentiments, and the consciousness of a divine power, in less improved minds.

I know that those who call themselves great on earth, are apt to estrange themselves from their inferiors; and the multitude, cast down by their high bearing, never think of proposing them as examples. But this springs wholly from the low conceptions of those whom we call the great, and shows a mixture of vulgarity of mind with their superior endowments. Genuine greatness is marked by simplicity, unostentatiousness, self-forgetfulness, a hearty interest in others, a feeling of brotherhood with the human family, and a respect for every intellectual and immortal being as capable of progress towards its own elevation. A superior mind, enlightened and kindled by just views of God and of the creation, regards its gifts and powers as so many bonds of union with other beings, as given it, not to nourish self-elation, but to be employed for others, and still more to be communicated to others. Such greatness has no reserve, and especially no affected dignity of deportment. It is too conscious of its own power, to need, and too benevolent to desire, to entrench itself behind forms and ceremonies; and when circumstances permit such a character to manifest itself to inferior beings, it is beyond all others the most winning, and most fitted to impart itself, or to call forth a kindred elevation of feeling. I know not in history an individual so easily comprehended as Jesus Christ, for nothing is so intelligible as sincere, disinterested love. I know not any being who is so fitted to take hold on all orders of minds; and accordingly he drew after him the unenlightened, the publican, and the sinner. It is a sad mistake, then, that Jesus Christ is too great to allow us to think of intimacy with him, and to think of making him our standard.

Let me confirm this truth by another order of reflections. You tell me, my hearers, that Jesus Christ is so high that he cannot be your model; I grant the exaltation of his character. I believe him to be a more than human being. In truth, all Christians so believe him. Those who suppose him not to have existed before his birth, do not regard him as a mere man, though so reproached. They always separate him by broad distinctions from other men. They consider him as enjoying a communion with God, and as having received gifts, endowments, aid, lights from him, granted to no other, and as having exhibited a spotless purity, which is the highest distinction of Heaven. All admit, and joyfully admit, that Jesus Christ, by his greatness and goodness, throws all other human attainments into obscurity. But on this account he is not less a standard, nor is he to discourage us, but on the contrary to breathe into us a more exhilarating hope; for though so far above us, he is still one of us, and is only an illustration of the capacities which we all possess. This is a great truth. Let me strive to unfold it. Perhaps I cannot better express my views, than by saying, that I regard all minds as of one family. When we speak of higher orders of beings, of angels and archangels, we are apt to conceive of distinct kinds or races of beings, separated from us and from each other by impassable barriers. But it is not so. All minds are of one family. There is no such partition in the spiritual world as you see in the material. In material nature, you see wholly distinct classes of beings. A mineral is not a vegetable, and makes no approach to it; these two great kingdoms of nature are divided by immeasurable spaces. So, when we look at different races of animals, though all partake of that mysterious property, life, yet, what an immense and impassable distance is there between the insect and the lion. They have no bond of union, no possibility of communication. During the lapse of ages, the animalcules which sport in the sunbeams a summer's day and then perish, have made no approximation to the king of the forests. But in the intellectual world there are no such barriers. All minds are essentially of one origin, one nature, kindled from one divine flame, and are all tending to one centre, one happiness. This great truth, to us the greatest of truths, which lies at the foundation of all religion and of all hope, seems to me not only sustained by proofs which satisfy the reason, but to be one of the deep instincts of our nature. It mingles, unperceived, with all our worship of God, which uniformly takes for granted that he is a Mind having thought, affection, and volition like ourselves. It runs through false religions ; and whilst, by its perversion, it has made them false, it has also given to them whatever purifying power they possess. But passing over this instinct, which is felt more and more to be unerring as the intellect is improved, this great truth of the unity or likeness of all minds, seems to me demonstrable from this consideration, that Truth, the object and nutriment of mind, is one and immutable, so that the whole family of intelligent beings must have the same views, the same motives, and the same general ends. For example, a truth of mathematics, is not a truth only in this world, a truth to our minds, but a truth everywhere, a truth in heaven, a truth to God, who has indeed framed his creation according to the laws of this universal science. So, happiness and misery, which lie at the foundation of morals, must be to all intelligent beings what they are to us, the objects, one of desire and hope, and the other of aversion ; and who can doubt that virtue and vice are the same everywhere as on earth, that in every community of beings, the mind which devotes itself to the general weal, must be more reverenced than a mind which would subordinate the general interest to its own. Thus all souls are one in nature, approach one another, and have grounds and bonds of communion with one another. I am not only one of the human race ; I am one of the great intellectual family of God. There is no spirit so exalted, with which I have not common thoughts and feelings. That conception which I have gained, of One Universal Father, whose love is the fountain and centre of all things, is the dawn of the highest and most magnificent views in the universe , and if I look up to this being with filial love, I have the spring and beginning of the noblest sentiments and joys which are known in the universe. No greatness, therefore, of a being, separates me from him or makes him unapproachable by me. The mind of Jesus Christ, my hearer, and your mind are of one family; nor was there any thing in his, of which you have not the principle, the capacity, the promise in yourself. This is the very impression which he intends to give. He never held himself up as an inimitable and unapproachable being; but directly the reverse. He always spoke of himself as having come to communicate himself to others. He always invited men to believe on and adhere to him, that they might receive that very spirit, that pure, celestial spirit, by which he was himself actuated. "Follow me," is his lesson. The relation which he came to establish between himself and mankind, was not that of master and slave, but that of friends. He compares himself, in a spirit of divine benevolence, to a vine, which, you know, sends its own sap, that by which it is itself nourished, into all its branches. We read, too, these remarkable words in his prayer for his disciples, "I have given to them the glory thou gavest me;" and I am persuaded that there is not a glory, a virtue, a power, a joy, possessed by Jesus Christ, to which his disciples will not successively rise. In the spirit of these remarks, the Apostles say, "Let the same mind be in you which was also in Christ."

I have said, that all minds being of one family, the greatness of the mind of Christ is no discouragement to our adoption of him as our model. I now observe, that there is one attribute of mind to which I have alluded, that should particularly animate us to propose to ourselves a sublime standard, as sublime as Jesus Christ. I refer to the principle of growth in human nature. We were made to grow. Our faculties are germs, and given for an expansion, to which nothing authorizes us to set bounds. The soul bears the impress of illimitableness, in the thirst, the unquenchable thirst, which it brings with it into being, for a power, knowledge, happiness, which it never gains, and which always carry it forward into futurity. The body soon reaches its limit. But intellect, affection, moral energy, in proportion to their growth, tend to further enlargement, and every acquisition is an impulse to something higher. When I consider this principle or capacity of the human soul, I cannot restrain the hope which it awakens. The partition-walls which imagination has reared between men and higher orders of beings vanish. I no longer see aught to prevent our becoming whatever was good and great in Jesus on earth. In truth, I feel my utter inability to conceive what a mind is to attain which is to advance for ever. Add but that element, eternity, to man's progress, and the results of his existence surpass, not only human, but angelic thought. Give me this, and the future glory of the human mind becomes to me as incomprehensible as God himself. To encourage these thoughts and hopes, our Creator has set before us delightful exemplifications, even now, of this principle of growth both in outward nature and in the human mind. We meet them in nature. Suppose you were to carry a man, wholly unacquainted with vegetation, to the most majestic tree in our forests, and, whilst he was admiring its extent and proportions, suppose you should take from the earth at its root a little downy substance, which a breath might blow away, and say to him, That tree was once such a seed as this; it was wrapped up here; it once lived only within these delicate fibres, this narrow compass. With what incredulous wonder would he regard you! And if by an effort of imagination, somewhat Oriental, we should suppose this little seed to be suddenly endued with thought, and to be told that it was one day to become this mighty tree, and to cast out branches which would spread an equal shade, and wave with equal grace, and withstand the winter winds; with what amazement may we suppose it to anticipate its future lot! Such growth we witness in nature. A nobler hope we Christians are to cherish; and still more striking examples of the growth of mind are set before us in human history. We wonder indeed when we are told, that one day we shall be as the angels of God. I apprehend that as great a wonder has been realized already on the earth. I apprehend that the distance between the mind of Newton and of a Hottentot may have been as great as between Newton and an angel. There is another view still more striking. This Newton, who lifted his calm, sublime eye to the heavens, and read among the planets and the stars, the great law of the material universe, was, forty or fifty years before, an infant, without one clear perception, and unable to distinguish his nurse's arm from the pillow on which he slept. Howard, too, who, under the strength of an all-sacrificing benevolence, explored the depths of human suffering, was, forty or fifty years before, an infant wholly absorbed in himself, grasping at all he saw. and almost breaking his little heart with fits of passion, when the idlest toy was withheld. Has not man already traversed as wide a space as separates him from angels? And why must he stop? There is no extravagance in the boldest anticipation. We may truly become one with Christ, a partaker of that celestial mind. He is truly our brother, one of our family. Let us make him our constant model.

I know not that the doctrine now laid down, is liable but to one abuse. It may unduly excite susceptible minds, and impel to a vehemence of hope and exertion unfavorable in the end to the very progress which is proposed. To such I would say, Hasten to conform yourselves to Christ, but hasten according to the laws of your nature. As the body cannot by the concentration of its whole strength into one bound, scale the height of a mountain, neither can the mind free every obstacle and achieve perfection by an agony of the will. Great effort is indeed necessary; but such as can be sustained, such as fits us for greater, such as will accumulate, not exhaust, our spiritual force. The soul may be overstrained as truly as the body, and it often is so in seasons of extraordinary religious excitement; and the consequence is, an injury to the constitution of the intellect and the heart, which a life may not be able to repair. I rest the hopes for human nature, which I have now expressed, on its principle of growth; and growth, as you well know, is a gradual process, not a convulsive start, accomplishing the work of years in a moment. All great attainments are gradual. As easily might a science be mastered by one struggle of thought, as sin be conquered by a spasm of remorse. Continuous, patient effort, guided by wise deliberation, is the true means of spiritual progress. In religion, as in common life, mere force of vehemence will prove a fallacious substitute for the sobriety of wisdom.

The doctrine which I have chiefly labored to maintain in this discourse, that minds are all of one family, are all brethren, and may be more and more nearly united to God, seems to me to have been felt peculiarly by Jesus Christ; and if I were to point out the distinction of his greatness, I should say it lay in this. He felt his superiority, but he never felt as if it separated him from mankind. He did not come among us as some great men would visit a colliery, or any other resort of the ignorant and corrupt, with an air of greatness, feeling himself above us, and giving benefits as if it were an infinite condescension. He came and mingled with us as a friend and a brother. He saw in every human being a mind which might wear his own brightest glory. He was severe only towards one class of men, and they were those who looked down on the multitude with contempt. Jesus respected human nature; he felt it to be his own. This was the greatness of Jesus Christ. He felt, as no other felt, a union of mind with the human race, felt that all had a spark of that same intellectual and immortal flame which dwelt in himself.

I insist on this view of his character, not only to encourage us to aspire after a likeness to Jesus; I consider it as peculiarly fitted to call forth love towards him. If I regard Jesus as an august stranger, belonging to an entirely different class of existence from myself, having no common thoughts or feelings with me, and looking down upon me with only such a sympathy as I have with an inferior animal, I should regard him with a vague awe; but the immeasurable space between us would place him beyond friendship and affection. But when I feel, that all minds form one family, that I have the same nature with Jesus, and that he came to communicate to me, by his teaching, example, and intercession, his own mind, to bring me into communion with what was sublimest, purest, happiest in himself, then I can love him as I love no other being, excepting only Him who is the Father alike of Christ and of the Christian. With these views, I feel that, though ascended to Heaven, he is not gone beyond the reach of our hearts; that he has now the same interest in mankind as when he entered their dwellings, sat at their tables, washed their feet; and that there is no being so approachable, none with whom such unreserved intercourse is to be enjoyed in the future world.

Believing, as I do, that I have now used no inflated language, but have spoken the words of truth and soberness, I exhort you with calmness, but earnestness, to choose and adopt Jesus Christ as your example, with the whole energy of your wills. I exhort you to resolve on following him, not, as perhaps you have done, with a faint and yielding purpose, but with the full conviction, that your whole happiness is concentrated in the force and constancy of your adherence to this celestial guide. My friends, there is no other happiness. Let not the false views of Christianity which prevail in the world, seduce you into the belief, that Christ can bless you in any other way than by assimilating you to his own virtue, than by breathing into you his own mind. Do not imagine that any faith or love towards Jesus can avail you, but that which quickens you to conform yourselves to his spotless purity and unconquerable rectitude. Settle it as an immovable truth, that neither in this world nor in the next can you be happy, but in proportion to the sanctity and elevation of your characters. Let no man imagine, that through the patronage or protection of Jesus Christ, or any other being, he can find peace or any sincere good, but in the growth of an enlightened, firm, disinterested, holy mind. Expect no good from Jesus, any farther than you clothe yourselves with excellence. He can impart to you nothing so precious as himself, as his own mind ; and believe me, my hearers, this mind may dwell in you. His sublimest virtues may be yours. Admit, welcome this great truth. Look up to the illustrious Son of God, with the conviction that you may become one with him in thought, in feeling, in power, in holiness. His character will become a blessing, just as far as it shall awaken in you this consciousness, this hope. The most lamentable skepticism on earth, and incomparably the most common, is a skepticism as to the greatness, powers, and high destinies of human nature. In this greatness I desire to cherish an unwavering faith. Tell me not of the universal corruption of the race. Humanity has already, in not a few instances, borne conspicuously the likeness of Christ and God. The sun grows dim, the grandeur of outward nature shrinks, when compared with the spiritual energy of men, who, in the cause of truth, of God, of charity, have spurned all bribes of ease, pleasure, renown, and have withstood shame, want, persecution, torture, and the most dreaded forms of death. In such men I learn that the soul was made in God's image, and made to conform itself to the loveliness and greatness of his Son.

My Friends, we may all approach Jesus Christ. For all of us he died, to leave us an example that we should follow his steps. By earnest purpose, by self-conflict, by watching and prayer, by faith in the Christian promises, by those heavenly aids and illuminations, which he that seeketh shall find, we may all unite ourselves, in living bonds, to Christ, may love as he loved, may act from his principles, may suffer with his constancy, may enter into his purposes, may sympathize with his self-devotion to the cause of God and mankind, and, by likeness of spirit, may prepare ourselves to meet him as our everlasting friend.

www.ingramcontent.com/pod-product-compliance
Lightning Source LLC
LaVergne TN
LVHW020922110826
845150LV00004B/744

* 9 7 8 1 4 2 5 5 5 4 5 8 3 *